Copyright © 2013

ISBN   978-0-9834831-2-0

Printed in the United States of America

The Irish Australian Monaghans

Warren Dent

Acknowledgments

Josie Abrahamson and Fai Dawson were enthusiastic supporters and wonderful editors for this tale about major family transition. Both ladies contributed in unique ways, Fai on forcing me to add more emotion, Josie on keeping my facts and assumptions straight. Josie also helped markedly with research into the family characters around whom this story is based, using resources to which I did not have access. Both deserve medals for their patience, serious input, and tolerance of my sometimes argumentative responses. In the end I take all blame for any historical inaccuracies, the judgments made, and interpretation of described political and economic events.

Author's Note

There is a branch of my Australian family whose roots are in County Donegal, Ireland. This is a fictionalized tale of the family's decision to migrate to Australia. It details the trials and tribulations they endured in leaving their homeland, crossing the oceans, and adapting to the new country when it was still a penal colony. All the principal characters are based on real persons. Obviously I have taken liberties with such things as certain peoples' names, dates, settings, and dialogue. I've kept names of public figures for authenticity, and reflected the economic times and conditions with as much relevancy as possible. Ultimately, this is a story that is representative of many Irish pioneering families in the early nineteenth century. These men, women and children helped lay the foundation of the culture that converted Australia from its ignominious beginning as a penal colony into a land of opportunity where wool, wheat and natural resources have contributed to world progress. The conditions these ancestors faced, their bravery, fortitude, and beliefs deserve more recognition. We owe them our lives and in many cases our livelihood.

PostScript
This book is written for both British and American audiences. Sometimes it deliberately uses American English spellings, at other times the Queen's English spellings. I saw no reason *a priori* to irritate only one group and not the other. Please tolerate this idiosyncrasy of mine.

Dedication

To all those brave pioneers who gave up everything they treasured in their homelands and travelled to an unknown land and environment in order to provide a new life and better opportunities for their families and ensuing generations. We thankful relatives applaud them.

Contents

PROLOGUE

The Monaghans were nervous and scared. All nine of them. They were not alone in their conflicting feelings of grief and hope. Members of the other sixty families crowding the ship rails were similarly disposed. All were leaving behind relatives and friends, trusting in their own judgment and initiative, wondering in part what was ahead, and at the same time, whether they would ever return.

And even though the Monaghans, like all the others, were on board by their own free will, that didn't make it any more comforting. They'd made the choice between living in the continued purgatory of the past two score years, versus that of the promises of a totally unpredictable new life in a country at the other end of the world.

Neither parent, nor any of the seven children, had even been on a ship before, and this brand new monster, the *Herald*, creaked and groaned continuously. Yet it hadn't even left the wharf. The temporary excitement and confidence they'd first felt on seeing her was gone. This was no longer a dream. Reality was upon them. What on earth would it be like in the vast ocean waters they had to cross? More than three months at sea awaited them.

For the umpteenth time Katie tried not to dwell on the pending voyage, and she tightened her grip on the baby, now nearly two years old. With husband Matthew they'd jointly decided that the devil they didn't know in Sydney, Australia, just had to be better than the one they had experienced for far too long in Drumcairn, County Donegal. So they'd filed their application for an assisted passage to the Antipodes, and the journey was about to begin.

There was no turning back now.

No doubt they would relive the heartache of leaving friends and relatives behind many times in the years ahead. But Matthew had been recognized in their village for his rational thinking and non-judgmental ways, and so the family's decision to leave was well respected. He'd never been a standup leader in village meetings, but when differences emerged he had a gentle way of suggesting fair solutions to conflicts, and was seen as wise beyond his years.

His love for his family and friends showed, for he rarely put his own interests first and was always on hand to help a neighbor out with house repairs or treatment of injuries. His children were well disciplined and raised to be courteous and sharing, emulating the examples set by their parents. Katie had grown up alongside multiple sisters and brothers and had learned to get along with others at an early age. She took charge of raising the children and worked hard to provide for them as best possible.

She hadn't thought much about it in advance but their trek across the country and the days here in town had really been wonderful for the children. They had learned that their situation was duplicated in many other villages in their land, and that strangers with common causes could become friends. They had deepened their experience of sharing with others, and had enhanced their flexibility in adapting to new eating and lodging arrangements.

She said as much to her husband, adding, "And of course the city here has been an incredible eye-opener. Perhaps in part for you and me too. It's been a long time since we were here as children and much has changed. The amazement the children evidenced at seeing things they'd never really observed before was wonderful to behold. It made me realise how insular and contained our lives really were back in Drumcairn. Lots of both positive and negative things to contemplate. I sensed early that there was an unspoken wish that they could have lived in a city, but I think as they witnessed some of the darker, less rosy, corners of life in a big town, that has been tempered a little. Have you sensed the same?"

"Oh yes. When I took the boys touring on their own, they expressed their interest and curiosity in an unusual way—by asking whether Sydney would be like this town of LondonDerry. At one point, Thomas was no longer at my side and I backtracked to find him playing with many of the leather articles hanging outside a merchant's shop. I forbade him to touch anything again and his irritation at me was obvious.

"A little later an ugly, snarling dog rushed out of an alley and tried to bite his ankle. He was surprised and very much taken aback. As old as he is, it disturbed him a lot, I could tell. Luckily I managed to kick the dog on the rump and it ran away. For a short time I was his hero father again."

Katie smiled fondly at her husband as he continued his story.

"Both boys were disturbed by the rubbish that seemed to have been thrown out of doorways and windows onto the street. Back in Drumcairn we had no rubbish to spare, but it wasn't just the waste that bothered them, it was that people didn't seem to care and had no pride. So the lessons were quite varied for them. I was pleased to see that their eyes were open to both pros and cons of city life."

The baby squirmed in Katie's arms, wanting to be put down. His hands reached out for his father, who helped lower him to the deck, where he studiously played with an iron bulwark and an errant piece of rope. Katie let him sit but watched carefully, as the little fellow could move amazingly fast when he spied something new that caught his attention.

Matthew turned back towards the rest of the children. They were all silent. Their hands gripped the deck rail tightly and their mouths were set in taut lines. Matthew sensed the apprehension running through them, just as it permeated his own body. He gripped Katie's hand.

The noise level from the docks decreased as the last access gangplank was removed. Contrarily, on board, shouted commands and responses increased as sailors climbed into the rigging and the lines securing the ship to the dock were released and hauled aboard. Slowly, inexorably, the hull parted company with the pilings of the wharf. The gap between ship rail and shore widened, and at last Katie released the pent-up anxiety she'd held inside, with giant sobs that racked her thin frame. Matthew dropped her hand and his comforting arm reached around her shoulders.

She raised her head skyward and whispered silently, "Lord, what have we done?"

Matthew gathered the brood close together and they knelt on the deck, where he offered a prayer. "May God hold us all gently in his palms, guide the captain and this ship safely to the new land, and bless all of us onboard in our quest to start a new life. We thank you, Lord, for your benevolence, and pray your forgiveness for past sins. Amen."

Katie's anxiety calmed as she listened to Matthew's soothing voice. Once again she reveled in his ability to carry on regardless. As they rose from prayer, she handed the baby to her daughter, Grace, and hugged her husband, whispering, "Thank you, Matthew, dear, from the bottom of my heart, for your strength and faith. I've turned to you many times for support in our life together. You are my foundation rock and I cherish your love for all of us. I'm scared for our future, but in my soul I know we will end up better off. I'll stay by your side forever." So saying, she reached up and gave him a tender kiss. This was not lost on the watching children, and small smiles eased around their lips and mouths. It was going to be alright!

Baby Connor was absorbed in his new surroundings. This was no time to be held, and he wriggled down Grace's tunic and led her to one of the large water barrels nearby. In his terrible twos, he commanded attention day in and day out. Some days his antics were fun; on others they were exasperating. There was an implicit understanding among the family members that they all needed to share in looking after him. Each had to take a turn in managing his rambunctiousness and satisfying his curiosity. The ship was full of unknown dangers for an energetic two-year-old, and while some laxity and tolerance had been granted back home in a familiar environment, here, without supervision, he was a potential disaster waiting to happen. Katie carried him more than anyone else, and since the strain on her back increased as he grew, she parceled him out to sons and daughters alike when she grew tired.

Few on board had acquaintances on the dock so the departure was eerily non-festive. A few desultory waves with handkerchiefs wiping away some tears were the norm. Like the Monaghans, most of the other passengers wondered what on earth was ahead. Those few left on shore shook their heads at the perceived bravery or foolishness of relatives and friends moving so far away. Not for them at all.

As the boat moved to midstream, more sails were unfurled, and the vessel made a pretty sight as she headed northward for the Irish Sea and the Atlantic beyond.

It was Saturday, April 10th, 1841.

The adventure had begun.

.

1. County Donegal, Ireland 1820-1840

A cold, drizzling rain swept across the verdant fields and gave way to a small sunburst between the low-hanging clouds. Matthew Monaghan, twenty, and Katie Whalen, eighteen, emerged from the front door of the old Presbyterian Ray 1 Meeting House in ManorCunningham, a mile and a half north of their new dwelling in Drumcarn, and exchanged a loving, thankful kiss in front of the friends and family well-wishers present at their wedding.

Among those happy with the union were both sets of parents and two of the grandmothers. John Monaghan and his wife Susan with her mother, Elizabeth Cooney, had been long-time friends of Katie's people through their joint association in this very church. Brian Whalen and his wife Nancy, together with Nancy's mother, Rebecca Farrell, had come from Letterkenny, five miles distant, for the occasion. They were from the poorer south side and had produced many children, most of the daughters having left home as soon as they could to serve as maids in wealthier households.

Katie's twin sister Elizabeth and her three brothers and four other sisters clapped and cheered, while Matthew's elder brother shook hands and kissed the bride. The group then moved to the horses and buggies for the treat ride into town for a simple wedding reception. The parents and grandparents had dug into their savings to create a festive event for this very special day, knowing the way ahead for the young couple would probably never be so good.

It was Friday, February 16th, 1821.

With the weekend honeymoon behind them the couple came back to the little hut they had arranged to rent on one of the farmsteads in Drumcarn. Matthew insisted on carrying Katie across the threshold. She giggled as he laid her down on the mattress on the floor, where they once again indulged in new pleasures of the flesh that they had discovered so recently.

The villagers had chipped in together, and at the nearby market had bought them a rooster and hen, as well as a sow pig, as a welcome gift. Newlyweds were given every chance to make a go of life in the village, the incumbent residents aware of how hard that life would be in the years ahead. Like many of the villages in the area, theirs was a tight little community where families readily helped each other out in tough times and shared simple family events together.

And while the villagers welcomed their new members warmly they also enjoyed a little fun. Entertainment, amusement, and games were all home generated in the small villages. And unbeknownst to the new 'youngsters' the established members were about to extract 'payment' for their welcoming generosity. Just after dark, when the children had come in off the road and the playfields, and the front doors were all shut, and crude lamps, if owned, were turned on, there was a knock on Matthew and Katie's door. An elderly couple asked if they could come in and chat in order to get to know the newlyweds better and to welcome them properly to the village. They stayed for an hour but left when it was clear that the young couple were tiring and running out of conversation. Not five minutes after their departure another man and wife knocked, voicing the same interests, and spent thirty minutes chatting with the newcomers. A third family came knocking, and a fourth. It was fun to see the youngsters trying to be nice in the face of the unending flow of good-wishers, when all they really wanted to do was be in each other's arms making love. The visits deliberately went on past midnight with the existing residents sharing tales with each other of the looks of apprehension the young couple provided at the entrance of each new set of visitors, and the surreptitious hugging and touching as they tried to keep up conversation.

Finally the villagers ceased their visits, but as soon as they figured the young couple were in bed, a relentless few silently gathered around the house and ran pitchforks back and forth across the stone walls and threw little pebbles at the one window and then broke into raucous song loud enough to wake anyone. When Matthew appeared at the door, eyes bleary, clearly disgruntled, and with his britches hastily pulled on, they all shook his hand, wished him goodnight, and retreated to their abodes singing and sharing mirth that came far too infrequently to the hamlet. A great night, a traditional welcome to new village members, and a source of new tales for the weeks ahead.

Back inside, Matthew flopped down on the bed and ran his hand over his bride's back, but got no response. Exhausted from the night's activities, she had finally fallen fast asleep. Frustrated and annoyed, Matthew did something most unusual, voicing his irritation in definitely not-pretty words—*"mallaigh, damnu air!"* It took a long time before he too fell asleep.

Drumcarn, later to become Drumcairn, was a microcosm on the Irish landscape. Some thirty-two traditional counties created a mosaic across maps of the country, with County Donegal defining the most northwest sector of the island, well recognized as one of the poorest areas. County Donegal was further subdivided into fifty-two parishes. Each parish supported a number of townlands, or areas of community. In County Donegal there were 2,836 official townland names plus another 1,500 or so place names, commonly labeled as 'unofficial townlands'. Drumcarn was just one of the over 4,300 such places in the parish of Raymoghy in the diocese of North Raphoe. A tiny blip on the canvas of the country, disarmingly similar to thousands of other small rural villages. But to Matthew and Katie, Drumcarn was home.

Blind bliss and happiness helped the young couple along. Matthew was a farmhand and Katie, so-called by nearly everyone, read stories to the children at the Raymoghy National School. She had never learned to write but she was a wonderful reader and storyteller and the young children loved her. Given her new sexual freedom it was no surprise when two cycles passed and her mother confirmed she was likely pregnant. The villagers were delighted as she announced her condition.

And not unexpectedly, given the family history, she birthed twin boys, Thomas and Patrick James, on the first day of the new year 1822. Matthew held her tightly and muttered, "Congratulations, Mrs. Monaghan. You have brought joy to my heart. What a wonderful New Year's gift. I love you and pray there will be many more fine babies to come."

"Thank you, father of our sons. I am sore and tired, but your love makes my soul glow, and I know our boys will grow up to be strong men like you. We are indeed blessed, Matthew. Please tell my mother and father on the morrow. They will be happy too."

Having children was a well-received and well-supported avocation of the times. There was no end of help in the village for the new mother. Katie's only regret was giving up teaching. The few pennies she used to earn were now foregone and Matthew worked extra hours whenever possible to make up the difference.

The hen kept them in fresh eggs, and the sow was mated and produced a healthy litter. Some of the piglets were given back as thank-yous to neighbours but two were kept for fattening and provided pork and ham at Christmas time. In due course another set of twins arrived on the seventh of August 1823. This time two girls, Grace and Eileen, were delivered by the midwife, and once again the village rejoiced. The babies were christened in the Presbyterian faith in the church at ManorCunningham. The family would trek there every Sunday with help from the neighbours in carrying the children. Church was the easiest meeting place for all the family members, and beyond giving thanks to God it was a location for fond social exchange.

Once a month there was a market in town, and if Matthew was able to take the day off on such Saturdays, he and his friends would take their excess produce and trade it for something different. Not that there was much variety in the farms of the area. Many farmers raised cattle and sheep and the crops were most likely potatoes and beets. Matthew worked his landlord's fields and his own tiny plot.

In the fifth year of their married life Katie produced another girl on the second of March 1826. Her name was Mary Jane, and two and a half years later a sister, Nancy, arrived on the fifth of August 1828. Matthew once again hugged Katie and affirmed his love for her and all the children, but this time his message ended differently. "My dear wife, the good Lord has been kind to us and blessed us with six healthy children, but I think we must ask his guidance for no more. The landlord has raised our rent yet again and we have less and less to spend. We've sold the chickens, and our vegetable plot has been taken away. Please do not condemn me for these thoughts, as I love our children, but I don't know how to feed them anymore."

Katie's tears were those of understanding. She nodded her head in acquiescence and raised the baby to her milk-laden breast. Her body was still relatively young and healthy but life was definitely becoming more unfair. Elsewhere, especially to the south and west in the county, the stories of hardship were becoming more prevalent and more disheartening. The pressures of the landlords on the farmers were becoming exorbitant, forcing increasingly burdensome demands on the working labourers. Since Matthew was one of the few in the village who could both read and write, he sometimes made extra pence writing letters for other residents. Even that source of income petered out over time.

By 1831 Matthew and Katie had pawned or sold many of their possessions, as had most of the villagers, keeping only the essentials. Every item was passed up with great reluctance and only after much discussion. Katie had first parted with a special bonnet her grandmother had worn on her own wedding day and given to Katie as a keepsake. It was the first hard decision. "It will be your turn next, Matthew," she had said. "This breaks my heart and I hope Grandma never asks about it, for I will not lie to her."

"I'm sure she would understand, dear, and she is definitely not likely to visit, for she grows more sickly every month, not even making it to church these days. I fear she will not be with us much longer."

The next time they urgently needed money Matthew gave up the one extra book they held in their home. It was a history of Ireland in Gaelic. "This has been mine since my tenth birthday, Katie. I was hoping we could use it to help all our children not only know more of our country's heritage but also as a wonderful source of our native language. But I'd rather give this up than the family bible. Heaven knows, perhaps one day that will have to go too. This is so hard."

"Yes, my love, but we need food for our babies, and others are in the same plight. This is the only way for now, until something changes for us. And I do not see the landowner demanding less in the near future. Some days, Matthew," she continued, "I truly despair. It is only my faith in the Lord and your love that keeps me going. We must do this for the children."

Over time, more personal items were sold. A pair of clogs, a wicker basket, and eventually clothing. Katie sadly gave up a soft green cardigan that her mother had made from scratch. She'd spun the wool, dyed it, made it into yarn, and knitted it to her own design. Its departure was doubly hard on Katie. The sentimental value was one thing, but it also kept her warm on cold winter days. The poor were becoming poorer, and the whole village suffered.

The plight of the peasants was being recognized in British parliament, but there was no action to curb the voracious and greedy demands of the land barons. A British commission appointed to inquire into the condition of the poorer classes in Ireland in 1833 described the condition of the bulk of the people, about 2.5 million, as follows:

> Their habitations are wretched hovels, several of a family sleep together upon straw, or upon the bare ground, sometimes with a blanket; sometimes even without so much to cover them. Their food consists of dry potatoes, and with these they are at times so scantily supplied as to be obliged to stint themselves to one spare meal in the day. There are even instances of persons being driven by hunger to seek sustenance in wild herbs. They sometimes get a herring or a little milk, but they never get meat except at Christmas, Easter, and Shrovetide.

As much as times and conditions were horrible, two small saving graces emerged. By 1836 the twin boys were fourteen years old and able to find small part-time menial jobs, and to help their father with some of his field tasks. And with the youngest child now eight years old, the twin girls were able to look after her, and Katie was able to spend time at servant work in one of the farm houses.

Buoyed with a little hope, the parents who had practiced contraception diligently for ten years became less careful in their love-making. On the first of November 1838, after their meagre supper, Katie took Matthew's arm and said, "Come walk with me, my love." The children wondered what was up as this was a little unusual, but they continued their chores and games while their parents trudged along the village road arm in arm to the work fields. A frost had fallen across the fields, suggesting a hard winter was ahead.

"I think I can guess what's on your mind," said Matthew.

"You should, my man, as it's happened six times before. I'm sure I am pregnant again. I have not used the towels this past month and from experience I think you have sired another little one. You are a virile man, my love, and I know how hard this will be for us. I'm now thirty-five years old and our youngest is ten. I will have to stop work for a while but at least the children can help with the baby. At my age there's a chance I could lose it along the way but I would hate that to happen, Matthew. Life is so precious."

"Well, my love, the deed is done. I cannot complain that our physical wants have led us here. And while in some ways I wish we were not bringing another child into our impoverished lives, apparently God wants us to, and so we will do as He bids. Thank you for sharing the news. And you are right, the elder girls should be able to help out a bunch. In fact, I suspect they will be excited when we tell them. Maybe with their help you will be able to be back at work in the farmhouse or school faster than other times. Whatever, we will work it out my love.

"Now, do you tell them tonight?" he asked. "Or later? They will be wondering anyway, and since the twins at fifteen are already with menses they are probably aware of your situation. Our daughters are very observant and astute."

"Oh yes, they probably have guessed already. There's precious little privacy in our home, my dear. I'm glad you are not angry, as that would be doubly hard on me. Thank you for your support. I know God will see us through."

She reached up and kissed his cheek, and his arm tightened around her, the other hand lovingly patting her belly.

Seven and a half months later, on the thirteenth of June 1839, a son, Connor, was born. The elder girls were ecstatic to have a new baby in the house. As anticipated, their willingness to help out allowed Katie to go back to her servant work quickly.

While the meagre income was restored, the darkness of poverty was closing in on them faster than they knew.

By the early 1840s most rural Irish families were in great economic difficulty. The majority were living in dire straits, being forced to pay excessive rents in the face of deteriorating crop productivity and prices. County Donegal was especially hit hard.

A report by Thomas Campbell Foster, who was appointed years later in 1845 by *The Times* newspaper as its "Commissioner to report on the condition of the people of Ireland," summarized the deplorable situation in the county. In his third article, written on 3rd September 1845, he described the towns he passed through. From Donegal town he:

"...proceeded to Glenties, a village which is the property of the Marquis of Conyngham. The whole of the country for many miles in the direction of Dungloe and beyond that town, in fact almost the whole barony of Boylagh belongs to this nobleman, together with the island of Arran on the west coast. Once in the course of his lifetime, two years ago, the marquis visited his estate for a few days. His chief agent Mr. Benbow, usually comes once a year and the sub-agents visit the tenants every half year to collect the rents. At short periods of a few years the farms are visited to see what increases in rent they will bear and this is the extent of the acquaintance of the marquis with his tenants. This nobleman himself, bears the character of a 'kind-hearted, generous man, fond of yachting and amusement and having an excess of distaste for every kind of business trouble'. From one end of his large estate here to the other, nothing is to be found but poverty, misery, wretched cultivation and infinite subdivision of land. There are no gentry, no middle class, all are poor, wretchedly poor.

"Every shilling the tenants can raise from their half-cultivated land is paid in rent, whilst most people subsist for the most part on potatoes and water. Every rude effort that they make to increase the amount of their produce is followed immediately by raising their rents in proportion, as it were, to punish them for improving; they are, naturally enough, as discontented and full of complaints as they are wretched in their condition."

Foster reported in minute detail what he found when he visited some of the homes, if such they could be called, of the 'noble' marquis' tenants.

"Into the cottages I entered. They were stone-built and well roofed but the mud floor was uneven, damp and filthy. In one corner was a place for the pig, with a drain from it through the wall to carry off the liquid manure, like a stable. Two chairs, a bedstead of the rudest description, a cradle, a spinning wheel and an iron pot constituted the whole furniture. An inner room contained another rude bedstead; the mud floor was quite damp. In this room six children slept on loose hay, with one dirty blanket to cover them. The father, mother and an infant slept in the first room, also on loose hay, and with but one blanket on the bed. The children were running about as nearly naked as possible, dressed in the cast off rags of the father and mother; the father could not buy them clothes.

"The men assured me that their whole food was potatoes and if they had a penny to spare they bought salt or a few sprats, but very seldom these. Instead of buying salt they sometimes bought pepper and mixed it with the water they drank. This they called 'kitchin', it gave a flavour to their food."

Moving to Dungloe, a village sixteen miles further, direct north, also owned by the 'ever-caring' marquis, Foster again described:

"Filthy and wretched cottages housing not only pigs but calves and ducks dabbling in a pool of dirty water in a hole in the mud floor."

While his report was dated 1845, he knew the conditions had been worsening for years. At first as conditions deteriorated, families squabbled. Wives complained about not having enough food to feed children and themselves adequately; husbands complained about the extra hours they were required to work to bring in the same pennies. Frustration led to anger, and sometimes to shoving matches. There were stories from other villages where men had simply up and left and walked into a river and drowned themselves. Which made things only worse for those left behind. Widowed wives retreated with children to parents' and sisters' and brothers' abodes, increasing the strain there. The cycle was vicious, with no winners other than the Marquis. Villagers wondered at their plight. What was the purpose of going on? To see their children withering away, malnourished and disheartened? There were no easy answers.

For many, the local conditions were too much to bear, and they sought to migrate elsewhere. The British had started the "Assisted Immigrant" Bounty scheme to Australia in 1836 for healthy citizens under forty years old. The reasons reflected a combination of events. Not only was there widespread rural poverty in Ireland, but a different form of poverty existed in England, Wales, and Scotland as well. There, the harsh conditions of the industrial cities also added to the misery. Migration to Australia became an attractive option for many, but few had the resources to pay for a berth even in steerage, which cost on the order of seventeen pounds.

At the same time, settlement in Australia by the British was outgrowing its convict origins and the colony was expanding at a rapid pace, creating an acute shortage of labour. The country was desperate for farm labourers, carpenters, bricklayers, etc. Towards the end of the convict transportation years there was also an imbalance in the male/female ratio. The colonial Australian government was forced into helping pay for the passage of migrants to obtain the people they so desperately needed. They funded this assistance by selling land. The parishes of England were only too pleased to take up this arrangement, as they were able to ship out paupers which were a great burden on their rates.

Matthew and Katie had watched people join the emigration ranks for five years. It was Matthew who finally brought the topic to a head. "As much as we have suffered here, Katie, I don't think we are being fair to our children and ourselves. I try to be optimistic but I have run out of energy to be so. I cannot see things improving and we are living in a state that I never wanted for us. It is shameful, and I am embarrassed for us and our children. I have thought long and hard, and as much as the kinship in the village helps, I think we must leave. Others have set an example by emigrating, and the bounty men weave a tale that has promise, even given their hyperbole and ability to make everything seem positive. I cannot see it being worse than what we have now."

"I've had similar thoughts, Matthew, but wondered if you'd feel ill of me were I to voice them. I dread the thought of leaving our families, but worry about our future here. I will follow you anywhere, and if that's to be Australia, so be it. If it's to stay here, again so be it. You and the boys have the best chance at earning income and for me that should probably be our main concern, so that we earn enough to feed us all. Even though the eldest girls are also farm servants now, and Nancy also brings in a little money as a child's maid, it's still not enough because we have more mouths to feed than others." She hesitated before continuing. "I do wish we had heard back directly from those who had gone to Australia before us instead of just from the bounty men and the town criers."

"Well, my love, if you are willing I will add our names to the list of the next bounty man who comes by. It's our last chance, as once I turn forty years old next year I will no longer be eligible. I hate to leave, but life here is miserable and I want better for all of us."

And thus it came to pass that in 1840 the Monaghans of Drumcarn townland made the decision to seek a new and better life elsewhere, before it was too late to do so.

It was with heavy hearts that they told their families of their decision. Both sets of parents and grandmothers had already passed on through sickness and malnutrition, but all the siblings with their broods were still around. The heartache was widespread, and sobs erupted in every conversation. The desire for survival with dignity rose paramount, however, and eventually it became clear to all that destiny for the Monaghans no longer lay in Ireland, but in a country far, far away across two mighty oceans.

Knowing that one of the most heart-breaking things Matthew had had to give up was the bible he'd owned for over thirty years, his elder brother placed his own well-worn bible in Matthew's hands and bade him good fortune. Katie's sisters had banded together, sought out spare pieces of fabric from various sources, and had hand-sewn two bonnets and a patchwork apron for her. A final gift from Katie's eldest brother was a blank diary. His request was that the family record their voyage to Australia in it. The gift caused a little consternation as Thomas and his father Matthew were the only ones totally skilled in writing. At fourteen, Nancy was the youngest of the children, not counting the baby at two years old. She had been a keen student at school, where she had been more commonly called by her nickname, Ann, a Celtic tradition in place country-wide. And it was too early for her to be learning to write yet. Katie looked at the children, especially Thomas. Anticipating the coming question, he nodded his head ever so slightly, at which point Katie turned and said, "Grace, I know you are learning but if you will take on the task I know Thomas would be glad to help you. Would you be willing to do this for us?"

She nodded yes to Katie's request, and the awkward issue was resolved. Grace hugged the diary to her chest, proud that her mother had sought her out. She kissed her uncle but the tears flowed anyway, with the realisation that this truly was goodbye to all.

The guilt that Matthew and Katie felt in leaving their brethren would weigh heavily for years to come, but the embarrassment at their poverty was festering in their souls, and needed to be overcome.

They started preparations to catch their ship to the future.

2. The country road
to salvation

The route to Londonderry was circuitous and crossed varied terrains. There was no alternative for villagers but to walk, for no one could afford horse and cart these days. Only young Connor needed to be carried and that function would be shared between adults and elder children alike.

There was precious little else to carry anyway. They had sold their furnishings, but had to simply walk away from the house. Two bags of clothes, a few sentimental keepsakes, pots, pans, simple plates and eating utensils, and that was it. The shoes they had on would have to hold to Derry and beyond. Over his shoulder and across his chest Matthew carried a small satchel with many coins and a few notes, plus all the papers from church and the farm owner necessary for passage on the ship. In an incredible surprise, the day before leaving, the farmer's wife had presented Katie with a small sachet of potpourri, in recognition of the service she had provided over the years. It was a simple gift that Katie was to treasure for the rest of her life, the nicest she had received since the day she was married twenty years earlier.

And so on Saturday 3rd April, 1841, beneath a mild spring sun, the family said goodbye to friends and relatives, and with tears in their eyes and sorrow in their hearts turned their backs on their home and headed for a new unknown.

In many villages throughout the country boys aged nineteen and girls aged eighteen would often be already married. Some would be 'required' marriages where the girl was pregnant, and shame was included in the situation. But many simply followed in their parents' footsteps, marrying young and starting a family immediately afterwards.

As the economy deteriorated, however, young men had less to offer eligible girls and fewer youthful marriages took place. That didn't mean that boys and girls didn't have sweethearts and favoured friends. And the Monaghan children were no exception. The twin boys both liked girls whom they saw at church and who came from other villages. Similarly with the twin girls and their boyfriends from elsewhere. Eight forlorn teenagers hugged and cried, sneaked kisses and touches, and promised never to forget each other and to stay in contact through letters and cards. Some of these special friends turned up to wave goodbye, which made parting harder on all concerned.

But turn away the family did, and headed down the road towards Derry. Broken teenage hearts littered the way behind.

The Monaghans weren't the only pilgrims on the road, and at the church rest point at the end of the first day they caught up with a family that had started out ten days earlier from Falcarragh on the northwest coast. Their route had taken them over Muckish Mountain and the infamous Bridge of Sorrows on the road to Kilmacrenan, northwest of Letterkenny. The bridge was a departure point memorialized in prose as:

"Standing on the bridge with the road down to Falcarragh at our backs we watch our departing relations and friends moving up this road to the top of the gap. They turn and wave, we wave back, they take a couple more steps and are gone into another world. And then, with our sorrow and our tears, we return to our homes while they pick up their steps going downhill from the gap, heading for the port of Derry."

The stone monument read:

"Friends and Relations of the person who was emigrating would come this far. Here they separated. This is the Bridge of Tears."

Sean O'Donnell and his wife Eleanor were making good time with their three sons and three daughters, Padraig, Liam, Niall, Shauna, Roisin, and Tara. The children had arrived in the world every two years and in alternating order—boy, girl, boy, girl, boy, girl. At twenty-two Padraig was a striking young man and Grace soon found herself fascinated by him. "Padraig, what did you do with the fishing boat you and your father owned?" she asked.

"We sold it to my father's cousin, whose boat had been smashed in a storm. He was happy to get it at a good price, but it was sad to pass it up as we'd had it nigh on fifteen years."

"What sort of fish did you catch?" asked Thomas.

"Cod and sole mainly, but our catch got smaller and smaller over time as more and more men came from the farms to the coast and started to fish. Towards the end there were days when we'd be out twelve hours and bring naught but two fish back in our basket. We rarely got to keep our catch and many days we would go hungry. Shauna and Roisin lost their jobs as maids when people could no longer afford to pay them, and so we had to decide what to do." Padraig looked sad as he continued. "One of my best friends, Rory, jumped off a cliff and his body was washed out to sea. That was the last straw for father and me as Rory often came fishing with us and helped mend the nets. Aye, that was a sad day."

"So that was when you signed up with the Bounty man?" asked Eileen.

"Yes," interjected Niall. "He'd been in the village before and other families had left, but this time Mother and Father talked to him at length, and well... here we are."

Liam joined in. "We'd lived in the same house since Padraig was a baby, so it was incredibly crowded. Padraig and I would often sleep on the nearby church floor overnight in order to make room for the girls and Niall. Was it like that for you too?"

"Not quite," said Ann. "Church was too far away to go there every night so we all slept together on the bare floor. We've never known a lot of privacy. Do you think it will be better on the ship?" No one really knew the answer and the conversation turned to common activities and how they all kept themselves entertained and amused. Sharing their feelings and experiences helped pass the time and consequently the road didn't seem so long and the rest stops were reached more quickly than expected. They all vowed to make sure they looked out for each other on the ship no matter where they found their space.

As the group journeyed northeast, other families joined in, and by the time they arrived in Derry two and a half days later, there were twenty-five emigrants in the band. All were poor, with common tales of disillusionment, and common fears of the unknown. In some cases elderly mothers and fathers had been left behind, and guilt lay heavily upon some of the souls. The comradeship helped a little and the exercise of walking was beneficial. Fortunately the weather was clear, if not exactly warm, and the little churches they stopped in overnight provided both physical and spiritual sanctuary. Catholics and Protestants alike were in the group with no discord. It was much later in the country's history that differences in religion created problems.

The children practised their bible reading each evening after supper and before the church wall lamps were extinguished. And each morning Nancy would ask the same question, "Will we see the boat today, Mother?" The children had been schooled in both native Gaelic and English. They could read in each but couldn't write in either, save Thomas. In particular Mary Jane was a little bit stubborn in fortifying her Irish roots. She loved the history of her land, and proudly studied her ancestral background and culture. And stubbornly refused to speak in anything but her native tongue at home. As they got closer to Derry they noticed that more signs were in both Gaelic and English, however, and they practised using the English language more often in their conversations, forcing Mary Jane to adjust. The Bounty seekers had made it clear when visiting the village initially, that once they were on the ship, English would be the more common language in use. As soon as the decision to pick up and leave was locked down they'd made sure they only talked to the baby Connor in English.

And so with over twenty miles behind them, they finally reached the outskirts of the city of Derry. They stopped and asked directions to the Presbyterian churches and found one quickly that would allow them to sleep on the floor overnight and organize meagre food rations for all. Matthew made a small donation and they lit candles and prayed their thanks.

None of the children had been to any town bigger than the local market town in their short lives, so Matthew clustered the family and said, "I want you to all hold hands and stay close. This is so much bigger than even Letterkenny, and it would be easy to get lost." The city was at first overwhelming. It had more streets, many of them paved, plus more houses, more taverns, more drunks, more noise, more smoke from chimneys, more people, more dirt, more horses and donkeys and wagons and carts, more merchants, more small factories and workshops, and a variety of goods such as bonnets and frocks and certain leather goods and baskets in styles and varieties that were totally new.

With frequent stops and longing stares they slowly made their way to the waterfront, where they encountered in awe the biggest river, the Foyle, that anyone had ever seen. The two youngest girls hesitated, and Katie held them close to her skirt as they approached the bank.

Small craft rowed to and fro delivering people and goods to the other shore. There were sailing vessels in dry dock, and constant movement of people and goods between warehouses and tied-up boats. It was hustle and bustle everywhere. So contrary to the peaceful, paced life of a rural village. This was another world indeed.

Londonderry history relates back to the sixth century A.D. when a monastery was founded there, although people had been living in the vicinity for thousands of years before that. The monastery church survived up to the seventeenth century and was used as the first place of worship by the London colonists who came in 1613 to build the walled city. As such, the city is Ireland's earliest example of town planning and is thought to have been modeled on the French Renaissance town of Vitry-le-François. Both cities are based on the grid plan of a Roman military camp, with two main streets at right angles to each other, and four city gates, one at the end of each street.

Completed in 1618, Derry's city walls are about twenty-five feet high and vary between twelve and thirty-five feet thick, with a circumference of about one mile. The four original gates (Shipquay, Ferryquay, Bishop's, and Butcher's) were rebuilt in the eighteenth and nineteenth centuries, when three new gates (New, Magazine, and Castle) were added. The walls have never been breached by an invader.

The Monaghans had heard about the walls, of course, as had every student of the country's history. Seeing them up close, however, was something else. They were mammoth and awe-inspiring to the youngsters. What must it have taken to build them? they wondered. Such an incredible feat so long ago. And to have stood over two hundred years as solid as the day they were completed. There was nothing of any comparison back in Drumcarn.

By now the children were awakening to a totally different way of life than that they had known since they were babies. At first there was some resentment. "Why couldn't we be living here, Father?" asked the persistent Nancy. It was hard to explain to her that her father's skills didn't apply inside an urban metropolis. Matthew knew farming. He was good at it, and being confined to a city existence would not be acceptable. Even the twins, nearing twenty, were now highly knowledgeable farmers in their own right with years of experience tilling the earth and looking after God's domestic farm creatures. Insurance men, publicans, salesmen, accountants, bankers, tailors, or general merchants were out of their domain of interest and skills. The closest they could come would be general labourers, and many of those they saw on the wharves and throughout the town were struggling on a day-to-day existence just as the family had done back in County Donegal. It just wasn't as obvious when the men could apparently afford to go to the pub at the end of each day.

The delights of the city—fresh-baked bread in the shops come early morning, fruit for sale, straight streets and big churches, protection from the great wall, and a select few pretty houses with dainty window gardens—were partially offset by certain other aspects. Well outside the walls trash mounted in foul-smelling piles, skinny cats and dogs wandered back streets, and rats brazenly ran along the river banks. Maimed beggars cried for alms in church doorways, and the more brazen who pulled at Katie's skirt as they passed by were somewhat intimidating and fearsome with their boldness. Matthew and Katie had a hard time explaining 'ladies of the night' offering their services in the daytime as they passed by small hovels. So much was new, so much was different to country living. There was good and there was bad, and for most of the children it was mainly confusing with far more questions than easy answers.

Historically, by the early nineteenth century Derry had become one of the most important and thriving ports in Ireland. In 1835 the value of exports from the city exceeded £1 million, making her the fifth largest port in Ireland. There was a large coastal trade with Britain in linen and agricultural produce. In 1835 linen accounted for 30% of exports; the provisions of beef, bacon, pork, butter, and eggs for 31%; hides and flax for 21%; and corn meal and flour for 12%, indicating a heavy reliance on agricultural produce. By 1838 Derry had trade links with sixteen ports in Ireland and with fifty-three ports in Britain. Between 1834 and 1850, 54 ships, over one hundred tons in size, were bought by Derry merchants. Twenty-eight of the ships were built in Canada.

3. Sailing salvation

The boom of the signal cannon's two shots reverberated along the coastline as the *Herald* anchored inside Quigley's Point and waited for the pilot ship. Baby Connor cried at the massive new sound that hurt his ears. The family could see the barque from their position on the city wall. Even at a distance it clearly dwarfed the other ships nearby. They watched as the sails were slowly furled and the three masts became fully exposed. The sun reflected off various small metal spots as the ship slowly swung in the breeze around its anchor chain. Everyone stared in awe.

In a strange way, the visage was somewhat reassuring. There she was, arriving on time just as the authorities had promised. Her immense size dominated every boat in the vicinity and as such she projected a profile of unchallengeable power and solidity. Irish and Scottish marine flags flew proudly from the centre mast. And suddenly, two more incredibly loud cannon blasts boomed through the bay.

Thomas and Patrick were openly excited as the enormous ship gradually eased into port. Up close she was even more majestic, with smooth, sweeping lines. Her wooden decks, rails, and cabins were highly polished and the keel in front was wrapped in yellow metal. The masts and the miles of rigging towered over the men on board.

"Patrick, have you ever seen anything so huge?"

"No," Patrick responded. "She looks as long as a football field."

As she approached the dock, sailors and wharfmen struggled to wrap the giant rope hawsers around the anvil cleats, and the capstans turned as strong men pushed them around. Gently, ever so gently, nine hundred and eleven tons of beautiful Canadian craftsmanship inched towards the pilings and eventually stopped firm against the pier. The sailors on board and the wharfies on the dock gave a mighty cheer. The *Herald* had arrived.

"Father, those ropes holding the boat to the wharf are as thick as your arms," piped up Eileen.

"Yes, daughter. And those men are as strong as oxen. Even so, it takes several to manage each line. I don't think I could be a wharfman."

The twin boys had been watching intently and the same thought struck them almost simultaneously. "Father, some of those sailors look no older than Patrick and me. Could that be true? Could we have been sailors had we grown up in Derry here, or London or Glasgow?"

"It's certainly possible, my sons. Who knows what opportunities you may have come across had we lived here. Mind you, I think a sailor's life may be less rosy than you imagine. Let's watch and learn once we are on the high seas. And girls, I wouldn't be thinking too hard about marrying a seaman. Many do not have any education and you'll find nearly all of them to be somewhat coarse and vulgar. You can see a number of them sitting by those barrels at the far end of the wharf, already drunk, as well as two others already carousing with women of low repute. They'll be no help in loading the ship now at dock."

The family watched as the gangplank was lowered and the local agent climbed aboard with a sheaf of papers under his arm. He was met by a gentleman they assumed was the captain, whence they both moved away out of view. From near the stern some crates and barrels were carefully unloaded representing valuable Scottish produce and whisky for the merchants serving wealthier citizens of Derry.

By nightfall an enormous range of extra provisions had been loaded. The two sets of twins had left the city wall and made their way down to the wharf, where they had endeavoured to identify and count the various types of boxes, barrels, bales, casks, pots, and bags that were carried and stored on board. There was brandy, gin, whisky, rum, and water in the barrels; salt and flour in the bags; raisins, hams, and dried herrings in the boxes; wine, salmon, and unknown provisions in the casks; and who knows what in the hundreds of cases of different sizes—perhaps produce and fruit, condiments, and spices. It was impossible to tell. Bundles of iron and tools, firkins of butter, big wheels of cheese, and pouches of tobacco all headed on board.

The four young adults were thunderstruck. There was food here that they hadn't seen in years. And in totally unbelievable quantities. They had to restrain themselves from running forward and stealing something to eat from the crates still piled in front of the warehouses.

"You mustn't think that way, Thomas," Grace chided. "The Lord will take care of us. Stealing is a sin. We must endure. It makes me hungry too. I wonder how fat the cooks will be when we see them."

The volume of supplies seemed endless and they were fascinated with everything they observed. Beyond the food and liquids, an amazing amount of rope, buckets, soap, canvas, chairs, tables, scrub brushes, shovels, axes, trunks, mugs, tankards, flags, oilcloths, bundles of timber, and bales of hay all made it on board. They wondered where they would find it all stored once they found their accommodations. Just how much room was there on this boat, and just how many people would be travelling with them?

As the last few lanterns were extinguished and the workers retreated to the nearby pubs, their raucous voices permeating the still air, the four teenagers walked back to the church, where they were handed bread and soup for supper, and sat down with their parents and siblings to recount the amazing sights they had witnessed. Nancy voiced everyone's thoughts when she said, "Maybe we'll eat something other than potatoes."

The notion brought faint smiles to her brothers' and sisters' faces, and mother Katie even admitted, "I hadn't thought of that, but you are right, dear. From what you all have described, it's possible we shall even see fresh ham or fish once in a while. Want not though. We will be pleased to take whatever we are offered."

At sunup in the morning they all went down to the ship again. The carpenters were building cages for the fowl—ducks and geese and chickens—that would supply eggs, and some of which would be sacrificed themselves later, as well as pens for the livestock, which would provide goat and cow milk. Amazingly, they were also creating two small garden plots in which numerous tomato plants were carefully placed. By noon they were done, and the animals were brought on board in order to start getting used to their new premises and handling arrangements. A number of entertaining incidents occurred during this loading phase. The loudest mirth occurred when the dairy cows refused to go up the gangplank and had to be pushed, and one vacated on the chap at the back. Another arose when one of the seamen carrying a cage of chickens slipped. As he fell, the cage latch released and three birds ran amok clucking back and forth across the dock, scattering people and goods, until they were eventually caught.

Matthew eventually checked with the agents and was told that the family could board either late that afternoon or first thing in the morning. If they boarded today they would have to sleep on the ship overnight. After consultation with the others it was decided that they would have many days sleeping on the boat, so they would wait until morning to board, spending one more night closer to their Lord on the church floor. Matthew had one other piece of news that he was reluctant to share, but at length his anger could not be contained. "The agent at Gilchrist & Alexander told me that the Bounty man had recorded our last name without the 'G' and that our name henceforth would be spelled 'M – O – N – A – H – A - N'. I demanded that it be changed back, that our family honour and history were at stake, but he said that that was how it had now been registered with British authorities as well as on the manifest going to Australia and that there was no way to change it. I'm angry that an ignorant Bounty man could change important things on us so easily, but there's little I can do apparently. We will have to live with a new surname from now on."

"Perhaps we can look at it in a different light," suggested Katie. "Tomorrow we truly start a new life. Maybe a new name will help us adjust to it. I suspect there will be harder things to adapt to in the future. We'll just take this as a signal that change will be upon us in unknown ways. I think the Lord won't really mind that much."

"Sometimes, Mother, you are the font of tolerance and wisdom," sighed Patrick. "I can live with the change, especially since the pronunciation won't be affected. I'm sure we all can."

Heads nodded and the discussion fizzled. But sleep came restlessly to most that night as the morrow's departure and its unknowns invaded all their thoughts.

It didn't help that a soft drizzle was falling from grey overcast skies when they awoke. And although it wasn't a long walk to the dock, their footsteps were slower and heavier as the reality of their situation set in.

4. The perils of
sea travel

The sails flapped overhead as they sought the soft breeze coming offshore and the *Herald* moved grandly up Lough Foyle. The city landmarks grew smaller and in an hour had been totally left behind. The weather was overcast but the wind going north was kind. Out past Magilligan Point they turned easterly in the Irish Sea, then southeast past Torr, and were abreast of Island Magee as the sun set.

Three hundred and four Irish immigrants had joined the seventy-one Scots on board at Londonderry. By any measure the ship was full, and very crowded. No one was happy with the arrangements. Most were amazed. Many were angry. And the sailors didn't seem to care much. Their own quarters weren't something to write home about either. Three hundred and eighty-two passengers had to find space in steerage, a low-ceilinged dark space beneath the main deck with a height of no more than seven feet.

The area was divided into three 'compartments'. Forty-four single men occupied the forward area, next to the crew's quarters, while seventy-one single females occupied the aft quarters, and some sixty families with their children were in the middle. Within each compartment, 'messes' were created. These were essentially groups of fifteen or so individuals, with an appointed leader responsible for making sure food rations were fairly shared. In the family area 'messes' were much larger since families tended to average two and one-half children each with sometimes five families in a 'mess'.

Passengers slept in tiers of bunks. They were provided with mattresses, but not bedding. Bunk space was cramped, and tables and forms occupied the spaces between tiers. Moving between messes was awkward to say the least. Containing small children to localized areas was impossible. Consequently, it didn't take long to get to know neighbours as youngsters were recaptured and returned to their parents.

The only saving grace was that the ship was new. The Scots, of course, being first on board, had chosen some of the best positions, but were open in providing advice as fellow passengers crowded their space. Arguments occurred but were quickly resolved as everyone realised this was to be their home for the next four months. Two days after getting underway, upon the advice of the captain, several committees were formed with the sole purpose of resolving conflicts and disputes among passengers. There was a certain military aspect to the regimen on board, based primarily on experience, of course, with convicts travelling under duress.

But the newness of the ship couldn't fully outweigh the ugly smells that emanated from the latrines and the animals on deck. At least due to the newness the rats and cockroaches were few and far between, unlike conditions on older ships. The passengers were urged to keep their rubbish contained and not left on the floors to attract same. Light was primarily supplied through hatches to the main deck, whence came the only fresh air as well.

In rough seas the hatches were closed, and people, luggage, and artifacts were tossed around mercilessly, often causing bruises, and in some cases broken limbs. As much as possible, however, the hatches were left open, which meant that when large rogue waves washed over the main deck, salt water poured into steerage and dampened the beds and clothes nearest the openings.

The surgeon on board was responsible for the health of the passengers. This included management of their diet, maintaining cleanliness, and treating the ill. Passengers were required to scrub down their compartments once a week and six crewmen helpers kept track of conditions, noting behaviour of troublemakers and adding notes to their records. A sense of discipline was necessary with so many immigrants on board, just as there was discipline for the crew. At first there was general resentment among everyone below deck, but after a while patterns of behaviours emerged that minimized friction and maximized co-operation.

In later years, meals were cooked in the main kitchens and handed out, but on the *Herald* passengers had to fend for themselves. The primary diet consisted of salted and preserved meat, ship's biscuit, flour, oatmeal, and dried potatoes. The usual ration of potatoes was six pounds per adult per week. Treats included raisins, sugar, tea, and coffee. The diet was coarse, monotonous, and offered poor nutrition, but it rarely ran short. Hanging stoves with protected coal burners allowed food to be warmed. The danger of fire from them was carefully monitored.

The cooks and senior officers were privileged, of course. Live sheep, pigs, and poultry were killed periodically to provide fresh meat for the captain's table, where fresh milk was also served. The cooks looked after themselves well and fresh meat did not make it to the steerage passengers. There was an allowance of fresh water—just under a gallon per day. But water stored in barrels often deteriorated and became undrinkable in a couple of months. Passengers then attempted to catch rainwater to drink or for washing. For the Monahan family, Ann's question was finally answered. Yes, they would eat more than just potatoes. But not immediately.

Outside Lough Foyle they all got their first experience of ocean waters. The wind increased and the ship rolled side to side and rode up and down in the waves and it wasn't long before many on board, being unused to the sea, were feeling squeamish and casting about in all directions seasick. Dawn of day two found them heading past the south end of the Isle of Man and by evening they were off Dublin at 53° N, 5° W. This second day out was Easter Sunday. The captain held a short Easter service topside in the morning, where sailors outnumbered the few passengers not yet showing discomfort. Ordinarily the Monahan family would have spent that revered morning in church-related activities.

By day three nearly all the passengers were seasick and below decks was a very unpleasant place. The wind picked up further and at times they made nine knots so that at nightfall they were just coming in sight of the Bristol Channel and saw a number of other boats in the vicinity. The Monahan children tried sipping some broth, which helped, as they hadn't eaten in nearly forty-eight hours.

Out past Land's End and into the Celtic Sea they encountered their first storm. The wind blew ferociously from the south accompanied by squall after squall of rain so the ship lay to for five hours and the hatches were battened down. Steerage was in pandemonium as the ship pitched and threw occupants and belongings back and forth. The Monahans clung to one another as the twin boys and their father anchored themselves on ribs and overhead beams. Squeals and curses floated through the fetid air as more seasickness resulted, and the floor through leaks from above became a soupy mess. As the storm abated and the hatches were opened there was relief all around but the cleanup was anything but pleasant.

Ann's little voice spoke for all. "Father, will it be like this all the way? I wish I had stayed at home."

"No, it will get better, I promise you, sweetheart. I know this is a horrible start to our journey but storms on the seas feel more fierce because we aren't anchored to the ground as we were back home. There'll be more storms I'm sure, but as you see the captain has gotten us through this one, and we will get a little used to them as time goes on.

"Mind you," he added, "I do think we could offer the Lord a small prayer of thanks. Let us all pray."

The next morning, there was sadness on the main deck as it was discovered one of the dairy cows and one of the sheep had died due to not being adequately secured during the storm. The captain was upset and publicly reprimanded two of the young sailors for their poor work. They were lucky to escape a whipping, but rather were denied any rum for two weeks as punishment.

There was a giant swell in the ocean on account of the currents off the Bay of Biscay. The wind stayed strong for two days but the *Herald* maintained nine to ten knots through the rolling waves, which increased in size as the boat neared the centre of the bay. As careful as the sailors tried to be, accidents still occurred. One young man fell from high in the rigging onto the deck, screaming all the way down. His fall was partially broken by a large coil of rope, but he was knocked senseless, and it was hours before he recovered. Ever afterwards his speech was more jumbled, his eyesight blurred, and his head was held at a slight angle to his torso. He was assigned simple duties on deck.

A carpenter repairing one of the animal pens hammered his thumbnail as the ship unexpectedly heeled over a few degrees when a larger than usual wave passed underneath. He swore horribly. His nail burst and there was blood all over his work. The next day the surgeon was forced to remove what was left of the nail and despite the extra doses of rum he had absorbed in anticipation the man's yells could be heard in steerage. The immigrants were learning how very cruel life on a ship could be.

By the time they were off the northwest coast of Spain the passengers had started to settle into regular routines. Seasickness had worn off as stomachs had adjusted to the vessel's movements. And once again Ann voiced opinions shared by many. "Father, it is so good to taste meat again, even if it isn't exactly fresh," she said after a welcome dinner. "And we haven't had raisins in years. They are so sweet. It is very cramped in here, but no worse than it was in our home. Although I still think I'd rather be on land than at sea forever."

Early next morning a cry from on deck had almost everyone scuttling above. A school of maybe thirty porpoises raced alongside and ahead of the boat. Smaller ones cleared the surface of the water by six or seven feet and the graceful arches up and over and down again brought smiles to all the faces along the rails. There was no question in anyone's mind that they were simply having fun, matching the speed and direction of the boat and simply cavorting for sport. Eventually they moved away but remained as the topic of the day while the boat ploughed on in calmer waters. The waters were now a deeper blue than had been the case nearer land.

Grace had written a few notes with Thomas' help in the diary over the past ten days but the porpoises brought forth quite an outpouring as she described the previous storm, the chaos in steerage, the food, and also a few words about some of the family's closest companions. "Mrs. Doyle is the one mother on board traveling without her husband, since he is already in Sydney. He is in the military, she says. She has a five-year-old son, Ryan, and a six-year-old daughter, Laura. She tells strange tales about the animals there and the native people, and I'm not sure we all believe her. She says the trip will get very hot, and before we land will get very cold again. She seems nice and her children are clean although they don't know a lot of English. We all try to help them learn.

"On our other side is a very poor family from Glenties. They arrived with no more than one sack of clothes, and Mother has loaned them our pans for cooking. I think Father makes sure they get a little more than their fair share of rations, as I've seen him hand out bigger handfuls of raisins and beans at times than he gives others. The mother and father and the two children are very thin and malnourished, although they constantly resist help from the surgeon. Their minds seem dull and they pray constantly. Father has forced the parents to do a little exercise with him on deck, and whenever they go they come back with more colour in their faces and look better. He has encouraged us to do the same with the children, and we've tried, but they are very listless, and their only joy it seems is to entertain baby Connor at times.' It took her ages to write so much, with frequent erasures and corrections by Thomas.

That evening as darkness fell, although the sea was calm and their progress almost non-existent, they witnessed an incredible electric storm far to the southwest. There was a great deal of lightning, and at every flash the whole ocean was illuminated. The horizon was so clear that had a ship been on it one could have seen it as distinctly as in daytime. Every three or four minutes there was a brilliant flash. Not even Matthew could remember seeing anything like it back home.

The temperature increased slightly every day now, and the creaking of the ship's timbers seemed louder as the wood reacted to more sunshine and heat. Some four hundred–plus miles west of Morocco a shout of "Land-ho" brought everyone topside once again to witness the island of Madeira way distant off the port side.

Each day after midday the captain posted a log of the distance covered in the previous day as well as their current location. From this point on they hoped to pick up the favorable northeast trade winds that would propel them across the equator and towards Brazil.

So far they had been making excellent time on their journey, now being out twenty-two days. The captain and some of the crew knew that as they approached the equator progress would slow and they could even become becalmed, but while the passengers were happy they did not speak of the future. As predicted, the winds picked up and on several days the ship covered well over two hundred miles. The heat, however, became more oppressive in the steerage area and soon young children were suffering.

A schooner coming the opposite way caused a bunch of excitement. She was out of Rio bound for Plymouth. Stopping broadside two hundred yards apart, the ships' captains crossed over and conversed on conditions. Passengers who had access to writing materials quickly penned letters home and these were placed in a waterproof bag and delivered to the England-bound boat.

The following day a baby was born to one of the young single women, but she had almost no milk to offer. A deputation of mothers approached the captain and he allocated some of his own milk ration to the poor child. People were immensely pleased at his benevolence. The baby prospered but a young girl, no more than two years old, succumbed to the heat, despite the surgeon's persistent attentions.

This was a very sad happenstance and seemed to affect nearly all the parents. Captain Coubro invited all those interested to a memorial service on deck. Katie and Matthew attended along with the four girls, leaving the baby with the twin boys.

Mary Jane whispered to her father, "Isn't there a reverend to lead the service?"

"One of the rules of ships at sea," he responded. "The captain is so empowered and has the responsibility in case no minister is on board."

The church service pennant was raised and the little girl was wrapped in her blanket and some heavy canvas. Weights were attached to her feet, and she was laid on a plank suspended at the rail. The captain empathized with the child's parents, recognizing their sorrow, devastation, and sense of helplessness, then read a psalm of comfort. He asked the parents to step forward and state the name of their daughter out loud for everyone to hear. He then intoned, "We therefore commit this child's body to the deep, to be turned into corruption, looking for the resurrection of the body when the sea shall give up her dead, and the life of the world to come, through our Lord Jesus Christ; who at his coming shall change our vile body, that it may be like his glorious body, according to the mighty working whereby he is able to subdue all things unto himself."

At this point the surgeon, Dr. Wark, tilted the plank, and the little body slid gently into the sea.

After the Lord's Prayer and the Benediction, the captain attempted to console the distraught mother and father with kind words, but nothing could really shake the despair they now felt. A small set of friends crowded around in support, but there was little in reality to offer. The couple had two older children, but for the moment there was only emptiness. One second their daughter was still with them, in the next she was gone. Gone to a grave with no headstone, in a place never to be revisited. Her winsome smile would exist only in memories.

The Monahan daughters, heavily affected by what they had witnessed, rushed back downstairs to look after Connor. "It was so sad," Mary Jane said to her brothers. "We must make sure Connor stays well." The children were well aware that several other youngsters were receiving the surgeon's attention for serious illnesses. Their plaintive cries during the night were pitiful and heart wrenching. Thomas voiced his siblings' thoughts when he offered, "I have a feeling before the week is out there will be more burial services." Sadly, his predictions were destined to come true.

The boys were intrigued with the routines and procedures the sailors had in trimming the sails, furling them when un-needed, and managing the complex set of lines used for rigging. There were days when they wished they could climb aloft, for it looked like a bit of fun and they longed to be high up and see the view from above. It didn't take long to exchange greetings with some of the lads when they were on break, and eventually two of the more friendly ones willingly spent time explaining the ropes and their purposes. It turned out that they were two brothers from Glasgow, Boyd being a year older than David, who was nineteen. This was their first time on a big ship, although their father owned a small steam-powered fishing vessel and for years they had helped him bring in the catch, so they were not uncomfortable out on the ocean. Their speech was full of fishermen slang and colloquialisms and there was a touch of bawdiness when they described life on the docks.

Grace and Eileen, protected by their older brothers, started to join in the conversations, at which point David and Boyd exaggerated both their responsibilities and capabilities, recognizing the attraction they presented. The girls were fascinated with the different brogue of the Highlands, and with the rugged features and muscles of men at work. Still, they seemed harmless enough, and when times were opportune the girls would meet with them alone.

At the end of one very warm day when most had sought constant shade, Boyd offered to wash Eileen's long hair to help cool her down. She sat on the edge of a packing case and leant forward over an empty bucket as Boyd handed her a fat bar of soap, and poured water over her head from behind. The water felt wonderfully cool on her scalp and she worked her fingers through the tangles, rubbing soap into her skin. She lathered up, and Boyd poured more water to help her rinse the soap away. Having emptied his bucket he walked around in front to get another. He halted as he caught sight of Eileen's softly swaying breasts, clearly evident beyond the front of her tunic, which had fallen forward. Without thinking, tantalized by the innocent sighting, he reached forward and happily fondled the glorious orbs.

Taken by surprise Eileen screamed and jumped up from the packing case, slapping Boyd hard across the face, and ran off with hair dripping. Grace followed after, yelling at Boyd and his brother.

The surgeon just happened to be coming up through a forward hatch as Eileen ran by. He had heard her screams and now observed her distress and teary eyes. He caught her and held her as other passengers came running forward. Thoroughly embarrassed, all she would say was that the sailor had taken liberties with her and should be dealt with.

Thunderstruck and bewildered, Boyd retreated way up on the bowsprit. He knew he had acted inappropriately and would be punished on the morrow. Momentarily he thought of dropping into the ocean, ending it all and escaping forever. It was David who finally convinced him to come back on deck and act like a man. Once back he was taken to the brig and held overnight while the captain decided the requisite response.

By bedtime, Eileen had calmed down, having told her story to her mother, who later shared it in whispers with Matthew. Matthew responded, "I did warn the girls earlier that seamen could be crude and vulgar. Guess I should have been a little more strident." While thoroughly annoyed by the unexpected coarse behavior she'd been subjected to, Eileen was also confusingly aware that the sensation of being fondled hadn't itself been unpleasant. After all, on maybe five or six occasions back home she had allowed her boyfriend to feel her breasts through her tunic. As she thought back, she was reminded of the warm and desirous feelings those episodes had created throughout her body.

Conflicting emotions flitted through her mind, and she surprised herself in finding a forefinger reaching over her mound and playing with the nodule just inside her slit. Her body awoke with the pleasurable sensations invoked, but she unwillingly stopped lest anyone realise her furtive activities. She wondered, not for the first time, whether in life ahead she'd ever have a room to herself where the word 'privacy' could finally be meaningful. Would some other handsome young man touch her, or more maybe, and make her moan like her mother did back home? The fantasy passed as she recounted the incident and a new thought lodged in her brain. Had she perhaps half deliberately exposed herself to potentially tease the sailor boys? Her body shuddered as another hormone attack travelled its length.

As they had supported each other for all their years growing up together, Eileen had no trouble recounting her night-time thoughts and behaviour in detail to Grace next morning. Intimate sexual topics were not something the twins readily discussed with mother, but they had no problem being open with one another on such matters. Eileen was concerned at the heaviness of punishment that Boyd would receive. He had after all helped her wash her hair, for which she was very thankful. It felt so much cleaner and more manageable this morning, and Grace, who had similar locks, was somewhat envious.

Fortuitously for Boyd, his 'crime' paled in comparison to another committed early that morning. One of the young sailors had cut the throats of two sheep because he 'was hungry for mutton'. Captain Coubro, after making sure the passengers were all below deck, called the crew together. "I'm going to remind you all again," he bellowed. "The animals are our food source for passengers and crew alike. Only the cooks may decide how to use the fowl and animals for the good of all of us. Irresponsible slaughter by anyone else is intolerable. We still have more than two months at sea and are lucky we can still use these two animals for meat, but not, unfortunately, as well as if they had fattened more before being culled.

"You men are paid to do the jobs you signed up, and were hired, for. Not to undertake new activities and exercises as you see fit. Discipline will be maintained or I will see that you never serve on this line again. Master Rogers here will receive fifty lashes under the surgeon's supervision.

"As for Master Boyd Duncan... We are a bounty ship. We get paid by delivering passengers in good health to the authorities in Australia. Any activity that affects such delivery negatively shall also be punished. Fraternizing with the passengers is not forbidden since I realised it is impossible to keep crew and passengers separated for the long period of time we will be away. But... any act that creates an injury or otherwise affects a passenger's well-being will not be tolerated. Mr. Duncan was helping a female passenger cool down yesterday but became overly personal and frightened the poor woman. She is not physically hurt.

"Mr. Duncan, you will be stripped to your britches and tied face down under the bowsprit for the rest of the day. You may want to pray that the seas are light. No one is to talk to the man except the surgeon. Do I make myself clear to all?

"You are dismissed."

5. Ship building, crew training

Captain James Coubro was livid. He walked back to his cabin seething. What was it that these men did not understand? Too often already he had had to talk to them about shipboard practices, behaviours, and expectations. To him it was simple. Just do your job. That's all that was required. Would they never learn?

In his mind he was taken back several months to an earlier time when he'd also become incredibly angry. It didn't happen often, which was why he remembered such situations with startling clarity.

The crew was on trial in the first run of the expensive new boat just out of the slips in St. John, Canada. The storm had come in quickly from the northeast, full of fury, providing exactly the test he had been looking for. But the sailors had not reacted smartly enough to his commands and already four of the square-rigged sails were torn and hanging useless in the pelting rain and wind. He expected more giant rips would follow and yelled once more for faster action by those high in the rigging. He had sensed the storm brewing and had called the crew together and given them his instructions. But many of the hands were young and inexperienced, and since the ship was brand spanking new, all the rigging was stiff, not helping the cause.

Fearing the captain's wrath, the experienced master sailors left their command positions on the deck and climbed the rigging directly, showing by example what had to be done. Two more sails fell useless but the majority were saved, and as the masts held firm, swaying before the gale, the boat succumbed to the merciless waves. Coubro had the anchors released and hove to in order to ride out the storm.

The next day they limped back into Saint John and set to work identifying the repairs needed. Coubro dismissed ten of the least useful crew members and sought out more experienced men. At least the *Herald* had proved her seaworthiness in the toughest of conditions and he gave a positive report to the owners and builders about her integrity. She'd been built with some of the finest Canadian timbers—black birch, oak, spruce, and hackmatack, the latter being soft wood used in the interior decor. As well, the ship's hull had been wrapped in the new special felt that underlay the yellow metal sheathing designed to better prevent bottom fouling. The *Herald* was the newest ship for the Anderson Company and was destined for travel between Britain and the Antipodes.

Six days later with sails re-stitched or replaced, with new hands on board and all sober, the ship left for the two to three week journey northeast across the Atlantic Ocean to Greenock, Scotland. Coubro stood before his crew and lectured them on discipline, doing their jobs earnestly, and his expectations. They made good speed and arrived early on Thursday 1st April 1841.

The ship was then officially registered out of Glasgow and the next four days were spent recruiting more hands, loading the holds with provisions, and eventually accommodating seventy-eight Scottish bounty passengers and their skimpy luggage bound for Sydney. The ship was twice the size of most regular barques, capable of holding four hundred passengers if needed, and spending four months at sea with rations, produce, and water to suit.

Captain Coubro had sailed to Sydney twice before on the *Portland* in 1838 and had a record of good timing and safe passage. The passengers on one of those trips had in fact set forth a testimonial to him. Published in the *Colonist* in Sydney on Wednesday 7th March 1838 was an article which read:

TESTIMONIAL TO CAPTAIN COUBRO
The cabin passengers per the Ship Portland, on her late voyage to this colony from Scotland, have presented an elegant Gold Snuff Box with an appropriate inscription, to Captain J. B. Coubro, the commander of that vessel, as a testimony of their respect and esteem. The box is of

colonial manufacture, and does great credit to Mr. Watt, the Jeweller, both for chasteness of design and neatness of execution.

TO CAPTAIN COUBRO, OF THE SHIP PORTLAND.

Sydney, March 6, 1838

DEAR SIR — We, the undersigned cabin passengers per the ship Portland, on her late voyage from Greenock, in Scotland, to this port, beg, on our own part, as well as on that of all the other cabin passengers by that vessel, to request your acceptance of the accompanying gold snuff box, which we are sorry it has not been practicable to present sooner, as our joint testimonial of esteem and respect towards you, as the commander of the vessel in which we made so long and so prosperous a voyage to this colony, from our native land. Wishing you a prosperous voyage to England, and hoping and trusting that the divine blessing may attend you in your future course, we are,

Dear Sir,

Your Sincere Friends,

JOHN DUNMORE LANG,

THOMAS DUGALL,

DAVID IRVING,

JAMES M'EACHERN,

W.T. ROBINSON.

Few captains ever got accolades from passengers or crew, so this was a marked event. As well, many of the crew of the *Portland* had willingly signed over to the *Herald* when they learned of Coubro's captaincy. John Dunmore Lang was a Presbyterian reverend and a pioneer in Australian religion. He became well recognized in the colony and was later to play a part in some of the Monahan lives.

The boat's agents, Gilchrist & Alexander, had found just over three hundred and eighty immigrants to partake of the British government's bounty scheme for the upcoming trip to Sydney. This time the ship would stop at Londonderry, Ireland, instead of Cork or Dublin, in order to pick up travelers from more northern and western climes.

The "bounty" system of immigration was the favoured method of assisted passage in the years 1837 to 1843. Ship owners and their agents were responsible for recruiting migrants, in conjunction with the Board of Immigration, and delivering them to

Australia, where they were paid on a per-head-landed basis. In 1841 the amounts they were paid were:

- Thirty-eight pounds for a man and wife under forty years on embarkation;
- Nineteen pounds for each single female fifteen years to forty years
- Nineteen pounds for each unmarried male fifteen years to forty years
- Ten pounds for children aged seven to fourteen years
- Five pounds for each child one to seven years.

In some cases landlords added to bounties to move people off their estates. As well, parents were often bribed to overstate ages of children who were just under the age acceptance limits. The flaws of the system were well known, but policing the requirements was difficult. Upon arrival in Australia, immigrants were processed by a government officer. No bounty was paid for any person who was not considered suitable due to age, health, or occupation, or who had died on the voyage. The ship owners therefore faced considerable risk. The ship's surgeon was usually given the responsibility of keeping immigrants healthy and fit until their arrival in Australia.

The Anderson Company and its agents, Gilchrist & Alexander, were delighted with Captain Coubro's capabilities and had cor ...cntly asked him to command the *Herald*, nearly double the size of the barque *Portland*. The new ship was to be a boon to its owners and to the agents, for 1841 would turn out to be the year of 'the great emigration'. Some 28,000 persons would migrate from Britain to Australia. To help their share of that number get there in good shape, Captain Coubro chose Dr. Wark as his surgeon based on their previous experience together.

Early in the morning of Tuesday April 6, 1841, the *Herald* pulled away from its berth in Greenock and headed south southwest down the Firth of Clyde. The pilot ship took command until Cummins Head, about thirty miles down the Clyde, was passed. It was the start of a one hundred and sixty mile journey into the

North Channel, past Ratlin Island and then southwest through Lough Foyle to Londonderry. Three hundred Irish citizens waited with trepidation for her arrival.

The Monahans were just one of many families due for the biggest shock of their lives.

6. Life on board

Coubro shook his head. He was extremely confident in his own abilities and in his practice of ship management. He strived to be fair and to set a good example for his crew, meting out discipline when necessary but preferring incentive as the carrot rather than use of punishment in the form of the stick. Especially when senseless acts occurred, such as killing the two sheep this morning, he became more enraged as understanding defied him. His recourse in such times was always some form of action. Once the punishments were under way he personally opened all the hatches and talked to the passengers as they emerged.

With his back raw, the sheep dispatcher was an ugly sight tied against the main mast. Young children were curious and resisted parents' actions to keep them away. For most adults it was the first time they'd seen any such sight and many were visibly shaken at what they perceived was inhumane and cruel treatment. Mutterings against the captain arose often throughout the day.

The two sets of Monahan twins raced to the bow, where they talked to David about his brother's penalty. The waves were medium sized and as yet Boyd had not had to endure the bowsprit plunging through a crest. Several older hands, however, had forecast a squall in the afternoon, pointing to dark clouds on the horizon. If the wind shifted to be more in their faces Boyd's experience would become much more uncomfortable.

Just after posting the ship's midday position, the captain had all the sails furled and the first huge raindrops started to fall. The wind picked up and swirled in varying directions around the boat, sometimes forcing a complete reversal in course. The passengers were shepherded below and the hatches battened down. The wind noise and the creaking of the vessel's timbers heralded the violence aloft. The ship rolled mightily as waves lashed the hull.

People wondered if the mast would snap since the wind sounded so fierce. It was a scary period. It was clear that waves were dashing over the bow as they could all hear the water carousing across the deck above and small leaks evidenced the fact.

But as suddenly as it had appeared, the storm passed. No more than an hour had gone by, although it seemed much longer. The wind died and the ship evened and stabilized. A light rain still fell. Everyone breathed sighs of relief. Several chickens had died from exposure but the other animals had all survived. No doubt sheep and cattle and hogs had bruises but they were hard to detect. Most were lying down against the back wall of their shelter and seemed okay. A couple of opportunistic passengers found empty buckets and filled them with rain water, which they then poured over themselves to wash down. A giant scramble to find pails followed as others tried to emulate the process. Some of the more brazen women even soaked themselves from head to toe, many revealing curves only husbands and serious boyfriends had seen before. One single woman and several single men stripped totally naked and got the best cleansing of all. As the rain stopped and the sun shone brightly through the clouds, steam rose from their bodies and the sight on deck was quite theatrical.

Away from the main crowd the two sets of Monahan twins had hastened to the bow. It was clear that Boyd had received a battering. The surgeon had him released and checked him over, finding several cuts on his head where either debris or fish had bumped into him as the bowsprit went under a wave. He was exhausted from the pounding and having to continually hold his breath, but after two drafts of rum, colour started to return to his cheeks and the surgeon declared he'd live to see another day.

Late in the afternoon the ship started slowing markedly. Even with full sail it was clear that speed had dropped way off that of the morning. The captain announced that they were approaching an area of calm winds just north of the equator between the two belts of trade winds, which met there and neutralized each other. Years later ships' occupants at this point would say they were 'in the Doldrums'.

The passengers had seen what was to be their last storm for days and the temperature now grew hotter and hotter, reaching ninety degrees Fahrenheit in the shade by dinner time. The very next morning they were almost becalmed. A schooner was seen at great distance from the stern. Slowly, ever so slowly, she caught up. Signals were exchanged and they learned she was thirty-five days out of Guernsey, bound for Rio de Janeiro. A slight northerly breeze came up and both ships took advantage, the schooner crossing behind them. Late afternoon was sad as two more children died and were promptly sent to the deep.

Day after day now the ship hardly moved. Grace wrote in the diary: "It is unbearably hot, the temperature below decks being one hundred degrees. It is stifling and many children are in distress. Cold towels are laid on their foreheads and sips of water are given constantly. Another baby was born yesterday. We could hear the mother screaming. Today the little boy was baptised by the captain, but we all wonder if he will survive. The mother's milk hasn't come in yet.

"Up top the deck planks are hot on the bare feet. Sometimes there is the faintest breeze but everyone seeks the shades of the sails and the masts and it becomes crowded. The sky is bright blue and everyone keeps looking at the horizon hoping to spot a cloud there. No sign of any in four days now.

"Our best friends are still the O'Donnells from Falcarragh, but their space is on the other side of the ship so we only see them on deck. I especially like Padraig, who is closest to my age. We have fun making up stories about the adults we don't know and the sailors. Where do they come from, what are their names, how old are they? Sometimes we learn the answers and are always surprised. I think Ann likes Niall a lot as I've seen them sitting together at the rail with their feet over the side. He'd better not touch her like Boyd did to Eileen or I will be mad."

No longer was Katie helping Grace compose her notes, as her daughter had grown quite competent at expressing herself. Matthew or Thomas would often still help her with the physical writing part, but they tried not to change what she wanted to say.

Katie did grin at Grace's latest entry, however, wondering how few years hence her feelings might change.

The passengers were bored and the sailors were bored. Passengers played card games in the shade, small children played hop-scotch and skip-rope when there was space but only in the cooler evenings. The sailors had three main forms of self-entertainment. One involved contests of arm-wrestling as bouts of strength. The other two involved races. One form involved seeing who could climb the rigging fastest; the other involved swimming. Many more men competed in the latter races since they got relief from the heat in the water. There were two favorite types of race. The first involved swimming around the ship, with two men diving off the stern and swimming alongside opposite hulls. Passengers ran from side to side to check progress and someone was always at the bow to see which swimmer got there first before heading back on the other side. There was great merriment and cheering as heat after heat progressed, culminating in an eventual winner receiving an extra share of grog and accolades from his mates.

A second swim race involved longer distance competition. Six participants would be rowed out in a long boat about half a mile off the beam. They would dive in together and race back to the stern of the ship. A shouted commentary from a sailor high in the rigging would give spectators information on who was leading, as sometimes with the swells it was hard to see from the ship's rail how the heads were aligned in the water. The passengers became enthusiastic supporters of select seamen and applauded all their efforts no matter who came first.

Finally a small encouraging breeze propelled the ship southward and everyone cheered. Their speed even reached four knots, and felt wonderful. Three vessels were seen in the distance, one of which had no canvas up except the fore top sail, which was torn to pieces with the wind. The captain, seeing her in such a state, steered towards her, coming within a quarter of a mile. It was obvious that there was no person on board alive, as the ship was waterlogged and almost sunken. She appeared to be loaded with timber and the Spanish colours were up. The waves were washing over her and every time the ship rose with the swell, water came out of the cabin windows. It was a large brig seemingly abandoned for many days. Her yards were all clean but a great number of her cables and bulwarks were broken. A very sad sight to observe. The other two vessels disappeared in the distance.

Grace couldn't resist writing in the diary about the strange vessel. She let her imagination roam wildly and even scared herself anticipating cockroaches that had grown to be the size of small mice and rats that were now the size of cats. Had they taken over the ship, eaten all the food so the sailors had died of starvation? Were there corpses littered below decks? Enough! Her sisters cringed when she read out loud what she had written. There was nothing wrong with Grace's imagination, although the pencil couldn't always keep up with her thoughts.

At the forty-five-day-out mark on May 25th the captain proclaimed they had arrived at the equator. They were due east of Macapa and due north of Natal in Brazil at longitude 35.15° W. A couple of huge albatrosses flew by but did not stay around. It was definitely time to turn southeast, but before that all hands new to reaching the equator had to be initiated into Neptune's Kingdom.

Late afternoon, the passengers watched as King Neptune entered a throne on the deck, wearing a red robe with a canvas hat trimmed in red cloth. He carried a shepherd's crook as a sceptre. The barber who accompanied him had his face, arms, and legs painted black. His tools included a wooden strop and a band of iron taken from around one of the casks. Next came the doctor, dressed in a black gown, with his 'medicine' in the form of a pail of grog. Behind His Majesty a great sheet of canvas hung between the rail and the longboat, full of water.

From the ranks of the uninitiated, two sailors were brought forward blindfolded. His Majesty asked their names, where they were from, and how long they'd been seamen, at which point he offered them a glass of grog as a welcome and ordered them shaved to be more presentable as they crossed the equator and entered his kingdom. The barber stepped forward and splashed their faces with water and soap and proceeded to 'shave' them with his rusty iron band razor. Their heads were then pushed under the water in the canvas until they eventually struggled free, to the merriment of the passengers. This continued until all newcomers had been so initiated, at which time several of the sailors brought out their flutes and fiddles, and everyone sang 'Rule Britannia'. Passengers joined in the dancing that followed until the lanterns were dimmed and the festivities ended.

Nineteen-year-old Patrick had a fine analytical mind and he was intrigued to try to learn how the captain estimated their latitude and longitude, as well as their speed at any point in time. He knew it took years to learn how to work the sextant for positioning so he didn't intrude on the captain to actually show him.

But to his delight one morning he came across two shipmates busy at the stern calculating the boat's speed. They held a wooden object shaped like a kite. It was tied to an especially long rope that had a knot at every six feet, and was fastened at the other end to a reel. They also had a sand glass, or so-called egg timer, whose sand took fourteen seconds to empty. The men threw the wooden 'kite' in the water, where it tended to stay put, and played out the rope while the timer ran through its sand. Mathematicians had calculated that for approximately every four fathoms of rope played out while sands slipped through the narrow glass neck, the boat's speed was one knot. If twenty fathoms played out as the sands finished then the boat was doing five knots.

How simple, how ingenious, Patrick thought.

Their target direction now was the Cape of Good Hope, and with a following wind they moved very fast across the southern Atlantic. Ten days from the equator a pod of whales was seen within a third of a mile from the boat, definitely a first sighting for many. They also encountered a large school of flying fish. The sailors launched two longboats and came back with a bunch that had landed unaided in them. There were so many caught over two days that the cooks shared fish soup with the passengers.

And although there was a lessening in the midday temperatures three more infants died in as many days. The sailor who had fallen from the rigging much earlier also succumbed, most people feeling he was probably better off as he never regained his full faculties and had been sadly getting worse over time. The little baby that had been born and written about in what was now being acknowledged as Grace's diary also died, and many folk were starting to get superstitious about the ship's environment. Especially as the rat population had seemed to grow in the heat. More traps had been set and the boys delighted in tossing the dead rodents at the squeamish girls before heaving them overboard.

The heat took its toll in other ways. Squabbles broke out more easily. Pushing and shoving occurred more frequently. Tempers rose faster. But one serious cause emerged as people started to complain that the rations they received were getting smaller and that there was not enough water being passed out. At the urging of several mess leads Matthew started keeping detailed track of weights and sizes. After a full week he and six other men asked to see the captain about the food they were receiving. Captain Coubro listened to Matthew's story and was clearly impressed with the records he had kept. He called two of the cooks in and made it clear to them that they were not to short-change the passengers any more. He further directed them to kill two sheep and serve fresh mutton that night as a gesture of reconciliation. When this action was announced below decks a mighty cheer went up, and Matthew was temporarily a hero again.

The heat also affected the sailors. They became slovenly, and several times the captain was seen on deck rousing the men into faster action. On one occasion a young sailor who was more thirsty than others had gone into the cooks' pantry and retrieved a bottle of wine. He got drunk and was caught fast asleep. His punishment was unusual, but to set an example he was made to 'strip to the gun' whereby he had to unbutton his lower garments and lie across a cannon where he received at short intervals twenty lashes with the 'cat' on his bare behind. He was then ordered to ascend the mizzen mast and sit on the cross trees all day without getting any food.

The sea kept on providing surprises. Large fish of the dolphin family, called grampuses, were seen close enough one day that the longboat was launched and several caught. And on a calm morning two days later small crabs appeared all around the boat. Various devices were used to try to catch them. Empty pails on ropes merely bobbed in the water until someone added a piece of lead in the bottom of one and it immediately sank below the surface and when pulled up had three crabs in it. The lesson was emulated quickly all around the deck and the cooks were presented with a fine haul of small edible crabs, the meat of which was shared with those passengers who wanted to try something different.

But other aliens were afoot. Cockroaches had been in evidence since the first day out but tropical heat encouraged breeding, growth, and aggression. They seemed to wait until nightfall before they came out of the cracks and crevices seeking whatever tiny crumb of food was about. Once again Matthew led the mess leaders in a campaign of cleanliness. As many as possible were killed on sight by a heavy boot, but during the day the floor was swept clean and food dishes were routinely washed. Sticky molasses was laid on the floor where well-known cockroach trails were observed and trapped many of the bugs as they sought the sweet liquid. Giving up the molasses was hard but it worked, and after five days the number of creatures seen had dwindled amazingly. Conversely, on the other side of the ship their numbers increased. Matthew shared the design of his campaign and the roaches started to be contained everywhere.

For well over two months Patrick had been observing a young girl, whom he thought to be about fifteen years old, located in one of the messes further towards the stern. He'd seen her many times, especially on deck, and noted how pretty she was and how tidily she kept her blonde hair in a long single braid falling over a shoulder or down her back. Their eyes had met on several occasions and he found himself fascinated by the flirtatious look she seemed to throw his way, but had not pursued making her acquaintance. He was probably the most introverted and shy child of the whole Monahan clan. He noticed other younger boys around the girl at times, like bees to a honey pot, he thought. She definitely was attractive and had a coquettish air about her.

As he returned from the latrine one evening in the dark hours well past midnight he saw her standing by a stanchion watching him. He could just make her out in the pale moonlight that slanted down from an open hatch further astern. As he paused to check she raised her arms and slipped off her dress completely. Her silhouette revealed her braid and well-formed standout breasts. She twirled and the distant light bounced off her buttocks. Patrick was rooted to the spot, enjoying the provocative display. She twirled again and he caught a quick glimpse of the blonde thatch between pale thighs. And then suddenly she was gone and he could see her no more. No doubt she had lain down beside family members.

He became painfully aware that his loins ached and that a bulge had grown in his pants. They were old britches, the legs of which were cut off above the knees to help tolerate the heat. Somewhat embarrassed and with the ache persistent, he tiptoed past sleepers and climbed to the deck topside. Keeping out of the light and in the shadows of the cabins he made his way to a dark spot near the stern. He swung his legs out through the gap in the rails, and quickly undid the top of his shortened pants. His member stood up thick and erect. He wrapped one hand quickly around the base and stroked slowly upwards. As he started a second stroke a voice whispered in his ear, "Here, let me do that for you." The girl who had helped create his predicament was kneeling behind him, her breasts rubbing across his back. Momentarily startled, he paused. She whispered again, "Sit back further so I can reach you." As he shuffled slightly she moved to his side, took his hand, and said, "Touch me," and guided his fingers between her legs, where he felt her wetness. Suddenly her mouth was around his penis and she was moving up and down. The pleasure was intense and his release didn't take long. She giggled at his speed and pushed his fingers further inside, gyrating on them until she eventually moaned softly and leaned back. "I'm Meghan," she whispered. "Shall we do this again tomorrow night?" And was gone.

As the family awoke around him in the morning he feigned continued sleep, kept his eyes closed, and examined his feelings. Part of him wanted more of what Meghan offered, another part felt guilty for being weak and unable to control himself. What was right? What was normal? Was it bad to want more? Was Meghan the wrong 'type' of girl, whom he should not get involved with?

The fact that they were so secretive said something wasn't proper. Would he regret it if they did it again? And what if they got caught?

He wasn't so innocent that he didn't know what certain activities could lead to. After all, for years eight Monahans had lived in two rooms, and when the parents were whispering happily and grunting at night the older kids knew exactly what was going on. Secrets were hard to keep in such close confinement. He'd seen his sisters' bodies, they had seen his. It was ridiculous to pretend otherwise. But his primary drive relative to the girls was to protect them, never to exploit or abuse them. Lustful feelings were reserved for outside the family. And it wasn't as if he could talk to anyone about his thoughts. He wouldn't want to anyway. They were very private and he would be incredibly embarrassed even to mention them. Sure, the boys had made jokes and told stories at school, but those were all channeled indirectly and never specifically owned or so acknowledged. No one ever mentioned a sister in any lustful or prurient context. It just wasn't done.

After eating some bread for breakfast he sauntered topside, wondering whether Meghan would make her presence known, or indeed whether she might have had second thoughts and had decided he was too naïve, or for other reasons not to see him again. He knew he definitely wanted to see her pretty face and full bosom again and so he surreptitiously kept watching for her to appear while pretending to be absorbed in other happenings.

And other happenings there were. Another huge school of porpoises was racing along the starboard side, some members frolicking ahead, some behind. There were so many of them that they spread along the ship's full length and beyond. Two enterprising sailors tried to harpoon one off the stern. After several throws they actually speared one and it was hauled on deck for everyone to see. No passengers had seen one up close so this was a novel experience.

A crowd gathered around the large animal admiring its smooth skin and dark eyes. Patrick turned away as one of the cooks brought his cleaver down, severing the head. It suddenly seemed wrong to reduce the majestic creature to nothing more than pounds of meat. But of course that was true for many food source animals. Maybe it was just the newness of seeing this one up close for the first time that affected him.

As he looked back towards the stern he found Meghan's face smiling at him from across the deck. He hadn't thought about her for a while with the porpoise episode at hand, but he found himself responding with a smile and he headed her way. "Good morning, Meghan. Did you see the catch?"

"No, I got here just as the cook came up. Tell me what happened."

So Patrick described the harpoon attempts and finally success, and how he sort of felt sad for the gorgeous animal. "They are so graceful in the water and are such a delight to watch as they have fun, that it seems wrong to kill one," he said. Meghan listened intently, admiring the sense of passion and respect he exuded.

"I agree," she responded. "Like trying to catch those huge albatross birds we saw. I just know the sailors will try again when we get closer to Africa. I don't want to see one caught. I know your name is Patrick," she went on, "because I asked some of the other boys who've met you. Such a strong name. Princely. Whence does your family hail?"

"Our home was a tiny village called Drumcarn in County Donegal by Letterkenny. We worked on a tenant farm there. It wouldn't surprise me if you'd never heard of it."

"I know the name Letterkenny as my father's grandfather was born there, but until boarding this ship we actually lived just outside Londonderry. My father had a cobbler shop, but people could no longer afford new shoes and eventually couldn't even afford to repair old ones, so Mother and Father sold off what they could and decided to emigrate, and that's why we are here. There's four of us including my elder brother, Quinn, who is seventeen. You must have noticed him since he is quite tall for his age. And I can tell you that while he is very tall his cock is not nearly as large as yours. I know because I've seen him make it go off. Now tell me about your family."

Patrick hesitated. Meghan talked so casually about subjects he thought were semi-secret and certainly not discussed between boys and girls at all. Finally he found his voice and told her about his parents and brothers and sisters. All the time though he was wondering, "Do all city children talk like Meghan?" Life certainly was different in other families.

Just as he was trying to think of something more to say three younger boys came up and joined them. Patrick watched and listened to their engagement antics for a while, then made his excuses and walked away to find his brother. He'd see Meghan again tonight for sure.

7. Will we ever
get there?

Matthew and his two sons approached Sarah, the seamstress who had cut down their britches when they entered the tropics. She was one of five needlewomen on board. Among the other sixty-six women with trades, forty-one were house servants, nineteen were nursemaids, five were farm servants like Katie, and one was a cook. In some cases they would trade their capabilities for something they needed in return, but since Matthew had helped everyone out with his general leadership acts Sarah was happy to do a little sewing for the men. One day after the other they each left the two parts of their britches with her, wrapped themselves in a blanket, and waited two hours while she stitched the pieces back together. Each thanked her profusely and promised themselves to help her however they could.

Adult female immigrants outnumbered adult males by one hundred and thirty to one hundred and four. But all the men had trade skills, whereas some fifty-nine females did not. If single in the latter group they were destined to be bride potential adjusting the imbalance of sexes in the new colony. Their future in some ways was more scary than was the future for those who had trades. And many were paupers, solely dependent on charity before they sailed, and would be similarly regarded once they arrived.

Sixty of the men were married, so forty-four were single. Match-making was a voluntary practical exercise that had commenced the moment everyone had found their sea legs and seasickness was a condition well past. Women of twenty and thirty years old who weren't shy had quickly worked out that if they could find a mate on board it would certainly give them a better start to life in Sydney. Consequently, posturing and exploration had started early and with seventy-one single women the men were in demand. Many of the men had little interest in the opposite sex and were happier left alone. And some women preferred the company of other women even though they recognized their pending situation at the end of the voyage.

Mixed groups of the young adults formed on deck and could be heard discussing what they'd left behind, the practices and procedures they missed, and at times local politics and religion. Protestants on board outnumbered Catholics by two to one, but that didn't seem to bother anyone and Sunday Church services were attended by both sects alike. After sixty days at sea it was clear that definite friendships had formed between select couples. Katie watched the women joyfully, sensing liaisons blossom. "I count ten couples Matthew, who could possibly stay together. I've even heard the word 'marriage' whispered and carried on the wind to my ears. I wonder if any will announce their intentions before we land and have the captain marry them. He does have that charter, doesn't he?"

"Oh yes, he can bless a child at birth, he can bless a couple in a union, and he can bless anyone who departs this life."

"I feel for the couples who have come together, for there is little privacy on board. I can see their love and desire easily, so others must also."

"Well, my dear, ahem, certain accommodations, shall we say, have indeed been made that you may not be aware of."

"What on earth do you mean, Matthew? Tell me."

"Well, way forward in the single men area, a tiny part has been partitioned off with some boards and canvas where couples may discreetly lie together. Since the men are sought after this was an arrangement they agreed upon and designed.

"I will admit, dear wife, that I have thought of taking you there at times, for my body is still responsive to my wants. But I do not think it would set a good example given how others regard me, so I have not mentioned it before."

"Oh, Matthew, I understand. It has been three months since we have coupled, and I am aware that others in the messes around us have not so restrained themselves. Somehow it doesn't seem right to do it here with so many people around. I hope you can wait further."

"I will try, my dear. I will try."

Sometimes he realised he didn't give his wife a lot of credit. He was well aware of the copulating couples in nearby messes but had doubted his wife was aware. How ridiculous, he now realised. She was simply being delicate not to acknowledge the behaviour. She hadn't reached out to touch or rub him since they'd been on board. Now he realised how she also had worked to restrain herself. They'd always enjoyed physical intimacy in Drumcarn, eventually realising that the kids would just have to pretend they weren't there when the wants arose, realising that privacy simply wasn't available. Their joint modesty came to the forefront when there were strangers, not just their children, in the immediate vicinity, however. He vowed to share later tonight his observation that Patrick was enjoying some middle of the night escapades that he could only guess at. Time to let the boy learn some things for himself. I did when I was his age, he thought. I can't advise him about everything in life.

That night, for the first time in weeks, Katie insisted that Grace write about the single adults on board and how out of initial groupings, several couples were now seen pairing off. Grace and her sisters were well aware of the single men and women seeking each other out, but Grace was surprised that her mother wanted her to write about them.

The girls had found a man on the other side of the boat who did carvings. He had amazing dexterity with a simple knife and would often be up on deck whittling on pieces of wood he found lying around or which others brought to him. Mary Jane had seen him carve a likeness of a saint on a flat piece of board that had been retrieved from the sea. She was thoroughly taken and wished she could have one as well. She summoned up courage and approached him. "Mr. Byrne, your work is beautiful and much admired. I would love to have a carving of a saint like the one I saw you do last week. But I have no money to pay you. Is there something else you would like that I may be able to offer instead?"

"Well, lass, I thank you for the compliment. I remember the carving of St. Anthony well. Where are you from and why do you want such a carving? Would you not prefer a small cat or a dog instead?"

"My family is from Drumcarn in County Donegal sir, and I miss the chapel in ManorCunningham where we used to pray. It had a grand window aside the pew where we always sat with a saint depicted there. I always felt he was especially looking after me."

"Well, that's a very noble reason, young lass. I tell you what. If you can find me a board like the one I used previously and if you can convince the cook to hand you two ripe tomatoes, I will carve you a saint. You are a pretty girl and you will have to use your guile on the cook, but let's see how resourceful you can be. Does that sound fair to you? What is your name?"

Mary Jane hesitated, for the produce gardens were sacrosanct. Her voice faltered a little as she responded, "My name is Mary, and I will try to get your tomatoes. Thank you, kind sir." After dinner she told the family of her quest and Grace wrote up the challenge in the diary.

Thomas offered immediate help. "I saw one of the packing cases broken behind the kitchen today. Let me see if any pieces have come apart or if I can break one for you. As I remember, the case is no longer usable." With that he ran topside and was back in no time with a rough thin piece of flat wood that would work perfectly. Mary Jane was ecstatic. Task one accomplished! She got up and gave her brother a loving hug.

They all discussed the harder issue; how to get a cook to give up two precious tomatoes. There were lots of them that had ripened beautifully in the tropics. All the passengers hoped they might be shared out sometime but so far the cooks had kept them for the captain, surgeon, and other officers up top. The conclusion was that the only way to get the tomatoes would be to trade other food for them. And that meant catching fresh fish.

If only they'd worked on this when all the crabs had been alongside, or if they'd been allowed in the longboats when the flying fish were about. It was difficult to foresee how else they could possibly contribute. But as sometimes happens when least expected, providence plays a hand.

Eileen was up at 7 a.m. enjoying the fresh air on a calm morning. She wandered along to the vegetable patches and animal houses thinking about Mary Jane's needs. A cook came out.

"Good morning, missy," was his bright introduction.

"What are you doing?" Eileen asked.

"Collecting some eggs for the captain's breakfast."

With that he entered the hen house and collected four eggs off the nest of straw. As he bent over his foot slipped on an egg that had fallen and broken on the floor. He went down with a crash and eggs and hens scattered all over. As he fell, his other foot knocked open the wire gate and one of the disturbed hens squeezed her body through the open frame and flew upwards—straight into Eileen, who had moved closer on hearing the cook's fall and the cacophony raised by the chickens. The squawking hen flapped its wings wildly but its claws had caught in the material of Eileen's tunic and it couldn't free itself. At first flustered, Eileen tried to help the hen get free but then suddenly wrapped her arms around it and held it close so it couldn't move.

The cook straightened up, shut the gate, and turned to the clucking hen. "Well, missy, I'm sure glad you were here. This is our best laying hen and had she gotten away we'd have far less eggs in the future. Let me remove her from your tunic. There's going to be holes left behind, I'm afraid. I hope someone can mend them for you."

He took the bird and put her inside the enclosure. Only one egg remained intact and he quickly picked it up. "This won't be enough for the captain. Would you like it, missy, for your breakfast instead?"

Eileen thought fast. "No, thank you. There are nine of us and one small egg would be hard to share. How about four tomatoes we could cut in half and fry? That would be nice."

"Four tomatoes? That seems a lot, but I guess if you hadn't caught the hen we'd be in a pickle. Okay, come with me to the vegetable plot and I'll even let you pick the ones you want. Just don't tell everyone how you got them, okay?"

Smiling broadly, Eileen took her reward down below, hardly able to believe her good fortune. Katie exclaimed over the rips in her dress, and Mary Jane couldn't believe how lucky she was. Eileen had been so smart asking for four tomatoes. Mary Jane got her two and they each got a small portion of the other two for breakfast. Mary thanked her sister over and over and finally said, "I'm not sure I would have done what you did, big sis. I think I would have kept on screaming trying to get that bird free, and let it fly away. I'm glad it was you up there and not me."

Mr. Byrne, the carver, was surprised to see the young girl approaching with two bright red tomatoes in one hand and a piece of wood in the other. "I'm impressed, lassie, for I thought you had little chance of securing those tomatoes. Now I will only ask you one question to which I expect an honest answer. Did you pick them yourself?"

"No sir, they are not stolen. One of the cooks gave them to my sister, who gave them to me."

"Hmm. I wonder how your sister got them, but I won't ask since my agreement is with you and I can tell you have answered me honestly. I will work on carving your saint for you, but you must give me a week for I have some other carvings to make first. Is that alright with you?"

"Oh yes, Mr. Byrne. But I will stop by now and then to see if you've started. I'm so excited to have my saint."

Late that afternoon the ship started rolling as waves built up. There was some amusement on deck at serving out the water to passengers at the after-hatch. The ship gave a sudden swing to one side, and water kegs, buckets, and other items not tied down were seen rolling in all directions, their owners having enough to do in keeping themselves from the same fate. A jar of rice was smashed and its contents spilled widely. A Scottish gentleman seated on a large coil of rope slid across the deck. Another swing of the boat sent him travelling back in the opposite direction. This happened several times to the amusement of all those watching.

The wind sprung up and the captain ordered the sails reefed. As black clouds then started to gather he had the sails fully furled and ordered the passengers below and the hatches battened down. In no time at all a pleasant morning had become a blustery, unpleasant evening. And it got worse. They ended up in the midst of a massive southern Atlantic gale which lasted a full three days. The passengers had been lulled into a false sense of security with over a month of good weather. Little food was passed down while the tempest raged, and that which arrived was sodden and non-nutritious. Some of the motion was so severe that some passengers got sick again, and many feared the boat would be dashed to pieces.

On the evening of the third day the hatches were opened and fresh air flooded below. Weary, bruised immigrants clambered up on deck. They were greeted with cries from seagulls and other birds, including the giant albatrosses. That meant only one thing—they were getting closer to land. Some of the passengers got lines to catch the albatrosses with a hook and bait in the form of pork fat. A piece of wood was tied about a foot from the bait to keep it near the water surface and it was hoped the albatrosses would swoop down and get snagged.

Simultaneously, sailors rigged a line aloft and hung ropes with hooks through the bait at the end. Two albatrosses were caught this way as they swirled through the air and swallowed the pork. Down on deck passengers were surprised to see just how large the birds were—some with wing spans more than twelve feet across. The sailors and officers were rewarded with albatross pie a day later. The cooks explained how they made the pies. First they steeped the birds in salt water overnight. They then boiled them in new salt water, and then boiled them again in fresh water with vinegar added. The large birds had a lot of meat and the final process was to bake the meat with salt, pepper, and vinegar to remove any fishy taste. The sailors declared their meal delicious, and the passengers listened to their praise with envy.

Mary Jane checked back frequently with Mr. Byrne but he had nothing to show her, until one morning he smiled and said, "Aye, it is finally done." He'd been working on it in secret and had wrought a beautiful carving for her. It was no longer a simply excised pattern on a board but rather was in the form of a large pendant, for he had cut around the robes of the saint and pierced a hole above the halo over his head. Further, he had passed a thin leather string through the hole so Mary could tie it around her neck. She was so overwhelmed she hugged and kissed the carver, thanking him over and over and indicating how beautiful it was and how thrilled she was. The old man reveled in her delight, knowing his artistry would be treasured for years to come. He'd done more than was asked and his soul filled with warmth at the reward of giving.

Two and a half months out the ship was in the vicinity of the Cape of Good Hope. They had crossed the Greenwich line at speed during the storm. June tenth had them at 34.2° S and 15.9° E, approximately one hundred and fifty miles west of Capetown. Four days later found them in the Indian Ocean headed almost due east for Australia. Passengers sighed with relief as the Captain announced they were on the final leg of their journey. They had maybe another thirty days ahead. He warned all that it was winter in the Southern Hemisphere and that it would get increasingly cold over the next few weeks.

The currents are strong around the Cape where the Atlantic and Indian oceans meet. Many ships travelling east are forced to the south, and the *Herald* was no exception. But Captain Coubro desperately wanted to see the islands of St. Paul and Amsterdam, destined to become French territories only two years later. These islands were located in the middle of nowhere, mainly providing checks on navigation since their latitude and longitude had been well recognized since 1838. Using only semi-manual navigation aids, finding them, however, was a bit like finding a needle in the proverbial haystack.

St. Paul is a triangular island located at 38.73° S, 77.52° E, some fifty-three miles southwest of the larger Amsterdam Island. It is the top of an inactive volcano, and is rocky, with steep cliffs on the east side. The thin stretch of rock that used to close off the crater collapsed in 1780, admitting the sea through a three-hundred-thirty-foot-wide channel only a few meters deep. Coubro wanted to anchor outside the inlet and hopefully go ashore and experience the active thermal springs. Only twenty passengers would be allowed to accompany him and the sailors. Many more than twenty volunteered so all their names were placed in a hat and the surgeon drew out the lucky winners. The three male Monahans wanted to visit, but none were selected. Meghan had included her name on a whim and when her name was called she offered her space to Patrick.

With the vagaries of current wanting to shepherd them southward, Captain Coubro worked hard against the current and winds to get a northward bearing. His seamanship was rewarded days later as they first sighted the western side of St. Paul. Sailing three miles along the south side he turned northwest and found the entrance to the 'Bay of the Crater' easily. Three longboats explored the rocky promontories north and south of the crater entrance, where in waist-level water the sailors, with large nets, searched for the unique island rock lobsters. In an hour they found six, which they then dragged under water into the shallow depths of the crater. As the tide ebbed it didn't take long to find bubbles rising from one of the hot spring vents, and to half cook the lobsters. Totally triumphant, the party returned to the ship, where their stories and catches held passengers and sailors alike spellbound till dinner time.

Heading east, the *Herald* avoided the bitter cold of more southern climes, but still the passengers dug out what sweaters and coats they owned, and many shivered at night. Two days from St. Paul they caught up with another vessel and 'spoke' to her. They pulled parallel to each other and rowed longboats between. The *Rajah* was a convict vessel bound from Woolwich to Hobart. She had left only five days before the *Herald* and had passed through most of the same storms on a similar track across the north and south Atlantic. The two ships travelled closely in the days ahead until the *Rajah* headed slightly more southerly to pass by the south of Van Diemen's Land.

A midday cry of "Land-ho" signaled the first sighting of Australia some fifty miles to the north somewhere near latitude 35.6° S, 116.6° E. A whole stretch of coast could be seen for about thirty miles. It was a major sighting for all the passengers. For some it was relief that finally the promised land was nigh, even though they had weeks yet to travel along the southern bight, through

Bass Strait, and northeast to Sydney. For many, however, it invoked feelings of fear and trepidation. What exactly lay ahead? How would they make out in this new land? Would it be worth all they had been through and all they had given up back home? The new friends they'd made with nearly three months at sea—would they ever see them again? Would there be housing for them when they arrived? Who would look after them and guide them?

The captain gave what reassurances he could, having been here twice before. Authorities would welcome them and the ship's agents would have organized temporary housing and would help them find jobs. Some church members would be on hand to help those needing spiritual guidance. Even so, he urged them to check the posted bulletins for advertised positions and to read the newspapers to learn about the habits and practices of the local people. Unfortunately, in the days ahead, as they were getting closer to their destination, serious bouts of influenza led to the deaths of more infants and two adult migrants.

The coastline receded out of sight as the bight curved northward. The travelling was fast but boring until early one morning, when two boats were seen ahead coming towards them. Between two sets of sails white foam could be seen. On coming close together it was clear that the whalers had harpooned a whale about fifty feet long and were pulling it along with a line from the two sterns. Patrick climbed up into the rigging a short ways and reported later that he could see its shape quite distinctly. The captain thought it could be of the sperm species and might be worth from eighty to one hundred pounds sterling, a truly rich amount

The course veered southeasterly and the captain announced Bass Strait was still 1500 miles away. But the winds became favourable and the ship made excellent time, so that on July 5th, the ship was roughly equidistant between King's Island and Apollo Bay, heading east before turning northwards. Land was in sight both to port and starboard and now some of the passengers' anxiety lessened with the realisation that the finality of their sea adventure wasn't far away.

Grace wrote in her diary. "We were all a-feared of what lay ahead, but now perhaps only nine days from our destination we are starting to realise that this terrible trip is nearly over and that we must prepare to go on land at our new home. I know Mary's pendant saint will guide her, and that mother and father will do their best for us. But there are so many immigrants that I wonder how we will all survive."

Now friendships took one of two forms. Some of them intensified, others languished in anticipated sorrow at parting. Patrick and Meghan made no secret of their feelings for each other, although trysts at midnight had fallen away for the moment. Matthew and Katie spent more time with Sean and Eleanor O'Donnell from Falcarragh, sharing meals where they could. Grace and Eileen would sit and talk with the sailors David and Boyd whenever the pair had time off. Boyd had sought out Eileen and contritely apologized for his behaviour. It didn't take long for them to become friends again. Katie wasn't quite sure about Boyd's intentions, but she kept from saying anything to Eileen, hoping her daughter's judgment would lead her appropriately. And, after all, Eileen had to start learning to look after herself. Katie couldn't watch out for her every waking minute any more. And she was eighteen years old, for heaven's sake. She noticed that Grace held hands with Liam while Ann would often sit with Connor by the rails and softly talk of Drumcarn. Mary Jane's impetuousness and outgoing personality usually had her surrounded by young boys her age and slightly older, and she never seemed at a loss for friends.

As they turned north past the southeast corner of New South Wales another ferocious storm broke upon them. They hove to in sight of land, where they could see small fires burning in the scrubland behind long sandy beaches—possibly natives cooking fish they had caught. It delayed them a day but since no damage seemed to have befallen the ship they continued on immediately after the storm dissipated. Meghan asked Patrick to meet her in back of the sheep shelter that night. She promised a present. And when secretly they came together he wasn't surprised when they lay down and she guided his penis inside her. "This is a safe time in my month, Patrick, and I wanted us to have something together we would never forget, as I somehow doubt we will see each other again after we land. Our fathers have different vocations and your father will look for farm work inland while mine will seek a shop in the town. Let us enjoy each other this first and last time." And they did. Maybe it was the first, but not the last, as youthful passion and energy experienced and enjoyed the pleasures of lustful intimacy several times. Hugs and kisses prolonged their parting and there were tears in both sets of eyes as they separated with the first light of dawn.

It was a proud Captain Coubro who finally turned his ship westwards to sail between the heads of Sydney Cove on Thursday the 15th of July 1841. This was his fastest trip ever, completed in the incredibly short time of only one hundred and six days. Temporarily holding against the wind off the growing village of Manly, the *Herald* fired her welcome cannons. The deck rails were awash with passengers admiring the rocky shores and bushland on either side of the Cove. It looked luxurious and not at all frightening. The harbour water stretched ahead, appearing welcome and calm after the enormous seas they had come through in the days behind. The sun shone on their faces and took the chill out of the air.

Slowly, the pilot ship steered their sea-home to a central spot off the Quay. The rattle of the anchor chain pierced the hearts of three hundred and sixty-two immigrants standing on deck, but they cheered anyway, thankful at last to have arrived safely.

The promised land was before their eyes.

8. Sydney, Australia & points west 1841/2

It took two days to land everyone ashore. Captain Coubro and Dr. Wark handed over their records to the immigration authorities and ship's agents. At least fifteen people had died along the way—one sailor, two emigrants, nine infants from teething and other complaints, two girls from influenza, and one baby. One other baby born had survived. The authorities regretted the deaths but were pleased with the number of single females and the variety of trades the men brought with them. Sixty-seven men were agricultural workers, twenty were carpenters, five masons, eight shepherds, and one each a gardener, butcher, bricklayer, and ploughman.

But a depression was settling in in the country. A daunting welcome.

As individuals and families were registered, the single men and single women were taken to special barracks, while families were allowed to return to the boat for temporary accommodation. The Monahans regarded their new environment with awe. There was no question that the cove they were in was beautiful. Coming down the harbour under sail they had been impressed with the relatively unspoiled shoreline, dotted here and there with sandy beaches, gurgling streams entering the bay, a large inlet to the north, and in a couple of places where bush had been cleared, small fields with grazing sheep. No industry lined the shores, no maritime buildings invaded the tree lines, no ugly wrecks littered the shallows. The aura was serene and peaceful. And yet at their anchor point there were all the signs of a growing metropolis. Nowhere near as big as Derry, but with vast spaces between buildings and a lot of activity both at the wharf and along the main streets that they could see from the boat. Local citizens were dressed like folk back home and the language in the air was English, not some foreign language they didn't recognize. Convicts in chain gangs were carting supplies, hauling rocks, and building structures.

It wasn't like Drumcarn with its soft hills and vast pastures, at least what they could currently see. There were hills, but they were half hidden behind heavily timbered forests along the shores. To the west the broad river rolled on with no end in sight. There were familiar seagulls and black crows but flitting among trees on the banks were vividly coloured parakeets, rosellas, and cockatoos, the likes of which they had never seen before.

As much as the scenery was intriguing there were realities that had to be dealt with. Matthew and the two sets of twins scoured notices on shore and read the newspapers they brought back on board, looking for jobs and lodging. The *Sydney Herald Daily* offered a large range of advertisements. From Cottages to be Let, Young Men wanted, especially in the grocery and haberdashery businesses, Cooks, Nurses, Governesses, Shepherds, Coppersmiths, and Bookkeepers. There was Land for sale, including sheep farms, and any number of miscellaneous retail goods available, most 'recently landed'. Of greatest interest were the ads stating 'Farmhands required', but there were very few of these. And some were dated, so possibly already filled. In a few cases an address was given, or the name of an agent. In other instances one simply had to reply to the newspaper.

It was a tedious and frustrating process to find work. And not inexpensive, as several opportunities were on the north shore of the harbour opposite the main city area, and one had to pay to be ferried across the water and then walk to the farm or location involved. It was the boys who found the first jobs working on a farm at Lane Cove on the north shore. There was a small two-room shepherds' slab cottage on the property that served as the first Sydney abode for the family. It was highly inadequate, taking them back to facilities similar to what they had in Drumcarn. Suddenly, reminders of home were everywhere, blighting their expectations.

Gradually, the timber industry on the north bank was creating open fields as the aged eucalypts were removed and the mills converted stately trees into slabs and more rigid supports for buildings. The land was sold to farmers, who ran small holdings of sheep and cattle and goats. Tanneries and soap factories started up and small industry found a new place to thrive. Limited employment opportunities appeared sporadically for young unskilled factory hands. Eileen found a job as housemaid further inland, and Grace, with her vivacious personality, found a position as a helper in a hotel dining room in the main part of town across the water. A small trickle of income started to come in but better jobs were scarce under the local recession.

It wasn't a particularly happy time. The family had travelled thousands of miles for three and a half months, through perilous seas in unsavoury conditions, hoping to find a new life. Not necessarily paradise, but certainly something better than Drumcarn. Yes, the skies were blue, the sun shone a lot, and adventure and intrigue abounded with all the newness, but day-to-day life was hard. There were no relatives to turn to for advice, succor, or simply comfort. They were alone forging their own way. Alone save for other immigrants in similar situations. Those with good savings, who were few in number, could rent flats or boarding rooms in the city itself, but the Monahans were not so fortunate.

With the multitude of families that had just turned up, and the recession, the agents were clearly overwhelmed and ill prepared to support everybody. Matthew and family soon realised that they could not depend on help from Gilchrist & Alexander. So they struggled on by themselves. Neither Matthew nor Katie could find a job, and they would take long walks along the foreshores and throughout the main town wondering if they'd made the right decision in coming. They asked everyone they met about possibilities but nothing opened up. The younger an applicant for any position, the more favourable the reception. Youth had energy, and limited alternatives, and could be 'molded' to do what was required better than older folk who both cost more and were decidedly more fixed in their ways. Ann found a job as a governess and Mary Jane found part-time employment at the local stone wharf helping dock the boats and collect fares.

No longer was Sydney just a penal colony, but rather a growing city that happened to have a penal colony in its midst. Some married convicts were even assigned to their free spouses if they were there. In multiple examples free-settler women became owners of taverns, but convict husbands poured the beer. The populace back home in England was originally deliberately not informed of this particular arrangement, in order to maintain continued justification of the penalty of transportation for the so-described 'vile and depraved criminals' in their midst. In eastern Australia, transportation to New South Wales ended in 1840, just a year before the Monahans arrived. It began in Tasmania in 1803 and ended in 1852. To Western Australia, where it began in 1850, it ended in 1868. So while no more convict ships docked in Sydney, the convict and military presence still abounded in everyday life.

Sydney Cove was formed between two headlands—the low-lying one to the east called Benelong Point and that to the west, Dawes Point. The town itself covered one and a half miles due south, along the depression between Dawes Point and Benelong Point, and included the hill behind Dawes Point, and the next deep bay called Darling Harbour. From beyond Farm Cove on the other side of town, there rose a hill in an area named Woolloomooloo after the Aboriginal term *Wallamullah*, meaning 'place of plenty'. Several considerable country houses, looking as though they had just arrived from England, graced the district, but instead of trees on the hill there was only a giant windmill.

Elsewhere in town, major streets were wide and in good order. Standard-type cottages were of a good size, many with verandas around them, with few that did not have a small garden, some with English roses, in front. On Sundays, military bands played in the streets, or by the wharves, and there was little to convey the notion that this was indeed the capital of a penal colony, beyond the presence of the military garrison, the local prison, and chain gangs at work. At the Quay where passengers first set foot on Australian soil, a new circular wharf was being started at the eastern end of the cove. The Tank Stream poured water slowly into the harbour at the other end. Citizens were proud of the new gas lamps being placed in the main streets as they added a factor of safety that all the women of the town liked.

They still illuminated their private homes with cheaper oil lamps, however, rather than gas ones.

Fifty-plus years after settlement, there were still many rough and unsavoury parts to the town, epitomized in an area northwest of the Quay known as The Rocks. As one travelled south from the Quay up George Street, the scenery changed from warehouses to commercial businesses. Except that the revolting prison was still in place even though citizen anger at conditions had eventually boiled over just a month or so before the Monahans arrival, forcing one hundred and nineteen men and thirty-nine women to be shuffled in clinking irons and head-hung shame along the streets of Sydney, accompanied by harsh catcalls, to new quarters out of main sight on Darlinghurst Hill. Crime plagued Sydney as it did in every other city in the world, and an expanded police force was funded to deal with the problem.

The constituency of the police force was strange as it was composed largely of men drawn from those groups which were traditionally regarded as most antithetical to the police—Irishmen and convicts. In 1839, fifty-three percent of the police employed in the district of Sydney were ex-convicts and Ticket-of-Leave holders. Convicts who had earned Tickets of Leave had certain degrees of freedom such as property ownership but had not yet been 'pardoned'. The general character of policemen was poor. Joseph Long Innes, as acting police superintendent, told a committee of the Legislative Council in 1839 that men of good character were unwilling to join the force. As a result, it included many persons 'wanting both in mental and physical ability, and presenting an appearance at once ludicrous and disreputable.' Over time, more soldiers were added to the force, so that by 1847 thirty-seven percent of the members were ex-soldiers. But in general the police were not perceived as an asset to the town's visage.

Despite the negatives of the town, it had much of the character of an English port. Yet there was something extra—a newness and lightness and space and a sun-washed sky not hidden by clouds— that contradicted the memories of certain dreary, sombre, smoke-filled British towns and cities. There was a hint of optimism and opportunity around every corner, brought about by the newness, the ongoing construction, and the nearby unspoiled beauty of the landscape. Even the need for infrastructure and the chain gangs at work couldn't offset the sense of progress and the recognition of the absence of any obvious restrictions on expansion. It was, in fact, a whole new world.

Beyond the old prison, or gaol, as the local population called it, were the Market Place, and the Old Burial ground with its pervading smell when southerly winds blew. Bathurst Street ran east at St. Andrews Church, and then north on Elizabeth Street there were new residences and Hyde Park under construction. Turning east on East King Street, one faced the huge Barracks at the top of the hill where newly arriving male convicts were first housed. North down Macquarie Street, past the General Hospital and the School of Industry, was Government Domain. Walking past the Government Stables one entered the Botanical Garden area bordered by Farm Cove. The gardens were still being established but already contained a number of unique Asian and local flowers, shrubs, and trees. There were Norfolk pines from which Indian rubber was produced, bamboos, plantains, shaddocks, geraniums, trumpet trees, guavas, and loquats. Magnificent specimens of the coral tree and mimosa were already in place. From the natural grasses, tubes were exported for gentleman's-canes.

At Farm Cove, Macquarie Point provided a wonderful vista of the harbour with views both east and west. It was one of Matthew and Katie's favorite stopping spots. With no job for either they were usually alone during the day. They spent much of the available time exploring the city. And with the available propinquity and absence of elder children they re-established the intimate physical contact which they'd chastely denied themselves on the voyage out. Fecund as she had been proven, Katie knew she was pregnant five months after arrival, and in July of 1842 she gave birth to a son, David. Another mouth to feed, but loved by all.

It then became more important to find a bigger house, and fortunately Matthew found one in late spring of 1842 across the water at Hen and Chicken Bay. The family was not unhappy to leave Lane Cove, as vagrants, outcasts, and illicit grog-sellers, for whatever reason, had started to inhabit the area. In the *Sydney*

Gazette of February 25, 1841, an article stated that Lane Cove was "the resort of disreputable people...as great a set of ruffians as the colony holds."

The economy had just started to turn around and jobs were becoming a trifle easier to find. Most were menial in nature, but one couldn't afford to be fussy. Plus, the city was expanding westward along the southern shore of the Parramatta River, where small settlements were springing up to support the growth in number of fruit, vegetable, chicken, and animal farms. Labour was needed to help manage the flow of goods to the city and in some cases to provide seasonal picking, packing, and animal husbandry.

There was much to get used to, of course, in the new land. In the Lane Cove and Hunter's Hill area there still existed mild skirmishes with the native aborigines. In the city of Sydney those aborigines who had adjusted to white man rule became trackers and guides, paid by the government. As labourers they were unreliable, their culture having never conditioned them to recursive everyday work. Alcohol became an unfortunate addiction and on the outskirts of settlements the women succumbed to prostitution. Smallpox had decimated the tribes in the area within a year after the first fleet arrived in 1788. As the disease was brought to the colony by slaves picked up in Capetown and Rio de Janeiro, the tribes had no medical or natural defenses against it. Those who survived were intimidated by this 'magic' of the white men, which could kill them off so easily. The Cammerraygal group of the Kuringgai tribe was the largest on the north shore of the harbour and was less affected than southern bank groups. In 1804, cowpox, a mild disease present in cows, was brought to Australia and used as a vaccine against smallpox. Several thousand people were vaccinated in Sydney including some Aborigines.

On the southern shores of the Harbour, where the Monahans now settled, civilization had progressed far more rapidly than along the northern shores, since Sydney town proper was located on the southern shore. By 1793 an overnight detention centre for convicts moving between Sydney and Parramatta had been established in Canada Bay, a small sub-bay inside the broad confines of the Hen and Chicken Bay area. The stockade was called Longbottom. Over the next forty years or so it was to be used as an overnight stopping point, a local prison, a work camp, police barracks, government farm and timber mill, and agistment land for police horses and government oxen. By 1840, when convict transportation finished, much of the area lay unused and derelict as the road to Parramatta had improved.

But in that year the land area near the river took on a new role providing the detention centre for a group of French-Canadian political exiles. The political, social, and economic grievances of the French Canadians of Quebec came to a head in 1837, when their claims for constitutional reform were rejected. Outright rebellion broke out in November of that year. However, the rebels were no match for the British troops, and were soon captured and tried. Some were executed, some were sent to Bermuda, the remainder sentenced to be exiled to Australia.

Fifty-eight French Canadians arrived in Port Jackson in February 1840 after a five-month-long journey in the hold of the *Buffalo*. The exiles' dismay at the first sight of Sydney was described by one of the prisoners: "On the 26th and 27th we came on deck as usual, and gazed with horror on this land…. Looking down from the deck we saw miserable wretches harnessed to carts, engaged in dragging blocks of stone for Public Buildings, others were breaking stones: the sight of this brought to us many sad thoughts for we believed that within a few days we too would be employed in exactly the same way."

The prisoners were transported up the Parramatta River to the revived Longbottom, where they were housed in cramped and filthy quarters. For up to twelve hours a day the convicts worked in quarry gangs, firing bricks, felling trees and sawing wood. Over time, they became involved with the settlers of Canada Bay, becoming well regarded because of their "exemplary" behaviour.

For anyone it wasn't the greatest place to raise a family. Added to general discomfort, Scarlatina was prevalent in the colony, causing a large number of infant deaths. Katie coddled David shamelessly. Grace, working at the local pub, started hearing repeated stories, brought by travelers on the main road to Sydney, of the growth in farms and the need for labour west of Parramatta.

The idea of moving further west started to find reception in Matthew and Katie's minds. The promise of a new, better life in the Antipodes had not emerged in the two years since arriving, and while all the children had grown physically and emotionally and could now write a little and were adapting well to the local culture, Matthew felt an increasing burden of guilt at being unable to provide as he wanted and had expected. The local depression hadn't been foreseen when they had considered leaving Ireland, and stoically he defended their decision to travel to the colony, but his restlessness grew with their continued helplessness. By 1842, the population of Sydney was one hundred sixty thousand persons, with the proportion of free settlers, as per predictions, up from ten percent in 1834 to nearly forty percent currently—a clear result of the cessation of convict transportation, plus increased advertising by the government to attract skilled labour and businessmen to the Antipodes.

As the summer of early 1843 faded into autumn, less than six months after moving, Matthew called the family together one evening. In a rare emotional state he addressed his sons and daughters. "I want to thank you all from the bottom of my heart for the faith you've exhibited in your mother and me as we've made this enormous change in our lives coming here to Australia. You have put up with conditions only slightly better than what we had back home in Drumcarn, and that is unacceptable to me and your mother. We were led to believe things would be far different, and while we don't regret bringing you all here we wish life were easier. You have all been uncomplaining, and incredibly supportive and opportunistic, and for that we can only say thanks. I'm proud when neighbours, acquaintances, and employers speak positively of you all. But we think we can do better than our life here in Canada Bay. As you know, the newspapers are full of tales of opportunity west of Parramatta. And while no one can be certain of the future, there are enough positive tales from the mouths of travelers that we feel obliged to see what might be there for us.

"So once again we are going to journey on. It will be hard because we don't have a lot of money, but the Lord has looked after us before and we feel he will do so again. In two weeks from

Saturday we will pack our small sets of possessions and take the main road west. We could take a boat up the river to Parramatta but that's expensive for all of us, so let's make sure our shoes are patched and that we only take what we really need. Start saying goodbye to your friends and let your employers know so they can plan your replacements.

"Anticipating your questions, yes I have looked at buying a dray and bullock, but the dray alone can cost anywhere between twelve and thirty pounds. A seat on the Bathurst mail coach to Penrith is over ten shillings each, and with eight of us to pay we would soon deplete our meagre savings. Even if we found work along the way, labourers' wages are only five shillings per week. So we must walk and use our money for food and lodging where necessary. I know I owe you all something better, and I will try, but I need your help, love, and support yet again. We'll start by staying overnight at our temporary church of St. John's in Ashfield. We know that the structure being built there will be one of the finest in the countryside. Maybe one day some of you may come back and see the completed structure for yourselves. It's supposedly ten miles from there to Parramatta and we should make that easily by the second day. Penrith is another eighteen miles beyond.

"I know I am asking a lot of you all. Thomas and Patrick, you are old enough at twenty-one to make your own decisions and we will understand if you want to stay behind."

Thomas interrupted quickly before his father could continue. "Father, there is little here for us, and Patrick and I have talked about staying versus moving on and had already decided if you asked we would go west with everyone. We've heard versions of those stories ourselves and frankly are looking forward to seeing what we might find. We're all strong, and others less able than us have clearly made the trek, so we all can do it too. I want to see the Blue Mountains and wonder how close we might get. For some reason I find them totally fascinating. Perhaps because they are the new frontier here and there was nothing so daunting back home."

Grace added her chorus. "Oh yes, the mountains are clearly attractive based on everything I've heard, although not for the faint-hearted. Bushrangers have found that they readily provide secluded hideouts and it pays to be armed when trying to cross them. The mail coach has been stopped several times I hear."

All at once everyone was talking and anticipating the trip to come. Both parents were pleasantly surprised and afterwards expressed their relief to one another at the solidarity of their family. Katie observed: "Maybe we don't give our children enough credit, Matthew. I guess the two sets of twins are essentially adults and totally capable of forming their own opinions and outlooks. Perhaps we should seek their advice more often."

"As usual, you are more perceptive than me, dear wife. They certainly still are a joy to my heart. All of them. One day they'll leave us. I hope I'll be ready when that happens."

Several years after the route across the mountains had been forged in 1813, Governor Macquarie urged the construction of a road from Sydney to Penrith. Sixteen sandstone markers indicated the mileage to both towns and these became the guidelines for the Monahans' progress west. In the early days of its existence the road was a major symbol of progress. Its point of departure was George Street and Sydney Cove, the genesis of the colony. Its route went west to Parramatta. Beyond, its symbolic character became more apparent, as the topography of long parallel ridges dipping down to the Nepean in prelude to the ascent of the great ramparts of the Blue Mountains on the other side of the river began to unfold. The road held a strange sense of promise to its travellers, a sense of anticipation quite unlike that felt on any other road out of Sydney.

And so it was for Mathew and Katie and the children. Ahead lay hope for the new life they desperately sought. The children took delight in counting off the miles. Every bullock team coming towards them stopped and they exchanged greetings. Matthew asked about work, Katie asked about housing and food supplies. Their first stop was Parramatta. The original aboriginal name for the town was Baramada, which to the indigenous Dharug tribe meant 'place where the eels lie down', an apt description as eels proliferated at that point in the river, attracted to the profusion of nutrients created by the saltwater of Port Jackson meeting the freshwater of the Parramatta River's catchment. For the Aboriginal tribes of Sydney who settled on either side of the Parramatta River some 11,000 years earlier, the river was an essential source of food. Fishing was undertaken by the whole community, women collecting shellfish and catching crays in nets of woven bark, men fishing from the rocks or in bark canoes with their multi-pronged spears.

With the white man's arrival it was not long before the river became the main roadway between the settlements, transporting the military and settlers, carrying mail and equipment, agricultural produce and timber. Over time many former governors of the colony had set up residence in Parramatta, and land grants had been given in early years to various farmers to create produce for Sydney consumption, so the town had a strong commercial flavour. But Matthew and the boys were farmers at heart, and while the commercial aspect offered potential employment for the females of the family, Matthew wanted to be on the land in open spaces.

And so they trudged on. The autumn air was refreshing and the rains held off. Walking was not unpleasant, but the risk of finding nothing ahead tugged at their minds and hearts. The mail coach on its return run from Bathurst stopped alongside one morning not far outside the town of Penrith, where the horses had just been exchanged. One of the gentlemen passengers turned out to be the manager of a large estate south of Penrith called Regentville. He was on his way to Sydney to purchase some special supplies for the owner, a trip he made frequently.

Despite the coach driver's desire to move on and keep on schedule the manager became intrigued with the Monahans' story and spent time asking about their background, history, and capabilities. He closely observed the two strapping twenty-one-year-old sons, the healthy twenty-year-old twin daughters, the two vibrant teenage girls, the two very young boys, and the clearly devoted parents.

"When you get to Penrith," he said, "take the road south towards Mulgoa until you come to the estate. We have many convicts working there and it would be good to have some free settlers like yourselves as well. Convict transportation has ended and we need more help both on the farmlands and in the house, the kitchen, and the laundry. There should be work for most of you, I should think. If I don't get back before you arrive, ask for Henry the cook, or George, the butcher, who will help you until I return in a few days. Tell them you met with Graham. I'll see you again soon." And with that he jumped back in the coach and the horses took off in a cloud of dust.

The Monahan family all started talking at once until Matthew led them off the road and found shade under a nearby eucalyptus tree, where they sat and smiled in disbelief, cut slices of apples, and drank from the water bottles they all carried. Was this the miracle they had secretly yearned for? Had God finally found them in this new land? Matthew led them in a small thankful prayer and Mary Jane kissed the saint carving hanging around her neck. Back on the road, their loads felt lighter and their steps were more energetic. The baby fell into a contented sleep and the milestone markers seemed to be reached faster. Their mood was euphoric, and even Matthew, the most stoic of all, burst into old Gaelic songs, and the family joined him.

Penrith's existence began with a weatherboard courthouse and lockup built in 1817, with an adjacent enclosed paddock of seven and a half acres for travelling stock. The town was very slow to become established, as it had two competitors in the close vicinity—Castlereagh, designated a town site by Governor Macquarie in 1810, and the important colonial estate of Sir John Jamison, named Regentville, to which the Monahans were now headed. By 1827, a courthouse had been added to the site of Penrith. It was set back a couple of miles from the ford, on higher ground, so that it would be less vulnerable to floods. A punt was operating at the Nepean River from 1823 on and by 1832 some inns were appearing nearby. By 1839 Penrith was "a long village, containing a few pretty and many new, raw-looking houses." The foundation stone of St. Stephen's church had been laid. Thus, Penrith was a roadtown from the beginning, becoming established not through an official surveyed approach as was the general pattern in the state, but from its relationship with the important western road which passed through it, and with the river which formed the prelude to the ascent of the Blue Mountains. This nexus was to become more important as time passed.

Even with potential salvation around the corner the Monahans did not seek accommodation in one of the inns, but slept peacefully in the open under a graceful willow tree on the bank of the Nepean. They were a frugal family, needing little but water and simple food on the road, accustomed to making do with whatever was available. The children had learned years ago to accept their lot and not complain. They turned eagerly south on the Mulgoa road as the late morning sun climbed high into the sky to their left and warmed their hearts.

The first view of Regentville took their breaths away. In the distance as they approached they could see an enormous mansion as a nucleus for a cluster of ancillary buildings of immense variety. The sun shone on the front pillars of the two-storey house and on some of the outbuildings. They had seen nothing comparable in their travels west, and the only edifice that came into mind was Government House back in Sydney. The structure was magnificent and the family was awed as their eyes swept back and forth.

"How can this be?" exclaimed Eileen. "It is so far from Sydney, and in the middle of nowhere. Are we sure this is not also a giant inn, rather than a house for a nobleman? Who could need all that space?"

"And what on earth are all those buildings, I wonder?" chimed in Ann. "The smoke from the chimney at right suggests that may be a kitchen, but could the next two be quarters for servants? They look like small houses with their windows. My, oh my. I wonder if Mr. Graham has come back—maybe passing us last night. Are you sure this is the place, Father?"

"Look," cried Katie. "That smaller building must be a laundry of some sort, for there goes a maid with a basket of clothes to hang on a line somewhere, I warrant. She even wears a uniform. My heavens, it's a very rich man who lives here for sure."

The men had wandered a little ahead and stood open-mouthed as they observed vast sheep paddocks, and grape vines and vegetable plots stretching between the road and the river in the distance. In shock, and now with a little trepidation, wondering if they were about to step way out of class, they all trudged up the main drive to the circular garden with its fountain splashing happily and small birds bathing in its waters. A broad-shouldered man with thick forearms sitting in a rocker on the front veranda rose as they approached.

"Graham suggested we stop by," Matthew said.

"I'm afraid he hasn't returned from Sydney yet," the man said. "I'm George and run the butchery here. How can I help you? Have you come far? You look thirsty. Let me arrange some lemonade."

With that he went inside and came back a couple of minutes later to find the Monahans sitting in the shade against the wall of the house out of the direct sun. Matthew jumped up and introduced himself. "I'm Matthew Monahan, from Donegal County, Ireland, and this is my family. We met the manager Graham three days ago on the road to Penrith, and he invited us here to work alongside the convict labour."

"Did he now? If that's the case we must look after you properly. I'll arrange to have some fresh bread and butter provided as well. Do rest up."

Little did any of them know how much George was enjoying himself. Ten years ago he had arrived at the estate accompanied by a guard from the Sydney garrison. He vividly recalled how he had been treated on arrival. Not as a convict, but as a man with skills to be used on the estate. He had been called 'sir', and a pretty maid had asked him to wait 'please' as the manager had been called away temporarily. He hadn't been treated so deferentially in years. Now he could reciprocate, and he treasured the opportunity.

A maid dressed in black with a white apron on and a white band in her hair carried out a tray with ten glasses, a number of little lace doilies, and a giant pitcher of lemonade. She set it down on the small serving table and George invited the Monahans to help themselves. Too nervous to speak up, the children mumbled grateful thanks and savored the soothing drink. Baby David gurgled and Katie raised him to her breast.

"So tell me your story," George requested. "I'm all ears."

9. Regentville
workers camp

In 1814, the convict ship *Broxbornebury,* with one hundred thirty-nine female convicts on board, arrived in the colony. In charge of the convicts was Sir John Jamison, now owner of Regentville. He had served as surgeon on the *Victory* and tended to Lord Nelson's wounds during the Battle of Trafalgar. He was knighted by the Swedish government for ridding their navy of scurvy through the forced use of fresh fruit and vegetables, the knighthood being subsequently confirmed by the Prince Regent in England.

John's father, Thomas Jamison, had been the surgeon's mate on board the *Sirius*, part of the First Fleet that arrived in Sydney in 1788. In 1805, as reward for his services as Surgeon General of NSW, Governor Phillip granted Thomas one thousand acres bordering the Nepean River near Penrith, thirty-five miles west of Sydney.

Inheriting the property upon his father's death, Sir John was granted many more thousands of acres to enlarge his initial cattle holdings to accommodate sheep and pigs, tobacco, and various vegetable and grain crops, as well as grapes.

Regentville was unique in many ways. By the time the Monahans arrived the holdings were enormous by any standard, covering over nine thousand acres, bordered to the west by the Nepean River, and employing over one hundred convicts in various capacities. There were maids and cooks and nannies and washerwomen in the house, gardeners and stable hands, plus myriad field workers looking after the sheep, cattle, pigs, vines, and grain crops. The estate was actually a little community in itself, with some extra buildings with rooms for selected managers and servants. To feed all the workers there were separate kitchens and ovens. The butchery prepared meat for the residents and their guests plus the workers. The field hands lived a quarter mile away in shanties and huts, out of sight of the main house.

And what a house it was. In fact, 'house' was an inadequate term to describe the edifice. The current mansion had been built in 1824. A great circular staircase rising two stories greeted guests coming through the front door. Aside from a kitchen, the house included a billiards room, two drawing rooms, a dining room, and nine bedrooms, with attached laundry and washhouse, an extensive cellar, and a 'multi-seat' privy. Nothing like it had been seen before and it became the social center of the area as Sir John was a great entertainer and became renowned for his hospitality throughout the colony. It also became the staging point for dignitaries headed for the Blue Mountains on the other side of the river. Governor Macquarie, Charles Sturt, and Henry Parkes had all stayed there.

Close to the mansion itself stood a number of outbuildings, including two more kitchens, a bakehouse, maids' quarters, and stone stables, large shelters for farm equipment and the butchery. Under command of the estate manager were the household working staff and six other men who managed different parts of the estate. One was in charge of the vineyard and produce; one was in charge of the cattle and sheep; one for the pigs, goats, chooks, and geese; another for the grains; then the butcher; and the last for estate mechanics and logistics, maintaining the fences, ensuring the water pumps and filters were in top condition, and that all the mechanical conveniences worked. Each had men working under him, all former convicts fortunate enough to have had skills in demand by Sir John when they arrived in Sydney.

There were no guards, and a curious honour system prevailed. As long as the convict worker reported for work and carried out his tasks he was fed and paid a small allowance. If he ran off, or 'went bush', he was reported to the police in Penrith, and all his privileges were revoked and he was no longer eligible for employment anywhere. Re-capture meant time on a chain gang building the roads through the mountains. Some who left became bushrangers, robbing settlers and travelers alike. They became a scourge to authorities everywhere outside the main towns.

On Sundays, many of the workers trudged into nearby Mulgoa village or Penrith town, further away but bigger. Pubs were always open, even on Sundays, and general stores were sometimes open in the morning solely for the benefit of these workers. They would come to buy clothes or boots, flour and sugar, or perhaps other cooking items such as pots and pans, and sometimes food, as they had to fend for themselves on the seventh day of the week.

Being so remote with no church or pub on the grounds, field hands and house workers made their own entertainment. Again, out of sight of the mansion, several large areas by the river had been set aside for employee use. The men had set up a soccer field with makeshift goal posts, and further away was a cricket pitch. The convicts spent time maintaining both areas given the importance in their lives, and it was clear that many of the men had participated in the sports back in England. Around the fields a running track had been established, and those few who simply wanted to keep fit would use it frequently. Matthew had never been an active sportsman but his eldest sons relished a game of football. It wasn't long before their skills were in demand on local pick-up teams.

For plain folks like the Monahans, the estate was simply overwhelming. The boys walked with their father and stopped by the stables. Thomas was stunned. "Father—look at this. Two separate buildings for the horses. I count fourteen stables and three loose boxes and a harness room in each building. But I only see six horses at the moment. I wonder if all the others are out being ridden or whether they are grazing at pasture."

"You could ask that stable boy at the end of the far building there, son, if you are really curious. Go on, he looks about your age."

"That's not necessary, Father. I'm sure there'll be many chances to find out later and I'm so anxious to see all these other buildings. "

Patrick interjected: "I'm not sure we should be here at all. What if the owner of this mansion were to suddenly arrive and see us poking our nose in everywhere. He might get very angry."

"Oh, Patrick," sighed Thomas. "Come on then. Let's explore out of view of the main house. Although I hope one day I can get to see inside. "

The trio crossed a grassy area to a long building that housed a series of large pipes and pumps along with troughs and steel tanks and numerous water outlets. Matthew addressed his sons. "Well, this is where the water pumped out of the river by the windmill is stored, then mixed with rainwater when available and pumped to the house, as well as some of the nearby fields, I imagine. There are probably other pumps in the outlying fields. But look how modern this equipment is. There were pumps on board our ship but not as sophisticated as these. This is an amazing place. Let's head to the river. I told Mother and the others that we'd meet them on the bank."

Mary Jane and Ann were crouched by the water's edge dipping their hands in the current and shaking the drops back on the rippling surface. "Mother, it is so cool and refreshing. Come wash your face and hands. Ooh, it feels so good," Ann cried.

"Don't you fall in, dear daughter. You might float away. Look at those sticks in the middle moving quickly downstream." The boys arrived and Thomas immediately spotted four rowboats pulled up into a little depression in the banks forty yards upstream. "Cor, I wonder if we'll be allowed to use these," he exclaimed. I'd love to row to the other side of the river. Look at the gorgeous bush to explore over there."

"Don't be silly," Grace responded. "I'm sure these boats will be for the owners and maybe the trusted staff, not for us."

Katie sought out Matthew, and linked her arm with his. "Maybe, just maybe, husband, the Lord is finally shining His light on us. What a marvelous place He has led us to. I have a feeling we will find life rewarding here."

Once the estate manager, Graham, arrived back at the mansion he quickly assigned Matthew and the boys to cattle, sheep, and pig management. Grace was assigned to the kitchen, Eileen to the laundry, and Mary Jane and Ann to the bedrooms and bathrooms in the main house. The family was ecstatic. They were given use of two small huts. The four males slept in one, the five females and the baby in the other. The girls were promised space in the servants' quarters when it became available. Space was handed out on a seniority basis and highly prized since only six rooms were available, sleeping two maids to each room. A small rental fee for the quarters was deducted from the wages each occupant received.

Suddenly there was more money coming in to the Monahan family kitty each week than they'd ever seen. Life had certainly changed for them all. But the huts were extremely primitive. Stout saplings had been cut and thrust deep into the ground to form corner and door posts. In some cases slab wood formed one or two sides, but the roof and other sides were comprised of great sheets of bark pulled from select gum trees and held in place with sinews of stringy bark acting like cord. The ground was the floor and had to constantly be swept to keep insects at bay. Over time huts had had pieces of tin added, along with anything else that would help conceal cracks, prevent drafts, or hold up the roof better. The camp was an incredibly motley collection of homemade abodes.

The estate itself was in constant flux. With well over one hundred workhands and varied schedules the place teemed with activity. At first it was hard to make new friends, but when the Irish brogue was finally heard, country men and women stepped forward, keen to know what information of home the new arrivals brought. The camp had an amazing collection of characters. Over ninety percent were convicts from every place in the British Isles, it seemed. And of course most of the encampment's population was made up of single men. Their grateful, and sometimes lustful, eyes constantly settled on the girls, who all had naturally curly hair, dimples, and sunny dispositions. Grace loved the attention, a little more brazen than her sisters, but all hoped their turn to live in the servant quarters would come quickly, for there were times when they felt distinctly uncomfortable at the over-attention they sometimes engendered.

Even Matthew's guilt started to ease. While the workdays were long, there was little rain and the fresh air of the countryside provided a healthy environment. They had free food twice a day except Sunday and while the rations were meagre it didn't cost a lot to augment them with purchases each weekend in Mulgoa village. Matthew's only regret was not sleeping with Katie each night. Some evenings they'd take walks after dinner to chat about their family and the new community. But with his wife's blessing, on certain days he would sneak home from the fields at midday and they'd have physical loving time to themselves, albeit in the presence of a four-year-old and baby.

There were other factors, less obvious, that affected them all. The surrounding presence of space, quietness, and beauty crept into their souls. The environs of Sydney had been noisy, with bullock teams, mobs of sheep and cattle in the streets, the sales pitches of street vendors, police whistles, factory clankings, and the inevitable crack of whips over chain gangs. Here in the evening, as the shadows of the Blue Mountains encroached, one could hear the parakeets and kookaburras and cockatoos in the trees across the river as they sought their overnight resting spots. Great herons flew along the banks and bullfrogs offered their mating calls.

There were no manufacturing outlets belching smoke and unpleasant smells into the air. There was no intimidating military presence. The convicts knew they were fortunate not to be working on chain gangs, and while serving out time for their pardons, they knew they were better off than many others who had travelled from Britain with them. There were no dark alleyways and confined slippery steps or buildings that seemed to lean on one another. No warehouses, no pompous government buildings with overbearing officials, no notices on lampposts of rules and regulations—just field after endless field, little creeks running into a river that disappeared in the distance, and the beautiful, enticing Blue Mountains close by with the fragrance of eucalyptus sometimes wafting in. Many of the convicts came from English cities, and indeed missed busy streets and the hustle and bustle that had accompanied their upbringing. But not the Monahans. This was a place of goodness, almost a step closer to heaven. They started to thrive.

Winter arrived, and it became colder, and more rain fell. The wind blew from the south up the river and the daylight hours grew shorter. The girls needed umbrellas to protect them on their walks to the big house, and mud became an everyday phenomenon to live with. Everyone grumbled but they all survived, for this wasn't the devastating cold of Europe. No snow here. A frost once in a while, usually welcomed, as it would be associated with a consequent sunny day. Katie knitted mittens and sweaters for them all. On sunny days it was often warm enough that the men shed layers of clothes and hung them on the wire fence of the paddock where they toiled. Water was always available in big barrels and clothing could be readily washed and rinsed at the river bank. Far better than Drumcarn in many ways.

And while the girls sometimes felt ill at ease due to the overwhelming male presence, there were occasions when life could not have been more fun. Some of the men were accomplished musicians playing harmonicas, accordions, fiddles, flutes, and even drums. Once in a while on a Saturday night, an impromptu gathering would occur around a bonfire, and the instruments would come out and hearty voices, lubricated with grog, would render songs from back home. Some of the lads were brave enough to ask the girls to dance, and that's when they enjoyed life most.

Matthew mourned the absence of a nearby church and some Sunday evenings he would lead a small group in bible study and prayer. The small camp gradually evolved with the general recognition of common good fortune even though nostalgia for the 'old country' was constantly implicitly reinforced. And yet beneath it all an Australian character started to emerge. A love for the outdoors and sunshine, an appreciation of nature in the birds and kangaroos and wombats and emus and native flora. Most of the camp inhabitants were accustomed to hard work, and while the aches and pains that accompanied it caused complaints, most felt that here there was potential reward to come, through the earning of Tickets of Leave and Pardons. A marked contrast to their lives 'back home' where all they had ever foreseen was endless work for the landlord. Subtle changes in language occurred as descriptions of phenomena and new situations had to be invented. 'Up-country', 'matilda', 'sheila', 'billabong', 'jumbuck', 'tucker', 'bikkie', 'mate' were just a few of the words that started entering everyday speech. Some were learned from travelling hunters and explorers passing through, some from aristocratic visitors to the mansion, where the maids listened attentively.

Of course, as in any small community, there were disagreements, dislikes, and divisiveness. Some men talked too much and were naturally quarrelsome. Some became angrier much faster than others. Some were very demanding, and some were violent. There were not many women present. All were convicts save for the Monahans and just a few others. Nearly all with less than salubrious backgrounds. Some had married in Sydney, but most unions were for convenience and had not been blessed in any church. These women when drunk would sometimes offer their services to other single males—many times leading to altercations, always to sore heads and morning recriminations. They were an embarrassment to the Monahans, but hard to avoid.

The older children had heard stories and seen examples of the effects of liquor on odd visits to Letterkenny, and heard the sermons of its evil influence in church and seen examples of prostitution down by the wharves in Derry. But here it was upfront and almost personal in presence. As such it was anathema of a different order and the children were repulsed. Katie and Matthew spent extra time discussing this variant behaviour, especially with the girls, who were offended at the pastimes and pursuits of persons of their own gender.

The two elder girls were singled out by a man from London named Gregory Turner. He confided that their lack of affectation and pleasant looks reminded him of his own daughter, who had died along with her mother, his wife, in an accident when a street car overturned and the horses panicked and trampled them. His first question on learning their names was "Can you read and write?"

Grace responded. "We can both read, and I started learning to write on the voyage out, thanks to my father and brother Thomas."

"Then you both must learn more for you will not be able to always depend on your brother and father. I used to teach my daughter and I'd be happy to teach you too. I even have the study books my girl used. I kept them as mementos."

Eileen responded quickly. "That would be wonderful, sir, but we wouldn't know how to pay you for your kindness."

"Ah, lass, I seek no payment beyond your company and willingness to learn. Please talk to your father. If he agrees let's start tomorrow evening after the dinner meal."

Not only did Gregory help the girls with writing, he also helped Matthew and the twin boys become acquainted with the property, its functioning and history, and the unwritten rules of getting along with the animal foreman and the other workers. A gentle free settler, salt-of-the earth type, without a single nasty component in his makeup. His reward was greater inclusion in Monahan family gatherings, and the loneliness that had befallen him started to lift away.

The boys' bodies hardened as they got back into hard work again. Thomas' outgoing nature helped create smiles around camp and he was especially noticed by the other lone girl in the squatter's camp, Bronwen.

Bronwen's job, paid for by the estate manager, was to keep the camp quarters clean. She would collect what little trash the roving dogs didn't take away, make sure the little gardens that some folks planted were tidy, collect the ashes from cooking fires and bonfires, sweep the paths when they were dry, check that clothes hanging on the lines were not falling down, and run small errands to the main mansion and back. Katie paid her a penny to wash their dishes and knives and forks every now and then, and others did likewise. She and her father had arrived as part of a convict family four years earlier, except that her mother had died aboard ship from consumption.

Thomas offered to help carry a load of firewood for her one day, which started their friendship. "Tell me about your home back in Wales, Bronwen, and why you came to Australia."

"Well, Thomas, Father was a shepherd on an estate north of Swansea, where we lived in a stone hut serving the farm's master. As the times got worse the master let two other shepherds go so Father's responsibilities grew. More sheep to look after, more hills to climb, more dogs to train and manage. He enjoyed the outdoors but then the master cut his pay and it became hard to buy enough food for us. One spring during the lambing he sold some recently born lambs to villagers to raise and have more food for themselves. With the multitude of new lambs that were born, he figured the master would not realise some were missing. And he was right. But he forgot the viciousness of men, and when he would not sell more to new buyers they told the master what he had done."

"So he was apprehended by the authorities and condemned to transportation? Someone must have had some pull that you and your mother were permitted to travel with him here."

"Oh no. We were fortunate, yes, but Father had served the master faithfully for over thirty years and he forgave Father, on the condition that he leave and be gone far away. The master did us a huge favour, for who knows what would have happened had Father been thrown into prison. We were lucky to get an assisted passage quickly, although our trip here was thoroughly miserable."

"Well, of course it must have been with your mother dying. I am so sorry. Was she ill before you started on your journey?"

"Yes, but the voyage itself was disastrous and she never had a chance to get better. We had no sooner left Plymouth than a massive storm came upon us. We lost the main mast and a bunch of rigging. We limped back to Plymouth, where we waited fifteen days for repairs. Many of the crew deserted and new inexperienced crew members were found. Several raided the food stores and left barrels and crates uncovered so that some of the food went bad. Many other crew members and a number of passengers threatened to mutiny unless the captain improved conditions. He ignored demands for a month and it was awfully distressing for everybody. Sailors became surly and refused to work, passengers threw food back at the cook. One night several crew members overwhelmed some guards and the captain and tied him to the mast. They unlocked the food stores, holding back other guards and loyal crew by holding a cutlass at the captain's throat. Two passengers who were cooks before being convicted prepared a meal for supportive crew and passengers alike, working all night. Steerage passengers had fresh meat and boiled vegetables for the first time in six weeks.

"Eventually the captain was released on the promise that rations would be increased and better quality food provided to steerage passengers and lower rank crew. The alternative was to be cast adrift with supporters in one of the longboats and left to their own devices. One of the consequences was that we now had to make an unexpected stop in Capetown to replenish supplies.

"Mother died not long after leaving there as it got colder and colder in the southern Indian Ocean. She was buried at sea on a day when we had icicles on part of the rigging. I'll never forget the grey low-hanging clouds and the little ice slivers driven at us by the wind. Mother deserved better."

Thomas reached out and took Bronwen's hand in his as tears gently ran down her cheeks. He was at a loss for words, although he felt Bronwen's pain readily. That she could talk about it so freely to a stranger moved him in ways he'd never experienced before. He stood rooted to the spot, nonplussed, then reached up and held her head against his chest as her sobs grew louder.

Later, Bronwen wondered what had prompted her to tell her tale to someone she hardly knew. Her father, Gwilym, had constantly tried to console her over the two years they'd been in the country. She knew part of his soul had died when Mother had been cast to the deep, and they had been a miserable pair for too long. Perhaps, she thought, it was the new vitality she saw blossoming in the Monahan children that had affected her. She had heard their story from her father, who had heard it directly from Graham, the estate manager. The Monahans too had been miserable but now she saw the subtle changes in them and realised her wish to change similarly. Unburdening was the first step to moving on.

It didn't take long before Matthew and Gwilym were out working the sheep together as Matthew and Patrick swapped job responsibilities. The Merino brand of sheep flourished in Australia, producing much finer wool than sheep in other countries. Wool grew to be the most important export from Australia for decades into the future. Although Gwilym had mastered the management of sheep in Wales, Merinos evolved from Spain and it had taken him time to learn the differences between the breeds in patterns and behaviours of eating, mating, fattening, and wool growing. The learning that Gwilym imparted to Matthew would turn out to be invaluable in the years ahead.

Katie was probably the least happy in the new community. Her lot was to look after young Connor and David, and there were no other mothers her age she could talk to. Those few women who were somewhat close to her in years tended to be coarse, ill-mannered, and generally surly. None had children as young as hers. After three weeks of meeting other camp women she still felt alienated and alone. It was a joy to have her family around at the end of the day.

One fine crisp morning she decided to walk to the mansion with the pretext of hoping to talk to Graham again. A couple of the creeks didn't have any form of bridge and she nearly stumbled on the slippery bottom stones as she carried David in one arm and held Connor close beside her on her other side, half dragging, half lifting him along. Her feet were icy cold but Connor thought it was great fun, and even where there were small rickety bridge crossings he wanted to try to walk through the streams instead. It was more of an adventure than Katie had bargained for, and when she reached the back porch of the mansion she slumped onto a bench to rest. She took off her wet shoes, gave some apple slices to Connor, and offered her milk to David. Just as she was starting to relish the sunshine and its warmth, a stout woman came out the back door and politely inquired why she was there.

"I was hoping to see Mr. Graham, ma'am."

"Well, I'm sorry, but he's not here. What was it you were wanting? Perhaps I can help."

"It's about my son here. In a way I'm glad I'm talking to you, this wouldn't have been as easy talking to a man. You see, my own milk is starting to dry up and I was wondering if there was a way we could get an increase in our rations of milk so I could feed him better."

"Well, I do understand. How many children do you have Mrs....?"

"David is my eighth, not counting two I lost along the way. And it's Mrs. Monahan. Katie Monahan. We haven't been here that long so I'm not sure of all the rules, you see."

"Well, Katie, you've come to the right person. My name is Lillian and I'm the assistant cook. I'm sure we can arrange something for you. Would you care for a cup of tea? I had just made some when I looked through the front windows and saw you coming. It will still be hot."

"That would be very kind, Lillian. Thank you."

Not three minutes later Lillian was back with two teacups, a teapot, sugar and lemon, and a plate of warm scones on a tray. "I thought your other son might like a bite to eat, Katie. He needn't be shy. What's his name?"

"Connor and he's four, but thinks he should be allowed to do everything his elder sisters do. Quite a handful, I assure you."

"Oh, I can well imagine, I've had to work with four-year-olds before. How did you meet Graham?"

And so Katie told the story of the family's arrival and trek westward. Lillian was a sympathetic listener, and the two women spent an hour getting to know one another. On her way back to the camp Katie reflected on how readily she'd been accepted. Ahead of time she had wondered if she would be told to leave the premises immediately and chastised for coming by. But no, Lillian had been welcoming from the start. So different to both Sydney and Ireland. Much more friendly and accommodating. Was it the rural setting? Was it conditioned by Sir John's own behaviours and preferences? Or were his people so happy they just naturally passed it on? Whatever the reason, it was appreciated. Two days later extra milk arrived for David, and Katie started alternating milk sources.

Not all was rosy, however. For some obscure reason, two lads a year older than the twin boys had selected Patrick as a convenient target for taunts and insults, and physical pushes and shoving. Benjamin and Paul worked as gardeners and were fellow convicts from Yorkshire who had been transported four years earlier for stealing. Instinctively aware of Patrick's shyness and sensitivity, they perceived he wasn't manly enough for them and constantly chided and made fun of him as he passed them by.

In typical bully behaviour, both being bigger and heavier, they would sometimes block his way on one of the narrow paths to the fields. Patrick would walk in the weeds or mud to avoid confrontation, the spiteful epithets ringing in his ears. Matthew calmly talked to the two boys, trying to change their behavior, but it only made matters worse, as the insults changed tone to "Weakling, have to get your father to talk for you now" style. Patrick became miserable, and to avoid the problem he would leave early for his job with the pigs and try to be home before Benjamin and Paul returned from their gardening chores.

One afternoon, however, the pigs had dug a hole under one of the fences, and after fixing things temporarily Patrick left his post to fetch some tools and more wire to finish the repair. He was headed for the equipment shed behind the mansion when Benjamin and Paul suddenly appeared, walking towards him on their way home at the end of their shift. The clouds were gathering and it was already darker than usual as the threat of a storm was becoming more obvious. The three approached a bridge over one of the creeks, arriving at opposite ends at essentially the same time. The bridge was nothing more than a row of planks nailed to two long beams stretching from bank to bank. The threats and challenges started immediately, and it was clear that the bullies were looking for a fight, and were not going to be content with just a little shoving and pushing. From opposite sides of the creek they glared at one another, and as much as Patrick wanted to avoid conflict he'd had enough.

Ben threw the insult that broke the camel's back when he scornfully asked, "Do you have more fun with the pigs than with the girls then, Patrick? Do you cuddle them better?" They met in the middle of the bridge, where Ben grabbed Patrick's shirt with both hands and lifted him in the air. Both Patrick and his brother Thomas had been working in the fields for years, pulling livestock out of the mud, hauling dead carcasses to the burn pile, and hefting sick animals across their shoulders to bring them to the barn. They were slight but wiry in build, with hard bodies and deceptively strong muscles. Patrick's mind dissociated itself from his body and instead of lunging for Ben's shirt in return, he swung his arms wide and with tremendous force pummeled Ben's ears with the palms of his fists. Surprised, and badly hurt, Ben released

Patrick, lowered his head, and clutched at his ears with their perforated eardrums. He bent forward at the waist as the pain registered throughout his body, and as Patrick's knee smashed into his chin, his teeth cut into his tongue and rivulets of blood started to flow. He swore and started to stumble forward as Patrick drove his knee hard and fast into the bully's crotch. As Ben finally collapsed onto his haunches yelling in pain, Patrick pushed him off the bridge into the water, where he lay quite still.

Paul saw his advantage and stepped onto the bridge, swinging the shovel he had been carrying. The flat blade caught Patrick near the top of his back, and he went sprawling over the edge of the bridge into the water, falling on top of Ben, whose head was now up on one bank gasping for air. Paul drove the pointed end of the shovel down at Patrick, who twisted out of the way at the last second so that the shovel hit Ben in the ribs, adding mightily to his misery. Patrick quickly reached back, wrapped two hands round the shaft, and jerked, pulling the shovel out of Paul's hands. With momentum lost Paul struggled to regain balance, and had nearly succeeded when Patrick's hands wrapped around his left ankle and pulled forward, sending Paul crashing to the bridge on his back with his head dangling over the other side.

Pain seared across Patrick's back from the shovel blow, but he struggled on to the bridge as Paul tried to pull himself up. Kneeling on the wooden boards, Patrick leaned over Paul's face and quickly dealt him the same painful ear blows he used on Ben. Paul cried out, "No more," but Patrick grabbed the bully's hair and pulled him totally up on the bridge, then lifted his legs up as well and delivered another ferocious kick to the groin whence Paul passed out.

Patrick was shaking, and tears started rolling down his face. Never in his life had he felt so angry and confused. This was another person, a demon, who had suddenly emerged in his old place, and he was frightened of what he had awakened. He felt bewildered and repentant and mumbled a small prayer over and over as he looked at the two twitching bodies he had felled. How did this happen? he thought. What have I done? He had taught his bullies a lesson for sure, but he had revealed a terrible capability in himself he was now ashamed of. It had all taken less than two minutes and he was scared at the level of violence he had exercised. A flashback told him this was what he had seen on the ship once shortly after sailing from Derry, when one of the new sailors had been accosted by two big burly seamen. They'd underestimated his boxing prowess, and in no time he had both bullies flat on the deck moaning pitifully. Patrick had reproduced some of the young sailor's moves, now registering that he remembered how effective they had been at the time.

Patrick gathered his wits slowly, and despite his concerns decided to include one more lesson for good measure. He stripped off both men's britches and shirts so they would have to walk home naked. He bundled the clothes up under his arm, retrieved the shovel, and took it with him as he continued his path to the tool shed. He left the bullies' clothes and the shovel inside. His shakes started to subside, but guilt lay heavily on his mind. His arms and hands hurt, as did his collarbone and spine, so that he had trouble hauling the wire and the specific digging tool he had selected. And he was still cold from the slight immersion in the creek. The storm broke en route and he was a sorry, bedraggled, wet mess by the time he reached camp.

He immediately told his father and twin brother his tale and asked his father for a prayer to help soothe his soul. "I'm ashamed, Father. I do not know what came over me. I could have killed them I was so angry."

"No, no, my son. You obviously realised and stopped way short of that. You have tolerated their behavior for a long time and I admit to being proud of the fact that you didn't shy from confrontation this time, as much as you feel bad about the damage inflicted. But you were dealing with bullies. I have no doubt you will never have trouble with them again and you will probably find some new grudging respect from others. We shall see what the gossip of the camp reveals. It might be interesting to see what those two are wearing tomorrow...

"Meanwhile, Thomas and I will rub some salve on the small cuts on your back. You do realise, though, that I will have to tell your mother in the morning. She hates violence, as you know, so I shall lighten the extent of your efforts. Just be prepared for a lecture in any event."

Time passed and the number of daylight hours grew. Many of the farm animals were pregnant and spring promised to be a busy time. Buds on trees turned into green leaves and blossoms, wildflowers opened their blooms, and by August the far bank of the Nepean was ablaze with the brilliant yellow of the densely bunched flowers of the wattle trees.

The land shone in the sunshine of clear skies. White lambs frolicked in the fields, young calves stayed close by their mothers, and litters of piglets rooted in the mud. Kangaroos raced along the river banks, fish jumped in the river, and contentment fell across the estate.

10. Homestead and camp relationships

Matthew was helping a young ewe deliver a lamb as two riders approached. One was Graham, the manager, and the other George, the butcher. George hopped off his horse, threw the reins to Graham, then bent down to help Matthew with his task. As the baby lamb straightened up and his mother licked him clean Matthew said, "Good to see you, George. Thanks for your help there."

"No problem, Matthew. Graham and I hear good things about how you are managing the flock. Indeed, we hear positive things about all your family. We're glad you are here.

"But I came to talk about the lambs. It looks like an incredible number of births this year, including some twins, I hear. That says the season has been good and the sheep are healthy. I've been talking to Graham here about doing something extra with the fat lambs. Culling more of them from the flock and setting up a larger segregated area on the lushest grass. As the nearby towns of Penrith, Castlereagh, Emu Plains, and Mulgoa grow we feel there will be more demand for lamb meat, not just mutton. And with the plentiful births this year we can keep enough lambs to grow wool and pull more into fat lambing to sell meat to the citizens of the towns. We'd like you to choose forty or fifty lambs to pull aside into a new paddock."

"That makes lots of sense, George. I'll be happy to do it. I'll get my sons to help tomorrow. We can use the dogs as well. I think the paddock two to the south probably has the most profuse grass, and since we rotated the sheep out of it this past winter it would be available now for the lambs. It will probably take me all day to do the culling as I'll have to first move the sheep in the next paddock to some other temporary spot."

George looked up at Graham. "You okay with that, boss? I trust Matthew's judgment on placement unless you have an alternate suggestion."

"Sounds good to me. By the way, Matthew, it looks like we'll have room for two of the girls in the servants' quarters in a fortnight or so as two maids are heading off to get married. Lillian now heads up managing the house staff and Miriam has become assistant cook. I'm sure Lillian will be talking to your wife shortly. Keep it as a surprise if you will. I know Lillian likes to be in charge. But just one notion for you. I know how rough it can be out here and you are free settlers while nearly all the others are convicts. As much as it might sound contrary, I'd be thinking of sending your two youngest girls along as I'm sure the elder ones are more able to look after themselves here. Just a thought. Up to you.

"But I must be off to check some fields further out before it gets dark. I'll see you later." So saying, Graham handed the extra reins back to George, turned his mare around, and set off for the nearest gate heading east.

Matthew waved then turned to George and said, "How about coming back with me and joining us for supper? I know everyone would like to see you once more. And an extra plate won't be hard to find."

"I'd enjoy that, thanks for asking. It will be good to meet your family again."

No one had forgotten the bread and drinks offered by George when they first arrived at Regentville, and they were all happy to re-visit with him. He was a friendly man with broad shoulders, a grin that showed a dimple, and enormous arms, heavily muscled. They sat around one of the crude tables in front of the men's hut and relished the rabbit stew that Katie and the elder girls had prepared. They found out that George's last name was Clarke and that he came from Erith in Kent. He arrived as a convict in 1832, and came straight to Regentville due to his past as a butcher. Connor, who had been well behaved up to this point, suddenly blurted out: "Is that where you hurt your thumb, mister?" Eileen tried to hush the boy, but George quickly replied, "Yes, I was still learning as an apprentice and one day I wasn't careful enough."

"Did it hurt?" the young voice continued.

"Oh yes. Very much, but I've forgotten about it now."

George didn't provide details of his crime but told them he'd received his Ticket of Leave three years earlier and so was essentially a free man. Matthew asked, "So why do you stay at Regentville if you are free to go anywhere? You've been here eleven years, which is a long time."

"There are lots of reasons actually. I've grown to love the rural landscape of this country. I was raised as a city boy. But when I compare the sunshine and fresh air and the fragrance of the forests and the sounds of animals on the land to the narrow alleys and the clouds and rains of London and the polluting black soot and the crowds of people and the crime and ugliness, I see no reason to move away. I do have plans to leave in one sense, for I have my eye on establishing my own butcher shop in Penrith next year. But even then to start I will still work here part time for Sir John until my trade grows. People have been good to me here."

"And is marriage and a family in your dreams, George, or am I being impertinent asking?"

"I've felt no need up to now, but seeing you folks and other families happy may change my views in time. We'll see."

George disappeared into the night, but the girls couldn't contain their fascination with him. They talked about his smile and his speech that was no longer pure English but was filled with local idioms and phrases. They were enthralled with his love of the bush and his descriptions of the Australian flora and fauna. And all of them admired his physique and massive arms. They wondered out loud why no woman had ensnared him, for he seemed a prize catch. New dreams entered more than one female head that night.

The following weekend, old man Turner, who had been teaching the girls to write, came by the huts mid-morning with a fresh glow on his face. "My nephew is coming to visit. I just got a letter. You'll all have to meet him for he's a fine lad. He arrived here over eighteen months ago as an assisted immigrant. I'd written to his father, you see, telling him young Robert should come out and make his fortune here. And he did. Come out, I mean. No fortune. It's a funny story, for apparently he arrived absolutely penniless. He told me the captain of his ship, the *Carthaginian*, gave him two pounds to help him come up country here to meet me. Aye, it was so wonderful to see him.

"But he didn't stay long, for the Blue Mountains were a strong beckoning force and he wanted to see what was on the other side. He writes from a small town named Hartley, where he has been working on a cattle farm. It's so good to hear from him and to know he's coming to visit. He's helping drive a mob of cattle to Penrith to sell. Should be here around the first of October. We'll have to have a little celebration when he turns up."

It was wonderful to see the happiness of expectation in Gregory's eyes. Over the next three weeks he read the letter over and over again. It was stuffed in his shirt pocket close to his heart. He shared it with his two writing charges and gave them more background on his extended family back in London and Scotland. The girls listened to his stories with attentive patience.

One evening their father came home quite agitated. The lambs had been docked two weeks earlier and he'd gone to check on the fat lambs and felt some were missing. He'd always kept meticulous records of births and deaths so the estate management knew exactly how the mobs were growing. He checked the fences and gates and the small shed in the next paddock but found no escape holes or hiding places. No one had noticed any great eagles in the last week that might have caught a free meal, and the lambs were getting too big anyway for them to carry off. Matthew was confused and annoyed and had come up with the distasteful thought that someone in camp must be stealing them to supplement their rations with extra meat. It bothered him immensely that there could be rampant dishonesty so close by.

Next morning he sought Graham's counsel. Graham offered an alternate possibility—that bushrangers had formed a camp nearby and were helping themselves at night. He promised to come by that evening and bring George along and a shotgun and see if anyone turned up. After dinner the three men, joined by Thomas and Patrick, headed across the fields to the little shack next to the fat lamb paddock. The shack was on the southern border a good two miles from the mansion and a mile from the workmen's camp. A line of thick foliage trees led from the shack to the Penrith-Mulgoa road.

They sat in the shack quietly sharing sheep tales until at a point well after midnight Patrick held up his hand to shush the conversation and said, "I think I hear horses." After a few moments George said, "Two of them, coming from the Mulgoa direction, but still quite a distance away. The wind is blowing their noise towards us."

Graham spoke up. "Okay, here's my suggestion. First, which of you Monahans rides best?"

Thomas indicated he had had more practice as the fields he oversaw were more extensive and his only way to track the cattle was to ride one of the estate's horses. "Right then, Patrick, you and your father go now to the lamb paddock and move any lambs that are near the road fence as far away as possible. When the lambs are settled, head back here and use this shack as your hideout. The rest of us will move down the tree line to the road and watch them come by. If they are the thieves they'll have to go another fifty yards to the lamb paddock and tie their horses to the fence while they hop over and try to catch a lamb. I'm pretty sure it will take two of them to chase one down. And of course they'll have to go further than they expect because the lambs will have been moved closer to the far end of the field.

"That should give us time to reach the horses and untie them. The horses may whinny at the presence of strangers, and that's a risk we'll have to take. Thomas, you tie one horse behind the other and ride them north to the main entrance to the estate, then back to the stables. Leave as quietly as you can, but if the robbers hear anything and turn around just take off. They'd have to run to catch you and my only concern is that they are carrying rifles with them. Tuck yourself down on the far side of the lead horse as you go, just in case. Although frankly I think if they are planning to carry off a lamb, rifles would get in the way and they probably are only carrying pistols on their persons. They'll leave the rifles with the horses.

"George and I will stay behind and lie in the ditch by the road so we can catch the bastards red-handed. They are going to wonder what to do without horses, and as they work that out we'll surprise them. Do you have that rope handy, George? I'm looking forward to using it. Now off you go, men, and move those lambs for us."

Matthew and Patrick raced off and George, Graham, and Thomas moved carefully down the tree line, listening intently. They heard the horses stop in the distance and indistinct laughter float on the slight breeze. They surmised the two men were relieving themselves and lighting up fresh cigarettes. The slow 'clip, clip, clip' of hooves on hard-packed dirt started up again and five minutes later the horses came into view. The riders were silent now, just cigarette ends glowing, so the three men melted into the blackness of the tree shadows just as the moon came out from behind a cloud, lighting up the road and fences.

As predicted, the riders went by, straddled the ditch, then dismounted and tied their horses loosely over two fence posts. Graham whispered, "I recognize them. They used to be troublesome convicts we had here at camp for a while. Clearly bushrangers now. Double down and let's go. They're over the fence."

Thomas made soft, soothing sounds as he approached the horses, which turned and regarded him carefully. Graham and George stayed back in the ditch so as to reduce any perceived threat. Thomas had a surprisingly easy time tying one horse beside the other and leading them both to the road. Graham had miscalculated one aspect of the setup, for as soon as Thomas swung himself up onto a saddle and had the horses headed north, the sound of their hooves reverberated once more through the stillness of the night and the robbers turned at the noise and started running back, shouting curses. The moonlight let them readily see a man in the distance riding away with their horses. As the horses' gait changed to a gallop, they stopped their running and yelling and stood stock-still, looking around. For now they realised that they'd clearly been expected, and they wondered if there were more men in a welcoming party waiting for them somewhere.

They both drew pistols from their belts and slowly walked back to the road, looking in all directions as they headed for the fence. Matthew and Patrick had left the shack once they heard the men yelling and were now watching from the sidelines of the fat lamb paddock. They could sense the men's nervousness and Matthew suddenly realised that if they created a diversion it might give Graham and George a better chance to apprehend the thieves. Just as the thieves climbed onto the fence Patrick and Matthew started yelling and screaming and running towards them, brandishing sticks that looked like rifles. One thief tripped and fell to the grass as he turned to face the commotion while the other also turned and fired a silly shot into the air, anticipating that the welcoming party was behind them and about to give chase. He stopped to help his partner up and that was his second mistake.

Two giant ghosts emerged from the ditch and charged the two robbers, who crumpled and went down like flour sacks. George wrestled the chap with the gun, pinning his hand against the fence post while punching him in the face. Graham's opponent had dropped his gun when he tripped, and Graham quickly kicked it well out of reach. His boot caught the robber in a vicious kick to the stomach, the next kick crunching his nose. The man's fight was all gone and Graham set to work tying his feet and hands while the man's nose dripped blood on to his shirt.

George's captive was the bigger and stronger of the pair and was applying all his strength trying to turn his gun on George. George felt himself starting to lose ground so with a deliberate feint he eased his grip a little, rolled his hand, and with a deft twist of his powerful wrist grabbed two of the gunman's fingers, bent them back and broke them. The gun fell harmlessly to the ground as the man's howls pierced the air. George calmly grabbed the robber's head with both hands and slammed it against the fence pole, knocking him unconscious. Breathing heavily, George stood up and started tying his victim's hands and feet.

Matthew and Patrick climbed over the fence and helped finish the deed. Graham turned to thank them. "That was great thinking to distract them, you two. I was worried about those pistols. Might have gotten uglier without your help. So thanks. Question is, what do we do with them now? Too bad we didn't get them with a lamb in their arms, but I don't think we'll have any trouble convincing the police about their intentions. We'll leave it to the authorities to find their hideout and see if there are more men in their party. I don't know about you, but I've had quite enough excitement for this night."

"Hang on," Matthew cried. "I hear hoof beats again, but coming the other way. Ah... there we are. I bet that's Thomas with one of the draught horses pulling a dray behind. What a smart lad."

Thomas had woken a stable boy back at the mansion, left the two new horses in his care, and hitched a single-tongue dray to the biggest draught stallion he could find. He grabbed a tarpaulin and extra rope and was back on the road in fifteen minutes heading for the fracas he was sure would have ensued. He was relieved to find his brother and father unscathed and Graham and George okay, although winded from fighting. They bundled the bushrangers in the tarp, tied it securely, and headed home, where a small crowd was gathered, having heard the stable boy's excited story.

Bushrangers were universally reviled, for they stole from settlers, often beating them and sometimes killing innocents. So the five men were treated like heroes, with multiple requests to tell their story over and over.

The police finally arrived late in the afternoon and indicated that the two thieves were part of a gang of four wanted for various misdeeds in the Windsor area. There was a cash reward on the gang's heads, half of which would be given to Graham to dispense as appropriate. The men were laid across the backs of their horses and tied down, ready to be led back to the cells at the Penrith courthouse. As the police were about to leave Matthew asked, "What happens to their horses when these chaps go to gaol?"

"Strictly speaking, the animals are now government property, but if we can establish their owners, for they are undoubtedly stolen, we will return them. If they aren't branded or otherwise identifiable we will sell them cheaply as we don't have a good place to hold them, nor do we really want the expense and bother of feeding and looking after them. If you are interested and we can't find owners I'll be sure to give you first chance of buying. Okay?"

"I'd definitely be interested in one," Matthew responded.

"And I in the other," chimed George.

The episode resounded around camp for a week then quietly integrated itself into the history of the estate. Work went on as before. The weather stabilized and the sun stayed out longer and the days slowly warmed. The routine was broken with two events. Ann and Mary Jane moved to the servants' quarters, each meeting a new roommate, and it became much quieter around camp in the Monahan area. Eileen and Grace worked hard to conceal their jealousy, and were rewarded when Gregory Turner's nephew, Robert Kitchings, finally turned up. One Friday evening he just wandered into camp as if he owned the place, went straight to his uncle's shack, shook his hand, and engulfed him in a bear hug which left the old man breathless.

The next morning Gregory introduced Robert to the Monahans. Robert was a strapping twenty-seven years old, sunburned on the face and arms, with a mob of unruly golden hair, and a smile that told of self-confidence and friendliness at the same time. His outgoing personality was infectious and in no time at all he had everyone laughing with stories of his arrival on the *Carthaginian*, and his travels westward over the mountains. He made Hartley sound like a place no one would want to move from with its strong Irish and Scottish communities, its delightful location among the hills, and the verdant fields for grazing in the district.

Grace found herself hanging on every word, mesmerized by his slight Scottish accent and the articulate tales he spun for them. She asked, "How long are you planning to stay at Regentville? Will you be going back soon?"

"No, I've no plans to go back at the moment as much as I love it there and now have some good friends. I thought I'd spend time here with my uncle if I can find a job; otherwise, I'll head to Parramatta or Sydney so I can learn more about the coach and transport business. As the towns of Lithgow and Bathurst grow and as the road across the Blue Mountains improves I think there'll be more and more goods and people transported along the Great Western Road. There's especially money to be made hauling goods up and over the hills."

It struck both Grace and Eileen that here for the first time was someone they'd met who knew what he wanted. Aside from George the butcher, that is. And, moreover, he was a free man. No convict encumbrances, no past to be ashamed of or to hide, and with good Christian values. He was stopping to see his uncle, a noble act in itself. The girls couldn't stop talking about him in bed that evening. Katie was pleasantly surprised to hear their infatuated girl talk. She wondered when the hormones would kick in more obviously, if they hadn't already. Truth be, Grace's hand was tight between her legs as she dreamed about the newcomer before falling asleep.

The police returned a month after the bushranger incident, bringing the two extra horses with them. Graham sent a rider out to the fields to inform the Monahan trio. They came running back to the homestead, where they found the policemen enjoying cold ales and biscuits on the front veranda. A police tracking party had discovered the bushranger camp five miles south of Regentville, fairly well hidden in a dell one hundred yards or so off the main road. But there was no trace of the other two members of the gang, who had probably fled when their companions never returned. There were plenty of small bones left by the extinguished campfire indicative of lamb dinners, however.

Graham gave half of the reward money to Matthew, and there was plenty left over after paying for one of the horses and saddles. Matthew asked if he could stable the horse with the estate stables and for a small weekly fee Graham agreed. Matthew happily added the remaining funds to the growing kitty back at their quarters.

At dinner that night Matthew laid down the rules. "The horse belongs to us as a family. I'm going to call her Splash because of that blaze on her nose. But since Thomas did so much with the horses that ugly night he can get first priority in riding the mare. In fact, Thomas, I'm relying on you to spend time taming her down, as I'm sure she's been mistreated along the way. Those bushrangers didn't look like animal lovers to me. Patrick, you'll probably want to help."

"What about us girls, Father?" Eileen interjected. "I'd like to learn how to ride. When will we get a turn?"

"Be careful how you speak to your Father, girl," said Katie. "We treat each other with respect here."

"Well, I see the boys always being given the first options when something new turns up. Are we girls never to have equal rights?"

"Eileen, that's enough! You are all loved equally."

"Well, Mother," Grace spoke up, "I must agree with my sister. We are just a year younger than the boys and I think at our age we need to be thought of equally with them. We're not back in County Donegal anymore. This is a free land with new rules and opportunities where women often work at men's jobs in pubs, bakeries, shipping offices, and such. We don't always have to play second fiddle to the boys, just because you did when you grew up."

Katie stammered to find words. "M... Matthew, do you have nothing to say in support of me?"

"The girls do have a point, my dear. Things are changing, and I think we'll all have to get used to a world with new values. Perhaps we can all sleep on it for now and raise the issue again when it's appropriate. I'm sure there'll be numerous chances in the times ahead."

Mary Jane had moved to a room on the second floor of the servants' building where her roommate was a twenty-year-old girl from London named Daisy. They knew each other, for both were maids assigned to bedroom and bathroom duty. But they worked different floors in different wings of the main house so hadn't spent a lot of time together.

It was a very strange feeling for Mary Jane, not only to be sharing a room with a stranger but to have a proper mattress for a bed. There were curtains on the window and a closet for her uniform and dresses, of which she had only two. Her first surprise came on the very first evening when Daisy ended her shift and walked through the door. She immediately started taking off her black and white uniform, hanging the pieces carefully in her side of the closet. Totally nude, she paraded in front of Mary Jane, pushing up her generous breasts with her hands. "What do you think, Mary Jane? Will that stable boy Eric be able to keep his hands off these later tonight? I doubt it. I've seen the tilt in his tight britches as he tries to look down the front of my dress. Here, help me put it on and you'll see what I mean."

Amazed and shocked, Mary Jane tentatively helped Daisy slip her dress over her head. "Here, see when I bend forward. Such an easy way to get any boy's attention. I'm going to meet him in the loft after late supper tonight. I may even let him touch me downstairs. I know he wants to. Have you done that with a boy yet?"

Mary Jane turned away, blushing and speechless. What was she in for, living here? Not even an hour had passed and she felt like an innocent child, unsure whether she wanted to stay or go. Behind her Daisy said, "I gotta go pee. Come on, I'll show you a shortcut to get to the privy."

Shaking her head at Daisy's crudity, Mary Jane followed meekly. Amazing how different certain people could be in and out of uniform, she thought. On her return she detoured to the downstairs room where Ann was sharing quarters. She knocked on the door, and hearing no response opened it up and peered in, only to see Ann napping on the far bed. As much as she wanted to talk to her sister she didn't dare wake her, and left silently.

She heard Daisy return late that night and pretended to be asleep. But in the morning Daisy was not to be denied the opportunity to talk about her nocturnal accomplishments. As they both changed into their uniforms Daisy whispered, "I made threepence by letting him touch me below. Next time he says he wants to taste me there. I can make a fortune this way. You could too if you wanted."

"Well, I don't," Mary Jane retorted angrily and somewhat disgusted. "And I don't really care to hear about your night-time adventures. Please keep your doings to yourself." She wondered what it would take to change rooms and roommates. A lot, she figured, since she'd just arrived. Better to grin and bear it for the moment. Maybe things would improve over time, although somehow she doubted it. Daisy seemed to have markedly different values.

A routine developed, and when Mary Jane was off shift for two days she would head back to her family at the convict camp. It helped to be away from Daisy among other things. Her big sister

Grace was promoted to a housekeeper position and Ann took her place as a kitchen helper and serving maid. Grace was becoming increasingly friendly with Robert Kitchings, who had been given a part-time job helping Thomas in the cattle pastures. The three of them got on well and Robert joined the family for dinner more and more often. One early November Sunday morning when they were all easing into the day over a late breakfast, Grace looked at Thomas and her father and said, "Do you think Robert and I could borrow Splash and go for a ride on the other side of the river later?"

Thomas piped up and said, "It's fine by me. I was planning to give her a wash and a brushing later, but that's all. If you'll do that when you come back, sis, it would save me a trip to the stables. Oh, and Father, I can vouch for Robert. Out with the cattle he often rides the estate horse I take there. He says he did a lot of riding on mountain horses when he stayed in Hartley, and frankly he's a better horseman than me."

"And what about you, Grace?" Matthew asked. "Have you been practicing riding somewhere?"

"No, Father. I'm just going to sit behind Robert and hold on tight, although if he offers to teach me to ride I wouldn't mind at all."

Katie's face clouded. "Just the two of you? Shouldn't someone else be going with you?"

"Oh dear, Mother, this is the new world. We don't need a chaperone at twenty years old."

Eileen looked up at her sister, a pout forming across her lips. "I wish it were me Robert would ride with. Why does he spend more time with you than with me? I like him too, and I don't think I'm any less attractive than you are."

"Of course you're not. We are *identical* twins, you know. In fact I'm amazed that twenty years after birth we still look so much alike. Remember as kids when we sometimes pretended to be each other just to have fun? Aunt Shauna could never ever get our names right, and even Uncle Paddy had trouble most of the time. But I'm sorry, sister, I don't want to do that to Robert. He's too nice to try and fool."

After lunch the pair walked to the stables and Robert attached the bit and bridle but left the saddle behind. He turned to Grace. "She's used to me riding her bareback, for what Thomas didn't tell your father is that we've also had her out in the pastures with us. She's strong but won't be used to the weight of two of us, so we'll go slowly and let her adapt at her own pace. Once we get across Emu Ford I think we'll just walk with her rather than ride. Are you ready?"

"Certainly, how do we get started?"

"I'll get on first, and sit forward. You reach up with your left hand and grab my belt. Then Eric here will cup his hands and hoist you by the left leg so you can swing your right leg over Splash's rump while reaching for my belt on the other side with your right hand. Coming home will be a bit harder. Come on, let's try it."

It took three tries but they finally made it. Eric was chuckling thinking of the stories he'd be able to tell his stable mates. Like how he had to pat the woman's dress under her bottom after it floated free over Splash's rump. The cotton chemise under the tunic was thin and he'd readily felt her cheeks as he maneuvered the fabric out of harm's way. Not many females rode horses, and it was always a treat to help them get organized.

Robert moved back a little and Grace wrapped her arms around his waist as Splash walked around the courtyard a couple of times while the riders slowly adjusted positions until they were both comfortable. Eric opened the gate and they headed for the main road at a medium-paced walk, Splash finding her stride readily. Grace's bonnet protected her from the sun's rays, although a faint sweat emerged on Robert's suntanned brow as there were few shade trees along the Mulgoa road in the Penrith direction.

After forty minutes they came to the bank of the Nepean at Emu Ford and stopped in the shade under a large willow tree now fully leafed out. Robert alerted Grace of his intentions to bring his right leg over Splash's head and to slide forward and down over her left leg while still holding the reins. He suggested that Grace then move forward and hold Splash's mane and head collar as they traversed the ford across the shallow part of the river. "And," he added, "as much as you ladies don't like to show ankle and leg, the more of your dress you can tuck up underneath you, the less of it is going to get wet."

Grace loved his lack of shyness and straightforward approach with a sensible suggestion. No euphemisms and silly words whose meaning was to be guessed at. "You don't want to get your dress wet, lady, then hold it up." Very clear. Was that some of the influence of the new country? Back in Ireland the suggestion would have been phrased with ridiculous delicacy and vagueness. Hurrah for the new land!

Robert walked slowly down the gentle slope of the bank alongside Splash and led her into the cool water. At this crossing point the water was usually only about two feet deep, but due to earlier spring rains it was running higher with a stronger current than normal. Unpredictable holes still existed in the base despite all the rocks that had been thrown into the area. Splash stumbled once and Grace reset her grip on the mane but they made it across successfully with Grace's clothing dry and Robert's pants wet to his waist. He led the horse off the road, tied her to a tree branch, and helped Grace down.

"Sorry you had to get wet. If you had been riding you'd be much drier."

"I'll dry off quickly once we start walking. I have some water here if you'd like a drink."

Robert pulled off the haversack strung across his chest and took out a bottle of cold water. He wiped off the mouth and handed it to Grace, who drank a hefty fill. After quenching his own thirst he returned to the river and filled the bottle again.

"Let's walk north in the same direction we rode. I've been that way before and it's very pretty and the ground is fairly flat. Plus I want to show you something special."

"Tell me about your life in England, Robert, and what brought you to Australia. Gregory has told us a bit but not really enough."

"Well, you know that Gregory is my mother's older brother. My mother was named Susan and she was born and raised in York. My father, whose name I inherited, was a sheep farmer in the town of St. Boswells just north of the Scotland/England border. One year he had his wool taken south to the mills in the Leeds area, instead of north to Edinburgh, because he'd heard prices were so much better there. He met Mother, who was working as a barmaid in a pub. I gather he was smitten immediately and stayed on much longer than anticipated. It was apparently pretty romantic because he headed the hundred miles back home, immediately sold his small farm, and rode back to marry Mother—all in a space of three months. Such love and devotion. When Father couldn't find a decent job in Leeds, they packed up and moved to Shoreditch in London. They married there in 1806 and eventually bought a grocery shop in Southwark on the south bank of the Thames. Apparently they scraped by for several years and I was born in 1816. It was late in my mother's life as she was forty at the time. I always suspected she'd been married and widowed before but Father never spoke of it if true.

"Sometime later, Uncle Gregory is not sure exactly when, we all moved to Lambeth. The timing was great because it wasn't many years later that the massive influx of refugees coming off the land looking for jobs in the city started. They had to eat and they bought their food and supplies at my parents' new shop which they had established in the area. I remember it well, but that's another story perhaps. My mother died of some woman's illness apparently when I was thirteen, and my father ran the shop for years after. I helped as much as possible when I wasn't in school. But he always wanted me to learn the 'ways of the land' as he called it, so after I had learned to read and write and helped out with the bookkeeping at the shop he sent me off to live with Uncle Gregory, who owned a small sheep farm outside of York.

"Uncle had never married and he was an enterprising fellow. We had four years together before he simply decided to go to Australia. That was in 1839. What little money he had left after paying the mortgage on the farm and other debts was used to buy passage to Sydney. I went back to London and worked in the shop. It did well initially with the surge of citizens. After a while, however, the economy was unable to expand fast enough to keep up with the massive labour inflow and many of the newcomers arriving from rural areas couldn't find jobs. People became desperate and turned to stealing and we had to watch their behavior in the shop much more carefully. It was very taxing, especially since we were selling groceries in part and people were hungry.

One time the front window was broken and food taken before the police arrived and stopped the mayhem. We replaced the window with a brick wall but Father became more and more upset and agitated. Good citizens moved away, and the streets became more crowded with hastily erected shoddy tenements providing tiny boarding rooms for a very low class of people. They operated truly ugly businesses in which they were knackers who rendered horses for glue, or gut spinners, varnish makers, and printer's ink makers. You wouldn't believe the horrible smelly and choking smoke pollution they caused.

"We survived nearly two years until the shop burned to the ground when a dirty bone bleaching business next door got out of control. Father died trying to put the fire out, as did the woman tending the bleaching cauldron.

"It was tragic. Absolutely everything was gone. I buried Father in nearby Northwood cemetery. It seemed as if my whole world had been emptied. There was nothing keeping me in England and so I applied for an assisted passage to Australia to catch up with Uncle Gregory.

"So there you are. I've told you far more than you probably wanted to know, Grace. Sorry if I've bored you."

"Not at all. I just feel sorry that you lost both your father and mother along the way. How very sad."

"My father made me spend time on the land, where I learned a lot and where I now enjoy working. I also learned a lot about running a store and the financial side of things. I know the knowledge will stand me in good stead later."

"I sense you are very realistic and practical man. You don't weep over the negatives, but look forward. I admire that. And you are very brave to come here totally on your own. You and Gregory both, I guess. Please let us stop for a moment."

Robert looked at her and promptly stopped walking. Almost before he was aware Grace turned, reached up, stroked his cheek, and gave him a loving kiss there. Robert blushed appropriately, but with a twinkle in his eye whispered, "That was very nice. Thank you. I do hope there might be more later."

"All in good time, sir." She slipped her hand in his, which enclosed hers tightly, and they continued happily along the faint path in the grass. Ten minutes later he asked, "Are you ready for a bit of a climb? If we turn here and climb the hillside to our left I'll show you a surprise."

"Oh yes, but you may have to help me, I'm not as athletic as you are."

"Follow me and I'll go slowly. We have to climb about seventy yards or so, I'm afraid, and there are a couple of steep bits I'll help you with."

At the outset the hillside was composed of dirt and grass and thick tree trunks, but after about twenty-five yards they came upon a rock face, which extended upwards for thirty yards or more. The rock was grey with strange vertical formations and indentations in which water seeped and ferns grew. Robert ascended along the side of the rock, gripping on to smaller tree trunks to haul himself upwards. Grace watched carefully, placing her hands and feet where he did. She also noticed how well his britches fit his bottom. After all, she rationalized, it was impossible not to notice, with him bent over right in front of her. A phrase crossed her mind—'steel cheeks'. She quickly reminded herself to concentrate on the task of climbing. Finally, the near vertical rock face started to slope back less severely, and at one point became almost horizontal.

Robert stopped and hauled Grace up the last few feet. "Let's rest here and catch our breaths before moving on. It will be much easier now as we will be walking along the top of this huge rock. Would you like another drink?"

"That would be most welcome, thank you, yes. But let us not stop long. I'm anxious to see what is ahead."

Robert set off across the undulating top of the rock for about thirty feet then paused at the edge of a large indentation that formed a cave going back just a few feet into the hillside. "Here it is. Step inside."

The colouring of the floor of the cave was a blend of almost orange and grey, and was clean except for a few dead leaves that had blown down from the trees above. "Oh my gosh," Grace exclaimed. "Are those aboriginal drawings on the wall over there?"

"I definitely think so. Look, this one is a goanna or lizard, and this one is clearly a snake."

"And over here, Robert, this has to be a kangaroo and this is a fish. And look at these hand stencils in this orangey ochre colour. How absolutely incredible! I wonder how many years ago these were drawn."

"Turn around and look out the entrance. There's a view through the branches to the right where you can see the river and the bank where we just walked along. Who knows, there could easily have been a native of the Gundungarra tribe sitting here watching us this very afternoon. He probably left as soon as he saw us start climbing."

"Oh my, to think we were being observed. Do you really think so? No, I see by your smile that you are pulling my leg. So be it, I will make sure I get even somehow. But thank you for showing this to me. It's very special indeed. How did you know it was here?"

"When I first came and visited Uncle Gregory, I spent every spare moment exploring the bush along this bank. I didn't go very far inland, mainly just north and south close to the river. This was my most exciting find. I didn't even tell Uncle, as I always knew I'd come back and I wanted it to remain secret so it wasn't disturbed by others."

"Good for you, but when we get back I intend to tell everyone I can and show it to them. It's far too important to stay hidden."

"Oh no. No, no, no!" Robert cried. "This was to be something special just between the two of us. Now I'm feeling a little angry."

"Look at me, Robert. I'm teasing you. If you remember, just a few minutes ago I told you I'd get even for pulling my leg. We Monahans can have fun too, you know." Playfully, she gave him another peck on the cheek.

"There. I promise this will stay our secret. Now I guess we have to make our way back to the river again. And I'm not sure that will be as easy as coming up. It looks very steep when I look down from here."

"Well, I will go first again, and if you did as you did coming up—

placing your hands and feet where I do—you'll be fine. The first part is easy back across the rock."

And so they slowly and carefully started their descent. They hadn't gone fifteen feet down alongside the vertical rock face when Grace called a halt. "Robert, there's a delicate little matter I want to raise. It is so steep here that I'm certain with this wide flaring skirt, if you turn and look up, you may see far more than a lady is supposed to show. I have no option. Are you able to keep your eyes looking to the path ahead?"

"The closer you stay to me, the less likely are such opportunities to occur. And I promise I will do my best, although it is tempting to have fun at your expense again. I think you've had more fun than me today. Come on, let's go. Close up the distance a bit."

Standing on the path at the bank once again and looking up, it was impossible to see any hint of the rock face or cave, both being totally concealed by the brush and thick foliage. "Thank you, Robert. Not only for sharing your secret with me, but for being a gentleman as well. I would definitely enjoy more walks with you. This was exhilarating, and dare I say, thoroughly enjoyable. I like being with you very much."

"You seem very secure in yourself, Grace. I like that, and I too would enjoy more excursions together."

They returned to the stables, where they hosed and brushed Splash down. Grace ran to the kitchen and got a couple of apples from Ann, and raced back with them as rewards for Splash. The horse had never been treated so well and nuzzled her nose against Grace's back.

In no time it was December and the heat rose accordingly. At the end of the day the male workers would often make their way to the river's edge, don bathing suits, and swim in the river. Two of the stable lads were the best swimmers, regularly winning races across the river and back. The Nepean was only about one hundred feet wide behind the mansion—short enough to make the races usually pretty close and exciting to watch. Not far downstream the depth of the river eased dramatically from fifteen to eighteen feet to almost five feet so that it could be forded by men on horseback, although carts would not make it across. It was here that the women would dangle their ankles and feet in the cool waters but without acceptable swimming garments would not venture further.

There were a couple of renegade females of course who, well after dark near this point, would slide down the bank nude, and enjoy the delicious feel of the cold water washing over their bodies from top to toe. Mary Jane's roommate Daisy was one of the cheerleaders. They'd come out refreshed and thrilled from their clandestine adventure and quickly get dressed before romping home. The stable hands had twigged to the arrangement and had found a suitable hiding place from where they could appreciate the young nubile forms. In the remote community of Regentville, one took one's entertainment and enjoyment wherever possible.

Sir John Jamison had promised a special celebration for Christmas. A couple of guests would be staying at the mansion but he had invited all the workers to a late Christmas dinner after dark. This was his annual thank you to all those who made his estate valuable. For the three weeks beforehand, an enormous pile of wood grew higher and higher in a field between the house and the entrance gates. Special benches and tables were constructed and a platform for musicians built. A patch of ground was raked and smoothed for dancing, and bales of hay for seating were placed in position. On the front veranda, extra lamps were hung and the rocking chairs removed and replaced with numerous serving tables.

On the morning of Christmas Day many members went to church early but were back after lunch and pitched in helping with the preparations wherever they could so all the work didn't fall on the kitchen staff. The butcher had arranged extra quantities of various pork, beef, and lamb cuts, and there was rabbit, duck, chicken, turkey, quail, pheasant, and cod fish as well. Many barrels of beer arrived from Penrith on a dray, and extra loaves of bread had been baked through the night. Bottles of wine from the estate grapes lined one of the tables on the veranda, and even Sir John was seen checking them over.

As darkness fell and the lamps were lit, workers came from every direction across the fields to the big house. The policemen from Penrith had been invited, along with many of the merchant shop owners from town. Two of the doctors and nurses from the Asylum Hospital in St. Marys came, as they were usually the ones to treat any accidents or illnesses on the estate. It was a grand gathering.

Sir John addressed the crowd from the veranda: "Welcome, everyone. Thank you for your toils this year, helping make Regentville a major supplier of produce and other goods to the markets of Sydney and Parramatta. With your help we have established new production records in every item that passes out through our gates.

"There will be two major additions starting early in the new year which I think you will appreciate. First, we will start constructing two sandstone buildings to serve as servants' quarters in the squatters camp. Second..."

But here he was interrupted with massive cheering from all the convict and free settler workers. It went on and on until he waved his hat for quiet. People immediately wondered how big the buildings would be, on what basis people would get rooms, etc., etc. Sir John was not about to elaborate.

"The second addition will be something quite different. As many of you know we have had a record number of lambs produced this year. More have been culled for the fat lamb market, but most will be grown for their wool. We have become one of the largest suppliers of wool to the Yorkshire and Italian markets. But next year we will have our own woollen mill, right here at Regentville, so that Australian citizens can get clothes made with fine wool for local prices and thereby avoid import taxes. So anyone who worked in the woollen mills back home, please see Graham tomorrow."

More cheers erupted, and Sir John waved them down again. "Now I'm not one for making long speeches, except when I want to impress the Governor on his visits..." Loud cheering and laughter erupted all around.

"But before we light the bonfire and enjoy ourselves I would like you all to recognize the staff that has worked all night and day to bring you the feast spread out on the tables here. Would all you staff people please step up on the veranda here with me. "

Applause and cheers filled the evening. Sir John and his wife beamed and shook hands with the twenty people who had climbed up beside them.

"Now, one last thing—a short prayer of thanks." Sir John waited for quiet, and the spectators dutifully bent their heads.

"Lord, thank you for our bountiful harvest this past year, and thank you for looking after all these wonderful people. Thank you for your son born to us this day. May we all stay safe in your and his hands along the pathways ahead of us. We are your servants. Amen."

The crowd echoed "Amen" and waited expectantly for the next traditional speech.

"And now, as has been our custom for nearly ten years, I'd like our eldest member, James Claville, to light the great fire. For those of you new to this event, James celebrated his eighty-ninth birthday this year—just yesterday. Graham—the torch please...."

James, more spry than most expected, walked quickly around the base of the pyre, touching his torch to the dry kindling in selected spots. Completing his circuit, he hefted the burning stick high onto the pile, starting another small fire halfway up. The crowd roared their approval and headed for the food and drink tables. The party was officially under way.

The musicians played, folks danced, people ate and drank, laughter filled the air, and everyone relaxed and enjoyed their host's munificence. Rejoicing and celebrating went on and on well into the early hours of the following day. The great mound of wood slowly burned down until a huge circle of glowing embers kept those who had fallen asleep warm, and those in love whispering to each other on the grassy fringes where light met dark.

11. Maturation, pairing, fauna

Those with early morning required duties were up and functioning on their regular routine the next day, but most people were slow to arise. Bronwen slept in, but in her half-awake state kept going over the evening's festivities and activities in her mind. She'd feasted on a new dish for her—duck—which she found delicious. She had eagerly brought some pieces to Thomas to try, and he was most grateful. They'd sat a little away from the heat of the bonfire and spent time in a group that included Grace and Robert, Eileen and Patrick, and Mary Jane. Ann was still helping with kitchen duties, but after an hour Patrick got up and went and fetched her, forcing her to take some time out, be with family, and relax a little as well. When the band struck up a waltz he led her to the dance ground and twirled her around. Thomas pulled Bronwen up and joined them, and not to be outdone, Robert did the honours with Grace. Eileen applauded from the sidelines, her infectious laughter bringing smiles to all the dancers' faces. After a while she and Ann changed places, whereupon Ann kept clapping and shuffling at the edge of the dance space. Then Ann and Bronwen swapped spots as the band played on. A young stable lad deposited himself in front of Bronwen, and when she returned his gaze with a smile swept her into the dance crowd as well. What fun that had been. Good people, caring people. When the music stopped they all collapsed, panting from exertion and laughter.

Bronwen smiled in her half sleep. They'd gotten drinks of apple cider to quench their thirst and grouped again back by the fire. She and Thomas leaned back to back helping support each other. Grace and Robert did the same opposite them in a tight little circle arrangement, spaces filled in by the others. Matthew and Katie came by with the boys, David fast asleep in his mother's arms. Eileen held him while Katie grabbed some food and drink and replenished herself. Connor wanted to get closer to the fire and had to be restrained. Just a normal four-year-old wanting to play. The circle of friendship grew larger as Gwilym and Gregory stopped by. At one point Gregory waxed a little nostalgic and talked about how it would be winter back home at this time, there'd be light snow in the streets of London, carol singers walking door to door, and Christmas trees decorated inside the homes with boxes of presents underneath. His story made everyone think back to the land and loved ones they'd left behind, and the mood became a little sombre. It was baby David who broke the mood with a yell that caught everyone by surprise. He'd woken up in Eileen's lap and needed changing.

The musicians were taking a break when Bronwen silently rose to her feet and started to sing. She had a beautiful voice and was proud to use it. It took a minute or two to realise she was singing 'Silent Night, Holy Night', for she was singing it in her mother tongue—Welsh. Tears fell from her father's eyes and while everyone else around the fire was first stunned into appreciative silence, at the end they showed their approval by clapping and asking her to sing it again in English, at which time they all joined in. The wondrous message of this song helped its universal acclaim, conquering the hearts of everyone in earshot.

Bronwen reveled in the recognition and the support from the crowd, but what she had really wanted was time alone with Thomas. She had come to admire his work ethic, sensitivity, and family values. He was a good man and would make a wonderful mate. During the evening she had dropped a couple of hints about going for a walk together, but she didn't get the response she had hoped for, and was disappointed.

Now, as she lay alone in bed in a semi-dreamy state she wondered why Thomas had passed on being alone with her more. She hadn't seen him show interest in any other girl. Perhaps he was more interested in boys? No, that didn't seem to be the case either. Was she not pretty enough for him, was her job too demeaning, was she of the wrong class, although certainly not a convict? Was it her lack of an education, or did she not bathe enough? Perhaps she had been too forward? Should she have made a little Christmas present for him? No one else had offered anyone presents, but that certainly would have set her apart. Thoughts nagged her mind, tumbling around without order and creating confusion and angst. She wrapped her arms around herself and cried into the pillow. I'd even let him touch my breasts if that's what he wanted, she thought. What must I do to capture his deep attention? Her waking decision was to talk to Eileen to see if she had any suggestions about how to win over Thomas.

Ann was one of those who needed to be at her post in the kitchen early to help prepare breakfast for the Jamison family. When she arrived, George the butcher was already there working with Miriam and Henry, the head cook. They were going over the spoils of the previous evening, looking both at what had been cooked and not eaten, and what meat was still raw. George knew which uncooked meats would keep longest, and which had to be eaten quickly. He divided the raw offerings into two piles, and Henry subdivided the 'cook soon' pieces into some for today's dinner, some for the morrow, and enough for the third day. George collected the remaining offerings. The 'eat later' pieces in the other pile were destined to be salted to store longer.

From the cooked meat pile Miriam separated quail, chicken, duck, beef, lamb, and pork to be used for sandwich meat. She turned to Ann and said, "Here, why don't you take everything else to the convict camp for dinner tonight. I hate to see so much go to waste."

George added: "And take these extra fresh pieces as well. But wait a minute, you can't carry all that. How about this? When your day is done, come collect me at the butchery. I'll bring a couple of sacks and we can carry the load back to camp together. Okay?"

"I'm sure everyone will be thrilled to have these leftovers. The food was so delicious last night. I'll have my father help provide the handouts so no one gets too greedy. There's enough here for everyone. Thank you all."

In the presence of the Jamison family the serving folks addressed their masters and benefactors using formal titles—'sir', 'milady', etc. But when the servants were working together they would use each other's first name or appropriate appellations like cook, housekeeper, nanny, or governess, depending on the structure of the communication. It seemed to be part of the more casual Australian culture that was emerging. Ann was still a little reluctant to call the butcher 'George', feeling a bit intimidated by his size and overt friendliness. As well, if she were honest to herself, she also felt secretly attracted to him, although many years his junior.

At the end of the day, she and George packed the meat into two bags and headed across the fields to the camp. In a way it would have been more efficient to have had Grace carry the meat as Ann was now staying in the servants' quarters behind the house. But she said nothing since this meant she had the chance to walk both ways with George.

As they started out she quickly said, "We were having a hard time until we met Graham on the Parramatta Road. I know Father has told you our story about coming from Ireland. And you told us you had your Ticket of Leave and why you stay here, but I would love to hear about your days when you were a boy at school and how you got into the butcher business."

George was impressed with Ann's sensitivity. She had very deftly avoided asking about his crime. Most people on meeting him and learning he was a convict wanted to know where he came from and what he had done and what penalty he had been given. "Did you leave behind any sisters or brothers?" Ann asked, trying to give him a starting point. She looked up and was surprised to see a cloud cross George's eyes. It was as if a veil had been quickly drawn there and removed and she wondered what was behind it.

He stammered a bit, recovered, and said, "I'm sorry, you've reminded me of something I hadn't thought about in a while and I'm ashamed. You see, I had two elder sisters and a younger brother. Jamie died at four months old and Mother died six months later. I think there were complications at his birth. And I was only four years old when Mother passed away so I don't remember her very well, except that she spent a lot of time ill in bed. The elder of my two sisters is named Mariann. She married a banker and has five children, whom I've never seen, and unfortunately will never get to see. I'm not eligible for an Absolute Pardon, which would allow me to go back and visit London. At various times I wonder what is happening in their lives but Mariann sends me a letter once a year telling me all about them.

"My father, bless his soul, is gone now too. He worked at two jobs after Mother died, to try and provide for us children. Our aunt came and lived with us for a while, and she's the only real 'mother' I knew. But she went back to Devon when I was thirteen. That's where my father originally came from. He was a tin miner. I owe my size and strength to him."

Ann interrupted. "Are you able to tell me what upset you a moment ago or is it too painful to recall?"

Once again George recognized Ann's sensitivity. Impressive in one so seemingly young. Obviously she was more grown up than what he had realised. "I'm happy to tell you, Ann, because it's about my second sister, Sarah. You see, she was born not quite normal. She didn't learn at the same rate as other girls her age, and while she could understand much, she had difficulty talking. She was the prettiest girl I knew, and she was so loving. Everyone cared for her and she was incredibly special. She had fine blonde hair and dimples in her cheeks and a smile that never turned off despite all her difficulties. She and I developed a relationship where I was her protector and she was my little supporter. She would help me with all my chores, and never complained. She could do simple things by herself, including making tea and soup and setting the table.

"But because of her innocence she was too trusting. Once in a while she would wander outside the house on her own and that could lead to trouble. I won't go into detail but boys would take advantage of her. I hated them for that and I nearly killed one of them in my anger one day when he went too far. That's not what I'm ashamed of though, for he had it coming, and I caused him to leave our village. No, I'm ashamed because I had forgotten Sarah in my prayers at the bonfire last night.

"As I started my butcher apprenticeship, many of the neighbourhood boys who had a better education than me, and were studying to be engineers and accountants, would bully me and give me a hard time, claiming that anyone could do my job because no real intellect was needed for it and that touching animals was 'dirty work'. I took up boxing, because my father had been a boxer making some extra money when he was a youth. Of course, I reinforced the bullies' statements but after I knocked one of them down once they didn't bother me much. The money I made boxing I sent home to my father to help pay for a nurse to manage Sarah. But I stopped going home to visit, thinking I was doing my part just by sending the money home.

"I was shocked one day when my father found me after a fight I had just won and told me that Sarah was dying. Even then it was a week before I went home. I hardly recognized her as she was all skin and bones and nearly comatose. I felt terrible that I hadn't been home in such a long time to be with her. She couldn't speak but I think she recognized me because she squeezed my hand when I talked to her.

"I've done some bad things in my life, Ann. Sarah never ever did a single thing bad. When she died and after I was sent away to Botany Bay I resolved to try and only do good—partly in remembrance of her, and partly for my own benefit."

He paused and they walked on in silence for a bit. Tears were running down Ann's face. She stopped as they crossed a little brook, turned, reached up, and kissed him on the cheek. "Thank you for sharing that story with me, George. I understand the pain of your memory now. You are a fine man to have loved Sarah so much. I admire you."

George reached out and took Ann's hand and they walked together the little distance remaining to the camp. There, several members who had seen them coming, and had guessed what was in the sacks based on previous Christmas celebrations, were looking forward to a more savoury dinner than normal. Two large tables were set up and the food spread on top evenly. When a couple of the more desperate women tried to steal more than their share, Matthew quickly intervened and admonished them heavily.

Heading back to the mansion there seemed little to say but Ann spoke up anyway. "George, I have this feeling that in the days before Christmas you and your team cut up far more meat than was necessary. Indeed, I suspect you anticipated providing leftovers for the convict camp. Would I be correct in my assumption?"

Once again George had to rein in his surprise. This girl was no girl at all. Everything she said and did showed her to be a very perceptive, mature young woman. "As long as you don't tell Sir John we'll keep that as our little secret, Ann. Remember, I too was a convict and have been more fortunate than those in the huts. I like any chance to help them out."

Katie was starting to sense a change in all her girls. They were definitely exhibiting more independence in thought and action. There was no longer a complete deference to their parents, which, admittedly, bothered her sometimes, but it certainly was nice to see them taking more initiative in their jobs and relationships and personal goals. Generally, she only saw Ann and Mary Jane on weekends or when their shifts changed. She was delighted that Eileen and Grace were both learning to write, Grace somewhat ahead based on help from Thomas on the sea journey and a little since. The two were constantly showing her their efforts and had even written letters on her behalf to friends and relatives back home. All the girls were showing emotional growth, hormones also playing a role in some cases. Totally normal, she thought as she reflected back on her own youth. She was happy that Grace had found a beau. And what mother could not like Robert as a potential son-in-law?

At the same time the boys, as she thought of them, were displaying serious adjustments to manhood. Their exploits with the bushrangers indicated how well older men considered their capabilities. They were civil and courteous, perhaps not the most outgoing, especially Patrick, but well respected. She was proud of all her family.

It was Mary Jane who worried her the most. Obviously she was not comfortable with her roommate, and Katie sensed there was more to it than what Mary Jane was willing to tell her. In the spirit of new liberties and new independence, at the bonfire on Christmas Day, Mary Jane had asked to be called Molly from that point on. 'Mary Jane' was too much of a mouthful, she felt, and she wanted to be distinct from the other Marys who worked in the mansion. Other youngsters at school had sometimes called her Molly and she had always liked the nickname. Katie realised her relationship with Molly was one of the more tenuous she had with the children. She just hoped that someone in the family was close enough to help her with whatever the deep-seated issue was.

On New Year's Eve, the workers once again migrated to the fields between the house and road. The hay bales had been left out since Christmas and it hadn't rained in the intervening week so they were still dry. Extra bales had been brought in and people either sat on them or leaned against them, watching the sky above the mansion's outline. Once again Sir John was a gracious host in ordering several cases of fireworks. The stable boys were given the honour of setting them up and firing them from the area between the stables and the river. They'd moved all the horses out to one of the paddocks down by the orchards so they wouldn't be as startled had they been left in the boxes.

Sir John and his family watched the festivities from the upper-floor windows at the back of the house, while the workers on the hay bales exclaimed with appropriate oohs and aahs as the varied colours, bangs and booms, and patterns thrust into the night sky. An old year fading away, a new one being ushered in. A final multi-coloured crescendo signaled the end and everyone cheered. 1843 was history.

Come morning, Eileen had just set off along the path towards the mansion when Bronwen came hurrying up and fell into step beside her. "Are you going to the big house for something special?" Eileen asked.

"No, I was really hoping I could just talk with you for a bit."

Eileen's curiosity was raised. "What would you like to talk about?"

Bronwen faltered. "Well... well... it's about girl and woman things. You see, without a mother or any sisters, I have no one to ask questions of. I... I... was hoping you might be willing to help me."

Eileen stopped, a little dazed. "Of course I'll help. You poor thing. I never even thought about your circumstances. But I don't know if I'll have all the answers for you. Would it help if Grace was with us too?"

"Well, I think if I'm going to be embarrassed I'd rather it be in front of just one of your family if you don't mind."

"Okay. My twin sister and I are very close and share lots of confidences, so if I can't help easily I'll go to her for advice. I get off an hour early this afternoon. What if I come home and find you, and we go down to the orchards to pick a few quinces and plums and bring them back. We can chat in private among the trees there."

"Oh bless you, Eileen. I'll be waiting." And with that Bronwen turned around and headed back to the huts. Eileen's mind turned over, wondering what specific problems or issues Bronwen was wrestling with. She had been spending time with Thomas. Was she in love? Hopefully she wasn't pregnant. She was far too young...

Around midday an unusual sight came about, for Sir John was seen in a dress coat walking along the path to the workers' camp accompanied by his overseer, Graham, and two other gentlemen, also well dressed, but carrying two tripods and two other bags presumably with equipment inside. Those few convicts destined to work later shifts in the day, or those with time off, gathered at the camp entrance, for word of the imminent arrival of the men had passed through the camp like wildfire.

Sir John addressed the group, saying simply: "We're here to choose a location for the two new buildings I promised. These gentlemen behind me are surveyors from Parramatta. Does anyone have suggestions?" Four arms shot up into the air. Sir John pointed to one of the men. "You, sir!"

"How tall will the buildings be, Sir John? If they are to be two storeys, then I suggest they be situated between here and the road. If they were placed between the huts and the river they would cast shadows over the huts preventing late sunshine in the camp, and as we know, the Blue Mountains already bring us darkness much earlier than in Parramatta, for example."

Sir John pointed to another man, who offered, "That is a good suggestion just made but another option might be to put the buildings on the south side of the huts. In winter the cold winds come from the south. If the buildings were close end to end, or if there was one big long building, we would have a space in front where the wind is blocked. That would make it easier for group meetings, for example."

The other two arms in the air were withdrawn at this point. Sir John responded: "Well, it seems there are a couple of options. We could have one large building and I see the merit of that, or we could have two separate buildings, one to the east and one to the south. I agree we do not want to block any late sunshine from the west. I'll let the surveyors check over both areas and determine the merits of each before we decide. And I'll talk to the builders as well about the advantages of one long building as opposed to two smaller ones. Excellent input, and I thank you."

Sir John and Graham headed back to the mansion, and the small crowd watched the surveyors set up their dumpy levels on the tripods and yell measurements back and forth to one another, writing down numbers in their little notebooks. An hour later they packed up, waved to the few remaining watchers, and also headed back. As the field hands returned in late afternoon they all heard about the visit and were pleased to know that Sir John was going to keep his promise.

Eileen left her laundry duties and once home exchanged her work tunic for a simple cotton dress and walked over to Gwilym and Bronwen's hut. Gwilym was still out with the sheep but Bronwen was sitting at their small table with her head in her hands. "Are you okay?" Eileen asked from the doorway.

Bronwen looked up and said, "Oh yes, I didn't realise the time. Just resting. Let me grab a big fruit basket and we'll be off." Eileen thought she looked a little embarrassed. What exactly had she disturbed?

The orchards were extensive and a fair distance away. They covered acres and acres, some trees having been planted as far back as 1820, over twenty years earlier. There were apples, oranges, figs, cherries, quinces, and plums, to name a few. Neither Bronwen nor Eileen had seen some of the fruits before coming to Australia, and Eileen had grown to love quinces.

"I don't know a lot about you, Bronwen, only what Thomas has passed on. Not even how old you are."

"It's so strange, Eileen. Neither my mother nor father ever told me exactly when I was born. The best I know is that it was in very late autumn or early winter time. English autumn or winter, that is, because mother once mentioned she was unprepared when the cold suddenly came on and I still wasn't holding my head up as a baby. One time she told me I was born in 1828, yet my father even today says it was 1827. I think it was later because of my smaller size. Over the years I've compared myself to other girls I've talked to who know their birthdays. I probably will never know for sure but for the moment I've convinced myself that I just turned fifteen a couple of months ago. I think that means I'm about your sister Ann's age."

"So tell me some of the questions you have or things you want to know more about and I'll see how I can help. By the way, some mothers are just plain uncomfortable talking about girl things. Grace and I learned much from one of our aunts, not mother, and in turn we've helped Molly and Ann. You don't have brothers. We do, which I think made it easier for us in some ways when we were talking about boys' bodies, for example. We lived in a two-room house—all eight of us before Connor and David were born—and there was little privacy for any of us. We knew what boys' 'willies' looked like and they knew what our 'muffs' looked like."

"Ah, there goes one of my questions. Thank you, you are already making this less embarrassing. You see, I didn't even know those words."

"Well, they aren't the only words for those parts, they are just the ones we use. Even Mother talks about little David spraying pee from his willy. You might hear 'cock' or other euphemisms. And muff could be replaced by 'quim' or 'madge' or 'cunny'. Context will usually make it obvious."

"So, talking about muff, sometimes when I'm lying in bed and think about boys I get a tingling feeling in that area. It's not unpleasant at all, and it makes me want to touch myself. I did once and when I rubbed a certain spot there I got all hot and bothered and then this impossible-to-describe feeling ran all through my body and startled me. Do you know what I'm talking about?"

"Oh yes, certainly. I don't know what the feeling is called but Grace and I have both experienced it many times and talked about it. Sometimes it comes on totally without warning, but other times there's an obvious reason. Back in Ireland, if I happened to see one of the boys' willy very stiff I would get that feeling and feel dirty. Eventually I came to realise it was a natural girl reaction and then I didn't feel so bad. We're obviously designed and built differently and we don't always see or know *all* the differences. When we observe them it can provide an intriguing education. It needn't be that obvious though. A good-looking boy or man can make it happen with a smile, or even if he just touches you gently—on the arm, say, or kisses you on the cheek. It's very hard to explain.

"I'm sure it's similar for boys," Eileen continued. "If they see a girl's parts that they're not used to seeing it can get them aroused. On our voyage out here, a sailor grabbed my breasts one day when I bent over in front of him, and he noticed more than I had wished for him to. I was shocked at the time, frankly more from surprise than from the actual touching. I screamed and he rightly got into trouble, but afterwards I felt a little guilty because it wasn't as if he grabbed me forcibly, rather he sort of fondled my breasts and nipples. I could still feel the sensation hours later, and I remember I had to touch myself in response."

"So, you don't think it's wrong to touch oneself?"

"Not really. I think it's an individual matter. It's not like I do it a lot."

"So what should one do when a man hugs you in a friendly way and your breasts get squished against his chest? Is that okay? I'm not sure. Or if tries to grope you in places? And if you feel his willy hard against your leg or lap? It bothers me even though it has only happened twice."

"Well, I think you have to be very careful. If you sustain the embrace or add to it in any way you are clearly encouraging the man. If that's in your interest so be it. Otherwise, you should back away immediately so your intentions are very clear."

"You probably have no idea how this all helps, Eileen. You are so straightforward and easy to talk to. I don't even feel embarrassed, whereas I was almost scared to ask things ahead of time. I thank you so much."

They picked some more plums and headed for the quince trees. Bronwen stopped and shuffled a bit then said, "But there is one other thing I want to ask you about."

"Okay, what's that, Bronwen?"

"Well, it's about your brother Thomas. I'm sure it's obvious to you and others that I really, really like him. And he's been very kind to me. But I don't sense he has the same level of interest in me that I have in him. It might be hard for you to talk about your brother but there are times when I'm with him that I wish he would want to—what did you say?—fondle, yes, fondle me. I've even wondered about paying closer attention to Patrick to see if that would make Thomas jealous and change his interest. Do you have any advice?"

"As much as Patrick and Thomas were great teasers when we were little girls, both Grace and I admire them. They are strong and sincere. They don't complain. They have always been supportive of everyone in the family. I think we've all come to rely on them. In fact, we probably take them too much for granted. They are like pillars we can depend on to stay calm in troubled times and to take initiative to help us move forward. And for each of them I only want the happiest of things in their lives. Yes, your interest in Thomas is recognized. I can't blame you, for he is an attractive man—not just in looks.

"My sense is that neither brother is ready to settle down yet. They still want to explore this new country, and expand their knowledge about farming. They've never needed support as they've got a sort of self-drive and self-reliance that we girls don't have to the same extent. I think after the desperate living conditions we had in Ireland, this land offers them a form of freedom that they never knew before. Perhaps it's Regentville as much as anything. While Irish at heart I see both of them relishing what they learn here. They are furthest along in adopting this country."

Eileen looked pensive, then said, "It's possible that neither wants to feel burdened in any way or restricted from whatever opportunity might arise here. That's all I can suggest, Bronwen. There are no negatives about you from Thomas or anyone in our family. In the main we tend to accept people as they are, unless they are really depraved like some of the old women in camp and a few of the men. I doubt very much that the idea of showing favors to Patrick would make Thomas jealous so I don't really know what to tell you."

Then she sighed. "Well, wait a minute... In thinking a bit more maybe I do know what to tell you. And this will be hard for you. Being 'straightforward,' as you say, I think you may get hurt because I don't see Thomas wanting a mate at this time. He would never wantonly be mean to you, but I suspect you are in for a broken heart if you look for something more permanent with him. It might help to look for other eligible men. What about that stable lad who danced with you at the bonfire?"

Silence was Bronwen's only response. A tear escaped her left eye and she wiped her sleeve across it. She stopped and grabbed a quince with an angry tug. A major sigh escaped her lips.

Eileen put an arm around her shoulders. "I'm sorry, Bronwen. I cannot be deceitful with you. Please forgive me."

"Oh, Eileen!" Bronwen wiped another tear away. "You are only confirming what I already thought deep down inside. I actually thank you for your honesty, as much as it makes me sad. You Monahans are all such lovely people. It will be hard to find another Thomas, but I intend to stay friends with your brother. Who knows what may come about in the years ahead. And I need to remember that I really am only fifteen."

In the days immediately following, Eileen didn't see Bronwen at all, but she was relieved on the weekend when the girl stopped by just as the family was sitting down to have lunch outside. She made room on one of the benches and joined in the conversation as if nothing was amiss. Eileen felt relieved and admired the young girl for her attitude. She remembered her first infatuation over a boy and was sure Bronwen would never forget hers.

The heat of summer stayed through February and even lingered into March. Robert and Grace spent more and more time together. On a Saturday when the weather had perceptibly cooled

Robert came by early in the morning excited about something he'd learned during the week from a traveller who'd just walked across the mountains from Bathurst. Robert's familiarity with the Hartley area had found a common ground for the pair of them and they'd gotten on well. Now Robert wanted to go explore an area where his new friend had seen both a lyrebird nest and a bowerbird courting ground. His friend had departed for Sydney, but from his detailed descriptions and directions Robert felt confident he could find the right spot.

The two animals of legend that the Monahans had not seen yet but had heard a lot about were the koala and the platypus. They were unique to Australia, as were many of the birds. The lyrebird was somewhat mythical so the possibility of seeing one was exciting. Grace, Patrick, and Matthew quickly voiced their interest in going. Molly generously volunteered to look after the two youngsters and insisted that her mother get out and see more of the countryside. The girls were all pleasantly surprised and pleased when she acquiesced almost immediately.

Thomas spoke up. "Robert, I'll go back with you to the stables and help you attach a dray to Splash that will save everyone walking. She should be able to pull four people. I imagine you have to travel a ways up the mountain road, yes? What if we all meet by the front gates in forty-five minutes, and depart from there?"

Two hay bales were added to the dray for support and Thomas waved goodbye as the others headed north towards Penrith. At the ford, Patrick and Robert first carried the bales across as the dray lipped the river surface. Detaching the dray on the other side, Robert took Splash back. He then helped Katie and Grace mount and walked alongside the horse, helping her stay steady through the current. This was the first time Katie had been across the river and she savoured the experience, thrilling like a little girl as the water topped her feet and ankles. They climbed back on the dray and headed for Emu Plains and the base of the mountains.

There Robert suggested they relieve Splash of a lot of the weight and that they all walk up Lapstone Hill to the government hut. With the cooler weather and the smell of eucalyptus and boronia in the air no one objected. It was a long uphill walk of three miles before they came abreast of the government station. They stopped and chatted with the corporal and his wife stationed there and admired the little garden they had planted in the shade of the big gums. A small creek, now with little water in it, flowed by the back of their premises providing drinking water and support for the garden.

Two miles further on, Robert stopped by the tree with the milestone mark. "Here's where we turn off," he said. "We need to look along the left-hand side of the road within a hundred yards of this marked tree to find two waratah bushes within two feet of each other. They should be blooming for us. Look closely, all."

Katie had already scouted a little ahead and she yelled, "Hurrah—here they are."

Robert gathered everyone around. "Here's where it gets a little more complicated. My friend says that about seventy-five yards straight in and down the slope the big gum trees get replaced by a substantial grove of large cedar trees. Somewhere underneath them, but well apart, are the two places we are looking for. We'll all have to be very quiet. I suggest we have a little lunch first."

They detached the dray from Splash and let her roam to a patch of grass. They then opened the bags of bread, fruit, and meat cuts, and sat on the dray to eat. A light conversation suddenly ceased as a warbling bird song cut through the air. "That's the lyrebird," claimed Matthew very softly. "They are supposed to be master mimics of all sorts of noises."

The song suddenly changed markedly, reproducing the sharp cracking sound of the whip bird, and then shortly after changed again to emulate the kookaburra, finally becoming a melody one could almost match humming. It ended with the hauntingly beautiful clear call of the bellbird. The group was enthralled by the enchanting varied song, which went on and on for a couple of minutes, repeating itself over and over. When it stopped, no one spoke, but listened intently hoping to hear it again. They were rewarded when a similar song emanated close by from the other side of the road. They strained to look in the trees but couldn't see the source at all. At least they knew they'd stopped in a good spot.

Down a slight slope the cedar grove came into view as

described. Crawling ahead under the low branches on a carpet of dried leaves, it didn't take long for Robert to find the satin bower bird playground. The little clearing had been built by the male and comprised a flat ground area with two structures of sticks shaped like parts of egg shells facing each other, rounded outwards and curving back in at the top to form a bower. He had decorated the dance stage with selected blue objects, including berries, flowers, and feathers. If a female were to be sufficiently attracted to the bower she would mate with him and lay eggs in a separate nest some distance away.

Katie was particularly intrigued with the information Robert shared. "It is so touching to think that the male is the one doing the decorating," she observed. "Wait, I have an idea. Turn away, everyone." And as they did she lifted the hem of her dress and picked at some of the stitches with her teeth. When loosened, she tore the cloth, extracting a rectangle of bright blue cotton that had been part of the external pattern. Triumphantly she laid it inside the bower. "Okay, you can turn all back now. See, I've added a gift from afar. I hope his little girlfriend likes it." The others grinned and applauded her creativity.

Robert spoke up. "Well, let's keep our eyes open now for the lyrebird. I gather sometimes they run together in small groups." He led them to the edge of the cedar grove and paused. Suddenly Matthew shouted from the rear, "There's one!" and pointed off to the left. A small brown blur streaked behind some bushes and was gone. Katie clutched Matthew's arm and whispered, "Why don't we just stand still here for a few moments and see if another comes by." Sure enough, a few minutes later a little female and a larger male dragging his long tail casually sauntered by on much the same path as the earlier bird. "Let's wait some more," Katie whispered.

Just as everyone was starting to get restless from standing silently, a lone male appeared. He too was dragging his tail, but as he approached a small rotting tree-fern log he started to raise it. It didn't come up much, but spread just wide enough for everyone to see the intricate lacework pattern between the two outer fronds. At the sound of an 'aaaah' from one of the viewers the tail came down and the bird disappeared in the undergrowth. No one wanted to crawl back under the cedar trees to find a dance mound. Seeing the birds themselves was great reward.

The women wanted to stay and see if more would come by, but the men had seen enough and headed back to the horse and dray. Ten minutes went by and the women returned, a little disappointed that they'd seen nothing more.

Robert's words were meant to console. "I think we've been very fortunate. As I understand it these birds are very shy, although some of the mountain residents have seen them in their gardens pecking at the flowers. We could have been waiting hours, and possibly not even seen one. Maybe it was your gift to the bower bird that made them come by, Katie. And at least we heard them singing to one another. That's a treat itself. We have some flasks of water on the dray. Anyone need to quench their thirst before we head homeward?"

The excitement had fatigued Katie and Grace both, so on flatter parts of the road they sat on the dray and were happy to be carried along. Where steeper downhill sections were encountered they got off to make it easier for Splash. Robert walked beside Splash's nose talking to her gently and encouraging her all the way down. At the ford they rested again, enjoying the shade of the weeping willows and allowing the horse to take a long drink from the cool water.

Summer morphed into autumn. The cherries had come in early but now extra hands were taken from other jobs to help with the harvesting of the other fruits. Many bellies were filled with the delicious offerings each day but as in the previous year the harvest was bountiful and Sir John shipped hundreds of barrels and baskets to the markets in the east. It was as if Regentville was blessed in every area of fruit, meat, and crop production. Sir John became richer and everyone around him benefited.

Even so there were malcontents who felt they deserved more, or weren't treated as well as others. As in any community, different family and educational backgrounds led to different values and experiences in individuals. The Monahans, who came from a rural environment, felt comfortable in the farm environment of Regentville, but there were those who arrived from the major cities in Britain who never truly adapted. Sometimes they responded with passive resistance by doing the minimum necessary, or less if possible, in their jobs. At other times their frustration and discomfort led to belligerence and less-than-thoughtful exchanges and inputs to conversations. A new young convict from Manchester was creating a fuss around camp with his constant complaints about the work and the hut and how there was a limit on the amount of grog he was allowed. Even some of the more dissolute older women were becoming tired of him, one slapping his face hard when he called her a 'beast's whore'. And when one of the older men, himself from Manchester, tried to find common ground, the youth sneered and called him a 'worthless nobody' and pushed him hard to the ground.

He appeared at one of the Monahan family's weekend evening dinners and started up a drunken tirade against the family. "Ah, look. Such a happy sight. All pretty and proper. Work hard, pray to God, and think you are better than everyone else. Why don't you all go back to your peasant farms where you belong, and fornicate with the animals. I bet you girls could learn a thing or two."

The mug in his hand slipped out and he stumbled to retrieve it. Matthew rose in indignation, responding with, "That's enough. Be gone from our table. We do not need the company of rogues like you."

Patrick and Thomas exchanged subtle glances, their heads nodding in unison. Quietly they got up from opposite sides of the table and approached the young man. Thomas said, "Father, he won't listen to any of us. We'll take care of things."

"Ah, here they come. The 'goody goody' boys who think they are men but are just poor little shepherds in disguise. Here, try some of my ale, boys, although beware it may be too strong for you."

Thomas' right fist to the midriff doubled the chap over and he yelled in pain then vomited up his drink. Patrick picked up the mug, tipped the remaining contents on the fellow's head, and placed it on the table. It took little to subdue the rogue on the ground, and in order to stop his continued yelling Patrick pulled one of the chap's shirts over his head and stuffed part of it in his mouth. The twins rolled him onto his stomach, and Thomas sat on his legs. Patrick then pulled the man's undershirt off and used it to tie his arms and wrists together.

Grunts and groans that sounded like muffled swear words came to the family's ears, but with a quick move Thomas picked up the body and threw it over one shoulder like a sack of potatoes and headed off with Patrick adding support. "There's no need to hurt him any more," their father yelled.

"No," Patrick replied, "we're just going to teach him how to swim."

It was a good walk to the ford on the estate and the twins swapped the kicking and muttering load every couple of hundred yards. Molly left the table, saying, "I want to see what they do with that ugly boy. He deserves to be punished for what he said." She soon caught up with her brothers but stayed behind a few yards so she didn't have to hear all the swearing.

At the bank of the river they put their charge down and started the next phase of his punishment. Patrick went to Molly and said, "This isn't a time for gentleness, Molly. You may see and hear things that aren't designed for delicate ears. It might be good to go back now."

"That's okay, brother, I've been growing up over the last few months. I'll just sit over here out of the way, but this piece of garbage deserves whatever lesson you might hand out."

"Suit yourself, sis, but perhaps everything you see or hear doesn't need to reach all family ears."

"Understood, brother."

Patrick marched back to where Thomas was keeping guard. "Is this the deepest part, Thomas? I don't want this idiot thinking he can walk back to shore."

"Well, it's deep enough, Thomas. But it is where we saw that giant eel the other day. Remember? I don't know if they come out at night, which is why we have to throw him from the river bank. I'm sure not going to walk in there and then let him go."

The noises behind the gag grew more vociferous and the

struggles more desperate. The boy's eyes were lighting up with fear.

"Do you think we should find out if he can even tread water? We sure don't want him drowning. Of course if he simply floats down to the sharp rocks at the crossing he could probably haul himself out, albeit pretty sore from dashing against the rocks and getting cut."

"Oh look, he's wet himself. Just like a little baby. Not much of a man here. That makes me want to pee too. Hold him down so I can pee on his feet. That way he'll remember us real well."

Fear in the boy's eyes turned to unbridled anger and he struggled even more.

"No, I have a better idea, brother. Here, help me pull his britches off. I've made this work before."

"There, now they go into the water first. He'll have a long chase on those—there they go."

Standing the nude, quaking boy up, Thomas shoved his face directly into the other's. "You are a pain, son. To everyone in camp. And you have insulted our family and especially our sisters mightily. We are peace-loving people but you have overstepped the bounds of decency. We are all different but we try to live in harmony.

"If you want to change you may come back to camp; otherwise, I suggest you be on your way elsewhere and we'll let the overseer know you went looking for greener pastures. The choice is yours."

They untied his wrists, which dropped by his side, all fight gone. They then took the gag out of his mouth with the youth whimpering, "I can't swim, that eel will bite me. Please don't throw me in."

With a quick nod Thomas grabbed his feet, Patrick his shoulders, and they threw him as far out into the cold water as they could, his screams sailing through the air till he hit with a giant splash.

Molly had come forward and picked up the shirts. "Are you going to leave these behind so he can cover himself up when he emerges?" She knew the water at this point was only four to five feet deep and that there was no eel and that he'd soon wade out but would have to track downstream to see if he could find his britches caught on some branches by the bank.

"We'll let you decide on the shirts, Molly. We've had all our fun. You might even enjoy staying and watch him running naked along the bank trying to find his britches. If he sees you, that will only embarrass him more."

"I'm coming back with you two. But I'm bringing his shirts. It might be more interesting if a group of us girls were here and we could make fun of that tiny willy I saw."

Thomas pretended to be shocked. "Molly, what happened to that refined sister we love?"

"We're not all as prudish as Mother, you know. And I want you to tell me honestly. Would you really have peed on him?"

"No, that would just have reduced me to his level. The idea was really to scare and belittle him more than anything. I'm pretty sure we succeeded at that. Come on, let's head homeward. I can hear him yelling and splashing back there, crying like a baby. I'd say justice has been served."

The young convict was never seen again, and while many in camp wondered why, the story stayed safe inside the Monahan family. Matthew wasn't quite sure he approved of all of his sons' actions, but not every disagreement and conflict could be settled peacefully, and he did agree that the epithets thrown at the family deserved an appropriate response. Certainly his daughters and wife relished the love and support shown by the two eldest boys. They'd always been loved. Their actions just reinforced the devotion.

12. A significant death,
a welcome marriage

The boiler heating the water in the laundry had been behaving temperamentally for a week. It took longer to get started and sometimes the water just didn't seem to heat properly, and the pressure gauge gave faulty readings. The workers had complained to Graham but he hadn't done anything about it. He had maintenance men who were trained as mechanical engineers and employed to look after all the machinery used at the mansion. But none seemed interested in fixing the boiler, as they were busy running new pipes from the river to help with expanded irrigation needs in the vegetable gardens and fruit orchards. It was a big job requiring co-ordination on ditch digging, pipe joining, testing, re-routing, and pump management.

Finally one morning when no hot water was forthcoming, Eileen stormed to the back door of the big house and demanded to see the overseer. When Graham finally turned up, she let him have it. "Sir, we've indicated for a week that we need help with the boiler in the laundry. This morning we have no hot water so everything will be washed in cold water and we'll have no chance of getting linen and household clothing rid of stains and marks. We need an engineer here now. Not tomorrow. Now."

Graham was a little affronted but realised he had put things off too long. He walked over to the maintenance facility and after fifteen minutes of arguing and cajoling came back with a young apprentice engineer carrying a box of tools. A little crowd had gathered, including George, who had just delivered his meat selections for the day to Ann, who was sorting them out on the big kitchen table.

The engineer could immediately tell that one of the hot water pipes must be blocked but he had no idea which. He pulled a large spanner out of his toolbox and tapped on one of the top pipes, listening closely to get an idea of how full or empty it was. Empty. Clearly a problem. He'd have to shut the boiler down and disconnect things and find the blockage. A side pipe he tapped on yielded the same sound. It shouldn't be empty at all. Obviously the bottom pipe, which looked a little corroded, would have to be where the problem resided. Anticipating he'd hear a dull, full sound, he tapped it solidly with the heavy metal spanner. The next second he was screaming in pain as hot scalding water burst from two ever-expanding holes under pressure. It hit his legs and midriff as he doubled over and dropped the spanner next to his foot. His scream rent the air in the rear courtyard, startling everyone who heard it. The man tumbled out the laundry door screaming in agony.

George had just opened the kitchen door to head back to the butchery and quickly realised what was happening as water poured out into the courtyard, running up against the fallen engineer. "Ann!" he yelled. "Get Graham to ride for the doctor, and bring fresh towels to the river."

With that he rushed to the young man, lifted him up, and streaked through the door between the stables heading for the river bank. Without hesitating he waded in and held the man's stomach and legs below the surface, letting the cold water do what it could to help soothe and take some of the pain away. Graham came running down the bank and walked out to help ease some of George's load. "He'll need a doctor, Graham."

"Yes, I sent one of the fastest stable lads to get the doctor. Thought I could be more useful here."

"I can keep holding him," George said. "Maybe you should go turn off the water supply to the boiler and check it's not burning the bottom of an empty tank. I'll be okay here for a bit. Poor chap's unconscious now from the pain I'll warrant. And here's Ann with the towels. I'll get him to the bank."

Ann lay down a large tablecloth and blanket and George placed the dripping comatose man on it. He made sure his head was down and his legs and midriff were above his heart. At least the man was breathing and his heartbeat seemed regular and strong. George lifted the man's shirt gently off his stomach and saw a series of small blisters forming. He immediately covered the skin up again. The man's pants were plastered to his legs and through a couple of small holes George could see how red the skin was, and to one side a whitish patch. He laid the towels gently over the burnt areas and talked softly to the man, whose eyes had re-opened and who was now murmuring incoherently. "Ann, please get me a glass of water for him. I need to keep him out of shock."

Eileen and others had rushed out of the laundry, avoiding the still hot water on the ground, and were standing around crying and feeling helpless. The raised voices and screams had reached the ears of the other engineers in the pump house, who also now gathered around. A couple of them ran after Graham to help contain the water flow and turn off the heat. They could see that the broken pipe was full of rust that had built up over the years, and they immediately felt remorseful for sending off the new boy to fix the problem.

Back on the river bank George asked if anyone knew the man's name. "Sean O'Leary," came the response from one of the engineers. Sean was now moaning in pain again and George cradled his head and said, "Sean, you'll be all right. The doctor is on his way. Can you tell me where it hurts most?"

The only word in response was "stummick," of no surprise to George since he suspected of all the areas affected that's where the skin was most tender. George bent closer to Sean's ear. "The top of your legs are very red and blistering. What about your privates? Are they burned too?"

Two words were whispered in response: "missed 'tween." George figured there must have been two holes in the burst pipe to start with—one which allowed the hot water to scald his stomach, the other his legs. He was probably lucky he got out when he did or the two holes would have become one large one and he'd have been scalded between the two areas as well. Oh, to be thankful for small mercies, he thought.

Eileen took the glass from Ann, whose hands were shaking, and bent down and caused a few drops to fall on Sean's lips. He responded immediately, searching with his tongue for more, so Eileen held the cup at his lips and tipped it slightly so he could sip. "Ann," she asked, "is there a little laudanum available somewhere in the house? Maybe ask Mrs. Jamison. It may help ease his pain until the doctor arrives."

Gradually some colour returned to Sean's face, which had paled considerably initially. His speech started to return to normal and the laudanum in honey applied to his lips helped him tolerate his pain better. After thirty minutes George and Graham picked him up and transported him to a spare room on the ground floor of the mansion usually reserved for less-important visitors. They put a pillow under his bottom and several more under his legs to raise them, again not wanting blood to rush to the affected areas. It was a good hour before the doctor arrived. He praised what had been done so far and cut away the man's trousers and shirt so he could work better on the burnt skin and blisters. Applying salve and fresh bandages, he declared that Sean would survive, but suggested he remain in the current room for two days before even attempting to get back to work. With relief all around Sean fell asleep and the spectators tiptoed from his room.

Back in the kitchen Miriam had made several pots of tea, and all those involved sat around the big table going over the events and soothing their nerves with the welcome brew. The doctor was highly complimentary of George's actions. "You cooled the burn areas immediately but not for too long, and then you positioned him with his heart below the affected areas. I would have done no different. You probably saved him from having much worse blistering and pain. Plunging into the river was very creative. I think I would have been looking around for pails of cool water. Well done, sir. He's going to be sore when he wakes up and for several days beyond, I'm afraid, but the skin will heal. He'll have some scars, but it could have been far, far worse."

The two replacement engineers knocked on the back door and asked if they could come in. They announced that they'd been able to find some new pipe that fit and they'd dismantled all the other pipes and found no more blockages. They'd added water back into the boiler and heated it up without any problems. The pressure gauge seemed to register correctly and was stable, so they felt the repairs were working and would hold for a long time yet. At that point Eileen grabbed a bread roll, cut a hunk of cheese off the round, and after saying goodbye to all, headed back to the laundry. Gradually the group dispersed. It was Daisy who volunteered to check on Sean every hour to see that he was comfortable. The doctor said he'd come by again the next day to check for signs of infection, but was pleased that clean towels had been used and the man's clothing not removed till he came. Those actions he felt would help prevent infection from occurring. Others crossed their fingers, hoping he was right.

The story of the disaster spread through the estate. George's quick-thinking action in carrying Sean to the river, wading in without hesitation, and holding the man and reassuring him through his screams and pain made him a hero in many folks' eyes. All the engineers insisted on coming by the butchery, shaking his hand and thanking him. None of them had the broad shoulders and the strength George possessed and they each wondered what they would have done in the circumstances. Far less to be sure. George shrugged it all off, but the girls in the mansion granted him renewed respect. They even started to vie more for his attention, recognizing the inherent goodness in the man. Ann quietly hung back, observing.

Something inside her told that she and George were destined to be together. The feeling emanated from deep within her soul. It had come out of the blue, and was calm and reassuring. A feeling definitely not to be denied and like no other she'd ever experienced. She beamed inside and felt her heart quicken. A warm glow settled throughout her body. The staff only said good things about him, and it was clear that he really cared for the people of the estate. She'd learned a lot in their walk to the convict camp and back. Yes, he was a good deal older than her but she'd never felt he was talking down to her or treating her differently than he did many of the older people around. Such an inspirational man. She watched as Daisy deliberately caught up with him in a tight corner of the room and brushed her breasts against his chest as they squeezed by each other. So obvious, she thought to herself.

It won't work, Daisy.

The apprentice Sean was up and about fully in a week. There were scars on the top of his legs and belly and it hurt to bend over, but he wanted to be back at work. The engineers admired his pluck. It didn't take long for the episode to merge with the past, especially with harvest season in full swing and the major irrigation project under way. Not only that, but clearing was going on for the two new buildings at the convict camp. It was a busy time.

Robert had heard Ann tell a little about what she had learned from George when he came for dinner. It gave him a new idea and he made a special trip to the butchery. "Ann was telling us all about your intention to establish a butcher shop in Penrith, George, and I wanted to ask you more about that. I think it's a grand idea, as there is every indication the town will grow and be a staging stop for settlers who want to take up pasture west of the mountains. They'll need to provision here and I see that need attracting other merchants and service people—wagon repairers, a blacksmith, hoteliers, storage providers, as well as implement and travel suppliers. The fact that St. Stephen's is already in place is an excellent indication that the church expects growth. So, if you get in on the ground floor, so to say, now, you'll be in excellent shape to build up your trade. I'm sure you are not aware, but my extended family back in London were butchers and I have a little experience in the trade as well."

George interrupted. "I totally agree with your views, Robert, and am pleased to see that someone else sees the future as I do, but I don't see how there'd be enough business to start that would require more that myself serving in the shop."

"Quite right, George, and I wasn't thinking of that. I was thinking more behind the scenes. You see, I have a background away from the shop counter. Basically I'm a man of the land. I presume you'll have some storage paddocks somewhere where you keep the animals fattening and then butcher them before delivering the carcasses to the shop. I was wondering if you'd be interested in having me manage that part of the business for you. Unless you are going to do that yourself as well."

"This could possibly work out, Robert, because I've offered to stay and help here on a part-time basis until I get well established, so I don't have time to do the actual animal management and killing per se. I have bought some acreage at Emu Plains across the river, and I've just started looking around for an overseer. I didn't know you had experience with butchering. Let's go out there and you can show me your expertise. I was planning lamb chops and loin for the Jamisons tomorrow."

The men walked to the stables and readied Splash and George's bushranger horse Maisie, waded across the estate ford, and rode off to Emu Plains. George explained the way he liked the lambs to be skinned and cut, and watched while Robert did an efficient and credible job. It was clear that he knew what he was doing. "I sure am glad you came forward, Robert. Certainly saves me trusting someone I don't know."

"Perhaps we can keep it between ourselves for the moment, George? You see, pretty soon I intend to ask Grace to marry me. Assuming she agrees, I think she'd be very happy to know we'd be staying in the vicinity, although I have to tell you that sometime in the future I would like to have my own farm."

"You'd help me get started so I think this is going to work out for all of us. We'll have to share an ale to celebrate when we get back to the mansion."

It wasn't too long afterwards that Ann brought disturbing news home one weekend. Sir John had suddenly turned seriously ill. For the past week the doctor had been visiting every day. Sir John's wife Mary was in a dither, rushing around with no real purpose, wringing her hands, unable to sit still, getting in the way of housemaids and cleaners, and generally being more of a nuisance than a help. The semi-hedonistic lifestyle Sir John had led for so many years was catching up with him. The news spread quickly throughout the estate and morale plummeted. While Sir John didn't present the best example of moral behavior, having had several mistresses and children by them, he was appreciated by the convicts who owed him their livelihood. The mood among the house servants who were impacted daily was despondent to say the least.

While last year's harvest had been good, Sir John had lost a much of his wealth in the earlier bank crash—especially being a founder of the Bank of Australia. His illegitimate children weren't particularly helpful on the estate, and they weren't regarded in the same light as Sir John. People viewed him as a charismatic, innovative, socially conscious leader. That his presence, his reign, his charm, and warm-heartedness might be in jeopardy, was hard to contemplate. He was an institution, their savant, leader, and employer. Without him their world would crumble, be ill-defined, and almost unimaginable. There was sadness everywhere as the realisation set in that the great man's life was coming to an end.

On June 29th 1844, at the age of sixty-eight, the flamboyant Irish-born son of Thomas Jamison, who arrived in the colony as surgeon's mate in the First Fleet, passed away. The whole estate was grief stricken. Sir John also owned grazing runs on the Namoi and Richmond Rivers and two other estates at Bathurst, and at Capertee. Fast riders were sent in all directions bearing the startling news. The governor of the state was notably distressed, as were many dignitaries and explorers who had spent time enjoying Sir John's hospitality at Regentville.

Two days after death, in a simple ceremony, Sir John was buried in an above-ground tomb in the graveyard of St. Stephen's Anglican Church in Penrith. Mourners paid their respects as high society men held hats against their chests, and women wore veils across their faces. Tears were evident in many eyes. Mourning at Regentville continued for days, as the loss of the man left everyone wondering what his departure would mean—for his family, for the estate, and for themselves. No quick answers were to be forthcoming.

A loud banging at the entry of Matthew's hut one evening stopped the newspaper reading that was taking place inside. Robert poked his head through the doorway. "Have any of you seen or heard from Uncle Gregory today? He left early this morning for the wool sheep fields but he's nowhere around and the gloves he always uses are not hanging on their usual peg at home. I suppose he could have gone swimming directly at the end of the day, but even so you'd think he'd be back here by now. I'm starting to worry that he might have had an accident. Would you mind helping me check with as many huts as possible to see if anyone noticed him today?"

Thirty minutes later as they all straggled back, the news was not good. He'd only been seen heading off in the early morning. There was no sighting of him since. Matthew said, "Let's grab some lamps and see if we can find him. Maybe you and I, Robert, can take the usual path to the sheep paddocks while the boys cut to the river, and walk along the bank and meet us out there. Do we need anyone else?"

"Probably best if it's just we four for now, Matthew. If we don't find anything tonight we'll ask for more search volunteers tomorrow. I hope he hasn't had a memory problem and just wandered off somewhere and gotten lost. He sure has aged markedly since I was here before."

There was no sign of Gregory along the regular track one would take to the sheep paddocks, so on arrival Robert and Matthew walked along the fence line towards the river to a point where they could see Thomas and Patrick's lanterns swinging to and fro coming towards them. They never faltered in their progress, indicating no finding along the bank. As the group reconvened, the discussion centered on how to search further. There were four good-sized paddocks to search, and one that had been left fallow. One man per paddock, four walking the boundaries of each paddock and then heading to the center to meet up, or random paths as the feet led one? They decided to search one paddock at a time by covering quadrants as best they could.

An hour later they'd finished two of the paddocks and were feeling discouraged. They all realised they could easily have passed Gregory if he were lying outside the circle of light each of their lanterns threw. They decided to walk back via the fallow field to save disturbing any more sheep and continue the search in the morning. As they closed the gate between the field and the orchard, Patrick noticed an old discarded shoe. He picked it up but the sole was hanging by a small thread, leaving a large gaping hole. "No wonder they threw this away," he said. "I don't think anyone could repair this. Looks like an old convict boot."

Robert's internal antennae quivered. "Here, let me see. Gregory sometimes wore an old dilapidated pair of convict boots that had been left behind in the hut he inherited. Where did you throw it, Patrick?"

Patrick retrieved the boot and handed it over. Robert studied it. "This could be Gregory's. I never looked that closely at them so can't really tell. Sure is worthless now. Let's keep going anyway." They skirted the edge of the cherry orchard, heading back towards the river a good quarter mile away.

As they passed the last fruit tree and were about to cross a section of lawn halfway to the river, Thomas, who was leading, spied a large lump on the ground just to the side of the course they were travelling, He rushed forward followed by the others, and found Gregory face down in the grass. He bent down, listened, and put a finger to his neck but there was no pulse. He turned around. "I'm sorry Robert. He's not breathing and there's no pulse."

"Let me check, please." Robert knelt and turned the old man over on his back. A speck of drool was at the corner of his mouth, and his face was contorted in a painful grimace. One hand was reaching up holding on to the front of his shirt, the other hanging lifeless at his side. He still had his gloves on.

Matthew knelt beside Robert. "I'm sorry, son. But it looks like he's gone to a better place. It's only a guess, but it looks like a heart attack to me. We'll have to get the doctor to tell for sure."

Robert stood up, put his hands over his eyes for a moment, and said, "I think you are right. Bless his soul. He had always been good to me. I will definitely miss the old fellow." No tears, but there was a definite quaver evident in his voice.

Thomas knelt at the man's feet where one leg had originally been over the other. In turning Gregory over the legs had separated and it was immediately clear that the left shoe was missing. "Patrick, can I borrow your lantern, please?"

With the extra light Thomas examined the sole of the exposed foot closely. After a few seconds he said, "He's been bitten by a snake. There are two red spots here close together. They're hard to see with all the dirt on his feet but there's little doubt. Look, I've rubbed the spot as clean as I can. I bet his shoe broke coming through that last gate so he took it off. As he was walking to the river to come home along the bank he didn't see a brown snake under one of the fruit trees and accidentally stepped on it with his bare foot. They're pretty venomous as we all know, but really aren't aggressive unless disturbed badly. There are a couple of blisters near the bite, whether from walking or the venom I can't tell. His heart attack followed from the poisoning. I really am sorry, Robert."

Robert again came closer and verified what Thomas had seen. "Well, I guess we should carry him back, men. He's already stiffening up. Let's head for the pump house."

Next day the doctor confirmed Thomas' assessment, and indicated to Robert that he'd make burial arrangements at St. Stephen's Church of England in Penrith for the following afternoon. The mood over the camp was downcast. Everyone knew there were snakes about and the only previous known bite had not been fatal. Brown snakes and king browns were the most venomous but no kings had been seen in the area so everyone assumed it had been a regular brown snake. As the story made the rounds people checked their boots, adding extra socks if they had them. Many came by and passed their condolences to Robert, who seemed quite stoic over his loss.

Grace assumed the role of closest comforter and the Monahans included Robert in all their meals. After lunch on the burial day Robert walked alongside Splash, who pulled the dray with Gregory's lifeless form wrapped in sackcloth. Eileen and Molly were able to get time off as were Patrick, Thomas, and Matthew. A number of other residents who had enjoyed Gregory's company trudged along the road to the graveyard at the beautiful church. Katie stayed back with the young boys and Ann couldn't break free. A short and simple ceremony saw the gentle man returned whence he came, and the mourners filed home in silence, Grace holding Robert's hand tightly the whole way.

Gregory's death brought Robert to new decision points. With all the family gone, there were no ties to any particular place. He had good friends back in Hartley, but the draw wasn't that strong. Grace clearly was the most important person in his life now. His desire to be with her permanently was growing, and he felt sure the feeling was mutual. But Regentville per se didn't present him with any opportunity to own his own farm or to go into the butcher business some of his family had been in. His first action was to go to Sydney and clean up his uncle's small estate, which basically consisted of a bank account at one of the main banks. Gregory had made him trustee and beneficiary.

On return he walked to the paddock where Matthew was checking the health of the fat lambs. Matthew saw him coming. "How was your trip, young man? Is the city growing by leaps and bounds?"

"It most definitely is. The road from Parramatta into the city is much improved and they are starting to work on the next section to Penrith. It is easy to see the shape of the new wharf at the Quay and more gas lamps have been put in place. I saw two new hotels and many more conveyances on the city streets. And the harbour had several ships at anchor. A thriving metropolis indeed.

"As you know, Matthew," he continued, "with my uncle gone there is no family holding me here and I am anxious to start my own farm somewhere. Your daughter is the most special person in the world to me now, and I would love to spend the rest of my life with her. I know I'd be taking her away from you but I would like your permission to marry her, and to have your and Katie's blessing for our union. I assure you I will do all in my power to be a good provider for her and to make her as happy as possible. I love her deeply."

A smile lit up Matthew's face. His eyes twinkled and his hand shot forward to take Robert's in a strong congratulatory grip. "There's a part of me, Robert, that wants to say 'what took you so long?' No matter. I'm delighted. We're all very fond of you and the two of you will definitely have all our blessings. When do you plan to tell Grace?"

"Well, she has tomorrow and Saturday off, but has to work Sunday. I was hoping I may take her riding tomorrow and talk to her then. Would that be acceptable?"

"I think that would work perfectly. I'd like to tell Katie tonight, she will be so excited, but that would allow us to have a celebration dinner on Saturday night. It gives me a day to make sure Ann and Molly can join us. Welcome to our family, Robert. You will make a fine husband for Grace. I'm very grateful."

The next day, not far from the climbing spot to the aborigines' cave, Robert and Grace sat on the grassy bank of the river dangling their feet in the clear water. "You know, in the creeks west of Hartley I've seen that strange creature called the platypus. It swims underwater and lives in a hole in the bank. Has this wide bill somewhat like a duck and four webbed feet and a stumpy tail. I think this river is too deep and flows too fast for any of them to live here. But I'd like to take you to Hartley and show you."

"Oh, that would be wonderful, but I doubt they'd let us go to Hartley without a chaperone."

"Well then, there's only one other way to make it happen. Will you marry me, Grace Monahan?"

Grace nearly slid down the bank as she quickly turned and gaped, mouth wide open, at the handsome man beside her. "Oh yes, Robert. Nothing could make me happier. I would love to be Mrs. Kitchings. I'd be so happy." She leant forward and kissed him on the cheek but he quickly turned face to face and they shared a longer passionate kiss that melded two souls together.

"Have you talked to Father?"

"Oh yes, he approves. I really didn't think he wouldn't, but he said he'd be happy to give us his blessing. He and your mother are going to arrange a big family dinner for all of us tomorrow evening."

"Oh my, I have to get home and tell everyone. I just know Eileen is going to be so jealous. Kiss me again quickly. Oh, I am so excited. I love you so much." It appeared that sharing the news with others was more important than spending extra time alone with husband-to-be as she stood up, shook out her skirts, and sought her shoes. Grinning happily, Robert followed suit, and they headed back to the crossing with Splash following behind.

While Robert brushed the horse down back in the stables, Grace ran to the laundry to tell Eileen the news. The two of them emerged laughing joyously and headed inside the mansion to find Ann and Molly. Soon all four were prancing and yelling in the courtyard and before one could count to fifty, work had stopped all around and the yard was full of maids, nannies, kitchen helpers, stable boys, and others joining in the impromptu celebration. Robert stayed in the shadows until Eileen came and dragged him into the melee.

At the family dinner it was Ann who asked the logical question everyone had been wondering about. "Where are you going to get married, and when?"

"We haven't really talked about that yet," Grace responded. "I don't want to put Robert on the spot now, but he's Anglican and we're Presbyterian. We'll work it out. I've been reading in the newspapers down at the mansion about some of the arguments going on over religion in Sydney. Especially as they affect education. Originally only the bishops of the Church of England were sent here and given land to build churches and schools. But as Catholic and Presbyterian clergy arrived they sought and were given recognition as well. One suspects in the future there will be some sort of nondenominational national school system alongside the church schools, just as in England and Ireland. There's a gentleman named John Dunmore Lang, who is a bit of a character, but has a Doctorate of Divinity and high moral standards and who preaches in the Presbyterian Scots Church in Sydney. He was one of the first clergymen outside the Church of England to be allowed to perform marriages here in the colony. I like what I read in his speeches in the paper and he actually has preached in Ulster as well. As far as when to get married," she finished, "I think that's up to Robert mainly."

"I'm thinking fairly soon, in early spring. I want to go to Hartley now and see my friends, stay for a couple of weeks, then come back here. Any time after that would work. In some ways the sooner the better.

"And actually I have a little surprise I think you'll all like. Not even Grace knows. I'm going to help George Clarke with the butcher business he will set up in Penrith. He's asked me to manage his storage paddocks and the slaughter of the animals there, preparing the carcasses he'll use to finalize his offerings at the shop. His fields are in Emu Plains across the river, so we'll try and find a little place there to live in so we won't be far away from you all. "

"Oh, bless you," Katie remarked as she jumped up and gave him a big kiss. "That's wonderful. I know it will be hard to see daughters and sons leave over time. Having them close by a little longer will help."

Grace smiled. She would be happy living close by. But she did wonder what other little secrets Robert might have planned that hadn't been aired yet. She made a commitment to herself to find out and see if she could avoid future surprises, no matter how pleasant.

With many months of co-habitation behind them, Molly and Daisy had actually been able to forge a relationship that, while not exactly sisterly, at least was friendly. Katie would have been shocked had she known the full transformation in her daughter, and Daisy's mother, were she close by instead of back in England somewhere, would have been surprised at some of the refinements in her first born. Instead of brazenly walking nude down the corridor to take a bath, Daisy now wore a smock or draped a towel around her. She scrubbed her hair more often, and had asked Molly if she would teach her to knit. Of all things she started to show a little pride in her maid's uniform, worrying if a spot was too conspicuous, and working to remove it if so. She owned only two dresses, but there was one of Molly's she liked in particular and which fitted. Once she'd seen the improvements in Daisy's self-care Molly was happy to loan her the dress on occasion.

Early in their togetherness Daisy had admonished Molly for being 'scared of her body,' the meaning of which Molly totally failed to comprehend. It took two months of persistent suggestions before Molly finally agreed to accompany Daisy one night and 'just watch'. At first she was very uncomfortable as Eric and Daisy stripped in the hayloft, but she'd vowed to stay and learn. Eric's fingers and mouth did their work and it wasn't hard to see Daisy's obvious enjoyment and satisfaction. And when Molly saw Eric's erection she definitely felt new stirrings. She bit her lip as the tingling intensified and lay back on the hay bale half squirming. "Go on," Daisy urged Eric. And before Molly knew it he was cupping one of her breasts, gently kneading the nipple, and with deft fingers rubbing her most sensitive spot below her mound. Molly couldn't stop herself and her spasms rocked her throughout. Daisy and Eric watched and smiled, until eventually, feeling embarrassed and very self-conscious, Molly sat up.

"You did well," said Daisy. "Now you know what I've been talking about."

Feeling humiliated, shocked, and yet nonplussed by the new pleasure she'd been exposed to, Molly wondered about the contradiction in feelings she was experiencing. She trailed Daisy back to their room with her head down, vacillating between being ashamed and confused. In bed she exclaimed, "I don't know, Daisy, I don't know. It felt good but is it right? Oh dear. I can't imagine paying Eric like you do. I think it would make me feel guiltier. But I suppose he'll want something in return." She could feel her own wetness, and a small shudder ran through her again. She wrapped her arms tightly across her chest and rolled side to side.

"Don't fight it, Molly. It's all very natural. And you don't need a boy every time, or even at all. I know you must have heard me moaning at times when I've pleasured myself in bed some nights. You can make it happen yourself too. You know how now. Will you be all right?"

"Yes, but I don't know whether to thank you or curse you yet, Daisy. Maybe the morning will tell. Night night..."

"Well, if you are ever up to it, you could thank me by rubbing my spot for me. I'd like that. And as far as Eric goes, well, he's told me before that he'd like to suck your nipples."

A week passed by with no recriminations or overt changes in behavior on Molly's part. In fact, in some ways, she told herself, she was happier to know about things that had previously only been mentioned in whispers or through vague coded comments, all of which at the time had left her feeling naïve and immature. The fact that her body could come up with such amazing feelings of pleasure was stunning. It was as if she'd been introduced to a new world. It had been there all the time but she'd known nothing about it. How could that be the case? How on earth could she not know? Was it the same for every girl? No, clearly not—Daisy knew somehow. How did she find out? Should I ask her or would that be too secret and personal? Oh, she thought, Eileen and Grace must know since they are two and a half years older. Did Mother tell them? I doubt it. She had enough difficulty telling me about the monthly bleeding. I doubt she'd talk about anything so, so... intimate. The word finally reached her conscious thoughts. I suppose all that grunting that went on back in Donegal was even more intimate. How naïve I must be. I think I need to talk to someone other than Daisy. Soon. Probably Grace before she leaves us. Yes, if she's getting married and thinking about babies she must know everything. I wonder what she'll think of me. Maybe I'd better wait. No, I need to know more now. Oh dear. It certainly is confusing.

Internal head conversations would come and go, starting up at totally unexpected times of the day, and disappearing as she realised she was distracting herself from whatever job she was in the middle of. Sometimes the recall would induce longing, although the intensity of the past experience would be well diminished. But after another week she could hold back no longer, and asked Daisy when she would be seeing Eric again. The consequent interchange was even more exciting and satisfying and Molly decided it was definitely time to seek counsel with Grace.

Summoning up her courage, she waited for Grace outside the servants' entrance one afternoon when Robert was in Hartley and asked if she could walk back with her. It wasn't hard to engage Grace as all one had to do was mention Robert and her face beamed and she would start singing his praises. Molly listened for a bit but finally interrupted and said, "Grace, before you go away and make your home with Robert I need some sisterly advice. You see...."

And she started describing the revelations she had been experiencing and the dilemma her mind and body kept throwing at her. They talked all the way back to the huts with Grace listening patiently, pleased that her little sister had sought her advice. Yes, she knew about touching oneself. The feeling in response was called 'orgasm'. No, she didn't know about tasting, no she hadn't touched a willy (other than baby David's when re-wrapping him) but she had seen them erect. Yes, she wanted to get pregnant and knew how to try and make that happen.

"Is this why you've been more moody than usual these past several months?" Grace asked. "I'm sorry you didn't seek Eileen or me out earlier. We could have eased your concerns. Don't delay next time. If you can't talk to your sisters about girl things who can you talk to?

"We won't tell you what to do or not do, Molly, for it's best if you make your own choices. But we're happy to share our experiences and what little we do know. One thing I do suggest you think about, however, is whether to continue seeing this boy Eric. He sounds strongly attracted to Daisy and threesomes rarely work out. If you are going to keep experimenting, you may want to see if Eric has a friend. I don't know that I'd trust Daisy's reactions if Eric ever started to favour you over her.

"So I'd be careful on two counts—not getting pregnant, and not getting in the way of Daisy's relationship with Eric. But, enough of this sermonising now. Come on, let's share a big hug."

Grace continued, "You know, I think I'm going to miss family terribly when Robert and I marry, although being only as far away as Emu Plains will help. There are ten of us now. Ten Monahans. What will I do when there's no baby crying, no youngster Connor needing attention, no Mother wanting help with the cooking, and no noise from everyone talking at once across the dinner table? I do hope I can bring a little one into the world quickly. Ooh, I can't wait. You'll be an aunt, Mother will be a grandmother. Hmmm, can you see Father bouncing a grandchild on his knee? I wonder how well he'll do. It's not as if he dotes on David a lot. Guess we'll just have to wait and see."

Ann was carrying the last dessert plates from the Jamisons' dining table to the kitchen when George walked in with a hamper of sausages and meat patties that the Jamisons had requested to take with them on an early-morning departure next day. They had official government guests in from Sydney and were going to take them up the mountains as far as Blackheath to see some of the views over the valley named after the Regentville hosts.

Ann grasped at an opportunity. "George, we have some leftover baked apple with honey that I'm about to clear from dinner. Would you care to share some with me on the river bank?"

Henry, the cook, rolled his eyes and grinned at George. "Go on, she's worked hard and she can take some time off, although you'd better check with Miriam since she made that dessert."

"Be off you two," Miriam rejoined. "But I don't want to hear anything if you don't like it."

Highly unlikely, thought George. Miriam's pies and desserts were always sumptuous. Ann retrieved the large serving dish from the table, transferred the remainder onto a smaller dish, fetched two spoons, and was out the door before anyone could change their mind.

"Your timing was impeccable, George. And frankly I was dying to try some of this dessert since it looked so good serving it. Thanks for turning up just now." As they walked to the bank, Ann kept chatting. "I hear Robert is going to join you in the commercial butcher business. I think that's terrific. He is such a pleasant man. We all love him and are so happy he and Grace are going to marry. When will your shop be ready?"

George didn't respond for a moment then tipped his head to the side and asked, "When are you next off duty, Ann?"

Surprised by the question instead of an expected answer, Ann stammered a bit. "...Th... The day after tomorrow, George, why do you ask?"

"Can you keep a secret?"

"Certainly for that long, and usually much much longer."

"Great. Let's sit here on the bank and finish this dessert and I'll tell you why."

They ate slowly, savouring the apple and honey mixture. 'Um's and 'Ah's of appreciation escaped their lips frequently and their eyes smiled at each other as the delicious taste satisfied their cravings for sweetness. George finished first so Ann held up her spoon, waved it, and pointed. "Okay, now tell me this big secret while I devour the last two mouthfuls."

"Well, it's like this, Ann. At this very moment there are two men building my new shop in Penrith. I'll be riding into town shortly to see how far along they managed to get today. We put plans together two weeks ago, cleared a portion of the ground last week, and the timber was delivered yesterday. Tomorrow I will join the men to help put the roof on and add the windows.

Ann watched George's eyes light up as he continued. "Finally my dream is going to become real. I've waited a long time for this. It's sort of exciting to have something that is totally mine. But I'd like to share it with someone. I was wondering if you'd like to come see the place on your day off? You could ride with me on my horse, and we could take some bread and cheese, maybe a little ham, for lunch. I'd make sure your father has no objections in advance."

"I'm overwhelmed and flattered, George. And yes, I'd love to see where your shop is and what it looks like. Will you actually finish building it tomorrow?"

"Oh no, but the main structure will be complete. There'll still be lots to do inside."

"Well, I'd be happy to come along and hear about your plans. What time would you like me to be ready? I'll organize some lunch for both of us."

"I have to go check on the animals first thing that morning but if we could leave around 11 a.m. that would work well. Would that suit you?"

"Certainly, and thanks for asking me to come along. This will be fun."

And what a magic day it turned out to be, despite the weather. A light rain was falling as they prepared to depart. George had Maisie hooked up to a small cart in which he had placed a number of builders' tools and some sharp knives and other butcher implements. Ann emerged from the kitchen with a wooden-handled umbrella and a large basket with the food and drink, and placed the basket beside the tools under the cart's canvas cover, which George pulled tight with the drawstrings in back. He lifted Ann onto Maisie's back, having her slide forward as far as possible. He then handed her the umbrella and the reins, and vaulted up behind her.

"I like this," he said. "Usually if it's raining I just get wet but if you'll hold up the umbrella with one hand I'll be able to reach round you and use two hands on the reins, and we'll both stay dry. And don't worry, we won't be going fast—Maisie will walk all the way since we're pulling the cart. Now hang on and we'll be off."

The road was a bit muddy, which made the going slower than normal as the cart wheels either clogged or bounced over the edges of newly forming ruts. Despite this, they made it to the new shop in reasonable enough time and George tethered Maisie to the tree in the yard, helped Ann off, and led her through the back door inside the structure.

The shop faced onto High Street almost directly opposite the magnificent St. Stephen's Anglican church. A front door led into a large room which stretched across the entire width of the building designed to be the actual butcher shop. A big picture window would let customers look in from the outside. A door at the back to one side of this room gave entry to a hallway which ran all the way to a kitchen at the rear of the house. Coming off the hall were three rooms. One was destined to be a storage locker for the meat awaiting display in the shop. The next was the bedroom with a window opposite the entry door, and the third was to accommodate a small eating area and arm chairs for reading. The kitchen had two windows looking out on the back yard and the door to the outside was opposite a small pantry area.

While George unpacked his tools, Ann set off wandering through the building. Her explorations were fast and she came back to the front room asking, "George, have you ordered any furniture yet? I don't know exactly what you will want in the shop itself but I certainly have an idea of what you will need in the bedroom, dining room, and kitchen."

"No, I haven't thought that far ahead yet. But I suppose I should if I'm going to live here starting next week."

"You'll need a bed immediately, a table, and at least one chair, and some kitchen implements at a minimum. And you need some wooden boxes out back for hay for Maisie. Later on you'll need curtains in the windows and barrels to collect water off the roof. And hooks in the beams to hang kitchen implements, and..."

George cut her off. "I know, I know, Ann. How about this? You could actually help me a lot. I have some sawing and nailing to do here. I wonder if you wouldn't mind walking down the road to Ben Atkins general store and having a look there at beds, tables, and chairs, and kitchen items for me. I don't even have plates or a knife and fork and spoon. Maybe you could ask Ben's wife for paper and pencil and make a list of things you see there that you feel I will need. Although please realise this is not Sir John's home, I'm not a bank director, and I won't need a hundreth of what he uses."

"Remember, George, where I lived as a girl we had almost nothing. I'll look at only the necessities for you. I hope Mr. and Mrs. Atkins are the friendly type."

After visiting with Mrs. Atkins at her store, Ann had a long list of domestic items George would need in the new abode, ably compiled with Mrs. Atkins' help. It comprised everything from cupboards to candles , and George was happy to have others do this thinking for him. Beyond the estate mansion, the last real home furniture he'd seen had been in his friend Mr. Eley's storeroom back in London, and he'd rather forget about that. For it was stealing that furniture that started him on the convict path to Australia.

He and Ann had lunch together sitting on planks of lumber laid across two tree stumps. George shared his plans for a stable in the back yard for Maisie and a shed for tools and miscellaneous items. Together they designed a simple sign for the front of the shop with the name "Clarke Butcher" on it. After walking around the township they packed up and prepared to head south back to the estate. The clouds were clearing and a soft pale light struggled through as the rain moved to the east, leaving only small puddles here and there for Maisie to splash in.

With the umbrella in the cart, Ann enjoyed the ride home, able to look around more and not just watch the road ahead as she had felt bound to do on the way out. Maisie knew the way so George relaxed and let her set her own pace. Ann leaned back, content, George's strong arms holding the reins encircling her midriff warmly. Not used to riding, her bottom felt a little sore, but she dared not complain. Riding was far better than walking all that way.

As they passed under a large tree, a soft breeze blew a few drops of water from the leaves above and her eyes drifted upwards as a kookaburra laughed, and the world felt good. She slipped slightly forward and found her breasts now nuzzling on top of George's hands still holding the reins tightly. Neither of them changed position, both cognizant and comfy in the delicate intimacy afforded. No words were spoken, but Ann let her head fall back further against George's chest and dreamily let the soft sounds of Maisie's hooves in the damp clay wash over her for the rest of the trip home.

As they slowed and turned off the road through the entrance to the estate, Ann sat up straight, turned, and smiled, her brown eyes twinkling in happiness. "Thank you, George, that was a lovely ride."

Pulling round the back of the mansion, he helped her down, retrieved the basket, umbrella, and tools from the cart, and walked across the yard with her to the kitchen. "Despite that spot of rain this morning, that was fun, Ann. Thanks for coming along and keeping me company today. I'll see you tomorrow."

Brushing down Maisie, George found himself in a reflective mood. More sugar lumps than usual moved between his pocket and Maisie's mouth as his mind relived the day's happenings and his concentration flagged. "Maisie," he said, "she got under my skin in a nice way. How did that happen? Such a sweet person, from such a terrible background. How did she come out so well? How can someone raised in such conditions be so cheery and uncomplaining? And I said I'd see her tomorrow? How did that come out so automatically?" Maisie turned, whinnied, and nudged him for another treat. "Oh, so you think you have something to say about this, too? You liked her as well? I think we both have good taste." So saying, he ran his hands up Maisie's face, brushed her mane one last time, locked her in the stall, and headed to the butchery.

Robert returned from Hartley, and he and Grace worked on wedding plans. They found a house they could rent in Emu Plains, and the whole Monahan family trekked over one weekend to approve. Robert acquiesced very quickly on getting married in Sydney at Scots Presbyterian Church, although that would mean most members of the family would not be present. After some discussion it was decided that Eileen would go along to be witness to her twin's marriage.

It was then that Robert announced he had two surprises to share with everyone. Grace tilted her head to the side in anticipation, wondering if surprises were going to be a way of life with Robert. There was still a lot to learn about this man, she realised.

Calmly Robert began his tale. "I've told you about my mother and father and Uncle Gregory Turner, but I need to tell you more about my father's family. Father was born in 1782, the third of eleven children, made up of six boys and five girls. His father was also named Robert and his mother Rebecca. I really didn't know my grandparents as they lived in the north country and I was born in London. Among my father's five brothers the second youngest was Ian, who arrived in the world in February 1796. Our family had little to do with all those aunts and uncles living far away. However, I vaguely remember being dragged along to Uncle Ian's wedding in Chelsea when I was five years old. He was living in London operating a butcher shop. I didn't understand family issues of course at that age, but later on I was told that Father and Uncle Ian had a falling out. Apparently brotherly love only went so far.

"It was much, much later that I learned that Uncle Ian and his wife Elizabeth had migrated here to Australia. They were brought out as hired servants of the Australian Agricultural Company in 1824, and once their company obligations were complete they were given a grant of one hundred acres of land by Governor Darling, which they took up in Camden."

Grace interrupted. "So you had two uncles already here when you arrived back in 1842, eighteen years after Ian arrived? Did you visit him in Camden?"

"Whoa there, Grace. Hang on a bit and I'll answer all your questions. But yes, I did have two uncles here, but no, I didn't visit Ian in Camden. You see, the Australian Agricultural Company was approved in England but local headquarters were set up in a town near Newcastle, called Port Stephens. The company was originally devoted to raising beef and merino wool for export to England. Again, remember my father didn't care for Ian and rarely spoke of him, so everything I knew came from Ian's older sister Dorothy, one of my aunts. And somehow she got something wrong, as I thought Ian had moved to Hartley, rather than Camden, which is why I went looking for him there originally."

"Then how did you learn he went to Camden instead?" insisted Eileen.

"Ah, so here comes the next part of the story. When I went to Sydney to finalize Gregory's estate I took time to have a look around Darling Harbour. It's a very busy commercial port with many warehouses and wharves. All sorts of ships, some delivering merchandise from the Hunter region, others with cargo from overseas, and there was one that was loading wool packs bound for England. It was fascinating to watch hives of activity everywhere I walked.

"As I made my way back to my hotel I detoured along Kent Street, and there in the middle of one of the blocks was Kitchings Butcher Shop. I couldn't resist going in, with no idea what I might find. Behind the counter was an older man, and yes, you've probably guessed it, it was Uncle Ian. Neither of us could quite believe the coincidence, but he quickly shut up shop and took me to his favourite ale-house back down at the docks. I think during that first visit we talked for two hours or more and I went back the next day as well before leaving for Regentville. One of his children was born in London before he migrated, one was born at sea on the ship, and four others were born out here in Port Stephens, and Sydney. Once he had his wool farm well established and running successfully in Camden—yes, wool, not beef—he sold it and came back to Sydney to open the butcher shop.

"We didn't mention my father but I think he was pleased to make contact with our line of the family again, and of course my parents are dead now anyway. His eldest son, named Cameron, is twenty-one years old. His youngest, Richard, is only nine years old. When we get married in Sydney I'd like you to meet the family, Grace. Based on what Ian told me, if there is a calm day, we might like to hire a boat and visit the emerging township of Manly, which is on a peninsula of land with the Harbour on one side and the Pacific Ocean on the other."

Matthew spoke up. "Well, that is an amazing story, Robert. To think that you end up meeting an uncle you haven't seen since you were a boy, in a foreign land, and purely by coincidence. It hardly seems real."

"Not only that, Matthew, but Ian says there's at least one other family member here. His eldest brother John had a son Ambrose, who was transported as a convict in 1828. He has no idea where he is today, unfortunately.

"Anyway, that's all the surprises I can think of right now. In a way it's nice to know there is family here, because unlike you I came out alone. Now I'm excited to show my kin my new bride. I know they'll be excited to meet her."

The Scots Church of St. Andrew's was the first Presbyterian church built in Australia, the foundation stone being laid by the governor, Sir Thomas Brisbane, on the first of July 1824. The Reverend Dr. John Dunmore Lang was paid £300 per annum as its first officiating minister.

On Tuesday 3rd September 1844, in a simple gathering, he pronounced Robert and Grace husband and wife. Both signed the marriage certificate in the presence of Grace's twin sister Eileen and a local parishioner. Robert was twenty-eight, Grace twenty-one.

Thus, the Kitchings and Monahan families were officially united in the first Australian marriage for both. A long way from their heritage in England and Ireland, and marking a giant commitment to their adopted country. Any children produced in the union would be first-generation Australians, part of a new society in a new land.

Before the wedding, Eileen and Grace shared a room at the Royal Oak Hotel in Miller's Road. Robert had a room to himself.

After dinner on the wedding night the sharing arrangement changed and the next morning found the newly married couple coming downstairs very late for breakfast. There was a blush on Grace's cheeks and a happy smile that nothing could change.

The trio wandered around town looking at the sights, with Eileen feeling distinctly awkward. She was glad when they finally stopped in the Botanical Gardens to rest. As Robert wandered off to check the view of the harbour the two sisters hugged and a few tears escaped Eileen's eyes. "I'm so happy for you, Grace. He's a lovely man and I know you will have a wonderful life together. I hope I can find someone as good."

"You will, sis, it's just a matter of time."

"I do hope you are right. In any event just don't forget to name your first daughter after me."

With a twinkle in her eye Grace responded, "Of course not— who knows, we may even have started making her last night."

13. Change is in the wind. Penrith 1845

By the time the new year was ushered in, it was obvious to all that George and Ann were courting. It had been incredibly hot during Christmas week and work productivity slowed as more rests were taken in whatever shade was available and more dips were taken by the men in the river at the end of the day. Bathing publicly was still not deemed appropriate for women. On free weekends in the early years of his employment at Regentville, George had set out to explore the bush on the opposite bank of the river. He was a frequent borrower of one of the rowboats tied up at the bank behind the mansion, and his natural strength allowed him to row without tiring for hours. He would tie up at some new point and explore the bush and hills and valleys before coming back and rowing home. In doing so he developed a strong love for, and appreciation of, the native flora and fauna, and never tired of seeking new paths and areas to explore. He did have one particular 'secret place' upriver that was a favourite escape point.

Over the years George had had a number of liaisons with members of the female staff. He was in and out of the kitchen every day and mutual attractions were a natural evolution of propinquity. Most of the young women working in the mansion were from city backgrounds and not entirely comfortable with the 'bush', where snakes lurked, unusual creatures lived, and it was hard to determine direction in the middle of the forest. For those unafraid, George would happily share his hideaway spot. In most cases the secrecy and beauty of the spot encouraged healthy uninhibited love-making, both parties engaging happily. It wasn't only George who suggested repeat visits.

One Sunday in early January, when the summer heat wasn't as oppressive as usual, he invited Ann to come with him for a picnic upriver. She packed a hamper and they headed for the river bank. Two of the rowboats had gone already and George could see them downstream. He always preferred to go upstream first so that coming home was always easier with the current pushing from behind.

He pulled out to the center of the river, turned the boat southwards, and set an easy cadence of strokes heading up river. A tiny breeze did no more than send shivers across the water and he smiled as the sun shone warmly on them both. Half a mile upstream they had left the estate behind and all that could be heard was the swish of the oars, the creaks of the rowlocks, and the calls of birds in the trees on the west bank. A heron by the soft grasses at bank's edge flapped his great wings and lifted gently into the air, flying downstream a few feet above the clear waters, settling again no more than fifty yards from where he started. A kookaburra uttered his joyous laughing song nearby; both sought to find him high in the branches but failed.

Ann lay back against some cushions, then half closed her eyes and luxuriated in watching George's strong arm muscles build and retract with the long, even strokes in a constant and seemingly effortless rhythm. Back and forth, up and down, swish and creak, swish and creak, up and down, swish and creak. Small beads of sweat broke out and glistened on his bulging forearms and forehead as the sun continued its climb. Ann wondered what maid might have cut his linen shirtsleeves off and sewed them neatly at the shoulder, although thinking further, more likely a convict tailor made that happen way back on the boat in the heat of the tropics.

The foliage on the banks blurred as she relaxed in the warm rays and the fresh air, causing her to lose focus on all but the smooth rhythm and movements of the boat and its rower. A wetness between her legs alerted her that she'd been fantasizing without realising it, and she enjoyed the sensations that followed with genuine pleasure.

Hoping to give nothing away, she stretched and lazily asked, "How much further, George? I'm being pampered here and thoroughly enjoying the ride, but surely you need to rest soon?"

"If you look ahead about half a mile you'll see a slight bend in the river to your right. Just beyond that, a creek enters and that's where we'll stop," he replied.

He watched carefully as Ann stretched again. The fabric of her light cotton dress and the chemise beneath pulled tight across her bust and the nipples strained to be released atop well-formed breasts. Oh, that view does make a man feel good, he thought. Please stretch again, young lady. And she did, as nonchalantly as before, and George felt some stirrings that hadn't been around in ages.

Less than a hundred yards past the bend, he pulled to his right and squeezed the rowboat into a wedge-shaped outlet where the creek emptied into the river. With the oars pulled inside, he jumped ashore and quickly tied the rope painter around a silver-grey eucalyptus tree. Back at the boat, Ann handed him the large picnic basket. He moved off and placed it by the tree then returned and helped her step up on the soft grassy bank. Oh my goodness, she thought as she stood vertically. Just as well he can't see my legs through this cotton dress. I'm more wet than I thought.

"This spot looks delightful, George. I'd like to stroll for a bit after sitting so long, before we open the hamper."

"Oh, but we still have a little further to go," replied George. "While it's delightful here on the bank I'm going to show you something special. Come on."

He picked up the hamper in one hand and held out the other, which she took readily. The full brush line started about fifteen yards back from the bank and beyond it was a small track heading uphill into the woods. Silently, they followed it for little more than three minutes until they came to a horizontal clearing beside the brook running down the slope. Forming part of the clearing was a small pool about ten yards across and fifteen yards long. The water bubbled in from above at one end and bubbled out continuing downhill at the other end. Large rounded rocks formed the far side of the pool with smaller flat rocks and the grass of the clearing framing the side they were on. It was as if man had ordered a holding basin for the stream before its final plunge to the river. The water was no more than four feet deep and beautifully clear so that the rock bottom was clearly visible. A couple of dragonflies flitted lazily between the grasses. George scooped his hands down and drank thirstily, replacing some of the sweat he had lost getting there. Ann quickly followed and exclaimed, "This is unbelievable, George. What an absolutely gorgeous spot."

"This is why I like the country," he replied. "Mother Nature has so much to offer and is full of surprises. I think this is one of her better ones."

Ann pulled a giant blanket from the bottom of the hamper and spread it on the grass. "Where did you get that?" asked George.

"The mistress of the house doesn't remember everything she owns, and I am only borrowing it, for it will go back in place this evening. It's not as if she checks the linen and other closets much, and especially not today with government officials visiting. Don't worry, George. I have no intentions of stealing it."

A half loaf of fresh bread, some delicious ham off the bone, which George had brought up to the house only yesterday, some tasty cheese, freshly picked oranges, and two lukewarm bottles of local ale emerged from under the flaps of the basket. Not even flies interrupted their lunch, although another kookaburra laughed, and once again they looked but couldn't find him. A whip bird cracked his notes and charmed them, annoyingly out of sight. Maybe the birds were shy, or maybe respectful as the couple chatted easily, sharing added details on the lives they'd left behind.

"You can swim nude here, Ann, if you like. I assure you that pool is perfect for refreshing oneself."

"I'd be too embarrassed, George, but you go ahead if you like. I'll stay here and watch the river through the trees."

Quickly he walked to the edge of the pool. Off came the shirt over his head, off came the boots, and then his trousers. He jumped in with an enormous splash, ducked his head under a second time, and after a couple of dives floated on his back, letting the sun warm him. Ann couldn't resist and sneaked a couple of looks. His physique was marvelous as she had known since the first time she'd ever seen him, but she was shy about revealing her own body. Partially in response to the constant close living conditions and lack of privacy she'd had growing up in County Donegal, partially because she was scared that exposure may lead to unknown activity. She wasn't that naïve that she didn't understand the whispered stories other servant women in the mansion sometimes shared.

George sat at the edge of the pool drying in the sun and in due course pulled his trousers on and headed back to the blanket spread on the grass. Ann marveled again at the ripples across his chest and the broad shoulders and muscle-bound forearms. "Maybe I'll go get my feet wet and cool off," she said. "You stay here and finish your ale."

So saying, she rose up, took off her boots, and ran to the pool's edge. With her back to George she hiked up her skirt and petticoat in front, sat down, and let her legs feel the gentle flow of the water and its soothing coolness. A huge smile crossed her face and she turned around. "Oh my, this is a little bit of heaven. I can see why you love it here. It's like something in a story book."

"We can come back again anytime you want, Ann. I enjoy being here with you."

George lay on his side watching Ann's back, admiring her long dark brown hair, thinking of nothing in particular. A bee buzzed across his vision and he refocused his eyes, watching it dart back and forth to the hamper, attracted by some smell from inside. Ann's laughter broke his reverie as she splashed her legs up and down and squealed like a little girl. A smile spread across George's face and he yelled, "Don't fall in!"

Ann swiveled and lifted one leg out of the pool. Five seconds later the other one followed, allowing George a glimpse of pale thighs before Ann staggered to her feet and her skirts rolled down. "Have you seen any animals drinking here?" she asked.

"No. I suspect I frighten them away. But I have seen birds on the rocks on the far side. There's a little depression between two of the rocks over there at the top end and I've seen them drinking and bathing in the small pool that forms. Cheeky little things with brilliant red and blue colours—bush rosellas, I think. There are all sorts of birds here. Nothing like what we saw in Kent.

"Further up the hill from here I found a cockatoo nest up in a tree. A parent was looking out of the hole in the trunk. I think she must have had babies, because when I approached she hopped down onto a lower branch, flapped her wings, and screeched at me as if to tell me not to come too close. She had a yellow crown on the top of her head and it raised straight up above her. She had a pretty strong-looking beak so I backed off. No point in being bitten, although I don't know if she would have gone too far from the babies in the hole."

"Oh, I wish I could have seen her."

"Well, we can come back another day if you like. It's a bit of a hike uphill and of course there's no guarantee the birds will be there. It was springtime when I saw them."

"I'd just be happy to walk with you and learn more about this wonderful bushland. Thank you for taking me out today. Now give me a minute and I'll pack up our lunch things. I need to go see a lady first."

"Watch out for poison ivy," George yelled. "We don't want any itching to spoil our day."

George was glad that the return trip was downstream as he didn't really feel like exerting himself much. He'd had a very pleasant, relaxing time enjoying nature and Ann's company. She was growing on him more and more. Ann watched contentedly as the sun shone on George's muscles plying their even rhythm in forming the strokes that carried them back. Too soon they reached the tie-up point. George helped Ann out and was tempted to kiss her as she leaned forward into his arms, but held back at the last minute. Later, he thought.

The new year welcomed in another finding when it became apparent that Grace was well along with child. Katie was ecstatic and started knitting baby-size booties, caps, and cardigans in anticipation of a winter arrival. On weekends Thomas would take his mother on horseback to Emu Plains where she would help her daughter with advice and plans. Robert was managing the feed lots and butchery for George, and looked forward to being a father. The whole Monahan family was delighted, as children were an important part of the family legacy. There was some amusement at the thought that Grace's child would have an uncle, David, about three years older. Would they end up as playmates, not caring about their relationship? The topic brought back memories of cousins and aunts and uncles left behind in County Donegal. The realisation that they hadn't thought much about family back home since Grace's marriage reinforced how well they were adjusting to their new environment. But it did move Katie to have Eileen write several letters for her to send away. Very little mail came from Drumcairn as most of the relatives back home couldn't write. Twice a year if they were lucky someone would carefully put pen to paper, but it dawned on Katie that the last letter had been nearly a year ago. It was quite probable that some folks had passed on in the meantime. The thought added a touch of sadness. But, she rationalized, as some go, so new ones arrive. It wouldn't be long before she would be a grandmother.

Other than Katie, it was Molly who was most interested in Grace's condition. She and Daisy had moved on in their sexual explorations and Molly was contemplating what she and Daisy called 'the big do'. Daisy had graduated from being tasted to tasting and producing liquid spurts from her partners, who now numbered three virile stable lads. She carefully stowed her monetary rewards in an old tin hidden at the back of the top shelf of the closet. One chap, bigger than normal in all dimensions, had wanted to see how well he 'fit'. Daisy had also been intrigued and had finally consented, telling Molly later that she had squirmed and screamed and that while it hurt a bit initially she'd been driven crazy with the sensations that followed from the movement in and out, and that there was nothing like it that she had ever experienced before. She and the lad had done it over and over, the intense pleasure demanding repeat performances. Only when she got a little sore had they stopped.

At nearly nineteen Molly was aware what 'the big do' could lead to. Grace had reinforced what she had suspected when they had chatted months before. Even in the short time she'd been working at the mansion, two unmarried maids had become pregnant and had left. She'd overheard one of them complaining she'd only 'done it' once and that, contrary to Daisy's experience, it hurt so much she wished afterwards that she'd never said yes. The remembered pain was exaggerated and her anger grew when she found later she was also pregnant. It just wasn't fair. Grace's pregnancy no doubt was also from 'doing it', maybe more than once, but she was married and that made a big difference.

Daisy was obsessed with her experience and sought more sessions with her new male friend. Molly observed her roommate carefully, but when Daisy hadn't become pregnant after three months of activity, she finally decided to try it for herself. While Eric had been replaced by Kevin in Daisy's preferences, mitigating Grace's concerns, Molly found Eric attractive, and playful trysts were still a once-in-a-while part of their relationship. He'd been challenging her to 'do it' for some time, and so shortly after one of her periods she agreed to 'try'.

Daisy had been right. After an initial hurt Molly's body rejoiced in a series of new revelations. Whereas previously on being stroked her pudenda had pulsed and tingled and surges of ecstasy had coursed through her body, now feelings started far deeper inside. They rolled forward and then backward, and forward and backward again, they made her squeal and moan, they brought sweat to her forehead, a flush to her cheeks, and took her breath away. Her back arched, her nipples enlarged, and eventually there was a mini explosion inside that sapped her energy but stayed lingering for precious seconds spreading its wonder widely. She was hooked. Nothing else felt anywhere near as good as this. Why had she waited so long? she thought.

Containing herself was difficult, but when her period arrived three weeks later, a giant wave of relief flooded her being. Daisy was her only confidant. And the mind battles started again with new conflicting thoughts. "Aren't good Irish girls meant to behave piously and stay chaste until married? Aren't we meant to turn a blind eye to the world of nature and animals around us and unlike them be pure in thoughts and behaviour? I'm not like women of the night who give away their souls with their bodies. Why can't I enjoy these pleasures of the flesh without worrying about incurring the wrath of God?"

There were no readily available answers. Her outlook responded in kind—one day moody and withdrawn, the next outgoing and all smiles. She knew her body and mind had some serious differences to work out. As Grace's profile filled out, and Eric's and her own desires heightened, her mental dilemma escalated and she wondered if moving away was a choice she might need to make.

George had received a letter from his sister Mariann in mid-December that indicated a sixth child was due soon. Reading it over several times had stirred some new feelings about family. He had almost forgotten the count of nephews and nieces Mariann had produced. The thought crossed his mind that perhaps it was time he reciprocated and contributed to that state. The notion of tying the knot entered his thoughts more frequently as his and Ann's familiarity blossomed into an ever-deepening relationship.

George had been his own person for a long time, and he was still a convict, even though his Ticket of Leave gave him a limited measure of freedom. Marriages of convicts to Free Settlers were taking place far more often these days and it was not uncommon for men to marry women much younger than themselves. He still had an eye for attractive female form, and other servants in the house had very pleasant styles, but he no longer seemed interested in the bedroom eyes cast his way and the risqué comments subtly whispered in passing.

"I think you're a goner, George, my friend," said Henry, the cook, one morning. "Ann's smart, pretty, and gracious, almost too good for the likes of you. What more could you ask for? And if she inherits any of her mother's proclivities she should bring forth ample children to keep you busy. Just tell me when you decide so I can let the other maids know and have them cry out of my sight. It's not long before you had planned to leave us anyway, and a wife would be great company in your new house in town."

Graham echoed Henry's views. "George, you've done well here. This area has become your home. You will never be allowed to go back to England, so it's time to settle down. You couldn't do any better than with Ann. It's clear she's a wonderful companion for you. And," he continued, "I want to share something in confidence that might help.

"Mrs. Jamison has consulted with the children, and none of them are interested in sustaining Regentville. Some probably resent the fact that John married her so late and she flaunts the title of 'Lady' as if she'd been born to it. The place was always his, not hers. I think after the harvest next spring and summer she will put the estate up for sale, and who knows what the fate of all us workers will be. It depends who buys the place. I suspect no buyer will want it all but will subdivide the holding, and new owners of the parcels will provide their own labour. The Monahans and others will need to find new employment. Again, in confidence, I've already started looking at new opportunities, as has Henry, although he probably didn't tell you."

"Well, that does add a new perspective, Graham. I appreciate the confidence," George replied. "Perhaps it's time for me to buy some of the cattle, sheep, and pigs here for my own stock. I have fenced in the holding pens I own and I've recently found me a stock manager."

"I think that would be very smart, George. Let's wait till the heat dies down and autumn has arrived so you are buying animals in good condition. Meanwhile, think how you are going to say goodbye to all your friends here."

After a week's self-deliberation George made up his mind. He went and talked to Matthew, who talked to Katie, who talked to Ann, who talked to and kissed George fervently as he asked her to marry him. There was no hesitation in her yes, just love in her eyes and heart.

It took ages to organize things, but on a Monday early in April 1845 George and Ann's application for permission to marry was approved by the authorities, and three days later on Thursday they were married at St. Stephen's Church of England. George was thirty-five, Ann eighteen. Unlike Grace, she'd never been a devout Presbyterian and was happy to be married in the grand new Anglican church. Ann's father, Matthew, was present and gave his consent due to Ann's age, while standing in with George was his good friend Henry Garner. Regentville had prepared a reception so they rode back after the service and spent time with all their friends and Ann's family. In a highly unusual act, Mrs. Jamison gave Ann one of her relatively unused lace tablecloths, and Graham, the estate manager, presented George with a bunch of new tools including a shovel, rake, pickaxe, and wheelbarrow. George and Ann were overwhelmed with the generosity shown. Henry's minions had prepared quite a feast in his absence and the front veranda was used for a buffet-style dinner of chicken and beef, corn and peas, and strawberries for dessert.

Ann watched the reaction of the maids as discreetly as she could. Carol, whom she knew had enjoyed some past intimacy with George, was surly, banging plates down on the table and dropping some of the cutlery. Gwenda sidled up to George with tears in her eyes, kissed him tenderly on one cheek, and melted away, her heart clearly torn. Yet most of the others were happy for Ann and openly congratulated her and wished her good fortune in married life.

As Graham made a little speech, tears formed in the corners of George's eyes with the realisation that an era and lifestyle were coming to a close. He'd lived and worked at the estate nearly thirteen years, and although he clearly recognized that it was a good time to move on, he was leaving a place that had become an important component of his overall being.

He wondered how many other convicts from his ship had lived these years as well as he had. Very few, if any, he imagined. Many would have served on chain gangs and suffered from the hard labour and punishments so easily handed out. But here he was, a shop owner, now with a lovely bride. Once again he thought how fortunate he was and how the opportunities here were so much better than they would have been back in London.

It was dark by the time he and Ann loaded up the cart and headed out through the gates with Maisie. The sky was clear and filled with brilliant pinpricks of light, warm and comforting, a gentle cloak wrapping the end of day. For a change, they decided to walk back to High Street, time being plentiful with no responsibilities on the morrow, both feeling content and happy, enjoying holding hands and talking about the day gone by.

Past the church and its memories from earlier in the day, to their own little house, designed and bought by George, but decorated by Ann. Definitely a joint venture, treasured by both. Before tying up Maisie and unhitching the cart, George insisted on carrying Ann over the threshold. They both laughed as he did so and she kissed him happily as he put her down.

Unhitching the cart, George told Maisie she'd have to wait until morning for a brush down, but he did fill a bucket with water and take the lid off the feed box for her. A last lump of sugar for the day and she was left alone.

George hurried inside to find Ann already in bed, sitting up with her hair brushed back wearing a simple white cotton nightdress tied with white ribbon under the bustline, a loving gift from all the maids at the house. He quickly washed using a bowl in the kitchen sink, pulled his blue striped nightshirt over his head, and hurried to the other side of the bed. The lamp on the nearby table shone brightly and he turned the flame down to provide a more gentle glow. "And how do you feel, Mrs. Clarke?" he asked, a big grin covering his face.

"Wonderful, Mr. Clarke," she responded, with as giant a smile. "This has been an amazing day. One minute I was Ann Monahan, the next Ann Clarke. I like the change. But the question is, are you sure you are happy with this new ball and chain, Mr. Clarke?"

"I was tired of being single, dear wife. I look forward to years of great company, and I can't think of anyone else I'd rather spend the time with. I love you, my woman. Now kiss me again."

And so she did. And after a while the kiss became more. "I've waited a long time for this night, George. Please show me how you'll love me," and she gently pulled his nightshirt up, reaching around and running her hands over his arms and back, loving the feel of his huge muscles. There was no real bashfulness, just eager anticipation. George had been with a number of young women during his time at Regentville, for he was an attractive man, not only in build and looks, but also in demeanor and attitude. Lust-fulfilling pleasure was something he savoured, especially when both parties enjoyed sharing to mutual satisfaction. The activity provided an opportunity for him to abandon, if only fleetingly, the harsh realities of a convict position. He often used the occasions to mentally escape his environment by directing and concentrating his energies in the pursuit of giving and receiving—sometimes more selfishly than others when his wants were paramount.

Now as he lay beside Ann, his desire was tempered by feelings of love and tenderness. He'd never felt the anxiousness of coupling with Ann that he had with others. He stroked her hair and gently rocked her in his arms, appreciating the sensation of holding a woman who had made a lifelong commitment to him. He kissed her softly on the cheek and curled her hair behind her ear. Ann moved his hand to the ribbons tied at the top of her nightdress and helped him release them. His lips brushed hers and his fingers caressed her breasts. She extricated herself quickly, removed her nightdress, and snuggled closer. George responded in kind. There was no rush; they had a lifetime ahead. He moved from the bed, took off his nightshirt, and extinguished the lamp on the wall. A single candle flickered on the chest of drawers on the other side of the room. They both sighed in mutual comfort in the small darkness that descended. "Married, I'm married," George thought to himself. Ann sensed his smile and cupped his face in her hands. She kissed him with all the love she could muster, and pressed her breasts into his chest. Her hands ran down his body. Gently George held her close, then made sweet love to her, considerate and caring. Eventually, they surrendered to sleep wrapped in each other's arms.

They planned to spend a few days in Sydney, where George had not been for many years, but where Ann had been just three years before. It took the best part of the day to make arrangements, with Ben Atkins and his wife agreeing to look after Maisie in their home paddock and to check the house now and then. George made a sign for the front door—"Back next Thursday"—and Ann emptied the cart of the wedding gifts and last-minute extras they had pulled from their respective quarters on the estate. They packed two small kitbags with their vacation belongings and strolled to the post office to wait for the 3 p.m. weekly coach service to Parramatta.

The horse-drawn coach service had been started ten years ago, running between Sydney and Bathurst. Penrith was the last stop before the start of the haul over the mountains going west, and on the reverse run, fresh horses took the stage to Rooty Hill, where another change took them on to Parramatta. If the coach was on time, they'd make it to Parramatta just on nightfall, where George hoped to stay at the renowned Woolpack Inn.

While waiting, they registered Ann's married name at the post office and filled out an application to change the shop business name to 'George and Ann Clarke, Butchers'. The coach pulled in only thirty minutes late, with the horses sweating and foaming from a gallop after fording the river. There were two other travellers on board, hailing from Mt. Victoria, where the coach had started its downhill run at sunrise. They also were planning to stop overnight at the Woolpack Inn before going on to Sydney next morning.

The newly married couple shared a hearty dinner at the inn with their new friends from the coach, but retired early, a bit sore from the bumpy ride, and tired from the morning's busy preparations after a short sleep the night before. With energies flagging, their lovemaking was short, and Ann fell asleep with her arms stretched across George's chest, her nightdress askew, and her breath blowing gently on his neck.

A deep sleep refreshed their bodies, but other re-emergent needs kept them occupied till mid-morning when they descended to the dining room and devoured a late breakfast. They then spent the day exploring the town, stopping outside the former Female Factory where women convicts had sewed clothes for the chain gang workers, visiting the new and old Government Houses, and moving on to the stockyards, where George checked out animal prices and got an estimate for droving cattle to his holding yards in Emu Plains. Early the following morning George and Ann carried their belongings down to the wharf to catch the regular ferry to Sydney, and by day's end they were ensconced in the newly opened Randall Hotel in the Rocks area close to the Quay.

Construction work on a new 'circular' form of the quay had been started four years before and they could readily see its shape as it crept westward towards completion. Even though George had arrived over a dozen years earlier, he experienced some unsettling feelings looking out over the harbour where the *John I* had berthed.

With memories stirred, he couldn't resist heading up Macquarie St. towards the Hyde Park Barracks, which still held male convicts, although transportation had ended over three years ago. Again, just standing outside the main gates gave him the shivers as he remembered his interment, and his trepidation when called to the warden's office. Ann noticed. "What is it? George, what's the matter?"

"I was held here for a week, Ann, when I arrived in 1832. After four terrible months at sea in horrible conditions, never knowing where we were or when we'd stop, scared of the violent storms and fearful of the guards, cramped into roach-infested quarters with two hundred other angry men, I thought that being on land would definitely be better. But the cells here were just as bad, the guards just as mean, the food just as awful. And every couple of hours during the day there'd be the screams of prisoners being flogged, and at nights the cries of despair. I was one of the fortunate ones not to be added to a chain gang, but to be offered a job in Regentville because of my trade.

"But they should burn this structure down. Especially now that transportation has ended here. I hate the place, but seeing it again helps me purge the memories once and for all. I'll be fine now."

"I probably have no real idea of what you suffered through, George. I'm sure the memories are truly ugly. I'm so sorry for what you had to put up with. No one talks much about what you all went through as convicts, but I can see how hurtful it must have been for you. Yet you seem to get along so easily with people. There must be a strong sense of forgiveness in you. Come on. Let's get away from here."

They turned away and left quickly, heading down King St. At the nearby courthouse they entered in order to check on the process involved for receiving a Pardon. George's original sentence handed down at Old Bailey was for life imprisonment. He'd already received his Ticket of Leave at Regentville, which granted him freedom to work without being tied to a master and allowed him to live within a given district of the colony before his sentence expired or he was pardoned. This inquiry was about something else.

A young clerk of the court, Edward Rogers, explained that in time, George would undoubtedly receive a Conditional Pardon for his crime, removing all conditions of the Ticket of Leave, but stipulating that he could never return to England. Only an Absolute Pardon would allow a convict that option, and Absolute Pardons were never granted to convicts sentenced to life imprisonment.

Ann quickly said, "I have no desire whatsoever to return to the places I knew in Ireland, even to visit, let alone live. But this means you can never go back to see your sister and your nieces and nephews, George."

"I know," George replied. "They would have to visit here, and I'm sure they don't have the funds for all to travel. It's sad, but unfortunately there's nothing I can do about it."

Ann watched the crinkles form on his forehead and his eyes close quickly with the deep pain of realisation. Her family and their descendants would be all around. What was left of his family was in an unreachable place. His mother and father were gone and he'd probably also never forgiven himself for not being more available to his other sister in her last months of life. Ann vowed to herself not to overdo the joy of her own family's presence, lest it reinforce the sadness he experienced when thinking of the absence of his direct kin.

Out of the courthouse, they turned left by Hyde Park and strolled past the Russell School for Ladies, hearing music lessons being practised within. On to Market Street and down to George St. by the cemetery and gaol, and then back to the Quay.

Two years earlier, in one of the most ambitious projects ever considered for Sydney, infrastructure was started on the so-called Argyle Cut between the north end of Kent St. and George St. Chain gang convicts supplied only with pickaxes and hammers basically were charged with removing a hill of stone to enable an easier transition of goods between Darling Harbour and Sydney Cove. A work that, in the end, took fifteen years to complete, much longer than anyone envisaged at its instigation.

Many other changes had taken place in George's absence, one he particularly liked being the new gas lamps put in the streets four years earlier. Ann had seen them before, but they added a factor of safety that all the women of the town liked. Even now, there were still some rough parts, their hotel being at the edge of a less savoury district. As long as she was with George, Ann didn't worry. She'd heard the story of how he had manhandled the bushranger trying to steal lambs, and had seen his strength in carrying the burned engineer into the river. And, lucky woman, she felt those huge muscles every night now.

On Tuesday, they traipsed through the Botanical Gardens and walked along the foreshore, enjoying the balmy breeze coming up the harbour. There was so much more to see and do and enjoy in Sydney compared to Penrith. They visited some shops, admired the new houses being built, and finished the day with a dinner of fresh ocean grouper, a fish not available in the Penrith region.

As much as the big town had a lot to offer, they were both anxious to get back to their new house and business. Wednesday morning saw them on the Parramatta ferry again, in the reverse direction this time, heading west. Another night at the Woolpack Inn and then the stagecoach dropped them off near the Penrith post office mid-afternoon just as a light rain started to make its presence felt. Rain always slowed the horses down as they moved a little more carefully on the slippery clay roads, so, as travellers, they were glad they weren't going any further.

George picked up their two bundles and they walked smartly home. They were both quite damp upon arrival, and as it had also turned cold, Ann quickly started a fire, hung their outer clothes in front of it on a foldable wooden rack, and made them some strong hot tea. There wasn't much in the larder beyond some old biscuits and beef jerky and so dinner was a poor contrast to those experienced during the past week.

One redeeming value to the evening was that it invited serious cuddling to keep warm. In bed, George spooned behind Ann, her bottom pushed hard into his lap, his free arm wrapped tight around her chest under one breast with his hand holding the other. What more could a woman want, thought Ann. I have a strong, reliable, hard-working man to look after me, we have our own home, and an income-earning business, and he loves me! She snuggled tighter, enjoying both the emotional and physical comfort of the moment.

George's hand tightened around her breast in response, and she thought, oh yes, there's one other benefit to this arrangement, and she lifted his hand and moved it under her nightdress to the hairs on her mound. The loving that followed made her glow inside and she fell asleep, deeply content, in the arms of her man.

Come morning, the sun struggled to push aside the rain clouds and George walked to Ben's house, where he found Maisie in the paddock behind. She whinnied gently when she saw him coming and raised her head in anticipation of his greeting. Ben must have predicted the rain of the previous evening because he'd put the blanket over her. George pulled it off and squeezed as much water as he could out of it, before leading his mare out the gate. He waved to Ben, who was finishing his breakfast on the back porch, and yelled, "Thanks. I'll come to the store later." As he passed the fruit trees in the side yard, he pulled off three nice apples, gave one to Maisie, and pocketed the other two for Ann and himself.

Back home, he hung the blanket on the clothesline and spent time brushing Maisie down. She absorbed the attention happily, having gone a week without it. George was anticipating a ride later to the holding pens with the cart to get meat for the shop.

While George was gone, Ann was planning a trip down the road to the general store to replenish their food supplies. She desperately wanted some fresh eggs, newly baked bread, milk, and flour, among other items. Her time in the kitchen as a maid at Regentville had provided the opportunity to learn much from Henry, Lillian, and Miriam, and she thoroughly enjoyed cooking and baking. George was in for some treats ahead as she had learned well the subtle use of herbs and spices to make flavoursome dishes.

Things were so different here. She thought back to the shack she and her family had been raised in, in County Donegal. So many years in such dire poverty. She felt ashamed that her parents had stood the conditions for so long without moving, although she also rationalized that they probably perceived they had no option at the time. No wonder her father had often seemed bitter. What must it have been like to work hard all day in the fields to come home to hungry children with no money to buy bread? She shuddered at the thought. How fortunate they all were now with jobs and free skies above. And in particular how fortunate was she to have a man so happy and smiling and determined to make good. He had a past that he could easily resent, but he'd mentally left it behind. She looked forward to her role in a new life with a loving man.

By the end of May, Ann had missed two periods, and random internal twinges previously unobserved added to her conviction that she was pregnant.

She was anxious to share the news with her parents and sisters but decided to tell George first. They were strolling home arm in arm after Sunday church service when she turned to him and coquettishly asked, "How much do you love me, George?"

"Well, it sort of depends on the day," he replied impishly. "Why do you ask?"

"I see all those pretty ladies in their best dresses in church and I see some of them look at you with longing in their eyes, so I just wondered."

"They are just jealous of you, my dear. Although I must admit," deliberately teasing her now, "that Penny Smithfield certainly has a gorgeous face and figure, doesn't she?"

Ann pulled her arm away, miffed, and huffed, "You are a rogue, George Clarke. I don't think she's as pretty as I am, and those tits are tiny, all pushed up with her corset."

George was enjoying this now. "Ah yes, that's possible," he said. "But you know there are those who say anything more than a mouthful is a waste, and..."

She interrupted before he could continue. "George, stop it. You are being mean to me, and here I was planning to share some good news with you."

Whoops, I've overdone it, he thought. How to recover? Thinking quickly, he said, "Well, I've also heard that you only tease the ones you love. I would never tease Penny Smithfield. And now that you ask, I love you bunches and bunches, Mrs. Clarke. I'm glad I waited all those years, and I'm glad you came along. No one before ever made me want to get married. You are more special than anyone else."

Ann stopped in the middle of the road as they were crossing, turned, grabbed his face with both hands, and kissed him long and hard, oblivious to the onlookers still coming out of church. George didn't object, but gently put his arm around her and pulled her close, whispering, "Let's hurry home and I'll love you some more."

Sunday noon in bed, flushed from lovemaking, Ann sat up. "Now, my cheeky husband, I told you earlier that I have some good news for you. I see by the look on your face you have forgotten already. Ah, men! Well, my lover, it won't be too long before things change, because I'm on the way to making you into a father."

George's grin lit up the whole room. "That's wonderful, darling! The best news I've had all week. Thank you, thank you, thank you. When is this little Clarke likely to appear?" Rushing now, words tumbling out. "I must tell Ben and also Henry and Graham at the estate. Have you told your mother yet? Will she be happy to be a grandmother a second time? What about your dad and your sisters? Do they know? I must write to my sister back in London. I think she had given up on me, now with six children of her own. Do you want a boy or a girl?"

Ann laughed. "George, relax, relax. I wanted you to know first, but I would like to tell my mother soon. I know she will be thrilled. Grace's baby can't be far away, and I believe your son or daughter should appear sometime in January, but I will see what mother thinks since she had eight of us. Maybe the two of them will grow up together here."

"Well, wifey, mother-to-be, let's ride down to the estate today, where we can tell family and friends. What a day this is! How long have you known?"

"When I missed my first cycle I didn't worry as we had been making love so much, and I just thought my body was adjusting to new patterns of activity. After another month, when I should have been flowing, I figured your seeds had worked their magic in me. I was due just a week ago... Well done, hubby!"

"I don't think it's just me, my lady. I hear it takes two, you know. You must have been ready as well. Whatever, I hope this is just the first of several. I like children and I especially like trying to make them."

"My sexy George. I like trying too. Let's not stop. But for now let's get ready to head up the road to Regentville. Mother will be so surprised."

She was surprised and delighted as well. Happy for her daughter and happy for herself to know she would be a grandmother a second time over. What more could she want beyond happy children and lots of babies. Katie had borne her twin sons Thomas and Patrick before she was nineteen years old and here was Ann following in her footsteps. Matthew shook George's hand and congratulated him, more animated than George had seen him in ages. Perhaps, thought George, Matthew interpreted the pregnancy as a deepening sign of commitment. He would have heard tales of George's roaming eye and pleasure-sharing adventures with the maids from employees who'd been around for some time. Maybe he had always wondered whether George was indeed ready to settle down. Whatever the reason, George was pleased with his father-in-law's reaction.

Molly ran to the big house, and in short order more visitors started to arrive. Maids brought food courtesy of Henry in the kitchen, and a bottle of wine appeared courtesy of Graham. Much to Matthew's chagrin, a couple of the servant girls couldn't resist a kiss and hug from George as they mussed up his hair and pinched his cheeks. Ann took it all in stride, knowing how popular he was among her old friends and how she was secure in his love and affection. Katie followed her daughter's example and made no complaints, helping array the food on the table and finding mugs for the wine.

Eventually it was time to head home, and as Ann said goodbye to all her friends, Matthew pulled George aside and whispered, "We've been told the estate will be sold, and there will be no jobs for us in the new year, so we will have to be moving on in a few months. We all like the countryside so we won't be going back to Parramatta or Sydney, but are thinking of heading west beyond the Blue Mountains somewhere. I wanted you to know so you could tell Ann at some later stage as I think it would be unwise to tell her right now. Unfortunately, unless something changes, Katie will not be around for the birth."

"Well, thank you for confiding in me, Matthew. I'm not surprised at the sale, but I am sincerely sorry as to how it will affect you all. I wish I could help in some way, but you are a hard-working, honest man and your children reflect the good Christian values you and Katie believe in. I'm sure something good will work out. Ann and I will be back here again before you leave, I'm sure, so we'll chat more then.

"For now let me gather Ann and take her home. It's been an exciting day. We'll see you anon."

George spent the next few months refining his business arrangements now that he could devote himself full time. He worked with Robert out at the holding pastures to improve the small butchery shed and add more fences and gates. In the meantime, Ann busied herself turning the house into a home. She also helped George where she could in serving customers. While she couldn't stand the killing of the animals, per se, she learned about the various cuts of meat and how best to prepare and serve them, which George had learned from Henry at Regentville. She and Jane Atkins established a friendship through mutual purchases at each other's stores. Often transactions were made in kind without coins changing hands. Each became an evangelist of the other's wares, and while Jane had no children she took an active interest in Ann's blooming pregnancy.

In the middle of June, on Wednesday the 18th, Grace laboured long and hard to deliver a baby girl. As expected, she was named Eileen in honour of her aunt, but complications at delivery and afterwards meant she would be the only offspring of her parents' union. For the first month after birth both baby and mother struggled for good health. In mid-August, fully recovered, Grace, along with Robert, decided to travel north to the only other

Presbyterian church in the colony, in order to have their daughter baptised. It was a picturesque journey north towards Castlereagh then northeast along the track to Windsor, where they rested overnight. Windsor was the third-oldest place of British settlement in Australia. Originally called Green Hills when established in 1791, it was in the center of a fertile area of land and at the same time near the head of navigation on the Hawkesbury River, renamed from Nepean. It was officially proclaimed a town in 1810 with a church, schoolhouse, gaol, and inn constructed quickly thereafter. Over time it became a hub for grain collection and distribution, with increasing commercial interests. A vigorous shipbuilding industry was established nearby.

Crossing the river, the Kitchings continued northeast towards Sackville, varying to the east along a twisting road until they came to Portland Head. Over forty years earlier, in 1802, just fourteen years after the arrival of the First Fleet in Sydney Cove, a small band of free men and women from Scotland and northern England selected their promised grants of land downstream from Windsor. With only the most primitive of tools they began the formidable task of fashioning homes in virgin bushland untrodden by white man.

To establish their farms on the rich flats along the river bank, they first cleared the gigantic trees and tangled undergrowth, overlaid with centuries of flood debris and twisting, climbing monkey vines. With families settled as comfortably as possible, these men and women then built a church and school. The sandstone church at Portland Head, later called Ebenezer, was built without any government subsidy or help of any kind. As such, it became the earliest church building in the country in which divine services were held every Sunday.

The church was well removed from the river, which meandered through the nearby countryside and was subject to flooding across the numerous U-turns and curves of its course. Looking at the structure that was more of a chapel than full church, Robert and Grace marveled at what had been built by strong loving hands so many years before when aborigines still roamed their tribal lands in the area. The Rev. John McGarvie, a disciple of Dr.

Lang, was the minister there and it was he who baptised two-month-old Eileen in the Presbyterian faith on Tuesday August 19th, 1845. For Grace the church and her daughter were to be her salvation.

There were times when she secretly and silently mourned the fact that she would never be able to bring forth another child into the world. She had always anticipated having a large family like her mother had produced. But it was not to be. They would have to be content with just one child. She'd certainly get all the love they could give her. Perhaps, Grace thought, she'd have to watch that she didn't overdo it, and make sure her daughter was not overwhelmed with too much coddling and protection, but would grow up with the right sense of balance between family relationships and independence. She vowed to herself to encourage interaction with young David as much as possible, and, of course, Ann's child. They were fortunate that Robert had found a job locally, although she knew it wasn't what he ultimately wanted to do, and that at some time in the future he would probably find something else, which could well take them away from family. They'd face that when the situation arose.

One Monday morning later in spring, Ann responded to a knock on the door to find her mother there, a little out of breath, having walked from the estate. "Mother, come in and through to the kitchen. I'll get you some water and put the kettle on. What brings you to town on such a fine day?"

"Well, dear, I wanted you to know that come the weekend your father and I and your brothers and sisters will be leaving Regentville and heading west. I just wanted to spend some time with you before we departed."

"George told me some time ago that Regentville had been sold, and that there would be no jobs after Christmas. I can't believe it's coming up so fast. I wish there was something here in Penrith so you could stay. Both George and I have been asking around but with no luck."

"That's very considerate of you, dear. We've been very fortunate with what we had at Regentville, but of course it's not just our family that's affected. Everyone is looking for alternate work and, in most cases, if something crops up it's usually offered to younger folk first. That's just the way it is. But even the twin boys have had no luck—too many people looking at too few jobs.

"I am so glad that you are happy," Katie went on. "I think you've married a good man. He has a business that will do well as the population grows. Everyone needs food no matter how poor they are, so there will always be customers. My only regret is that George is a convict, and if I could have made it happen I would have preferred to see you marry a free settler. At Regentville all the work hands except a few of us were convicts so there was no stigma there. I just hope it never gets in the way of your life here."

"Obviously I thought a lot about it, Mother, when George and I were becoming serious about one another. Things are changing as more convicts and free settlers marry. George's crime was one of foolishness and he has become a highly responsible person. Yes, he chased a few girls. Or they chased him. Who can blame them? But I see all the goodness in him and love him dearly. He is unselfish, smart, and genuinely thankful for the opportunity to make up for his early mistakes. In a couple of years he should receive his pardon and he will be completely free. I look forward to that day for him."

"I see all those qualities in George you mention. A part of me wondered at first, however, if you married him because he offered you such a positive alternative to the poverty you had grown up in. I certainly would have understood that, but I've come to realise that it isn't so. I think you would have married him had he been a station hand working the cattle on the estate."

"You are right. Having the business just means that life will be somewhat easier if the shop succeeds, and I intend to do whatever George needs me to do to help make that happen. But if I had to sleep on a dirt floor somewhere as a farm hand's wife on a cattle or sheep station—I'd do it.

Standing, Ann moved to the sink and filled the pan with more water to heat on the stove. "Now, are you ready for a second cuppa, Mother?"

"I listen to you, Ann, and I already hear your Irish brogue accented with Australian tones. Yes, I'll have a second cup, please. We all have to adapt to this new land, but I think it is easier for you who are younger than it is for your father and me. Just never forget your heritage, young lady."

"No, Mother. I'm proud to be Irish, but I'm also happy to be here in Australia. And that means the children will all be first-generation Australians, with a mix of Irish and English ancestry. That's fine by me. Speaking of which, this baby keeps poking me with its elbow or feet. I have to change position but I love knowing it's growing inside me. I'm just sorry you won't be here when it's born. I'm sure some motherly advice would be helpful at the time."

"I'm sorry, too, as I'd love to hold my second grandchild as a newborn and be able to help you. Let me give you a few thoughts now since I won't be around in the new year."

For the next hour, Katie passed on suggestions and answered a multitude of Ann's questions, some topics decidedly intimate and meaningful only to mothers and mothers-to-be. Ann wondered how much she would remember when the time came.

Finally it was time for Katie to head back to Regentville. "Here," Ann said. "Take some of these sausages George made this morning. The young ones will love them. And thank you for coming. Thank you for your advice, your support, and your love. I know we will both miss you all when you are gone, but we'll wait to see you next weekend when you come by to start along the main road west. I'll tell George to have plenty of supplies for you."

Nine months to the day after being married, on the 10th January 1846, Ann gave birth to a healthy boy. They named him William in honour of George's father. He was a noisy little fellow, but Ann came through well, remembering almost all of her mother's tips, in the presence of her friend Jane, who ably assisted her.

The news spread fast through the village and George was kept busy answering the door and receiving gifts of food and clothes. A week later, Ann proudly took her first walk down High Street with William in the pram, stopping at each store, showing her baby off, and thanking folks for their kindness.

A month later William Clarke was baptised at St. Mary Magdalene Church of England in the adjacent village of St. Marys to the east. In the last six months, Ann had come to prefer this church over the one where they'd been married, and despite the incredible closeness of St. Stephen's, she and George now regularly attended the church in St. Marys, a short distance down the road to Sydney.

Two Monahan sisters now had brought children into the world. A new generation of the Monahan lineage was under way. The family's focus was definitely on the future. Ireland had been left behind in many ways, yet was still present and would remain in others. Children's names were strongly family oriented, the cooking of potatoes still followed old traditions and processes, and the crocheting of Gaelic patterns in blouses and tablecloths was a treasured activity. The Australian influence was coming but old patterns died hard.

14. Crossing the Blue Mountains 1845

Ann remembered the day the whole family had come by to start their trek west over the mountains. She admired the tenacity, bravery, and adventurous nature of her parents and brothers and sisters. Their departure took her back to the time four years before when she had been part of the walk along the great Western Road from Hen & Chicken Bay. It was a crisp November morning when she and George added parcels of both fresh and seasoned meat into the hampers the family had prepared. Matthew had made the Jamisons a good offer on an old single-spoke dray which they hitched behind Splash and onto which they loaded their scanty possessions. It was not a heavy load so once in a while the two youngest boys could sit up there and rest. Everyone else walked alongside.

There was no rush, the eight remaining family members intending to take their time and explore along the way. Due to deliver in a couple of months, Ann stayed behind while George saddled up Maisie. Molly patted Ann's abdomen and the women had a little cry as they said their goodbyes. Ann kissed her father and wished them all good fortune, partially torn not to be going with them. George hefted three-year-old David up in front on Maisie and they all headed for the river. At Emu Ford they had no trouble getting across with four strong men maneuvering the dray and hefting the youngsters on their shoulders. On the second pass George put Katie and Molly on Maisie's back to save them getting their skirts wet, and then followed up likewise with Eileen. The women enjoyed the attention.

George accompanied the group across the flats to Grace and Robert's place in Emu Plains. There, once again sad goodbyes were shared, Molly holding baby Eileen till the very last moment. Ahead lay the first part of the road up Lapstone Hill, and the first test for Splash and her load. David sat atop Patrick's shoulders but six-year-old Connor cut a little swagger, determined to be like his big brothers, and walked. As George waved and turned around to head back to Penrith he grinned and wondered how long it would be before Connor also wanted to be carried.

The first route over the mountains had been established by Gregory Blaxland, William Charles Wentworth, and Lieutenant William Lawson in 1813, although many others had tried and failed before them. In July 1814 William Cox, J.P. Lieutenant and Paymaster of the NSW Corps, was commissioned by Governor Macquarie to convert the route found into a roadway. In six months Cox and his team accomplished the incredible feat of building a passable road from the Nepean River to Bathurst, a distance of 102 miles. The group consisted of a superintendent and guide, a storekeeper, doctor, constable, tools overseer, carpenter, blacksmith, miner, two bullock drivers, twenty labourers, a sergeant, corporal, and six privates of the Royal Veteran Company as guards.

In those earlier times the method of making roads was very primitive. An alignment was made by blazing the trees along a route which presented the least difficulties. A track was cleared and grubbed along this path. The road was then graded, and bridges and small culverts constructed where necessary. At every mile of completion a tree was especially marked to record the distance. Large rocks were blown up with gunpowder, while boulders were levered out, or removed by block and tackle.

Lapstone Hill was the Monahans' gentle introduction to the ascent beyond. A couple of miles beyond the top the family reached the remnants of Cox's first depot at Blaxland. There were good sources of water and pasture available so they unhooked Splash and let her graze, and set fires to cook dinner and make a perimeter for sleeping through the night.

Man's worst fear of crossing the mountains wasn't animal attacks but rather that of being accosted by bushrangers. The numerous valleys and gorges were pockmarked with old caves, creating secluded hideaways for these rogues who mainly held up travelers for money and food. Generally speaking, the fires kept wombats and possums and snakes away. The slopes were generally too steep for kangaroos or emus to roam and they were rarely seen in the vicinity.

As the group settled in for the night Katie turned to Matthew and asked, "Do you have that pistol you bought handy? This is the first time I've been away from a dwelling in years and I'm a little scared, to be truthful."

"I understand, dear. But you are surrounded by three strong men. I think anyone will be hesitant to try us on. Try not to worry."

Rustling in the undergrowth and the shadows of a pair of curious flying foxes silhouetted by the moon kept a couple of the girls awake but eventually peace reigned and tiredness from the long uphill walk and the emotion of departure helped them all sleep.

Grilled sausages and bacon and fried eggs with bread filled their stomachs in the morning, and they all drank from the freshwater stream nearby, keeping the barrel of water on the dray for future needs. Brightly coloured mountain lorikeets flashed through the foliage across the road, with one cheeky enough to alight on Splash and try to pull hair off her mane. Splash seemed unconcerned but it made the young boys laugh to watch the funny antics of the bird trying to secure nesting material.

One of the games they developed walking along was to see who first could find the next mileage indicator. The road builders had diligently marked trees along the left-hand side of the route. David, just learning to count, loved being first to spot the numerals carved in the trunks. That is, when Connor let him, of course. While the road now twisted and turned more often and was essentially more northerly in direction, the ascent was not too demanding and Splash made no complaints. The children (which, to Matthew and Katie, meant all sons and daughters) now engaged in watching and listening for birds and for checking for wildflowers that could be seen from the road. Brilliant golden wattle was found in sunny spots, and everywhere were the eucalypts ranging from stringy-barks to giant silver gums. The beautiful red waratah was generally found in the lower mountains in the sandstone-supported soil and it took Eileen wandering off the road at one point to find one. Spring brought a profusion of blooms and colour and the family rejoiced in the new offerings they discovered.

A couple of miles from their morning starting point they observed a team of four bullocks with a dray full of wool bales coming downhill towards them. The driver and his helper slowly pulled to a stop and waited for the Monahans to come abreast. "Good mornin' to you, Mr. and Missus and family. Where would you be headin'?"

"Not exactly sure, sir," answered Matthew. "Somewhere over the mountains where's there's some land for grazing."

"Let me tell you then, think of just this side of Bathurst. Lots of fertile grazin' land available. Rolling hills, lots of rivers. That's where this wool came from. Headed to Sydney we are. Need to make Penrith by nightfall. Can you spare some grub for us? We haven't eaten since yesterday."

Katie opened a hamper and passed over a loaf of bread. "There you go. There's water for your bullocks about two miles down the road off to the right if you want to unharness them."

"Thank you, missus, but if we unhook these miserable beasts we'll never get them yoked up again. They can drink as we cross Emu Ford. We'd best be getting on now. Thank you kindly for the bread. Best wishes to you all." And with multiple cracks of the whips, and some yells and curses, the wagon started moving again.

"Father, were those men convicts?" asked Molly.

"I suspect they were. They probably had Tickets of Leave and passports to move between Bathurst and Penrith but nowhere else. I'm sure the wool agent in Penrith will put their load with others and send them down to Sydney. The drivers will probably haul back other supplies to shop owners in Bathurst or help people like us move goods over the mountains for a fee. Those bullocks are incredibly strong and now that the original road has been improved in parts their journey is a little less hazardous for them."

The family walked on. The road wound through thick forest now. It was narrow in parts as the road makers had selected the easiest path through the massive gums, and in places there were still vestiges of small stumps in the road which Splash avoided but which necessitated the men watching where the wheels of the dray tracked. Sometimes they had to back up a little and have Splash move diagonally across the road to avoid potentially breaking wheels on hard stumps. Still, it was a pleasant morning and at noon they stopped at the twelve-mile mark where a sign nailed to a tree indicated 'Spring Wood'. They found a small creek off the road to the right where they led Splash to drink. But they didn't tarry long for lunch, anxious to keep moving up the ridges. Bread and cheese sufficed to keep hunger pangs away at least for a few more hours.

Matthew was surprised they hadn't encountered more people on the road already, although he knew that could change easily over the next hill, or the one after that. Late afternoon they stopped at the fifteen-and-a-half-mile point after a steep climb which took its toll on the two young boys. Splash also was wheezing a bit. An hour earlier Matthew had sent Thomas and Patrick ahead to scout for a creek not too far off the side of the road. Success had drawn them to the current spot, and while there was no pasture available they tied Splash to a tree with a long lead so she could reach the creek with ease.

As the sun was setting at the end of their meal, Patrick suddenly shushed everyone and said, "I hear horses."

"Which direction?" asked Molly.

"Coming downhill. Must be three or four."

Around the bend four horses suddenly appeared. Two were pulling a short dray on which two bedraggled men sat with wrists and ankles bound by rope and secured to the flat bed with chains. Alongside rode two uniformed troopers. They clearly had no intention of stopping but as the Monahan family waved, one of the troopers shouted, "Bushrangers," pointing to the two prisoners on the dray.

"That may be a good sign for us," Patrick muttered. "At least the constabulary is actively looking for these vermin."

Two miles along the road next morning, the group stopped at a crude sign indicating the nearby presence of 'Caley's Repulse', a cairn of stones supposedly marking the spot where in desperation, George Caley in 1806 had turned around on his fourth unsuccessful attempt to find a route across the mountains. Others attributed the cairn to Patrick Hacking, formerly quartermaster on the *Sirius*, who in August 1794 had also tried and failed to cross the 'impassable barrier' of the mountains. Yet others attributed the stone pile to aborigines of the area from the Wiradjuri tribe, although this does not seem consistent with other revelations of their culture.

The terrain was still difficult but was marked with new varieties of eucalypts. When a patch of coarse grass pasture was found near the twenty-first mile marker it was taken as a signal that a stop was in order, and Splash was allowed to graze while the family again had a quick lunch. The game of spotting mile markers had by now run its course and was replaced with identifying the different birds seen. They had observed many new ones, but their names were unfamiliar so their size and colouring were the identifying features. The white, yellow-crested cockatoo was the most common with its ear-shattering screech. These were followed by the red and blue crimson rosellas, which often flew across the road in front of the group but rarely alighted in the trees nearby.

It was easier to look for birds during stoppages. On hearing their calls the family members would look around trying to identify them in the tree branches. In the thicker groves it was nearly impossible but every now and then someone got lucky. The most spectacular bird they saw was a huge black cockatoo, holding a pine cone in a claw and cracking it loudly, dropping pieces to the ground as it searched for the meat inside. His crest rose magnificently, matched in presence and strength by his strong beak. Everyone wished they could see him up close, but that was not to be.

Very late in the afternoon they halted at so-called Jamison Valley, stopping outside the second storage depot put in place by Cox during his original road-building efforts. Over time the depot had been converted and enlarged from a shed housing supplies to what was now called the 'WeatherBoard Hut'. A few small rooms were available to rest in overnight. And a simple meal could be had. A garden decorated the front approach and a stream behind the inn had channels running off to help water the plants. A clearing on the uphill side of the shelter had obviously been used many times before by travellers, and as the group stopped to contemplate the area the proprietor's wife came out the front door and welcomed them. It must have been a standard greeting, Katie thought, when the woman asked, "Where are you headed to?"

"We're not quite sure," she responded. "It depends what we find along the way. But we're looking for grazing land for either sheep or cattle. Someone has already mentioned just this side of Bathurst as a good wool-growing area. If you have some suggestions we'd be very happy to hear them. Everything is very new to us here."

"Well, Bathurst is a long way away. Tell me, are you all Irish or some Scottish?"

"We all hail from County Donegal in Ireland, close to Londonderry. Why do you ask?"

"Well, in the major valley at the bottom of Cox's Pass there is a large village emerging which is settled by Scottish and Irish families as I understand. You will want to stop there and learn about the surrounding land, which apparently is well suited to raising sheep and cattle because of the lush grass, although it is somewhat hilly."

"Thank you. We'll definitely ask around when we get there. You are most helpful."

"Now, would you be looking for rooms tonight?"

"Maybe for the youngsters. Can I have a look?"

What Katie saw inside was not very attractive. There was one room that had a real bed; otherwise, most of the rooms still had dirt floors, some with tree stumps protruding, and where beds were formed from large sheets of stringy bark. Most rooms were dark without a window and in one, which smelled of urine, she saw a swarm of bugs moving across the floor. It didn't take long to turn around and head outside.

"I think we'll just stay as a family and sleep under the dray as we did last night, thank you, missus."

"Well, before you leave tomorrow morning, do spare an hour and take the track that starts across the road over there by that large cypress tree. It leads to the edge of enormous sandstone cliffs and there's a very pretty waterfall you can see from one spot.

Definitely worth your time. And if you like native flowers the bottle brush is in bloom right now about a quarter mile along."

"Thank you, that sounds fascinating. We'll definitely have a look."

The view from the top of the cliff the next morning took their breath away. For mile after mile green hills stretched into the distance beyond a vast valley named after the late owner of Regentville. They'd never seen anything so magnificent, and the tinge of blue in the air from the fine eucalyptus oil reinforced the naming of the ranges they were crossing. The vista made them realise just how difficult it must have been years before to find a way through these hills. Their appreciation of the road they'd been travelling grew, and thereafter complaints about its state were minimized.

The red flowers were just as described, like thick brushes used to clean bottles through a narrow neck. Little finches and wrens were busy flitting in and out of them, along with bees gathering pollen. And while the waterfall was a long way away they could see the sun reflecting off wet rocks, and were amazed at how far the water fell to the pools at the bottom. "It makes me want to go exploring," Thomas remarked. "I bet those pools would be fun to swim in."

The proprietor's wife had told them where water and grass was to be found at further spots along the road, so they meandered on, confident that they would not have to search hard for water or pasture for Splash. Their target for the day was milepost forty, a good twelve miles ahead. Before they got there they watched for a spot around milepost thirty-three which allowed them to view a picturesque opening called Pitt's Amphitheatre on the south-west side of a glen, the opening being circular in shape and revealing mountains and valleys beyond mountains and valleys. The vastness of the country they were traversing became more and more apparent the further they climbed. There was nothing comparable in Ireland that they knew about, and the views were a revelation of how little this new land had been explored and how much was still unknown about it.

The air was fresher and the night noticeably cooler when they camped at day's end. Where the road had been blasted through solid rock earlier on the route it now looked more like granite than sandstone. What a job men had done just thirty years earlier. The family had detached Splash to graze and had just settled down around a blazing fire to cook their meat for dinner when they clearly heard voices on the still air. Surprised, they listened intently, finally realising natives were in the vicinity. They'd all seen the odd native in the town of Penrith or along the river bank, but there was something eerily uncomfortable about encountering them in their own environment. They could hear the voices, but had no real idea where the speakers actually were. Splash's ears pricked up and Thomas moved to comfort her. He rationalized to the family: "They know we're here as they are familiar with the fact that people like us travel this road often. And their senses are attuned to the forest and valley environment. I bet they've known we were coming along the road from a mile or two back. If they wanted to hurt us they would have made their presence felt by now. They're probably watching from behind trees in the gloom of the shadows.

Just then Connor stammered, "F...Father, lu... look." And he pointed half ahead to the right, where a tall black man stood on one leg, his other leg stretched out and down at forty five degrees and hinged inwards at the knee with the foot planted back on the knee of his vertical leg. He held a spear upright in one hand, and draped about his shoulders was a cloak of fur—possibly possum skins, thought Patrick. A dirty loincloth covered his privates. He stood absolutely motionless, simply surveying the scene.

A woman with nothing more than an old cotton skirt on came up behind him and ventured past, heading towards the fireplace. The girls retreated, startled by her wildness and unkempt appearance. It was Katie who realised the woman probably wanted food. Katie moved to the fire and using a thick stick with a pointed end retrieved a small rack of lamb that was roasting over the coals. Carefully she turned to the aboriginal woman, walked a few steps forward, and laid the lamb meat on a rock. She gestured that the meat was for the visitor, whereupon with a swift movement the woman picked the meat up by the end of a bone, deposited it in a woven bag slung behind her back, turned, and was gone, melting into the shadows without a sound. Her mate had also disappeared and all that could be heard was the crackling of the flames and the hiss of fat oozing from the remaining meat.

"Good for you, Mother," said Molly. "I was scared stiff. How are you feeling? I think you were very brave. Do you think they'll be back for more?"

Patrick responded, "If they had wanted more I don't think they would have disappeared so fast. But I agree. You did well, Mother. Let's eat and enjoy the last of our fresh meat. I think tomorrow we should reach the little hamlet of Hartley on the other side of these mountains. I saw some dark clouds gathering late this afternoon, so it may well rain tomorrow. Let's hope not."

Inspired by Patrick's assessment they set off earlier than usual the next morning. A mile uphill they spotted their aboriginal friends from the previous evening standing on a high rock watching them. As they came abreast the old man raised his spear as if in salute, and they all waved back, grinning in friendship. They bypassed the Scotch Thistle Inn without stopping, determined to try to get to Hartley before it rained. Around lunchtime they reached the highest point on the road and shortly after they arrived at the little tollhouse at the top of Cox's Pass. They gasped as they looked down the precipitous slope to the valley floor six hundred feet below. The valley looked lush and rich and they could see the small River Lett flowing westward in the opposite direction to all the streams they'd seen as they came up the road from the east.

While Cox's original road had been improved in places over time, it still looked like a formidable descent. Thomas pointed out a bullock team with a load of household belongings halfway down, moving incredibly slowly towards the bottom. The constable at the tollhouse said, "If you look closely you'll see a massive log chained behind the dray. The weight and the drag of the log on the roadway help the bullocks from slipping and moving too fast or losing their footing. That's why you see all these stumps up here where drivers have cut down thick trees. The real problem is that they take them off at the bottom and leave them there, but no one brings them up again. You are going to have to be careful with that light dray you have there.

"Here's what I've seen work best," the constable continued. "No one on the dray. You all have to walk, including the young'un. Do not put him on your shoulders in case you slip. Let's see now. Mother, you walk with his little majesty holding his hand. You, girl...," pointing to Molly, "you take the other youngster. Now you...," singling out Eileen, "you and your father walk either side of your horse. Real slow, real steady. Hold her bridle, but not tight. She'll find her own footing. You're only there to reassure and guide her. Talk softly to her all the way down. And as for you last two strapping chaps, your job is to hang on to the back of the dray and be dragged with it, using your feet as brakes. You'll be fine, I'm sure.

"Now, mark my words and be off with ye. I'll wave when I see you at the bottom."

And so they slowly and very carefully descended the most famous part of the road that had opened up the country west of the Blue Mountains for settlement, agriculture, and trade. Eventually the road became level. The toll collector waved from on high and the family laughed and hugged each other. They'd made it on foot fifty miles across the Blue Mountains. A journey well worth rejoicing.

Initially, the area at the foot of the pass had been called the Vale of Clwydd, after a namesake vale, Dyffryn Clwydd, in North Wales. By the 1830s there was a need for a police station and courthouse between Penrith and Bathurst to manage bushranger problems. The village of Hartley was born and by 1837 both the courthouse and the police barracks had been built. By 1840 a town, with sixteen streets laid out in a grid system, had been surveyed, although most of it was never completed. When the Monahans arrived in late 1845, there were sixty two residents and twelve houses. A church, post office, general store, inns, and a stagecoach house were part of the town's welcoming environment.

Never had any place looked so inviting. This was almost full civilization compared to the sparseness of buildings they'd come across in their trek. It was with tremendous relief and hope that they hitched Splash to a fence post and crossed the veranda of the Collits hotel. Its galvanized iron roof, water tanks, and chimney, while well short of the grandeur of the mansion at Regentville, beckoned them in. Pierce Collits met them at the entrance and in a strong Irish brogue that made them all smile stretched his arms wide and said, "Welcome travelers. Welcome. Come on in and say hello." He stood aside and they trooped in and sat at a long trestle table.

Matthew shook hands with the proprietor. "Matthew Monahan and family of County Donegal. My wife Katie, Thomas and Patrick, Eileen, Molly, and Connor and David. We are so pleased to be here."

"Mary," Pierce yelled. "Can we have some food for our new guests? Now who'll be drinking my ale, and is it milk for the young'uns?"

The rain started falling and Thomas and Patrick rushed outside to move as many items as possible off the dray and under the veranda roof. They didn't mind getting wet at all. They unhitched Splash and took her around the back of the inn to the stables, where she welcomed a feed of hay and apples. Back inside, the rain was making an incredible din on the roof and conversation ceased while they all recognized how lucky their timing had been.

Dinner was fresh cod caught in the river, accompanied by spring vegetables grown in a garden behind the inn. And as a celebration for their efforts Matthew splurged on soft beds for everyone for the night. They were the only guests and the Collits treated them like royalty. The next day Pierce took them on a tour of the town through muddy streets and introduced them to many of the residents. No one could fail to notice the predominance of Scottish and Irish accents, and by day's end the children were begging their parents to stay. Here was old-world comfort and friendliness as well as frontier interests. Men and women alike seemed genuinely at ease although none proclaimed to live in luxury. Community spirit was at the heart of their existence.

At the general store Matthew met up with several farmers buying provisions and asked them about land and grazing conditions. He also checked in at the courthouse to determine land availability and prices. He was pleasantly surprised at both the reasonableness and quantity of un-owned land in the area.

In 1842, St. Bernard's Catholic Church had been built out of local sandstone. It indicated the religion of the majority of residents in the area, and while the Monahans had no quarrels with those of other faiths, they were a little disappointed that there was no Presbyterian church present. The Reverend Colin Stewart, actually a Presbyterian, conducted services in the local courthouse in 1839 with permission from Governor Gipps. Thereafter it was used for Anglican services. However, the Monahans were told that, just as had been the case at Regentville, while there was no Presbyterian church per se, there were several resident families of the Presbyterian faith who met in private homes on Sundays. Reassured, over dinner Matthew arranged to rent two horses the next day and to go looking at land with the twins.

The beautiful setting of the vale with its lushness and fresh water, the close community of expatriates and their friendliness, and the availability of inexpensive land had enormous attraction for all. The fact that the next nearest town was still fifty miles away, as far again as they had just come, detracted from any interest to go further.

It seemed that the Monahans had finally found a place to settle in the new land.

15. Hartley geography.
People, pardon

It took two days of exploring before the men chose a forty-acre lot five miles south-west of Hartley between Blaxland Swamp and Good Forest, two tiny hamlets with naught but a pub each for a marker. Mount Blaxland rose nearby to the north and the low undulating hills and valleys displayed rich green grass courtesy of the overnight and previous days' rains. Access to the site was along little more than a two-wheel track that followed the contours of the land mainly through forests of eucalypts and beside or across creek beds. In fact, there were numerous creeks crossing the property they chose, one of the major attractions for the Monahan selection. All ran roughly to join Cox's River, which ran in a south-westerly direction. What's more, land surrounding the plot was still available in several directions. In signing the deed of sale at the courthouse Matthew made it clear to the clerk that he planned to buy many more coterminous forty-acre parcels as returns from the farm would allow, and that he should not sell any such parcels to others without contacting Matthew first.

The immediate major task was to build a livable abode on the property, and to that end they first had to buy tools. At the general store they bought a two-man saw, axes, rope, block and tackle, chain, wedges, pickaxes and shovels, crowbars, a number of bricks, gloves, and strong boots. They paid cash for their purchases but established a line of credit for other provisions. They let it be known that they were looking for horses and some cattle for breeding.

Full of energy and thoroughly excited, the three men cut down trees, then sliced and diced them into crude slab planks and built a shanty with a small fireplace. Eileen went along not only to cook and help with light chores, but also to push for small feminine touches.

Katie and the others stayed at the inn and explored the environs while the men built their home. The River Lett was a constant drawing card. It was nowhere as wide or deep as the Nepean and meandered through fields with river-oaks and willows shading its banks. Several fording spots had been built by piling large stones that had been freed up by the building of the road down Cox's Pass. When the water was low many of the rocks were exposed, making it easy to cross. Often the Collits or other town residents would join them in walks through the vale and show them some of the local treasures and special points of interest. By chance they met one of Robert Kitchings's friends and through multiple interactions with residents, reaffirmed that the town was everything Robert and the proprietress at the 'WeatherBoard Hut' had said.

Molly had a keen eye for the animals and birds of the district. The family saw their first echidna crossing a track late one afternoon. Connor chased after it, but it disappeared into the scrub with ease. In one of the small tributaries they discovered turtles sunning themselves on the rocks, and everywhere there were wild ducks which made great eating. It was a paradise compared to what the family had endured for the past three years and Katie constantly had to remind herself that it was not a dream.

The community recognized its good fortune and although the work was hard on the farms, every weekend there was rejoicing in the pubs with men on accordions, flutes, harmonicas, and fiddles playing Irish folk songs and Scottish dance tunes. Food was plentiful, beer was plentiful, and camaraderie was plentiful. Even Katie started to relax and enjoy herself. Molly was a flirt of the first order and was never at a loss for a partner in the dances, her beguiling smile quickly enhancing her popularity. At the end of two weeks after starting out, the men and Eileen came back into town with news that the new abode awaited the rest of the family. Eileen took Molly aside and said, "Make sure you enjoy yourself this weekend, because where we are going is lonely, and rough. The inn will look like a castle by comparison."

Katie led the way to the general store to buy some more domestic supplies. Then they loaded up the dray and waved goodbye to their new friends as they headed into the bush. They promised to return on Christmas Day when the whole village planned to turn out for a celebration in the afternoon.

Molly and Katie had to hold back their shock at first sight of the primitive slab hut. Once again they were back to two large rooms plus a kitchen and eating area. The wind whistled through cracks between the vertical timber slabs, and it was clear that rain would seep through the roof in places.

A couple of neighbours from nearby farms had come by while the men were building and introduced themselves. As soon as the message had spread around the area that the whole family was now present they came again, bearing gifts of food and passing on local knowledge and advice with genuine interest in everyone, especially the young boys. Matthew bought his first two beef cattle from one of the visitors as well as three laying hens. One neighbour offered to supply them with milk since his dairy cow produced more than he and his wife needed. Another brought a bushel of apples and invited the family to help themselves from his trees.

The Monahans planted a vegetable garden and were directed to a river five miles away where bream and cod were plentiful. Their cottage was on a slight slope with a hill at the back. From the front entry way they had a 180-degree view of rolling hills, thick forests, and blue sky. There was no question that the location was idyllic, and that the spirit of community that had pervaded the village of Hartley readily extended to the countryside as well.

Matthew sensed his daughter Molly's frustration. As much as the wildlife was abundant and attractive she missed the social interaction of people her own age. Matthew discussed the situation with Katie and they decided to buy Molly a horse so she could get back to Hartley more frequently and also visit some of the neighbours. But first Matthew had a surprise for Molly, Katie, and the youngsters. One day, on a pretext of showing them a new plot of land and suggesting they have a picnic there, he led them across several large meadows, over three small hills and though two shallow valleys, coming eventually to the edge of a gentle meandering stream.

After Matthew urged everyone to be quiet, they lay down on the bank and looked into the clear slowly moving water. For a few minutes there was nothing but the sound of the breeze in the gums above and a slight rippling sound from the brook. Then suddenly a flash of brown caught their attention as a platypus emerged from its burrow just above the waterline and dived towards the bottom. Even Molly was taken aback to finally see what she'd only heard about. How weird it was! She could clearly see the black bill widening out at the front, the short bushy tail, and the four webbed feet splayed outwards as the animal turned to and fro. It looked to be about eighteen inches long but she knew the water magnified it a bit so she wasn't sure. Thick like a small possum in body size but a rich brown colour rather than possum grey. Mesmerised, she lay on the bank and watched long after the others had withdrawn. It looked as though it used its bill to scoop up food from the bottom of the creek—maybe worms, insects and roots, although it was difficult to tell. The platypus would surface and clearly chew whatever it had gathered. Molly wondered if this was a female since it dashed back to the burrow every now and then but emerged again after a few minutes. She wondered if there were babies hidden away deep inside.

Everyone approved of the outing. Even young David scampered across the field laughing as he tried to catch errant dragonflies and butterflies. It certainly was a pretty country with its lush open spaces, clumps of eucalypts and willows, the multi-coloured parrots, and the little streams coursing down the hillsides. But there was little for Molly and Eileen to do beyond gardening and cooking, and while the boys helped their father build fences and a shed for tools and plant fruit trees, the girls became bored. Matthew and Katie revised their plans slightly and arranged to buy a horse that both girls could share. The girls were thrilled and it fell to Thomas to teach them both how to ride.

As 1846 progressed, the horses allowed the girls to ride into town more frequently and to explore their environs more widely. Good Forest, near Lowther's Creek, was in the tribal lands of the

Gundungurra aborigines. Had the family continued on further down the track from Hartley they would eventually have come to the later-named Jenolan Caves, called Binoomur, or "Dark Places," by the indigenous peoples. The old natives knew the caves. They penetrated them as far as the subterranean water, carrying sick people to be bathed in this water, which they believed to have great curative powers.

Their knowledge of the caves went back a long way, given an aboriginal dreamtime creation story about how this whole cave-riddled area of countryside came into being. The story describes an almighty struggle between two ancestral creator spirits; one, a giant eel-like creature, Gurangatch, an incarnation of the ancestral rainbow serpent, and the other, a large native tiger cat, called Mirrangan. The scuffle resulted in the gouging out of the land to form the river systems of the Cox and Wollondillly rivers and the resultant caves.

It was a long and fairly steep descent from Good Forest to Binoomur, so the girls and their twin brothers set out early one morning, determined to learn what they could about the area. The girls of course rode side-saddle, and the boys laughed at their discomfort and tentativeness. Why couldn't females ride like the men? Surely their long skirts would hide everything important, except their ankles, and the boys had seen those plenty of times. It certainly slowed things down. An hour out they paused and rested the horses by a shallow pool. Streams and rivers in this area flowed southerly or south-westerly as the contours of the land changed. On foot they walked down a narrow valley following a tiny rill of water which disappeared over a precipice. Below, and in front, was the analog of a grand 'bay' or 'gulf' covered with thick forest. The cliffs of the precipice diverged on either side, showing headland behind headland, like one sees on a bold sea-coast. The cliffs, almost completely vertical, were composed of horizontal strata of white to orange limestone. In the distance another line of cliffs extended across the view, making as if to surround the entire valley in its contrasting dark green with minimal blue haze. The entire vista in its magnificence took their breaths away. There was nothing like this in Ireland, nor near Regentville.

After letting the horses drink from the cold water in the stream they continued their journey downward. After another hour or so they finally reached what looked like a giant sandstone arch alongside a blue-green river. At the time the caves were known as the 'Fish River Caves'. The track continued through the arch, heading uphill. To the left and right under the overhead rock formation were dark cave entrances of various sizes, and with differing access. A couple of them were near the track, but most would require clambering over a series of large boulders to reach.

A group of aborigines sat on the bank of the river which disappeared underground some thirty yards beyond their campsite. At first they didn't acknowledge the new arrivals in any way, but when Thomas alighted and started walking towards them, conversation stopped and all eyes warily watched his approach. Thomas stopped and hailed them but got no response. Aborigines that lived closer to villages often picked up aspects of the white man's language. Similarly, missionaries and certain government officials picked up various components of select aboriginal dialects. But these particular natives didn't appear interested in communication. A huge goanna lay roasting in the coals of their fire, and their spears and throwing sticks were spread out on the grass. Thomas's assessment was that they were about to eat and weren't to be deterred from that activity. He smiled, waved, and backed off, at which action the small band of natives visibly relaxed.

Moving on under the arch the young explorers spotted more natives near two of the cave entrances. They seemed to have been squatting behind ridges of rocks, but at the sound of the horses had emerged and shown themselves. One young lad, bolder than the rest, came bounding down from his perch, clearly gesturing for food. Eileen reached in her saddle bag and handed down four apples, the smile on the youngster's face as rewarding as any 'thank you'. They all noticed that one of his teeth was missing, and Patrick explained that apparently at male child-to-adult initiation ceremonies knocking out a tooth was part of the ritual. Molly wondered what else was involved but didn't dare ask.

After lunch the twins gathered some dry grasses and old broken tree limbs and formed a pair of primitive torches. The women carried extra grasses and they headed to one of the more accessible cave entrances. Inside, it didn't take long to reach the limits of daylight penetration. The walls were cold and already showing signs of 'perspiration'. Lighting one of the torches, they moved cautiously forward, travelling slightly downhill across uneven rocks but along a path clearly established by the natives. It got progressively colder as the passage widened and they could hear the sounds of running water way ahead. Turning a corner after lighting the second torch, they found themselves in an enormous cavern, the ceiling of which could not be seen with their limited torch light. But there was light enough to see a sparkling shawl of limestone spreading across a sloping rock surface and a formation like a rasher of bacon sticking out from a wall when they held the torch behind it. And everywhere were stalactites and stalagmites in various lengths and thickness. The scene was like something out of a fairy tale, and the foursome found themselves whispering to each other in reverent tones.

The second torch started sputtering, bringing them quickly back to reality, and they hurriedly used the extra grasses the women had carried in to relight. On the way back to the entrance they met up with a group of natives coming in. Four men and two women, naked as the day they were born, had their torsos decorated in ochre and white clay designs, and ashes rubbed in their hair, presumably in anticipation of some ritual ceremony to be carried out inside the cave. One man was carrying a small dead wallaby, the other a fish at the end of his spear. One of the women was carrying some roots in a large piece of bark. Patrick wondered if they might be antagonistic, feeling the white man's group might have violated sacred ground. However, contrary to these concerns, the natives seemed to smile in recognition that others might have appreciated but not disturbed their special place.

The ride home seemed shorter than the trip out, but only because the wonders they had seen were a continued source of conversation. Actually the track in parts was quite steep and every thirty minutes they would walk beside the horses for a while rather than ride them. They refreshed themselves and the horses at the creek they'd found on the way down, and arrived back at the homestead with an hour's daylight to spare. Matthew and Katie could scarcely get a word in edgewise over dinner as the four related in detail every element of the day gone by.

The beauty and peacefulness of the countryside around them was heart-warming to all the family members. They had come a long way from the low rolling hills, plains, and moors of poverty-stricken Drumcarn in County Donegal, to a place they could never have imagined before leaving. No longer were they tenants to greedy and tyrannical landlords. They were their own people. They owned their land, they had clear skies above, and their future was in their own hands. There was much to be thankful for.

Back in Penrith, Ann also felt good. She rocked her baby, William, gently, looking into his little face, reflecting on how well things were turning out. Her mother's letter, written by Eileen, had been full of positive news and happy thoughts. It seemed that far better times were at last falling on the extended Monahan family. She wondered what her mother might have thought twenty years ago when she had rocked Ann as a baby, in times when the outlook would have been far more grim. Was there any spark of hope for change then, or just resignation of one more mouth to feed? The family certainly did not have much in terms of material possessions in the years when she was a baby, child, and young girl. They did have love, and that was the foundation that had held them together. Despite all the hardships they faced, belief in themselves and one another had pulled them through. How remarkably different it was today. She smiled at the sweet thought.

The clientele for George's butcher shop was growing steadily, and other signs of progress in and around Penrith were very encouraging. Right across the road from the shop, labourers were hard at work building a Catholic church, St Nicholas of Myra. More small communities like Castlereagh, Emu Plains, Mulgoa, and St. Marys in the nearby countryside were adding new residents every month as the migration of Irish and English settlers continued west from Sydney. All the merchants in Penrith were benefitting from this rural growth. The village was developing a cloak of civic responsibility and emerging as a natural trading centre.

Ann and George became good friends with Robert and Grace, often sharing meals, especially on weekends when the workload for the men eased back. As income started to become reliable Ann was able to add more feminine touches to the home behind the shop. George built a proper stable and added a smart front fence. They planted a small vegetable garden out back, which became Ann's pride and joy. The year 1846 rolled on. A punt was added at Emu Ford as more travellers heading over the mountains declined to get wet crossing the Nepean, and were willing to pay to keep dry. The road from Parramatta was improved and the mail coach from Sydney to Bathurst now ran three days a week instead of two. Progress inched along.

Eventually, the months passed into 1847, and by March Ann knew she was pregnant again. She hoped it might be a girl this time, but she knew she'd be happy either way. She confided in Grace first, somewhat hesitantly knowing her sister could have no more children. But Grace was thrilled for her and looked forward to being an aunt a second time around. George was also a happy man. He had a real love for children, so the more the merrier. Grace was helping Ann learn to write, and together they composed a letter to their mother with news of the town, Ann's decorating adjustments, the children's progress, and mention of one more to come.

Molly's horse allowed her to escape the mundane trappings of home when she felt the need, and actually provided the chance to take up a partial governess position at a nearby farm. The Langford family lived five miles away, and when their current live-in governess had had to leave they asked Molly whether she'd be interested in the job. Molly readily welcomed the opportunity to look after the education of their young brood four days a week. It gave her something to challenge her mind and fill her time.

She stopped at the Post Office on her day off to chat with the postmistress, who handed the letter from Ann and Grace and said, "I also have some letters for the Langfords if you wouldn't mind taking them. They arrived the day after they were in town. And who knows when they'll be back again. How is your job going looking after all their children? I don't envy you that chore."

"No trouble to take their mail. Actually I love their children, although there are days when some of them can be a trial. But poor Mrs. Langford doesn't seem to be getting any better, and I worry that she may not come through. You know, they've hired John Evans' wife to do all the cooking now, so she's moved into the house while John still stays out in their shack in the sheep meadows."

"Yes, Dr. Lawrence was pretty pessimistic about Mrs. Langford's chances. Such a lovely woman, but I think that the tenth child was one too many. But who am I to talk when I only had one. Just me and the mister now looking after the horses for the mail coach and filing the forms for folks."

"Oh, Ruth, you and Barry are wonderful people. We all love you. Anything new in the village we don't know about?"

"I presume you heard that David Boyd is fixing up those storage yards just off the main road west of town? He's going to build some special loading gates, so it's easier to put the cattle and sheep on the wagons for transport to market. He'll loan out the yards on a daily basis, so I think everyone will benefit by speeding up the process and avoiding damage to the animals."

"Sounds like good thinking to me. Projects which aid a number of folks are always the most likely to succeed. I'll mention this to Father and Mr. Langford. Any newcomers this past week?"

"Well, we've had a bunch of folks staying at the inns overnight, but most have been travelling on to Bathurst. The coach boys tell me there's a lot of building going on and people taking up claims there. The garrison has been strengthened because there has been increased cattle stealing apparently and the farmers are up in arms. These new types of bushrangers will use a hot piece of iron bent to the right shape to change the brand on a cow's hide. It's easy, for example, to make a 'C' into an 'O', and letters like 'I', 'L', 'P', and 'V' are easily converted.

"Another practice I've heard about is to steal young calves before they are branded at all, and add a false brand to their hide. Why do people have to be so dishonest when there are so many opportunities to make a decent living these days? Beats me. The only good news is that it doesn't seem to be happening around these parts. I think the famers' lands are harder to get to, the animals are spread out more, and of course there's a bunch more sheep here, although I'm hearing more folks are getting into cattle."

"Well, Father keeps a mix of sheep and cattle. Each have their advantages and he doesn't want to be dependent on just one species if the markets aren't good at a particular point in time. You've probably heard he's about to buy a fifth plot and put it in one of the twins' names. It's time they had their own holdings. At some point I hope they'll marry and settle down. They are twenty-five now—both a great choice for some lucky woman."

"And what about you, dear? Aren't you about to turn twenty-one? I know you live out of town but I would have thought you'd have several suitors by now. When I was your age, back in Glasgow, my biggest problem was keeping straying hands from wandering under my skirts. I gave in eventually, and look where it led me. Don't you ever say a word to Barry. He still thinks he is the only man who asked me out twice."

Molly blushed, and Ruth noticed quickly. "Ah, so you do have someone of interest. Good for you, lassie. I couldn't see someone so young and fresh and attractive being unattended. Hmmm. Not my place but I'm wondering if there's someone on the Langford place who's taken a fancy to you. Lots of eligible men there looking after those vast flocks of sheep. Most are convicts, I guess. Does that matter to you?"

Still blushing and not looking directly back at Ruth, Molly shuffled and answered, "Well, my younger sister Ann married a convict butcher back in Penrith, and you know I rarely think about it. When we lived at Regentville they were all around. Some were worse than others but that's true in any bunch of men. And frankly, most of them were transported for petty theft trying to find food. I'd want to know a convict's crime. If he was a murderer I think I'd move on as I wouldn't be able to trust him. I know convicts tend to talk to one another about their crimes but less so with us free folk.

And by the way, yes, my birthday was last month. I sure don't feel any different."

"Well, how about one more cuppa before you hit the road home? Always enjoy visiting with you, Molly. Thanks for spending time with an old lady."

"An old lady with a young heart and mind, Ruth. And yes, I'll have one more. Can always stop and pee in the bush."

"As long as you watch for snakes and other crawly things."

"You know, we've been lucky in that respect. We haven't seen a lot of snakes on our property. Mother still cringes at the sight of them. Once in while we see a kookaburra perched on one of the stumps at the gate with a snake dangling from his beak, so I'm glad those birds are around. They are good to have in the area. It's the wedge-tailed eagles I don't like, as they will go after the newborn lambs. The twins deliberately sleep out during lambing season to be around when the eagles come. But I know John Evans on Langford Station has the dickens of a time with those huge birds. Of course he has hundreds more lambs to look after than we do. I'm afraid I'm one of those who feels good when I see an eagle that has been shot and hung up between two trees with its wings outspread. I'm just not sure it's a deterrent to keeping others away. I love all the other birds—especially the mountain lorikeets—but those predators make my blood boil as they deprive us of income. It's too bad to have to kill them—I really wish they'd just fly to Bathurst or anywhere else." She gave a little laugh. "Sorry to spoil your tea, Ruth. I got carried away."

"No, it's quite alright, dear. I sympathise with your concerns. I love all elements of nature, I must admit. I don't even like hearing when horses or bullocks have to be put down. So sad to see one of God's lovely creatures hurt and incurable. Better indeed that they not suffer further, but I could never be the one to put them out of their misery."

"Sometimes it's a cruel world, Ruth. That's just the way it is. Like with stillborn or even deformed babies. I admire mothers who have such deep love that they can keep going. I hope I am never put to the test."

"Well, you have to find a husband first, dear. You need to get past that hurdle before any other."

Molly smiled. "You sound like a grandma, Ruth. But I must be off. Please remember me to Barry. I'm sure I'll be back in less than a week. Even if I don't have to, I'll probably make up an excuse. Sometimes it's lonely out in the bush."

Katie reread Ann's letter for the third time, this time out loud to everyone gathered around the dinner table. Ann's descriptions of all she was doing in her little house made Katie speak out longingly.

"Matthew, with the property we've just bought at Yorkey's Creek, do you think we could build a real house there? Not a slab hut like this, but something like Ann and George's home, albeit bigger? The twins could live here and the rest of us move there? What do you think?"

Matthew turned to his eldest sons. "What do you think, boys? Shall we design something more grand and buy lumber from Bathurst and build Mother a nice house with a stone fireplace and chimney? With wood, not dirt, for the floor, and include a big veranda facing the western sun where she can sit and rock and count the parrots and other birds flying by? Maybe we could even add real glass windows so the sun could shine inside as well. Not quite a palace, dear, but I think I know just the hillside where we could place it."

The twins' heads nodded in agreement, and Katie responded, "Oh, it sounds wonderful. Thank you, hubby. Just for that I'm going to bake a special pie tomorrow night. Would a mixture of peaches and apples be okay with everyone?"

Molly took the Langfords' mail with her next day. Their farm was five miles further down the road towards the caves but short of the precipice overlooking the valley ringed by the limestone cliffs. As she pulled up to the veranda and tied her horse to the rails the children came swarming out to meet her.

"I'm so glad you are here," Beth Evans yelled over the din. They've been an absolute handful this morning. Even the elder girls had trouble getting the youngest ones to eat their breakfast. They are so happy to know you are coming after the weekend days without you that they are all keyed up waiting. Sure wish you could live in here even though there wouldn't be room."

"How's Mrs. Langford this morning, Beth?"

Beth came closer and whispered, "Very badly, Molly. Bruce has gone into town to fetch the doctor. I made him go although he didn't want to. But she's been spitting up blood all week and concealing it from Bruce. But not from me. Today was worse than ever. She didn't even want to say hello to the children. I've told the eldest girls that I think their mother is very, very sick, and they must be prepared to be strong in case she doesn't get better. I just can't tell them I think she's dying. I think that's up to their father or the doctor.

"I'm just supposed to be the cook, but I'm much more—nurse to the children and Mrs. Langford, and on the other hand confidant and empathiser to Mr. Langford. Which is sometimes hard to handle. You'd be surprised to know some of the things Bruce tells me. Some are most intimate and embarrassing. I always thought he was a true gentleman, but I think his wife's disease has completely unnerved and depressed him and he brings out all the negatives when he's down. I don't really know how to help.

"But enough. The children need your attention. I hope you have something really entertaining for them today as I suspect they also are affected by their mother's sickness and absence, especially since they don't understand. And if you happen to see John wandering around please tell him about Mrs. Langford's situation. I won't see him today for sure."

As Molly herded the boys and girls along the veranda one of the older hands came by.

"Good morning, Andrew. How are the crops doing?"

Andrew was a Scot who was born in Mull in Argyllshire in 1810, the eldest son of Duncan Fairweather and Ann MacDougald. Duncan was a "farming man and plowman" and apparently had felt that opportunities in Australia would be better for his family than those that were then offered in Scotland. Duncan and Ann and their eight children, ranging in age from sixteen to twenty-eight, sailed out to Sydney on the *British King,* arriving in Port Jackson on

28 February, 1839. They eventually came to the Hartley Valley and found work on Lowther Park station, a property some two and a half miles west, accessed from the road leading to Good Forest. Initially, Andrew drove the ration cart which supplied food for the convicts working on the roads in the area. A stockade had been built at Hartley to house the convicts when they returned each night from their work. One of his brothers took over the job when he got the opportunity to work on the Langford station managing the limited crops planted there.

Andrew was older than Molly by about the same difference as George was older than Ann. Neither thought it unusual to be able to get on so well together. To Molly's question Andrew responded, "No change, Molly. No new bugs, caterpillars, or insects to fight today, thank heavens. But I did kill a six-foot snake yesterday that had gotten up on the veranda. Scared the kids terribly. Can't say I particularly like snakes, and there are plenty around here, although I've rarely seen them that long. This wasn't one of the poisonous ones, but I used it to educate the kids about not picking up what might look like an old stick until they really checked it out. You can just see it hanging over there on the barbed wire at the paddock entrance. "

"Ugh, I hate them too, and mother is positively scared to death of them. She wears big boots even inside the house sometimes. I'll reinforce the message to the kids of being careful. Thanks for telling me."

"Aside from snakes do yell when you want to educate the little ones about all the vegetables we grow here. I'll be happy to show them where carrots and peas come from. By the way, I've planted some passionfruit vines. We'll see if it's hot enough next summer to produce decent fruit."

If she arrived early at the Langfords' Molly would often spend time with Andrew, chatting about the histories of their respective families, finding common ground in social and educational interests. Andrew was well read and often shared lessons he had garnered from old books.

Today, she was running late. She led her charges out into the fields. First a couple of games, then a lesson in geography, followed by a trip to the creek to see what insects they could find. She had scrounged some preserving jars from the kitchen to put their catches in, and had a couple of small nets for collection purposes. After lunch the smallest charges took a nap, and to the rest Molly read stories or encouraged individuals to practice their own reading skills. End of day allowed her to pack things up just as Mr. Langford and the doctor came riding up. She nodded as they crossed the veranda but they were too intent on purpose to engage in conversation.

She felt sad for Mrs. Langford, whom she hardly knew. For Mrs. Evans she had mixed emotions. Beth had always been a chronic whiner so it was ironic to hear her complaining about Mr. Langford, although Molly did appreciate that listening to another person unburden his soul could be emotionally draining. She knew because she had to sometimes listen to Beth's husband John unburden his when they made love. She wasn't really interested in his emotions beyond those that rejoiced in full-blown coupling. The two had met some months back, well before Beth moved to the main house to become cook. The separation had left John far lonelier than before, feelings he found he could share with Molly and get ready empathy. As she rode towards his shack she quickly dismissed the guilt that sometimes arose. Making out with a man whose wife wasn't far away added a stirring element of excitement through its danger of discovery.

Her body had been hungry for attention ever since leaving Eric and Daisy behind at Regentville. For two years she'd had to suppress her desires except for the odd instance of self-pleasuring on a rare occasion when she was completely alone. Having a horse, even if shared, allowed her more freedom, and while the increased social interaction in the village of Hartley had its rewards, especially the enjoyment of the reactions of males she flirted with, there was nothing like full sensual excitement. At first her mind played with her senses but the first time John's hand had run up her leg the mind's games had raced away. Conscious of rhythm methods and withdrawal techniques, she still feared pregnancy, and wasn't always as careful as she should be. The sensations of ecstasy from coupling kept her wanting more, and there were days she wondered if and possibly when it would all catch up with her.

As anticipated, Mrs. Langford passed away and it was a sad congregation that attended her funeral at Bowenfels cemetery. Mr. Langford had trouble coping afterwards, but his eldest daughters, aged nineteen and twenty, took over with aplomb. Andrew helped them with understanding and managing the books of the farm's doings and by October the household was back on an even keel. Beth Evans still cooked, but Molly was replaced by a live-in governess who could give day-in, day-out attention to the younger children. The writing was on the wall for more change, and late one Sunday afternoon in early November Molly made a final visit to her lover John. His protestations fell on deaf ears as Molly indicated she thought he'd soon be joining his wife in the big house helping the daughters manage things as Mr. Langford became less and less able to do so. Their coupling was fierce and intensely passionate, with Molly shedding tears and surprising herself in so doing. She didn't dare look back as she climbed on her horse and sadly rode home.

Two months before, in early September, back in Penrith, Ann had birthed a daughter. She was named Mary Ann, partially reflecting her own name and that of George's sister Mariann. Like William, Mary Ann was christened a month after birth at St. Mary Magdalene Church of England in Clydesdale, South Creek, St. Marys. With a baby and a toddler, Ann's days were busy, so George had to spend more time serving in the shop, forcing him to be more efficient in travelling back and forth to his holding yards.

Incredible news arrived in December when the Sydney newspapers ran advertisements for the sale of Regentville. Much of the land had already been parceled off and sold, but now the mansion itself was going.

A portion of the splendid estate of Regentville, consisting of 1560 acres, about 600 of which are cleared and stumped, and about 150 under cultivation. Together with the elegant family mansion house, garden, grounds, vineyards, etc. To be sold by auction by Mr. Lyons at his mart on Tuesday the 21st December.... The following valuable improvements have been made on the Hawkestone Grant; first, "Regentville House", substantially built of stone with a tasteful Colonnade in front and on each side, surmounted with an Iron Balcony from which there is a delightful prospect of the adjacent country. It contains an Entrance Hall and 15 rooms, viz; 2 drawing rooms, 1 dining room, 1 breakfast room, 1 study, 1 library and cabinet, 9 bedrooms, the principal staircase is also stone built and circular. A wash-house and laundry are attached, and there are spacious cellars under the house. The right wing consists of an immense coach-house with store above; the left wing contains the billiard room. The out offices are also stone built, and consist of 2 kitchens and a bakehouse communicating with the house by a covered way, a servants' hall and 7 bedrooms adjoining; the whole being under one roof. All the above offices are contained within an area of 180 feet square, enclosed by a substantial stone wall about 10 feet high. In the rear of the foregoing, adjoining the wall, are the handsome stone stables, which consists of one 10-stall and one 4-stall, with three large boxes and two harness rooms. The lofts are over the whole of the above stabling, and are about 160 feet in length by 15 feet breadth. the stable yard is enclosed by a paling, and contains also 3 loose boxes, slab-built, with loft over them. Adjoining the stable yard at the back lies the Garden, covering about 4 acres, full of choice fruit trees, vegetables, etc., and contains the gardener's house. In the rear of the garden, a shed is partitioned off, and railed in to accommodate about thirty colts; it is well secured by a substantial fence, and has a paddock attached with contains stockyards and draughting yards. The Vineyard is on the left of the house, and contains about 7 acres of terraced vines, and 3 1/2 acres of field vineyard. It also has a stone built house, containing four rooms, a large cellar for manufacturing wine, with wine press and still. Immediately in front of the wine cellar there is a large dam, receiving the water from two gullies: is about 300 feet in circumference, by about 10 feet in depth, and has never been dry.

It was a sad time for Ann and George as the estate was realigned and the mansion and surrounds were converted into a hotel. Regentville had been an influential part of many convicts', and a number of free settlers', lives. Now the sanctuary it once was for them, along with its magnificence, style, and vitality, was gone. Regentville had endured as a distinct unparalleled microcosm of Australian society, neither reproduced nor emulated anywhere.

Few convicts probably had it as good as those who served at Regentville. Not only was Sir John Jamison a well-respected master; the whole environment was incredibly unique. A giant house essentially in the middle of nowhere, built like a fine English mansion. Only government houses built for crown appointees offered any sense of similarity in style and purpose. And no convicts served in those, as they represented the values of members of the peak of the upper classes of English society. Completely at the opposite end of the social spectrum to the supposedly wretched, immoral, and depraved criminals they were sent to guard and reform.

For Sir John's convicts, authoritarian rule was almost non-existent. In general, convicts assigned to Regentville had no wish to hurry and leave, except those who missed cobblestone streets, brick houses, a plethora of pubs, the noise of trains and coaches, nearby churches and shops, and crowds. For those folks, even though there was a beautiful river at hand, it had no wharves or warehouses or grand sailing ships, as did the mighty Thames. In a different vein, for others, even the beauty of the unusual birds and the kangaroos and the wombats couldn't overcome the existence of snakes and bushrangers and strange insects. When they could, convicts so affected applied to work for a different master in Sydney or Parramatta. Their experience at Regentville usually stood them in good stead, and it was a rare circumstance when Sir John did not put in a good recommendation for them.

The conversion of the mansion at Regentville to a hotel was a notion that was unfathomable to most, and many were happy to leave the area and not have to see the desecration that would befall their adopted home. As upsetting as that was, another great sadness was the potential loss of friendships that had developed and been nurtured over time, some covering a decade or more. Graham decided to go back to England, and George never heard from him again. Henry, however, moved up the mountains to Blackheath, where he worked in the kitchen of the Scotch Thistle Inn, hoping eventually to become the head chef there, or move on. He and George kept in touch once or twice a year.

For now, George and Ann were forging their own identity and environment, no longer influenced by the backdrop of Regentville. Their circumstances and outlook were heightened considerably when George finally received his Conditional Pardon on 1st June

1848, seventeen years after committing his crime back in London. The Ticket of Leave, which he had received eight years previously, had allowed him to purchase the land for his shop and holding yards, and no longer be assigned to a master, but he was still a convict subject to the Crown's rules and authority. The Conditional Pardon freed him completely from his convict status.

The initials 'CP' and the date were added to his previously issued ticket of leave. The Conditional Pardon was granted on the one condition that he could not return to England or Ireland. Original copies of the pardon were sent to England and duplicates remained in Australia, one of which was given to George.

It was a time of great rejoicing. Had he not been transported from England sixteen years prior, George would still have been in gaol there since his sentence was for life. Gaols at that time were not an attractive proposition as George well knew from his short incarceration at Middlesex before being transferred to the hulk *Retribution*. He had been spared rotting away in a fetid cell till he died. Instead, he had walked across green pastures under a blue sky, felt the sun and the wind and the rain, bathed in cool clear running waters, seen live flora and fauna in a new land, earned an income doing something he enjoyed and was good at, and married a free settler of his own choosing. What on earth more could a man have asked for?

Only one thing.

To be free.

And now he was.

On the following weekend Ann baked an enormous cake and George fixed sausages and chops for a giant outdoor party held in place behind the shop for all their friends, including merchants and customers alike. Even the pastor from St. Mary Magdelene church came along. A local publican helped with a discounted barrel of ale and two constables came to participate and give 'approval'.

George nursed his hangover until noon on Sunday and the couple missed church, but Ann was up early as usual with the two youngsters. After a bite to eat, George saddled up Maisie and headed to the river and Emu Ford. He wanted some time alone to reflect on his good fortune so he followed the road up to Spring

Wood, where he turned right for Yellow Rock. When he reached the overlook of the Nepean he made a small fire between the rocks and boiled the billy to make tea. He listened to the birds and the silence and thought how back in London he could never even have conceived of this place. His mood was sombre and reflective, as once again, he realised he could never feel totally bad about his misled pugilist friends of old. Without their urging he never would have stolen and would never have ended up here. Life did take funny turns at times.

Back home, he felt a need to share his feelings with Ann. As she started preparing the evening meal in the kitchen he sat at the small table and asked, "Did they have hulks on the River Foyle at Derry?"

"I didn't see any, George. But then I was in shock walking so far and then arriving in the big city. I was only thirteen and had never been to a big city. I hated the crowds and the noise and my younger brothers and sisters were scared all the time. None of us really knew what was happening and why we had left home. We just trusted our parents. We were so poor we slept on the floor in a church along with many others and were lucky to get soup and a crust of bread for dinner from the nuns. We waited four days before we boarded, and we all cried as the ship left the wharf. Maybe there's a part of me that just doesn't want to remember. I know there were other big boats on the river but that's all. Whether they were hulks I don't know. We'll just have to ask my father when we finally visit the family. I'm sure he'll know."

Then she said, "I do remember Father making a lot of fuss about the wall around the city. It dates back to the seventeenth century and is eighteen feet thick. While waiting those four days we walked along the top and viewed the layout of the streets to the four gateways. I remember wondering what sort of people must have built the wall and what sort of wars there were over one hundred years ago that required it.

"I know there were ships that took convicts directly from Ireland to Australia, but I think most of the Irish convicts who came here had moved to England first to try and find jobs. They suffered there like the native English, were forced to steal to buy food, caught, convicted, and transported here. I'm sure you had Irish brethren on board the hulk where you were held, George."

"Oh yes, we came from all over, Ireland, Scotland, Wales, but mainly England, of course. There were some chaps I had trouble understanding, their brogue was so thick, and they often formed their own little groups. At least my time on the hulk was relatively short, but I really hated it. The only good part was when my father and sister came to visit and brought fresh food. When I hear your stories, Ann, about how you were raised, it makes me feel bad that I complained about our conditions. I can't really appreciate how you all slept and ate together in such a confined space, especially with animals there too."

Ann responded, "At the time, we youngsters didn't know any better. All the other farm labourers lived the same way. The only difference we knew was the church and the farmer's house, which we never went in, but which Father saw sometimes when loading the hay or animals to send to market. When I think back to how we all slept together on top of straw on the earthen floors I shudder. And we were so cold in winter with few blankets between us. The only way we really kept warm was by crowding together and letting our bodies heat one another up. Boys and girls together. And if one was sick, they were always put in the end position to infect others less, but that was the coldest spot so often didn't help. And woe betide anyone who had to get up to the privy in the middle of the night. There was no privacy, and while we were conscious of that, there was little we could do about it. I remember my brothers being sneaky and feeling me up, touching my breasts and other parts and if I made a fuss my parents just ignored it. It was the same for my three sisters and when we could we tried to always sleep together but one of us at least would have a boy cuddling behind. Everyone knew when one of us had our period and it was often embarrassing, especially with the boys teasing us. We all had to pretend not to hear when our parents made love. Behind their backs we called it 'grunting time'. But through it all we survived and I still love all my sisters and brothers. I'm just so glad that you and I don't have to raise our children that way.

"For all of us little ones," she continued, "the church, and the little school classes held there and at the national school, were our salvation. We all learned to read and do our sums, but as soon as they were old enough, the boys helped in the fields, and we girls helped at home, preparing meals, looking after the younger ones, although at peak harvest times we also helped in the fields. I want our children to not be scared of hard work, but I want their lives to be better than what we had growing up."

George replied, "As a boy raised in northwestern Kent my memory blurs on those sorts of details. I think it's because my mother died when I was only four. There was a lot of sadness after her death and Mariann, who was eight, wasn't really old enough yet to help out much. I remember our aunt Joyce staying with us immediately afterwards for a while, and there were some friends who brought food or we went to their place for supper. Eventually, Grandma Clarke came from Devon and stayed several years, until I was about nine. By then, Mariann and I were running the house and looking after Ruth while Father worked two jobs. Church was part of our life, too, as was school. We weren't poor like your family, and the house we rented was adequate for our needs. There were many others just like us. The big difference, of course, was that we lived just outside London proper but had access to shops and parks. For me, the Thames was close by, and as a lad, we had fun on the banks, playing and watching the big ships. Of course it never crossed my mind that I would end up incarcerated in a hulk on the river later on.

"There are times I remember back to the magnificence of London. It was the centre of the universe for us youngsters. Churches, cathedrals, Houses of Government, the Royals, theatres, galleries, shops, warehouses, up and down alleys and side streets. Always busy with traders and merchants and the militia personnel. Anyone of importance lived there and that's why I wanted to work in London. But, while it was great when I was a boy, it certainly was not as pleasant by the time I ended up working there. The factories cast black smoke over the city nearly every day and it smelled bad. More people became beggars with their hands out at every corner. Ladies of the night became obvious in the daytime. More police were added as crime increased. I'm not proud that I was part of the cause. In the end, my greed was my undoing. It brought me here as a convict, but now I'm a free man. Thank heavens, because I love living here, much better than London."

A look of understanding passed between man and wife which implicitly recognized that the past was the past, and while it had shaped both their lives in definitive ways, it was now behind them. The hellish journeys and experiences they had both gone through, and which had brought them to this place at this time, had cast indelible impressions on their hearts and souls.

So be it.

For now, they had each other in a new place, in a new time, in a new life. Their children would grow up knowing only joy and thankfulness, benefiting from a deep, dependent, and devoted love between their mother and father.

They joined hands and prayed.

16. Shame 1848

Molly's pregnancy stayed secret for months, but eventually there was no way to avoid telling the family. She decided to brave it when the twins were over for dinner one Sunday evening so that everyone would learn at the same time. After Connor and David had left the table, she pulled herself forward and shakily started: "I have… some news for all of you. I'm afraid you won't particularly like it, but you need… to know. And that is… that I'm going to be having a baby."

With head bowed, unable to look anyone in the eye, she continued. "I'm sorry, Mother. I'm sorry, Father. I know it's something you probably dread hearing, but it's my fault, I have sinned, and I have to live with it. I'm sorry to everyone else as well, especially if it brings shame on the family and you are all hurt by my indiscretion."

Tears started flowing, and Eileen quickly jumped up and came around the table to hug her, saying, "It will be alright, Molly. Really."

Father threw down his napkin and got up and paced back and forth to the doorway. His face was contorted as he tried to control his angry reaction. He said nothing, and shortly went outside and started walking towards the front gate. Katie wrung her hands, then formed them in prayer fashion beneath her chin, and looked down at the table. "Oh dear, daughter. What have you done? This isn't the way we raised you, may God have mercy on your soul. I must go look after your father, but we will have to talk later."

And with that she was gone. Silence lay heavily across the room. Thomas and Patrick stared incredulously, wishing they'd been mistaken in what they'd just heard. Patrick at last spoke up. "How could you, Molly? How could you? You have wounded

Mother and Father to their core. They will never think of you the same way again."

"I know, Patrick, I know. I don't expect forgiveness. I have to live with my sins, but please, I beg you, don't judge me too harshly. I shall love this baby with all my heart and raise it as well as I can. I know it will be a problem for all of us, not just me. I truly am sorry, I truly am."

Patrick and Thomas exchanged glances and slowly stood up from their chairs. Patrick started to head to the door, but Thomas leaned to his left and kissed Molly on the head, said, "Bless you," and walked outside. Patrick followed suit, and a fleeting look of undeserved relief crossed Molly's tear-stained face.

Eileen unwrapped her arms from around Molly's shoulders and said, "Come on, let's go out to the orchard and chat a little."

And suddenly the room was empty. The young boys came inside and wondered why it was so quiet, having no understanding of the minor calamity that had just befallen the family.

"Eileen, I know everyone will want to know, but please don't ask who the father is. I will tell when the baby is born, not before. I have my reasons, believe me please. Any shame should be contained within our family, and not spread unnecessarily. It will be hard enough on you all, with the community wondering. But what you don't know you can't lie about if you are tempted. You may have to explain that to Father for me, as I think it will be some time before he speaks to me again."

"Yes, he was clearly terribly upset. But Mother will calm him down. She's the rock of support he needs and depends on, as much as it looks the other way sometimes. I think she will accept your wish to not reveal the father's name, although you can't blame us for wondering, and guessing."

"I would do the same were I in your shoes, so yes, I understand, but I've thought long and hard and will stay silent on that score."

Katie and Eileen wondered at her secrecy but also felt for her as women, one knowing motherhood, the other hoping to know one day. With Katie's prudent support behind the scenes, Matthew eventually was able to ask at breakfast one morning: "When do you expect your baby to arrive, daughter?" Using the term 'daughter' instead of 'Molly' indicated his lingering discomfort and arm's-length position, but it was a major step forward, for which Molly was grateful.

Attempting to ameliorate things even further by involving her mother, she responded, "Mother thinks the middle of August or so." Katie had become more accepting of the notion that what was, couldn't be changed, and that one of her new obligations was to pass on her baby-making experience.

The situation still festered deep in Matthew's soul and he found forgiveness almost impossible. With Molly he was reserved and courteous, but the warmth was no longer there. Despite his wife's gentle coaxing, empathy just wasn't ready to be seen yet.

But about a month after the dinner revelation, a hint of mellowness started to creep into his discourse. Truth was that he was starting to feel guilty for not loving his daughter more openly and for being unable to accept her condition. He finally rationalized that Mary Jane was twenty-two years of age and old enough to make her own decisions. He'd married at age twenty when Katie was only eighteen, and they'd had the twin boys within a year of their public commitment. If they could take responsibility for raising children at that age, then so could Mary Jane, albeit alone, but really not alone—there was family all around.

Time was the cure-all, and one morning as she pushed back her chair to leave the breakfast table Matthew helped her heave herself up and gave her a loving hug. Katie turned away and smiled, secretly pleased that harmony would once more assume its place throughout her home.

As her pregnancy advanced Molly stayed home, never straying far, Eileen using the horse to go to town to buy needed supplies and pick up any mail. The family assumed that that arrangement suited Molly because most likely her suitor was someone located in the village of Hartley, where she had travelled often. She stayed silent on who that might be.

George had written explaining his conditional pardon and the freedom he felt on being on a par with free settlers. He reiterated his love for Ann and the delight his two children provided. Long before now, Matthew had forgiven George for his crime in London. George's love for Ann was obvious and he had proved himself to be a sincere man, good-hearted, helpful, and selfless. Matthew's eldest sons had similar qualities and he loved them all. He was surprised that the twins were still happy to live with Katie and him. After all, they were gown men and should be pursuing their own lives. They were mature enough to make their own decisions, however, so he didn't push them.

Baby Jane was born at Mary Jane's home at Good Forest on Saturday 26th August. Mother and Eileen assisted and the little girl arrived with fine voice. Mary Jane scrutinized the little wrinkled face to see if it was her or John's features that showed, with some relief when she didn't see much of John there. She wondered, had he known, would he want to see his new daughter? Would he feel guilt at his fickleness and stay away, or would curiosity dominate? And for herself, what now? A torn life with no husband or baby's father to help raise the child? Would her love be strong enough to withstand the scorn, the behind-her-back whispers, the eyes of shame that would be cast her way then hastily be withdrawn as she stared back? Would there ever be another man who would take her and her charge into his life and love them unconditionally? That was probably too much to ask. She knew her family would help, but they too must wonder about her. Conflicting emotions rushed hither and thither through her heart and mind. They subsided as another plaintive cry of life claimed the need for attention, and even though she was exhausted, an inner strength allowed her to spill her love in a smothering kiss on her baby's forehead. We will survive, you and me, she thought. We will survive.

A week later Thomas and Eileen rode off together to the nearby Langford property on a friendly neighbourly visit. Mr. Langford didn't recognize them at first, and clearly his brain was no longer functioning perfectly. Beth and John were glad to see them, as was Andrew. And the eldest girls immediately pestered Thomas with farm management questions.

He was glad to eventually break free and ask John how well the flocks were holding up after the recent cold rains. John invited him to check some of the ewes heavy with lamb, and they rode off together as Thomas had hoped. He delivered Mary Jane's message about the baby's birth and how she was going to name her daughter Jane Evans. She would keep John's fatherhood secret as long as she could out of respect for his married state, but she anticipated christening the baby at some later stage, at which time the information would most likely become public as the Presbyterian Register of Christenings was open. She'd be asking Colin Stewart, Minister of the Vale of Clwydd, to perform the ceremony next time he was passing through Hartley—possibly some time in December.

John swallowed hard, readily owning up to his paternity, and passed on his good wishes to Molly and baby and said he'd stand by his fatherhood in name, but no more. He'd face the music with his wife in his own way, well before December, so there'd be no unexpected public humiliation for either of them.

Back at the homestead Andrew asked after Molly since he hadn't seen her in ages, and he missed their lively discussions. When told she was well, he said he'd drop by in a week or so to say hello and return the call. Thomas and Eileen couldn't quickly think of a reason to suggest the visit may not be appropriate, so promised to look forward to his company.

Molly nursed baby Jane and thought about John. He had touched a corner of her heart as they had come to know each other. There was an innate goodness within him, and a small part of her soul wondered why she, rather than Beth, hadn't found him first. Not that there had ever been a chance of that, but there had been some emotional bonding between them that she had relished, and which added a soft corona around the physical tryst. She justified to herself why he hadn't found a reason to visit, pretending she understood, although deep down she was hurt that his own child meant so little to him. Plentiful sighs and large intakes of air prevented her bursting into tears. There definitely was a price to pay for her sins, she thought for the umpteenth time. But as she felt the beat of her little one's heart on her breast, once again she knew they would survive.

There was no concealing baby Jane's cries and need for attention during Andrew's visit, and Mary Jane didn't try to hide her situation. Andrew was too much of a good friend and she felt guilty enough in not having talked to him at all in the past four months or more. She felt at ease breast-feeding in his presence, albeit contrary to customary practices, and wasn't at all surprised at his smiling support for both her and her daughter. It would have been indelicate to ask about the baby's father and Andrew gave no hint of needing to know. As Molly didn't talk about future plans, he assumed she'd stay home and raise the baby where she was, at least initially.

Molly enjoyed his company and invited him to come back whenever he wanted. She certainly wasn't going anywhere. Her only request was that he not publicise Jane's existence, as she wanted to do that when Jane was christened. He was back two weeks later, at the end of September, with startling news.

Apparently with no fanfare, and just one day's notice, John and Beth Evans had left Langford Farm, heading for Parramatta, where John's brother lived. Their reasoning seemed vague and unconvincing to others on the property, as the couple talked about not wanting to be so remote and to take advantage of the benefits a growing city was sure to provide. They'd never voiced such interests prior that anyone could recall, and folks weren't aware of any recent correspondence John had received from his brother that might have triggered the move. No matter; one lunchtime they loaded up their dray with what minimal possessions they owned and left.

Since Beth had been the Langfords' cook, her departure created new issues for the family. There were other shepherds to split responsibilities and help manage the vast number of sheep on the estate and it wouldn't be that hard to replace John if necessary. But cooks were not in ready supply in the district, especially as the townsfolk had learned. Bathurst was attracting most of the travellers from the east. Few were taking up residence in the Vale of Clywdd and vicinity. Andrew reflected the situation to Molly and her family, saying times were going to be a little rough on the property for well into the new year.

Surprisingly, Andrew showed enormous interest in Molly's baby, and would happily walk from the house to the homestead gate and back with her in his arms, talking to her in his Scottish brogue about the land she was born to. There were young children in the Langford family but no babies. And while Andrew was closer to forty than thirty, he seemed to have genuine affection for the little girl. His visits became more frequent and on weekends he would often spend time with Patrick and Thomas working in the pastures. It was clear that he was far more interested in managing cattle and sheep than growing vegetables. The Monahans soon realised he also had excellent training and background in animal husbandry and enjoyed working with him.

In early November Mr. Langford died from a stroke and a pall fell over the property, although his passing was a blessing in many ways. Two weeks after his funeral, on one of his visits, Andrew confided in Thomas and Patrick. "The daughters have realised they cannot manage things as they stand and are considering selling off some of their stock and also some of their land. The house you are building for your mother and father is nearly complete, and I presume one of you will take over the dwelling here, but perhaps this might be an opportunity for the other of you to have a separate range if that is of interest."

"Thanks for letting us know, Andrew. Actually, as a family we'd been talking just a couple of nights ago about buying yet another property or extending this one. But we hadn't thought of doing anything until we sell some fat lambs and calves early in next year," Thomas replied.

"I don't know how much you know about the property," Andrew responded. "But I'd be happy to help out any way I can. I won't do anything until you discuss things further within the family. But I know the Langford girls hold you Monahans in high regard based on Molly's time there and the occasional visits you've all managed. I wouldn't be at all surprised if they'd be willing to hold the land and stock for you if you indicated an interest. And if it's appropriate I can let them know for you."

"Thomas has seen some of the land, but I would welcome the chance to look over the parcels they are thinking of selling off,"

Patrick said. "Assuming you are coming back again next weekend, perhaps you could check if that would be possible. You're a good companion, Andrew, and we all appreciate and enjoy your interest in our doings, and especially your support for Molly. Circumstances are a little out of the ordinary there, but it's not hard to see the genuine interest you have for Molly and her baby. I'm not much for words, but... I just wanted to say thank you for that."

"Your sister is one of the smartest, sweetest women around. I'd like to meet Grace and Ann also one of these days. I can't imagine that they don't have lots of the good characteristics that all you Monahans seem to possess. I'll be back next weekend. Please say bye to Molly for me."

Patrick turned to Thomas after Andrew left. "He's one of the best, isn't he? I have a lot of time for him. Does good work, always thinking of others. Do you think he knows that John Evans fathered Molly's baby?"

"If he didn't know before now, John and Beth's hasty departure should certainly make him wonder, I would imagine. You know, when this has happened to other girls or women I've always thought badly about their morals and behaviour. When it happens to our sister, whom I love, it makes me wonder what exactly the difference is between right and wrong. I feel uncomfortable about what might happen when she has Jane christened later and all the village and farming families in the area know. But I imagine if she can overcome any negative emotions, feelings, and thoughts and keep a brave face to the world then I should be able to as well. And I imagine if anyone says anything nasty and derogatory about her morals they'll be on the receiving end of a fist. Guess I'm just proving that blood is thicker than water, right? Family comes first. Always."

"Yes, indeed, brother," Patrick agreed. "We need to make sure we support her no matter what. I'll be right beside you with another pair of fists if ever needed. Speaking of which, I haven't seen you glancing sideways at any women in ages."

"Too busy on the farm and building the house, brother. I could say the same about you."

"Yes, but I don't know that I have any real yearning to get married," Patrick said. "I just can't take to that looking after babies stuff, you know. It amazes me how comfortable Andrew is with it. And it's not even his baby to whit. But I think you wouldn't mind some young'uns eventually. True?"

"Yes, I sort of like babies," Thomas replied. "But I'm in no rush to find me a wife just yet. At least not till I find someone who can bake a pie as good as Mother's."

"Right, I hear you, but I don't believe you for a minute. The first time some pretty gal offers you time under her skirts you'll be gone."

Thomas' face grew red and unable to hold it in he doubled up with laughter. "Oh, Patrick, you made me remember a crude joke. Did you hear the one about the new hand on the sheep station who thought he'd ... Ah no, I'll wait till I'm more drunk and can tell it without thinking whether I should or not. How far away are those Christmas celebrations in the village? We've worked incredibly hard these two years and I feel like I deserve a break for a while. Might rest up around end of year. Even take a trip to Sydney for a change of scenery, or maybe Bathurst to see what everyone is so keen about. We'll see..."

Over the next month the Monahans and the Langford ladies spent time discussing the possibility of a land and stock purchase. To their surprise the Monahans found the sheep and cattle not in as good a condition as their own. It was clear that John and the other shepherds hadn't spent enough time checking for diseases and insects, and that a bunch of extra care and attention would be needed if the Monahans were to buy the stock. Thomas was the main naysayer, and Patrick knew he had in mind the small holiday he longed for. Buying these animals would negate that opportunity for sure. In the end they bought eighty acres and ten head of cattle, borrowing forward against the upcoming sales of lambs and calves, but leaving the purchase of sheep for later determination.

The hot weather of summer was ahead and while the properties benefitted from the shadows of the hills creating shade, and numerous streams for drinking water never seemed to run dry, hot winds reaching eastward from the plains could be a major challenge to unhealthy animals. While the farmers in the area helped one another out, the ones who prospered most were those that kept their stocks healthy, producing the most calves and lambs which then fattened best during their growing period, and whose sheep produced the finest wool. Sometimes it was a fine line between success and failure, which is why men with good experience were so valuable.

Matthew and family now owned three distinct properties, each carefully selected for the quality of grass in the pastures, the availability of running water, and the presence of groves of shady trees. Small sloping hills helped animals exercise and keep in shape, but they still needed constant examination for a variety of diseases, any of which not treated quickly upon occurrence could decimate flocks and herds in quick order. The Monahan farms were set in beautiful surroundings, and there was no one in the family who didn't appreciate their environment.

The two youngest boys, nine and six, had never seen Ireland, and were only now becoming fully aware of their homeland. They had no memory of the tedium, poverty, and hopelessness that all their siblings and parents had suffered. That this was paradise by comparison was meaningless. Molly was their primary tutor, although others helped with special subjects where they had expertise. Matthew and Thomas insisted on teaching them to write in order to provide them every advantage in this new world. The boys were privileged in ways they only started to comprehend years later in life.

Even Andrew helped teach the boys. His specialties were geography and history. His visits became more regular, and it was clear to all that Molly occupied a place in his heart that was growing more special over time.

The village of Hartley made preparations for Christmas. Long ago the residents had overcome the fact that back home in Scotland and Ireland there might be snow on the ground, and for sure it would be cold, and fires would be burning in the fireplaces, carolers would sing at the front door, mothers would be cooking special treats, and there'd be presents under a small Christmas tree by the frosted-over window. Some of the village residents received cards from relatives reminding them of the traditions that they used to enjoy and perpetuate in the old country.

For more than a few it could be a time of nostalgia, as they remembered family, and perhaps special presents that still held place on the mantelpiece or hung on the wall in the bedroom, jewellery that had been in the family for generations and had been passed on lovingly, or sachets of dried flowers whose perfume was only a memory, and small wooden toys carved by a loving uncle. The community spirit of Hartley was readily found in the churches where the congregations sang hymns with gusto and relished their Saviour's birth. Farmers from miles around came to town with their families to share in the camaraderie and good cheer of the residents. The inns were full and private residences opened their doors for the countryside visitors.

After church on Christmas Day, a giant picnic was held on the flats by the river. Every family contributed food of some form— fresh vegetables from their gardens, fruits from the orchards, a side of lamb, pork ribs, beef cuts, baked chickens, smoked fish, hard-boiled eggs, slices of ham, rounds of cheese, tartlets, pies, butter, cream, and dripping, fresh scones and bread, petit-fours, and creative dishes lovingly produced by amazing culinary talents. Several fire pits on the river bank were used for heating water and cooking the meat. A large clearing of grass was cut by scythe and a special area set up for dancing. Five large drays were lined up along the river bank, three for all the food and one for the kegs of beer donated by the pubs.

The last dray held the bands, for there were several which had considerable talent with men on violins, drums, flute, and accordions, and in one case a piano as well. There were aging 'lassies' who in good humour would render their personal versions of the Highland fling, well cheered and appreciated by the crowd. Not only were the ladies a hit but the father-and-son combo playing the bagpipes brought smiles to every face. On the far bank of the river another area had been cleared for what was locally dubbed the 'Lowland Games', where still-sober men would toss the caber to see who could heft it the furthest. Many residents turned up in kilts proudly displaying their lineage and clan designs.

It was a wonderful sharing occasion. The sharing extended in an unusual way in that the stockade was opened and chain gang convicts were invited to participate along with the local garrison command. In the years since the stockade had been in place, not one convict had used the occasion to try to escape, something the local citizens were proud of. Yes, the men had chains on, and their beer intake was well monitored, but primarily they relished the good food that was offered them on an equal basis with free settlers.

The Monahans, the Langfords, the Fairweathers, and their neighbours converged on the village, along with nearly two hundred other adults and children from the surrounding area. Ordinarily there would be a few aborigines hanging around, but for the days of Christmas they all 'went bush', as if recognizing the special nature of the event for the 'white man'. All the farmers tended to bring meat, and the Monahans were no exception. For them it was a time of giving, to be able to offer to others more than they received. They were highly thankful of the goodwill that had befallen them in coming to this new land, and they wanted to pass on their thankfulness in meaningful form.

Andrew's father, Duncan, and Matthew met for the second time. Duncan was some twelve or more years older than Matthew, having been born in 1788. His wife Ann, five years younger, was about ten years older than Katie, but they all seemed to get on well, and spent more time together than in their first meeting, clearly due to the growing liaison between Molly and Andrew. The Fairweathers were a healthy, robust family, in great contrast to the Langfords, where both parents had passed on recently, far earlier in life than normal. As with all such gatherings the men formed groups discussing farm prices, the new loading pens, and emerging husbandry practices, sharing trials and experiences. The women grouped around children and babies, more interested in discussing domestic elements and home-making functions. Molly was approached by many of the women to learn more about baby Jane. All the village residents had heard she'd been pregnant and given birth, but this was her first public engagement, and many were naturally curious. Some were standoffish on the principle that immoral behavior should not be condoned, but those women were vastly outnumbered by others who admired Molly for not terminating her pregnancy or leaving the area in shame, but staying and proudly raising a daughter with love. Jane was now four months old, and her gurgling smiles were a delight to witness.

Still, Molly was conscious of being shunned by some. It hurt, but she tried to empathize with their perceptions, knowing full well that she may never truly understand their feelings, and that past relationships might never be repaired. So be it. She had survived a hard life in Ireland, and, no matter what, she would love this little girl as if she were the most valuable person in the world. If those shunning her could not overcome their inability to recognize the love she would offer, then perhaps she had no need of them. She worried also how her brothers, sister, and parents would respond to the inevitable questions, the head shakes and downcast eyes, the mutterings and step-asides. Long term she would owe them all much for their support. She felt fortunate that her family was with her. How terribly hard this would be were she alone.

The day after Christmas was called Boxing Day, wherein families visited relatives and friends and exchanged gifts in boxes. Andrew sought out where the Monahans were staying and presented Molly with a pair of tiny wooden kangaroos that he had carved in his spare time. Side by side they emulated perfectly how they looked in mid-stride, racing away to another destination. Molly was overcome with emotion, having expected nothing. With the bountiful offerings from the day before there was still enough food to feed almost everyone again. On the 'commons', as the celebration area came to be called, people proudly showed off their gifts and made promises to see each other more often, knowing full well that the best of intentions were just that—intentions. Some would come true, some wouldn't. But this was a time of reunion and community, of respect and helpfulness, and of the love of fellow man. These were proud people, proud of their heritage, proud of their willingness to take risks, and proud of their accomplishments. Their common bond was the survival of the journey they had taken to this unknown land, coupled with what they had had to do to overcome hardships once arrived through dint of hard work, faith, and a deep belief in themselves. The outlying farmers refreshed their ties to the town and went home with full bellies, happy hearts, and heads held high. Life here was definitely positive!

The minister who was to baptise young Jane had plans to spend the next two days in the countryside visiting and consoling some of the elderly farm people unable to join the festivities. He promised to be back the day after. Molly decided to stay in town instead of making the long trip home and then returning two days hence. Ruth and Barry had an extra room with a bed and were happy to have Molly stay with them. Their only daughter had married two years before and gone with her beau to Sydney. They hadn't seen her since, so in a way Molly was a surrogate daughter they could fuss around for a while. Eileen promised to ride back on the morning of christening day to provide support for her sister.

And so on Friday the 29th December 1848, Molly and baby Jane, accompanied by Eileen, Ruth, and Barry, walked to the church on the north side of the village, where they would formally welcome the little girl into the Kingdom of God. When the minister bade them enter, Molly asked for a little time alone, and handing her baby to Eileen, she went forward and knelt at the altar. From a pocket in her skirt she brought forth the carving of the saint that she had earned on board the ship to Sydney. Faint etchings of blue paint that had been added long ago outlined the saint's robes. Holding the small wooden figure tightly between her hands, she bent her head to her fingertips and closed her eyes. Her prayer was simple: "I know I have sinned, Lord, and ask for no personal forgiveness for I am not worthy. My daughter, however, is an innocent who deserves no shame. I have given her life and I will love her forever. I just ask you to help guide us both in the years ahead through your care and devotion. For that I will be eternally thankful and grateful. Amen."

Baby's birth and christening dates were dutifully recorded with John Evans named as the father.

Back home, the family had a small celebration. Already at four months old Jane was a well-behaved, happy child, adored by all. David, now six, finally had someone younger and smaller to wonder about and help care for. He showed all the elements of a loving uncle at an early age. With Jane's father's name officially recorded there was a question of how the community's curiosity would manifest itself when folks eventually heard. Based on the receptivity the family had enjoyed at Christmas time with the villagers at large, Matthew and Katie expected little comment, but gossip was a way of life in every community, and undoubtedly there would be questions.

The first 'test', as the family considered it, came when Andrew turned up on New Year's Day with well wishes for the year ahead. Conversation over dinner centered around recollection and discussion of events at the wonderful Christmas gathering in the village. As the dishes were being cleared, Molly asked Andrew if he'd like to enjoy some cool evening air and walk the baby outside with her. He agreed and they set off across the fields where shadows of the hills slowly spread eastward.

Molly brought the subject up directly as soon as they were out of earshot of the dwelling. "Well, Andrew, now you know that John Evans was the father of Jane. Does that make you feel any differently about me? I made a mistake, I regret it, but it is something I have to live with. I can't undo it."

Andrew stopped, turned, and looked Molly in the eyes. With a gentle countenance he softly said, "No, Molly, it changes nothing, and let me tell you why. There are two reasons. Long ago I had guessed that John was Jane's father. You see, one day at Langford's I had gone for a ride after taking fresh vegetables into the big house for the evening supper and the next day's salads. I was just emerging from the tree-line on the hill well above John's shack, when you and he came out together. I saw him kiss you and help you get on your horse.

"John and I used to chat frequently so I knew that he was lonely, although not unhappy that his wife Beth worked and stayed in the main house. Frankly, I think the arrangement was better for both of them. Beth could be surly, stubborn, and superior, rarely recognizing others' needs, and almost childish in her self-centeredness. John's frustration and unhappiness at his treatment by her would be taken out on the very animals he supposedly watched over. I've seen him kick ewes having trouble lambing, and be unnecessarily cruel to baby lambs during marking. Deep down there was goodness in John, probably in Beth also, although I didn't know her as well. I just think they weren't good as a couple—the fit wasn't there. You happened to come along at a vulnerable time. When John and Beth left in such haste that made me feel even more positive that he might be little Jane's father."

"Thank you for telling me, Andrew. It helps in a way, and it reinforces my affection for you, in that even knowing all that, you have still been so supportive. But you said there were two reasons your feelings aren't changed. What else is there?"

"It's because you aren't the only one who has sinned, Molly. Back in Scotland I found out the week before we were to leave on the *British King* for Australia that a lass I had lain with was pregnant. I've always wondered whether she kept the baby and if so whether it was a boy or girl. I suppose in some mystical way Jane is the answer.

"For a long time I felt horribly guilty, especially because it seemed I was running away and abandoning the girl. But I couldn't stay. I was the eldest son and my parents depended on me heavily. I've had to live with guilt, and regrets, and one other thing different than your situation—and that is I don't know the outcome. Sometimes it gnaws at me. I've had my torments and nightmares, probably as you have. But life must go on. Like you said, there are some things we just can't undo. To this day my parents don't know and I'd prefer to keep it that way. So perhaps that helps you see why I might have a different understanding than others. Never will I speak ill of you or Jane. You are both too precious."

With tears in her eyes Molly turned and handed Jane to Andrew. She then reached up and wrapped both hands around his neck, pulling his face down to hers, and kissed him passionately. She released him, saying, "You are almost too good to be true, Andrew Fairweather. Thank you for believing in me and my baby. Maybe she does indeed represent the spirit of your unknown baby as well. That would be nice."

By the end of January, Andrew and Molly were engaged and busy making plans for their future. Both families were thrilled, and

Molly fairly glowed with happiness. Out of the darkness had come light, in a wonderful, unexpected way. Her mood was infectious, and everyone benefited.

In 1843, on arrival in the area, the Fairweathers had bought two hundred acres of prime land. It was on a parcel of this land that Andrew and Mary Jane planned to build a home and raise a family. Molly planned on using her full name in her married state, although the family and Andrew would be allowed to still use her nickname. Like the Monahans, the Fairweathers primarily ran cattle and sheep along with a small effort in general farming. As both families grew in wealth and relationship in future years, they bought land together between their existing properties so that the joint Monahan/Fairweather farming properties eventually extended over some eight hundred acres. For now Andrew's mother and father had gifted Mary Jane and her husband-to-be forty acres to start.

Because of their proximity to one another, the wedding took place at the Monahan residence at Blaxland Swamp on Monday 19 March, 1849. Colin Stewart, the Presbyterian minister who had christened Jane, rode out from Hartley to conduct the ceremony. It was a simple, short service binding Andrew, who was thirty-eight, to Mary Jane, who had turned twenty-three a little over two weeks earlier. Mary Jane's father signed as a witness along with the husband of Andrew's younger sister.

Eileen wrote to her sisters with the news, and Ann wrote back indicating she was due to deliver Clarke child number three sometime in May. The family was expanding again.

Katie secretly wished that Andrew and Mary Jane would have a child of their own quickly, so that Andrew could be a true father to his own progeny. But she said nothing. For at the same time, he seemed devoted to Jane and she didn't want that to change. She wondered if John Evans would ever hear that Mary Jane had married his working associate at Langfords.

Three of her four daughters were now married. In the weeks following Mary Jane's marriage Katie sensed an increasing restlessness in Eileen. Her two younger sisters had husbands, as did her twin, but for her there was no one in sight. Her elder brothers were out working every day and while she enjoyed teaching Connor his school lessons, she longed for companions of her own age. With Molly gone the horse was available to her at any time, and she volunteered to ride into town for errands more frequently than before. As she was a fine young woman, the merchants enjoyed her visits and many an elder storekeeper wished she'd get to know his son. But no one in town caught her eye, and Eileen started to feel lonelier than had ever been the case before.

As the weather cooled down and autumn moved into winter, Thomas decided it was a good time to take a break and enjoy a small vacation as he had promised himself. More and more people were talking about Bathurst as the new frontier. Everything pointed to its becoming a central hub for inland business. Government was parceling out land lots, supporting merchants and growers alike to settle there, and increasing the size of the garrison stationed in the town along with pushing professional infrastructure and services in the form of a larger constabulary, a courthouse, and government supply station. An increased schedule for the coach service between Bathurst and Penrith was already in place, and more dignitaries and government officials were visiting every month. Talks about improving the road across the mountains and beyond were being discussed and funds were being allocated for the purpose.

Because of all the attention, Bathurst seemed like an appropriate place to explore, but Thomas was just as interested in the country between Hartley and the emerging town. He'd only travelled a few miles west of Hartley looking for land but had heard of fertile valleys and small plains that he would like to see. So he started preparing for a two-week trip, the longest he felt comfortable being away. He and his horse would travel light, as he would hunt along the way to provide food for his journey. There seemed to be enough rivers to supply water, although he anticipated taking a couple of extra canteens for good measure. He planned to take his time and enjoy living off the land, so to speak, and exploring at will.

He spent extra time with the farm animals and added some finishing touches to the house so his brother wouldn't be unduly bothered by his absence.

Two days before he planned to leave, Eileen surprised them all at dinner by asking, "Would you consider having me come along as companion, Thomas? I know you are set on exploring places off the beaten path and have no pressing interest to reach Bathurst quickly. And frankly, I would relish having something more to do than teach the boys their sums and read to them…"

Katie interrupted: "Eileen, I think Thomas was looking forward to having some time to himself. Goodness knows he deserves it. He's been working so hard for all of us that I think we've come to take his presence and contributions for granted."

"Yes, Mother, I agree, and I love him for all he's done for us. But I think he can also speak his own interests. And it's not necessary to decide right this minute."

Turning to Thomas, she added: "Thomas, I won't be offended if you say no. It was a thought that just occurred to me today—partly out of envy, I suspect, as I've watched you making last-minute preparations. Please think about it. I promise not to be a burden, and would be happy to ride with you wherever you want to go."

Finally Thomas spoke up. "Dear sister, Mother is right. I was looking forward to being off on my own following whatever whim caught my attention, but you make me think about something new. And that is that I haven't been alone in twenty-odd years. Maybe I'd get terribly lonely out there…"

Now it was Eileen's turn to excitedly interrupt: "So does that mean I can come along with you, dear brother? Having a female alongside won't get in the way of your 'walkabout' spirit as the aborigines would say? You wouldn't regret it?"

Thomas chuckled and he sputtered words. "Hold on, little sister, not so fast. I still have to think about it. Because I imagine you wouldn't want to rough it quite as much as I'm prepared to do. You'd want a tent to sleep under and an extra dress or two—maybe some home-made bread to take along, and who knows what else. I'm not sure I want to slow myself down managing an extra load."

"Well, I have a solution for that," Eileen retorted. "Let's take a packhorse to carry both our loads, making things lighter for our own horses. Surely we have one strong and healthy enough in the stables to keep up with you and me. Would that help?"

Thomas had to admit that would work, but now instead of just himself and his horse, there'd be another human and two more animals to worry about. He really wouldn't be as free as he had anticipated to do exactly what he wanted. On the other hand, maybe it would be fun to have Eileen along. And he could definitely see how bored she was becoming with the current situation at home here. "Let me sleep on it before I decide, Eileen, and I'll give you an answer tomorrow. Meanwhile, Mother, would you please pass the pie again? Thank you."

Katie reflected on the dinner conversation as she and Matthew sat together on the porch watching the shadows grow longer across the fields in front of them. "I think we did something right in raising our children, Matthew. They clearly care for one another. There are many families where brothers and sisters cannot stand each other or their parents, and end up leaving home in spite. We've never had that problem. I do feel for Eileen, who has younger sisters already married and with children, but I daresay her time will come. It crossed my mind that if she goes to Bathurst with Thomas she may even meet some young eligible gentleman there, but maybe I'm hoping for too much."

"Yes, we've been blessed with our children, that's certain. When you think of what we've been through in the last ten years, what we've required of them, how they've trusted in us, we're very fortunate parents indeed. Think back to when we were their age, Katie. Just as we never imagined then the future as it is right now for us, I'm not sure we know what our children's lives will be like in twenty or thirty years from now. It would be nice if some stayed in the area with us here, but that's not a hope we should cling to. We probably have no idea of the opportunities that will face some of them and what dreams might come to pass."

"As long as they are happy, using their own definition of 'happiness', I won't ask for anything more. And while I think of it, husband of mine, you deserve a mighty thanks from the bottom of my heart in making me happy. This wonderful home that you and the boys have built—I couldn't ask for anything more. Remember what we had back in Drumcairn? This is a palace by comparison. Sometimes I wonder what would have become of us had we stayed there." She sighed before continuing, "While I feel for all those we left behind, I'm so glad we made the decision to migrate. There are times when you are out working in the fields and the youngsters are off with Eileen somewhere, and the only sounds are the sounds of the bush—leaves rustling in the breeze, the screech of a white cockatoo, and otherwise just a stillness—that I sit out here and remember the stillness of County Donegal. A sad stillness, a lonely stillness, stillness born of fog on the moors, of the grey clouds, and the same gloominess day after day. Of puddles in the road from the rain, reflecting the bleakness of the surrounding fields. I think that at the time we just took the sounds and silence for granted. We really didn't think about them. But when I conjure them up in my thoughts these days I'm glad we are no longer there living around them. For they were the sounds and the silence of despair. Here there is constant hope. We are lucky people, Matthew."

The sense of wanderlust Thomas wanted to evoke and satisfy in his planned adventure tormented his soul that evening, and his sleep was quite restless. But after quaffing down an early breakfast and completing some last-minute chores in the paddocks he returned to the homestead for morning tea and a chat with Eileen. Her loving smile warmed his heart and reinforced his decision: "Okay, young lady, start packing, we leave early tomorrow morning. But I intend to hold you to your promises, so be prepared."

Eileen jumped out of her chair, threw her arms around his neck, and nuzzled a great big kiss on his lower cheek. "This will be so exciting. Thank you from the bottom of my heart, Thomas. You are the best brother a girl could have."

Patrick laughed out loud. "And here I was all these years thinking I was your favourite, Eileen. Guess I've learned my lesson. I'll just have to find someone else."

To which Eileen responded by hurrying around the table and planting an equally loving kiss on Patrick's cheek. "There, that should keep you happy till I get back, big brother. Now stop your whining." Her smile made them all laugh.

17. Brother and
sisterly love

Thomas and Patrick spent the day grooming the three horses, checking their shoes, cleaning saddles and blankets, packing the small tent, and filling saddle bags—scolding Eileen for the amount of goods she felt were necessary, eventually cutting her load in half—and testing pistols, rifles, shotguns, and knives needed for hunting and possible protection against bushrangers. The camaraderie was heartfelt and spread to Katie, who baked extra bread and dampers. Even the young boys got excited at all the preparations but had to be constantly steered away from the guns and knives to which they eagerly gravitated. It was a special time for all.

A slight drizzle the next morning couldn't dampen spirits but necessitated a change of clothing to add the waterproof skin capes and broad-rimmed hats that would minimize the impact of drops falling off the giant eucalypts along the road to town. A last goodbye wave at the gates and the pair were on their way heading out of sight.

It didn't take long for Eileen to ask: "So what made you change your mind and decide I could ride along, brother?"

"I think a number of things contributed, sis. When I thought about it, the idea of company appealed. And then you've been looking so forlorn and unmotivated lately that I thought getting away would be good for you. Plus, I realised at some time you will find a husband and be gone from all of us, and if I still wanted I could go off then by myself."

"You are an unselfish man, Thomas. I thank you. I'm not sure about the marrying bit and its timing, we'll just have to see. I will try very hard not to be a burden on this trip."

"I know, so for the moment let's just get to town, where I need to buy a few more small supplies, and then head west. It looks like the sun should break through by the time we get to the general store. Keep your fingers crossed."

Eileen had to work hard to disengage from conversations with store owners as Thomas focused strictly on the necessities he wanted and minimized his conversations. She was determined not to be a thorn in his side. As predicted, the sun shone through as they passed by the new loading paddocks and ramps on the outskirts of town. They peeled off their jackets and allowed the horses to walk at a leisurely pace, enjoying the warmth of the sun on their fronts. Thomas' target was a small region named Cooerwull beyond the end of the Vale of Clwydd. Not a hard ride at all, but his real interest was to make camp there, check out an unusual rumour he had heard, and perhaps do some hunting along Cox's River to the west.

Apparently, more than ten years previously, a local farmer named Scott Brown, who had migrated from Methven, Perthshire, Scotland, to manage James Walker's property at Wallerawang, had recorded finding coal in one of his paddocks. Brown's property was named Cooerwull after a small bluebell-like flower that grew in the area. The man was quite the entrepreneur, and among other activities he established a flour mill to process wheat grown on his property and in the surrounding district. The mill was situated on a brook and was initially driven by a water wheel. At the time Thomas and Eileen were in the vicinity, the mill was being transformed to use steam power and years later would be converted yet again to manufacture woollen tweeds. The foresight of Scott Brown wasn't obvious initially, but he was a genuine pioneer, and his discovery of coal eventually led to the formation of the town of Lithgow with large collieries and steel mills.

The pair descended into the huge valley on the zigzag road and readily found a large grassy area by a brook, where they tethered the horses after they drank, and pitched camp under two large weeping willow trees. Thomas went off hunting while Eileen roamed the banks of the brook looking for turtles and platypuses. She found neither, but half a mile upstream she came across a mother duck and her brood of ducklings on a good-sized pond that had formed, and where the surface current was so slight it was difficult to discern. She sat on the bank and dangled her feet in the cool water, checked her reflection a couple of times, and then let her mind empty of all thoughts, watching the baby ducks and their joyful movements across the water surface. It was the most rested she had felt in months.

In the thirty minutes it took Thomas to reach the eastern bank of the Cox's River he hadn't seen a single animal that might be good for dinner. Birds, an echidna rushing across his path, and the baying of a wild dog, or dingo, to use the aboriginal term, were all that caught his attention. Maybe he'd find a fat duck or swan by the river, although the thought of killing one of the regal black swans didn't appeal much. Such fascinating birds, seemingly full of grace and pride with a hint of aloofness, and totally unafraid of man. He'd only ever seen one before, but its sereneness and majesty had made an indelible impression on him, and he had left with a feeling of awe. How could they affect him so?

He rode south along the river bank. The eucalypts were sparse and his horse made it across the few streams entering the river without any trouble. Beyond a set of rapids he could see the top of a waterfall where clouds of spray from the falling water blew back up and over the rim. Surprisingly noisy. After a quick look he retraced his steps back to where a small natural dam had formed and the water stretched behind it in a miniature lake. Before tying his horse to a tree he retrieved the two halves of a long fishing pole and screwed them together, then dug up some juicy fat worms from the muddy side cliffs of the bank. Forty minutes later, just as his head started nodding from the peaceful environment and the warm sunshine, the rod nearly jerked out of his hands as some creature tried to rid itself of the murderous hook beneath the surface. It had to be a cod. He just hoped he could land it to use for dinner tonight.

His instincts said to respond vigorously, rather than play with the fish, especially as his line was short. Standing abruptly and whipping his rod backwards, he was surprised when a nice five-pound cod came flying out of the water towards him. It flopped on the bank and a quick strike with a rock made it eligible for dinner. Why not try for another, he thought, but after an hour had passed with no luck he decided he should be satisfied with what he already had. Backtracking to camp, he found the shadows of the nearby mountains already lengthening, even though there was plenty of daylight left. The western sun was down behind the nearby peaks, although the high sky overhead was still a soft, waning blue.

He removed the saddle and let his horse roam while he prepared the fish for cooking. Down by the stream he selected a number of rocks and made a circle out of them to contain a fire. As he walked upstream picking up dead branches he heard a familiar "coo-ee" as Eileen hailed him walking back in the opposite direction from her sojourn. She helped gather twigs and bark for kindling and recounted her adventures and halcyon episode by the pond. Thomas was amused by the details of her reverie, never having ever let himself relax to a similar level of contentment and bliss. Maybe even at this age he could learn something from his younger sister.

They sat by the fire watching the stars come out, and revelled in the tranquility of the evening. Once in a while one of them would break the silence with some remark about family, but neither was interested in detailed discussion. The only close-by noise was the mating calls of the frogs in the stream, some of which were so bellicose that they both burst out laughing. Eileen wondered out loud: "What female could ever be attracted to such a roar?" Ah, the mysteries of nature.

Based on somewhat vague directions picked up in Hartley, the next morning Thomas sought the route to Scott Brown's farm. He followed what was little more than a track roughly paralleling the meanderings of a rivulet, and eventually they came to the mill. A workman there directed them to the farmhouse, where Scott and his wife happily served the visitors morning tea. The ensuing discussion was inspirational for Thomas as Scott described some of his dreams and plans. As a well-off Presbyterian with philanthropic leanings, his current activities involved building a Presbyterian boarding school, to be named the Cooerwull Academy, a

Presbyterian church in Metheven, and a school house in Bowenfels. Unforeseen at the time by Thomas and Eileen, several Monahan grandchildren were to attend these institutions many years hence.

It was coal that was of paramount interest to Thomas. Scott showed him the tiny mine and explained how he felt there were major coal seams in the area and that he envisaged using the coal to eventually power his mill. It occurred to Thomas that commercial quantities of coal would dramatically change heating and power capabilities in the surrounding towns and villages, and that being an agent in Hartley for coal distribution could be a valuable business proposition. He vowed to keep in touch with Scott.

As they travelled further north and west they entered the lands of the Wiradjuri aborigines. The first few miles northward were through a verdant valley, where pastures with grazing animals were in evidence and in some cases large fields of vegetable crops showed lines of planting with expectations for the coming spring. Turning west towards the end of the valley, they travelled a little over a mile before coming to a signpost pointing northwest to Wallerawang, whereupon Thomas turned right and left the main road. In the Wiradjuri language Wallerawang meant 'place near wood and water', clearly referencing the hills to the north and a giant lake not far from the main road turn-off. The Wallerawang station was established by a James Walker in 1824, although Scott Brown of Cooerwull managed the property much of the time. The station had become a major rest point for travellers between Sydney and Bathurst, one guest in 1836 being the famous natural historian Charles Darwin, who stayed overnight at Wallerawang farm as a guest of Mr. Brown.

Instead of camping in the region, the siblings now headed in a south-west direction, skirting a major forest and hills to the east. Thomas pushed hard along the flat land, his intention being to reach sight of Evans Peak by day's end. Eileen started to feel a little sore from saddle burn, not being used to riding so much in a condensed timeframe. But, remembering her promises, she concentrated on enjoying the sunshine and the vistas that unfolded, and kept her complaints to herself. It definitely was a great relief, however, when Thomas finally called a halt not long after they first viewed the round rock formation on the summit of Evans Peak. A year after Blaxland, Wentworth, and Lawson had discovered a route across the Blue Mountains in 1813, Governor Macquarie sent 'Assistant-Surveyor' George William Evans to confirm and extend their discoveries. Coming eventually to the strange formation, Evans named it after himself, the accolade being approved and proclaimed by the Governor in 1815 as he passed by on his trip to Bathurst.

After checking the horses, feeding them, and brushing them down, the pair built a raging fire and ate cheese and bread and some dried beef well after darkness had fallen. The night was cold, consistent with the middle of winter, and both added an extra sweater when away from the warmth of the fire.

"Okay, Thomas, my bottom is saddle sore, as that tender part hasn't done as much riding as yours. Do you have an extra blanket I could put on the saddle tomorrow morning to help?" Eileen tried to sound as matter-of-fact as possible so she wouldn't be perceived as complaining, but Thomas had already noticed that she didn't sit by the fire for long before getting up and crouching on her haunches. "That's not the best solution, sis, as the blanket would only cause you to slip and slide, making you less stable and adding to your discomfort. If only you women would wear pants. The secret is to wear something under your dress and add padding tight around your bottom. I don't suppose you brought anything that would work."

"No, I never thought about it in advance. Silly me. I could add extra petticoats, I guess, but they will only puff out my dress and make it harder to get on and off. Plus I'd look like a china doll in a box all wrapped up ready to be given as a gift to someone. And as it happens I only brought one extra anyway and I'd better save that in case something happens to the one I'm wearing. Do you have any brilliant ideas?"

"Sure," Thomas responded with a laugh in his voice, but a little irritated internally. "You could always walk, or sit backwards, or ride bareback, but I suspect none of those options really appeals. It's a pity you are in mixed company. We men would just peel everything off and walk, letting nature's sunshine and a good smathering of Beaufort's liniment work its magic. And well, maybe an ale or two as well."

"I promised not to complain and I'm ready to ride some more, but by the end of tomorrow I think I might have to stop for a day if we can't think of a remedy. Two days out and it's been wonderful so far. Travelling around like this has been both educational and enjoyable. I'd like the joy part to stay with me."

"Well, I actually can think of one thing. It's a bit strange but may work if you're willing to experiment a little. In one of my packs I have a set of tools wrapped up in an old supple kangaroo skin. I think it's of a size that you might be able to wrap it around your bottom and private parts and add some padding that way. The question would be how to tie it on and keep it in place. We could see if it would work in the morning light if you'd like to try it."

"Sounds a bit odd but I don't think I have much choice. Is the skin clean inside? Maybe I could wash it in the creek yonder if it's been wrapped around dirty tools. Also, I have some straight pins that if I put them in the right place may work. Do you have any leather thongs I could try perhaps?"

"Not that would be long enough, I'm afraid. No wait. I have some dried sheep gut holding other bundles in place. I could possible tie three together and form something workable. This would be a real first, sis. We'll just have to see what the morning brings. But washing and drying the skin will just make it harden, so I don't think that's a good idea. It really should only be dirty at one end close to the tools because otherwise it is skin wrapped around itself. "

"You are so smart, brother. But if I could get that 'roo skin now I could check it over and see if it might work. Please, dear brother, please? And if you can also find those sinews now so I can work on them I'd be ever so grateful."

Reluctantly, Thomas got up from the fire and searched his saddlebags, finding the large tool bundle after pulling out many smaller ones. He wondered if the whole trip would be like this, catering to his sister's special wants, despite her earnest and sincere promises of not needing extra attention. Please Lord, he thought, let this be the last.

The crisp morning air woke them both early. Thomas built a fire and made tea and dampers and they cut an apple into pieces and shared it. Eileen was anxious to try out her new 'costume'. She retreated to the tent and after five minutes called Thomas to come look. "I'm showing you just because you had the idea and you are family. It works like a dream. See, the 'roo skin is big enough to completely cover my backside and muff and provides sufficient overlap that I can pin it easily. I've cut a number of slits in the skin and threaded the sinews through and tied them in front so I have a safety net as well to keep it on. I know it won't interfere with putting on my underskirt and dress."

She then laughed. "I doubt this will ever become a new fashion, brother, but you just may have invented a new bush underwear garment for us country women. Well done. As I said last night, you are so smart. The next test is to see how it holds up in the saddle and whether it does as you suggested, keep my delicate bottom from getting any sorer. By the way, it does feel much better this morning after a good rest. Let me finish getting dressed and walk around a bit to see how it works."

Turning westward before reaching the base of Evans Peak, they rode only a few miles before reaching the bridge over the Fish River. They let the three horses graze and walked a few hundred yards along the bank until Thomas found a spot below some rapids where he thought he might try fishing again. Anticipating Eileen's interest, he had brought two rods along and helped bait her hook with freshly dug worms and they sat side by side enjoying the stillness interrupted only by the soft sound of the river running over the rocks in the rapids. Eileen's rod quivered first and Thomas proudly helped her land a ten-pound cod. True to its name, not ten minutes later the river yielded another cod, to Thomas, perhaps a pound lighter than his sister's. He expected her to crow about her prowess but she didn't, being thankful for her new outfit he had created for her. They stayed and caught four more good-sized fish before lighting a fire and cooking one for an early lunch.

Eileen was ecstatic over her new 'protection'. There were few good-sized trees around to provide any privacy, so she stepped into the water up to her knees under the bridge and adjusted and tightened the sinew thong slightly and removed the straight pins she had used, sensing they weren't adding any real value. She emerged all smiles, and complimented Thomas again on his ingenuity. She added, "Of course, you realise you will never get this 'roo skin back, don't you? I'll have to show other family members at some point, and come to think of it, given where it's been you may not want it back anyway. I think you might want to shoot the next kangaroo we see in order to replace it."

"I'm one step ahead of you, sister. Here, follow the direction of my arm and you will see several mounds in a field about half a mile away. I'll warrant those are 'roos resting. Thought I might take my rifle and see if I can bag one—we have fish to eat tonight and tomorrow and I don't really like the gamey kangaroo meat, but replacing the hide would be worthwhile. I hope there's an old male in the group as I hate shooting young females in case they have a joey in their pouch. I'll be back shortly."

The 'roos saw him coming, and while several stood up to check, they offered no signs of fleeing their spot. They seemed to be Western Greys, a common variety in the area. About one hundred yards away the animals became restless and more stood up. Thomas counted twenty, far more than he expected, but he now saw that the ground undulated more than he had anticipated and most of the group had been lying down in a swale of short grass. He stopped and crouched on one knee, unslinging the gun from behind his back. He picked out what he thought was a large male which was sniffing the air and lined up a head shot. The crack of the rifle made the rest of the group rise and look around nervously. Thomas' quarry dropped instantly and as he rose and started walking forward the group moved off as one, not with urgent strides, but in a very deliberate gait, heading for another resting area. He paused to watch their graceful movements—the heavy tail helping give them lift to their jumps forward. As always, he was amazed by the distance even a small 'roo could cover in one bound. He held a certain reverence for the strange creatures but they ate up good grazing grass and he was not averse to killing one now and then.

Thankfully, he had indeed chosen a large male, which he skinned quickly, bringing the hide back to the river for scraping and further cleansing. He spread it fur down on the packhorse's back to help it dry out.

The pair mounted up and headed west. The valley offered excellent pasture land with the timber line high on the rolling hills on the flanks. The floor of the valley was flat, creating no strain for the horses. Eileen was the first to see a dust cloud in the distance approaching from the opposite direction. "I hope that's not bushrangers, Thomas."

"Unlikely, sis. The country is too open here. They're more apt to operate in forested areas where they can disappear back to their hideout more readily and where it's difficult to follow. That's a pretty good-sized dust swirl and moving fairly fast. Could be horses pulling an empty or possibly light dray back to Penrith, or the mail coach. Bullocks pulling a load would be going much slower and not kicking up so much dust."

They pulled off to the side of the road and waited. Eventually they sensed the oncoming riders slowing down, and finally identified them as a group of four soldiers with varying states of uniforms clinging to them. They were all sweating even though the day was far from hot, indicating they'd been riding hard. The leader stopped alongside and asked, "Where are you two off to, pray tell? Bathurst, perhaps?"

"Yes sir," Thomas responded. "We're going to see what it offers newcomers these days." Which was certainly true enough, although he had no intention of giving them complete information. For all he knew these were convicts in stolen uniforms, so best to be careful. "You sure are travelling light with only that packhorse," the leader said. "We've just booked some cattle thieves into the prison in Bathurst and are out looking for some of their accomplices. By any chance have you noticed any strange activity involving cattle in your trip so far?"

"Can't say as we have, sir. Sorry. Glad to hear you are out catching up with the rustlers. They deserve everything they get in terms of punishment. We've seen nothing in this valley or the one northeast of Evans Peak. Don't think you'll find any cattle there."

"Well, thanks for letting us know. We actually think they are hanging out more to the south anyway and once we reach Evans Peak we'll turn off that way. Much obliged to you. Hope the rest of your trip goes smoothly. You've probably got another thirty miles or so to go yet." Tipping his hat to Eileen, he muttered, "Nice to meet you, ma'am. Safe journey both." He whipped his reins and the four horses moved off smartly. Definitely not convicts, thought Thomas. No convict would tip his hat to a lady.

"Why do men steal?" Eileen asked. "Guess I'll never really understand."

"Me either, sis. Obviously they weren't brought up with the same morals and standards we were. Even though we were dreadfully poor, temptation wasn't there. Not that there'd have been much to steal anyway. I guess they are just lazy men taking an easy way out to try and earn a few shillings. Very unfortunate."

They rode on along the valley, remarking the existence of a dark tree line a couple of miles distant that indicated the river meandered somewhat in the same direction. Comforting to know that water was not that far away if really needed. Gently rising ground and local plains tended to be the norm now as they continued westward, and Eileen started to experience a sense of boredom. At the end of the day they turned the horses northward and marched to the bank of the Fish again, where they made camp. Eileen searched for branches, bark, and small twigs, relishing having activities to perform, no longer just sitting in the saddle. Two fat ducks coming downstream were quickly shotgun dispatched by Thomas, and one of them helped provide a very fulfilling dinner along with one of the fish caught earlier. Eileen removed her new under garment feeling much better than the previous day. It had worked beautifully!

After feeding the horses and brushing them down, they sat by the fire and recounted the conversation and exchange with the militia. "Now that we've re-joined the main road I expect we'll meet more travellers tomorrow," Thomas said. "The mail coach should definitely come through if it's on its regular schedule, as it is due in Hartley at the end of the day. And I expect wagons bringing goods from Penrith and Sydney to be going our way. They'll be slower than us, but if they've travelled through the night we may catch up to some in the morning. We may even hear them if the frogs don't drown us out with their choruses.

"But tell me, sis, how are you feeling about the journey so far?" he asked. "You seem to be having a good time but are you really glad you came or are you having second thoughts?"

"That should be obvious. Are my smiles not enough? I love being out in the wilds and I'm very satisfied being with you."

"Only satisfied? I thought I deserved more than that. After all, I don't create underwear for just any woman I know. And other than yesterday I haven't pushed you too hard. I will say you look great—the brisk air suits you, especially when it brings out the colour in your cheeks. I don't know why some man hasn't snatched you up long before this. If he could see how the sunlight makes your hair sparkle after you wash it and how pretty your face is when you smile, you'd have men falling over themselves to be with you."

"Well, you certainly are full of compliments tonight and I thank you for them. You are more observant and more poetic than I ever knew. How is it, dear brother, that we grew up so close physically for so many years yet we still have new things to learn about each other?"

"For me, sis, it's wonderful to have a female I feel I can talk to. At home I am always working with Patrick and we talk about the same things every day. In many cases I'm sure we could end each other's sentences. I don't think we males are as interested in some of the softer topics of life as you females may be, or perhaps it's fairer to say we feel it is unmanly to talk about them. Don't get me wrong. I love my twin brother and I know we'd do anything to help each other, but it's so good to have sisters too."

Thomas paused and then said, "One question I've been dying to ask you confidentially is what do you really think about Mary Jane having a child before being married? We all supported her and I have no trouble with that. For I still love her dearly. And sex is such a delicate topic. But her action begs the question. Did she get pregnant from a one-time stand or was she playing around before, perhaps even before John Evans? Patrick and I were pretty shocked when we first heard about her condition. And I think Mother and Father were as well, as much as they tried to not show it. It seemed so contrary to the family values we'd all been raised with. I know in some sense the answer to my question doesn't really matter but it makes me wonder if I ever really knew Mary Jane or if deep down she was, and still is, someone different than who I thought she was. I mean will she stay with Andrew, or end up with someone else? Is she basically fickle and insincere, or did she make an honest mistake?"

"This is hard, Thomas. I have extra information but I don't want to betray Mary Jane's trust. I can understand your and Patrick's questions and concerns, so I'll tell you what I can. First, though, let me test your level of trust and sharing. On board the boat coming to Sydney towards the end of the journey Patrick got very friendly with a girl named Meghan. In schoolgirl parlance we would have characterised her as a girl with 'a bit of a reputation'. Do you know what I mean by that term?"

"I think so. She was forward with the boys, kissing them, letting them touch her breasts, maybe elsewhere. Overly flirty. Teasing."

"You got it, especially the early parts. Grace and I—based on nothing more than our intuition—both think she and Patrick had a fling and that there was sexual activity going on. Can you confirm or deny that without compromising your relationship with him?"

"At the time Patrick was pretty unsure of himself, but today I think he'd admit to the liaison directly were you to ask him. He wouldn't discuss any details but I don't think he'd shy away from the question at all. In his words as recounted to me, it was a new experience, full of new revelations and sensations. He wondered if I'd had any similar experience along the way. The answer to that is no."

"Thanks for sharing that. In reciprocal fashion I can tell you that when Mary Jane was Molly at Regentville she too had some sexual experiences. Her roommate, Daisy, was also a girl with an emerging 'reputation' and she helped educate Molly with co-operation from a stable hand. For whatever reason Molly wasn't able to limit things until we moved away. The fervour, interest, and desire never really disappeared and the accessibility to John Evans was too hard to resist.

"I guess we're all made a little differently and that's how I think about it. I've stopped trying to relate it to family and Christian values because I can't see an explanation. In a sense Mary strayed. She knows it but she accepts it as something in the past, and life is here to get on with. I have incredible respect for Andrew, who treats baby Jane as his own. I don't know if I could do something like that in an analogous situation."

"Yep, Andrew is a keeper. Both Patrick and I like him. Like you, we both give him a lot of credit."

"Maybe I'll find someone as loving and considerate as Andrew, although a part of me seeks adventure, as evidenced by coming on this trip. Who knows who I'll end up with. Same applies to you too, for that matter. Guess we'll both stay virgins until the time is right."

"Nothing wrong with that. Good to chat, sis. And actually over the last six months I've come to think there is a bit of wanderlust in you. Maybe you'll meet an adventuresome type in Bathurst. There should be plenty there. We'll see. Time now for some sleep."

Anticipating a straightforward ride of about a dozen miles to Campbell River, Thomas was in no rush to get away next morning. They had camped in a small forest watered by the river and Thomas was anxious to try out something he'd seen once before. He and Eileen waded through a shallow area and walked on about a hundred yards among the thin grove of eucalyptus trees. Thomas pulled a large square of bleached linen from his pants pocket. Motioning Eileen to be quiet he waved the white cloth slowly back and forth high above his head.

A soft gasp from Eileen made him turn towards her as she pointed off to her left. There, as anticipated, two curious emus were slowly walking forward. Turning back, he found four more coming from different directions. Eileen had seen emus before but not as close as these had ventured before stopping. They were strange birds in that they couldn't fly but could run very fast, and even swim. They had large clawed feet on incredibly strong legs which had been seen to rip metal wire fences. They fed on plants and insects and could go without water, like camels, for long periods. They'd also been observed ingesting stones, glass shards, and bits of metal, presumably to grind food in their system. They were wary of man and their only natural predators were dingos and eagles. Thomas had once inadvertently come across a nest where baby chicks had recently hatched, guarded by a vicious parent which poked at him while making loud noises in his throat, but standing his ground by the babies.

Their curiosity revealing nothing to eat, the six emus silently retreated whence they had come, leaving Eileen and Thomas both smiling at the unusual event. Thomas offered his flag to Eileen, saying, "Here, amaze your friends sometime."

"How did you know they were here?" she asked.

"I didn't," he replied. "That was a bit of luck. I thought I heard one of their sounds during the night but wasn't sure. I'm surprised to find them so close to water. They must have recently sought it out after roaming the plains."

"Well, that certainly was a bit of fun. Do you have more surprises for me up your sleeve?"

"I'll never tell... Let's get going down the road."

As Thomas had predicted, in the three hours it took them to reach the Campbell River, they encountered two heavily loaded bullock-driven wagons hauling supplies to Bathurst, and the mail coach going in the opposite direction. The coach didn't stop, but they rode alongside the supply wagons for a while briefly chatting with the drivers and helpers. One load was the extensive household furnishings of a bank manager's family which was moving to Bathurst, and the other carried a large variety of barrels, boxes, crates, baskets, tables, chairs, and tools, which by their nature were clearly destined for a store offering both hardware and general goods. Conversations with the drivers didn't reveal any information more recent or newsworthy than what Thomas and Eileen had picked up in Hartley a few days earlier. The loads were compelling evidence of the growth of Bathurst and added to Eileen's excitement to view the town ahead. The bullock teams stirred up an amazing amount of dust, which also helped limit the verbal exchanges. Thomas wondered how the men could put up with the conditions for such extended journeys.

Crossing the bridge over the river, Thomas followed the western bank for about half a mile south until he found a suitable spot to camp. A number of trees provided shade from the unusual warmth of the day, and of particular value was a small backwater lagoon that joined the main river through a narrow channel. Grass was abundant and the three horses relished fresh feed and water. It hadn't been a strenuous ride at all, rather a dusty and hot one, and horses and humans alike appreciated the restful shade of the willows and eucalypts. Thomas planned to go hunting further south but decided that swimming and bathing in the lagoon first would provide welcome relief from the dust and heat.

On letting Eileen know his intentions she smiled and said, "That sounds so good. Maybe I'll do the same. Can I come and watch you, and make sure there are no big fish or platypuses in there?"

"Up to you, sis. I'm not bashful, just dirty at the moment, and that water looks very inviting. See you at the pond." With that he grabbed a bar of home-made soap from a saddle bag, stripped off pants, shirts, and shoes, ran to the pond, and jumped in with a huge splash. He found the water was shallow enough to stand near the edges, and he enjoyed soaping his hair and body and rinsing off repeatedly. He yelled to Eileen, "Could you please bring my britches and shirt so I can wash them too?"

She complied, throwing him his clothes, and thought, you do indeed make a pretty fine specimen, dear brother, with an attractive build—everywhere. The clear water and dappled sunshine concealed nothing. "Stand back—I'm coming in too." Clothes were dumped on the bank within reach and with a hearty laugh she launched herself into the cold water. "Ooh, you didn't tell me how cold this was. Throw me the soap please."

Thomas climbed out, threw Eileen's clothes to her, and walked along the bank to a spot where the sun shone through the branches, where he stood feeling the warmth soak in. Eileen was a bit surprised he didn't turn to check out the view she was providing. Surely he wasn't embarrassed to see a girl's body after all those years of their close family living environment.

But no, guess he had no need to ogle his sister. In one passing glance he'd realised how attractive her body was but he didn't need to stare. He just hoped that she'd only expose her pert breasts and blonde patch to the right man, unlike their younger sister's behaviour.

As he warmed up he yelled, "Now, do you want to come hunting with me? Try a rifle shot at a kangaroo maybe, or a possum in a tree? I'm heading back to camp to hang up my wet clothes and get into clean ones."

Both felt better after bathing and changing clothes and they elected to walk south with a rifle each. Half a mile upstream, Thomas stopped and pointed to a tree twenty-five yards ahead. Eileen couldn't identify what he was pointing at so he whispered, "Goanna, second main fork, twenty feet up." She still couldn't see the animal until it moved its head slightly around the trunk. "We can get five yards closer probably," Thomas indicated. "Any further and he'll climb higher and be harder to see. Would be good target practice if you want to have a shot. Wait til he presents more of his body before shooting. Aim for the belly as the head is too small."

Tree-climbing goannas, or lace monitors, were far different from the common small garden lizards. They could weigh nearly ten pounds, and grow to six feet or more. With a diet of small animals they could be fierce predators. Aborigines enjoyed their meat after roasting, but most white folk wouldn't touch it.

Eileen had learned to shoot years earlier but hadn't held a rifle for some time. She raised the barrel, patiently waiting until finally the reptile changed position and exposed more of his underneath. Her arms and hands stayed steady although she was feeling tired from holding them up.

As she'd been taught, she held her breath as she sighted, and gently squeezed the trigger. The loudness of the shot surprised her but she was gratified to see the reptile fall from its position. "Good shot," Thomas cried. "I sure would have been upset if you'd missed from that distance, but you got him. Unfortunately, you can't gloat over your kill because he fell directly into that first fork and he's stuck there. The crows and hawks will be here shortly, no doubt. You'll have to admire him from the ground, I'm afraid. You were very steady. I'm impressed."

With a swagger to her walk, Eileen followed Thomas further along the bank of the river. She smiled as a kookaburra sang its laughing song, feeling quite proud of herself. She realised she really was enjoying this trip with her brother. They had talked more than would ever have been the case at home, through which she'd come to appreciate the man much more, and she'd found the wilderness exciting. She'd shown restraint and flexibility in adapting to his leadership and interests, and not objecting to any of his pursuits. They'd been fortunate with the weather. Perhaps it wouldn't have been as much fun had it rained a lot, but no matter what, she'd do this again anytime.

The trees thinned out and in a meadow beyond the forest edge a group of small wallabies was also managing the day's warmth resting under a lone tree. At the same time as they were sighted, two ducks came into view on the river, paddling downstream. "You have a choice," Thomas whispered. "Duck for dinner, or a wallaby skin for whatever purpose you think of."

"Which should I take?"

"Well, we really have enough food for supper and a shotgun would be better for duck shooting. Plus, you made a great short-range shot earlier, how about practising something a little more challenging? Those wallabies are at least one hundred yards away and offer relatively small targets. But you could use the trunk of this tree to prop the rifle against, and that would help. Want to try?"

"Sure, why not?"

"Good for you. Do you see to the right, an extra fifty yards back, a second group? I'm going to try a shot at one of those. There's no breeze at the moment but with the distance you are shooting your bullet is going to lose some height as it flies, so remember to aim a bit higher than the target area on the animal you select. I will wait until after you've shot, for I'm hoping when the group scatters that my group also gets the message and moves off so I can practise a moving target shot. I'm going to shoot from a ground position so I won't be in the way of your tree-propped shot. Okay?"

How could she argue with that? She felt confident enough to also try a moving target shot, and maybe there'd be a chance later, but realised she needed to prove myself with the long-distance still kill first.

"Let's do it," she whispered back.

The crack of her shot reverberated in the bush behind them, but Thomas saw no animal fall, and a small swear word escaping his sister's lips confirmed his suspicion that she'd missed. The animals moved away a short distance in seemingly desultory fashion, but the second group where he was focused stayed still. Maybe her bullet had just made a hissing sound as it passed them by, the lack of impact not sufficient to make them flee in panic.

"That's too bad. What happened?"

"I think I just wasn't steady enough and jerked rather than squeezed the trigger, sending my shot a tad off course. Darn."

"Well, why don't you try again? They are not that much further away. Do you see the two on the left flank looking like they are staring at us? I'd go for one of them. Tell me which one you select and I'll watch the other one, which is sure to take off after you drop yours."

"I'm setting up on the slightly taller one on the left. Get ready."

Thomas watched as the animal dropped dead to the ground, and focussed on the fleeing mate. He swivelled to lead its flight path by a small margin and squeezed off his shot. Right on. Another kill.

"Wow, he was moving fast, Thomas. That was a great shot. Well done. Let's go see our trophies."

"Glad you got yours. Went straight down. Want to guess exactly where you got him? What did you aim for?"

"I targeted the base of the throat hoping to get a chest shot. What about you?"

"I just aimed for the middle of the body. About all one can do when they are leaping away like that."

With two skins in hand, they meandered back to their campsite, washed the skins, and hung them over two low branches to dry overnight. Full of renewed energy, Eileen led the efforts in collecting material for a fire and in preparing the evening meal.

Satiated after a tasty meal and with the inevitable frog chorus starting up she asked, "Do you and Patrick talk about getting married and raising families, or is that not on the list of personal aspirations and desires?"

"We differ there. Patrick doesn't seem that interested in creating a family. He looks at what Mother and Father went through in raising the first six of us and their continued commitments to Connor and David. He feels that caring for children limits too much what one might want to do in life. As much as he's thankful he was born and is alive he doesn't feel any compulsion to bring others into the world. You've probably noticed how he has less interest in relating to his two young brothers than do the rest of us . Too big an age gap for him to reach across.

"I think," he said, "that it won't be long before he will leave us on a major journey to see other parts of this country. It's possible he could be gone for as much as a year. He absolutely loves this adopted land and is happy managing stock at the moment. But he often says there's more to life than stock keeping. As much as our sea voyage was somewhat traumatic he says he'd like to go sailing again. Maybe he'll visit Van Diemen's Land—it seems to have some fascination for him. Don't be surprised if the stories we tell back home of our journey hasten his interest to explore."

"Maybe he dreams of finding another Meghan?"

"Don't be so cynical, sis. Surely you remember his delight in learning how the sailors measured our speed through the water, and how he wished he could ask the captain about the sextant used to calculate latitude and longitude? Also, he was the one who climbed the rigging to see the whale towed by the whaling ships. He climbed up without thinking about it—it just came naturally to him."

"Okay, you're right. Sorry. What about you though? Do you feel similarly about children?"

"Nope. That's one of our big differences. I understand his feelings, but I want to have children who will grow up and live a full life in this land. I believe it won't be long before convict transportation to all the states here will cease and the country will grow under the ingenuity of free settlers. There will be opportunity in forms we can only imagine today. For example, when the railways eventually reach out across the country massive population shifts will occur and various new types of industry will arise as the flow of goods from inland are able to reach the ports more easily. Look at what the railways are doing for England. I predict something similar will occur here."

"I'm impressed with your thinking, Thomas. Very profound, and it's hard to argue with your ideas. Perhaps the harder question is do you have any desire to get married soon so you can start bringing those little ones along?"

"Marriage will happen when I meet the right woman who has similar interests. There's time yet but it has crossed my mind to keep my eyes open. I probably need to get into Hartley and other towns more often to help myself in that regard."

"Yes, I don't think women are going to come wandering in the farm gates looking for a potential husband."

"Come on, sis. There's that cynicism again. I'm not naïve, you know, and I don't expect to be chased. As I said, when the time is right I'll know it."

"Guess I just want you to be happy, brother. And to see those children sooner rather than later. I'm glad you want to help me with my aunt status."

The coals in the fire were almost totally burned out when Thomas suddenly jumped up and started walking around the area sniffing the air. "There's another campfire in the vicinity," he said. "Probably aborigines. I can't tell exactly where it is. Maybe we'll see it in the morning."

Somewhat alarmed, Eileen asked, "Do we need to be wary, Thomas? Do you feel safe? Should we keep the guns by our sides tonight?"

"I don't think we need to worry. This is their country. I'm sure they already know we're camped here. They would have come looking for food or some other handout by now if they needed it. I'm sure we'll be fine. Hopefully the horses will let us know if anyone approaches." With an unseen smile on his face he added, "They probably got their thrills earlier this afternoon spying on your white body taking a bath in the lagoon."

"Oh, you miserable man, even suggesting that. I see you laughing to yourself. I hope you are enjoying your little effort at making me feel awkward. Ha, I will get even at some point later, just you wait."

Rather than turn down the road the next morning Thomas elected to follow the course of the Campbell River as it flowed north. Not far past the road bridge they spotted an aborigine family walking in the same direction on the opposite bank. They marvelled at how these people could travel the land with no shoes and little clothing. Their nomadic life seemed so purposeless in a way, and beyond easy justification.

"Those are most likely the ones whose fire I smelled last night. One child walking and see, the woman is also carrying a little baby on her back. The mother is probably quite young. No harm coming from that group."

They waved but got no response so continued on their route. Sometimes they would be in the tree line bordering the river, sometimes in the meadows further out. The terrain was similar to what they'd come through previously but the birds seemed more active along the river bank. They spotted ducks and black swans on the water and brightly coloured kingfishers that swooped down for their small fish prey. Clearly there was an abundance of food for the gathering, but Thomas wanted to make sure they reached Bathurst by day's end as he had promised Liz a hotel room as a change from outdoor sleeping. He was smart enough to recognize that she would relish the comfort of a real bed where one was available.

An hour later they came upon the confluence of the Campbell with the Fish flowing in from the east. The waters combined smoothly and of course the volume they now walked beside increased dramatically. George Evans had named the river in 1814 after the then governor of the colony, Lieutenant-Colonel Lachlan

Macquarie. It was on its eastern bank, downstream a few miles, that the town of Bathurst was founded and now awaited them.

As hunger pangs signalled lunchtime was nigh the pair emerged from the final grove of trees and saw the buildings of Bathurst ahead. They re-joined the road and happily trotted across the bridge into the centre of town.

Tying the horses to the hitching rails in front of the Angel Inn, they walked inside the pub and ordered two large pints of ale. Their presence as 'husband and wife' newcomers was immediately assumed by the existing throng of patrons and the silent smiles of welcome made Eileen feel good and wonder positively about what adventures might be in store ahead.

18. An Irish diversion.
Bathurst

At the same time as Blaxland, Wentworth, and Lawson were finding a route across the Blue Mountains, back in Cork, Ireland, in one of the many inner-city slums, a baby boy named Jeremiah Slane was born. His mother wasn't sure who the father was but a gentleman named Slane was one of the ones she had fancied most in the previous year. The boy was small but had a strong voice and a belligerent character even as an infant. By age ten, he had learned how to live off the streets, with instinctive fighting skills, a beguiling smile, and a natural predisposition for 'wielding the blarney'. He could keep a straight face through the most innovative lies and exaggerations, and was able to fool many upright citizens and judges with his disarming personality, skirting the law repeatedly. It was a tough, stressful life that enveloped Jeremiah but he was born with an innate will to survive.

Cork had a history dating back to the sixth century. The ancestor of the modern city was founded between 915 and 922 when Viking settlers established a trading community. Over the centuries, much of the city was rebuilt, time and again, after numerous fires ravaged the setting. At one time the city was fully walled, several sections and gates surviving the years. The medieval population was about 2000 people, but the city suffered a severe setback in 1349 as almost half the townspeople died of bubonic plague when the Black Death arrived. In 1491 the city played a part in the English War of Roses, but by 1577 one description of the city concluded it was "so encumbered with evil neighbours, the Irish outlaws, that they are fayne to watch their gates hourly...they trust not the country adjoining [and only marry within the town] so that the whole city is linked to each other in affinity."

Between 1540 and 1690 different religious wars engulfed the city with Protestants and Catholics alternating control and influence. In the late 17th and early 18th centuries French Protestants arrived, fleeing from religious persecution at the hands of Louis XIV of France. Their influence remains today in the names of buildings and families in the Huguenot Quarter and French Church Street. Many new buildings were erected in Cork in the 18th century. Parliament Bridge was built in 1806 and a new Custom House in 1818. Cork County Gaol was built in 1825. St Mary's and St Anne's Cathedral was built in 1808 but it burned down in 1820 and had to be rebuilt. Trade in the port expanded considerably with merchants exporting large amounts of butter and beef to Britain, the rest of Europe, and North America.

The ending of the Napoleonic Wars after 1815, however, reversed economic progress. Prices for agricultural produce declined by one-third to one-half of the wartime prices. Cork Harbour no longer regularly hosted fleets of the Royal Navy and this caused a major decrease in trade. The return of the currency to the gold standard led to a contraction of credit and the subsequent collapse of many banks. After 1824, Irish industry was exposed to competition from the far more developed British economy.

The combined impact of these developments was catastrophic for the textile industry and the provisions trade. Unemployment in Cork rose to very high levels. Remarkably, the population of the city stayed stable due to the massive influx to the city of migrants from the economically depressed rural areas. But the high levels of unemployment served to depress wages and contributed to the poor living conditions in the densely populated inner city.

To Jeremiah, history meant nothing. Hunger, a lack of education, an almost non-existent and certainly non-caring mother scrounging for her own existence through prostitution led him to crime, and by the age of fourteen he was well known to the city constabulary. Stealing was his specialty and his gilded tongue made confessions to priests and sergeants a game. But his native smarts and small size had made him realise that survival was easier with a job, and he was lucky enough to be taken on as a carpenter and joiner's apprentice in a distillery owned by a patron of the establishment where his mother had a room. He joined a local gang, tattooing his loyalty in indelible initials on the inside of his left arm. Fights left him with scars on an eyelid, in the center of his forehead, and on the little finger of his right hand. He never learned to write and would have had trouble in any event unless selecting to be left-handed, something not encouraged in the times. He was wiry, tough, indefatigable, and fearless, with an enigmatic grin that made adversaries underestimate what they were up against.

He was unreliable as a worker, for his concentration level was limited. The authorities finally caught him for the fifth time and charged him with theft and vagrancy. At his trial on April 7th 1828 he was sentenced to gaol for seven years, but was quickly transferred to the list for transportation to Australia.

The aging barque *Governor Ready* was chartered by the Commissioners of the Navy for transportation purposes shortly after her arrival from Van Diemen's Land early in 1828. A detachment of the 63rd Regiment of Infantry embarked at Gravesend on Tuesday 12th August and five days later she sailed from Deptford, arriving at the Cove of Cork on the 27th. A part of this bay, which is about three quarters of a mile wide, forms one of the most beautiful harbours in the world. Both shores consist of high hills, at the time covered with palaces, villas, country-seats, parks, and gardens. On either side, rising in unequal height, they formed a rich and varied enclosure. By degrees the city proper advanced into the middle of the picture, terminating on the brow of the highest hill with the imposing mass of the barracks which looked like a fortress.

No one visited Jeremiah on his sixteenth birthday in the city gaol, and no one came to the wharves to wave goodbye when, on September 18, he was marched on board the *Governor Ready* along with two hundred other male prisoners, destined for Sydney town. The prettiness of the city cum harbour setting was totally lost on the incarcerated convicts.

After minor repairs and provisioning, the vessel left with the morning tide on the 21st September 1828, captained by Master John Young, with Thomas Braidwood Wilson as surgeon. There were five free-settler passengers on board but the convicts were a motley lot, coming from Cork and other counties including Tipperary, Waterford, Kilkenny, and Limerick. Most of them were being transported for various forms of theft. However, there were seven like Jeremiah who were deported for vagrancy, three for rape, five for manslaughter, at least seven for murder, and five soldiers convicted of desertion.

Amazingly, and totally at odds with voyages by other convict ships, the *Governor Ready* arrived at Sydney on 17th January 1829 after an almost pleasant passage during which there was no disharmony among the prisoners, who were unusually accepting of their lot and fate. The prisoners were mustered on January 20th and were landed six days later on the 26th January—auspiciously the anniversary of the founding of the colony. By the time the twenty-four pounders were discharged at Dawes Battery to celebrate the occasion, the prisoners were all ensconced in the Hyde Park Barracks.

While this particular trip was trouble-free, circumstances on the high seas could be totally unpredictable. Contrary to the trip out to Sydney the return trip had alarming consequences. The *Governor Ready* effected some minor repairs, re-constituted the decks for non-human cargo, and left Sydney two months later on the 18th March, heading initially to Hobart Town. The plan was then to proceed to Mauritius and pick up a cargo of sugar to take to London. However, on the eve of the Sydney departure, Captain Young received intelligence indicating the failure of the sugar crops in the Isle of France. At Hobart, instructions were received to pick up spices instead, from Batavia in the East Indies.

And so on April 2nd the ship departed to the south, anticipating turning west in order to pursue a route north along the west coast of Australia. The voyage started out badly with massive storms, contrary winds, and turbulent seas that held progress almost stationary for two weeks. Captain Young switched intentions and proceeded to make excellent progress up the east coast and into

Torres Strait. But on the 18th of May the ship struck a coral reef which immediately penetrated the hull way beyond repair.

The thirty-nine crew and cabin passengers abandoned ship and in three longboats set as their destination Melville Island, north of the Australian coast in the Timor Sea. This was the only inhabited place in the vicinity that the captain was aware of, albeit several hundred miles distant. The weather and seas were favourable until just before reaching Melville, when they were driven past in a violent gale and forced to head for Timor. Providence smiled and they arrived on June 4th having covered well over 500 miles in the small boats. Sea voyages were definitely not for the faint of heart in those days.

Back in Sydney, with his natural bravado and blarney, Jeremiah Slane quickly convinced the local military authorities at the Barracks that his carpentry skills and experience were top-notch even though he was young. As a consequence he was assigned to Mr. Michael Mitchell at Lower Portland Head to work as a ship builder. Lower Portland Head provided specialized outposts for the main shipbuilding efforts in the Windsor/Pitt Town area, 15 miles upstream.

Michael Mitchell had arrived as coxswain in 1820 on the female convict ship *Lord Wellington.* He found a position as ship's carpenter with John Grono of Windsor. The men became friends and Michael travelled with Captain Grono, going seal hunting off New Zealand in 1823 on the Grono-built ship *Elizabeth*. Later, in 1827, Michael married John's twice widowed daughter, Jane Grono, and became a family member. They had six children in the years to come, Jane having delivered two previously by her first husband.

John Grono was one of Australia's early 'characters' whose shipbuilding and sailing efforts contributed to the history and culture of the country. He arrived in the colony in May 1799 from Wales as boatswain's mate on board the HMS *Buffalo*, along with his wife Elisabeth and three children. In 1801 he took up land in conjunction with James Ryan on the Hawkesbury River, north of Sydney, where they grew wheat. But by 1803 he was in the shipbuilding business. His first ship, the *Speedwell,* ran aground only eight months after being launched, and the consequent financial strife led him to undertake seafaring voyages, hunting seals in the waters off the southern end of New Zealand. He was very successful over the subsequent years, bringing back 6,000 skins in 1810 and ending up as captain of the *Governor Bligh* in 1811. Numerous explorations in New Zealand led him to name Milford Sound, Elizabeth Island, and Grono Bay on Secretary Island. His last trip in 1813 netted a cargo of 14,000 seal pelts and three stranded sealers whom he rescued from Secretary Island.

After retiring from his New Zealand maritime adventures, Grono set to expanding his shipbuilding and farming enterprises. His life had many ups and downs, however. Before the financial crisis that set him to seal hunting, his family suffered a horrible incident at the hands of a bushranger named Patrick Wright, who violently assaulted one of his children. Wright was sentenced to three years hard labour for the Crown, during the whole period of which he was exposed in the stocks for a period of two hours every Saturday. Further, he was denied "every hope of commiseration, and lived as the object of reproach and scorn."

Jeremiah Slane arrived in the Windsor area just in time to witness the launch of perhaps John Grono's most famous ship, the *Australian*. The launch of this locally built ship was avidly described by an educated supporter in a letter to the editor of *The Sydney Gazette and New South Wales Advertiser* published on April 2nd, 1829. In part it indicated that Mr. John Grono had been engaged for more than two years in the construction of the largest ship ever built in the Colony, which he would have completed long before, except for difficulty in procuring a sufficient number of good carpenters... The vessel was one hundred tons larger than any ever built in the Colony... Not only were her timbers of Colonial growth, but her iron work also was of Colonial manufacture. The *Australian* was rated at two hundred seventy tons, being eighty one feet four inches in length at the keel, and one hundred feet over all, in the upper decks. The main breadth was twenty feet. She had two decks, and drew no more than nine feet of water, a remarkable achievement of the times. The outer planking was two inches thick, each plank being from ten to fourteen inches wide. Moreover, the boat was covered with a coating of oil and lime, and sheathed over all. The masts and yards were of black-butted gum, and were procured, though not shipped by launch time. All the materials from stem to stern consisted of blue gum, black-butted gum, iron bark, or apple-tree... The cordage was made entirely of New Zealand flax with the main cable twelve inches in circumference, consisting of three immense strands...

The actual launch into the Hawkesbury River was met with resounding cheers by workers and visitors alike. Grono's work was recognized by the governor, who granted him twenty five hundred acres of land containing a considerable quantity of blue gum which would be used in further shipbuilding.

Jeremiah was immediately put to work on helping complete the *Australian* and stayed on to build the next Grono ship, the two hundred-ton *Governor Bourke*, which was eventually completed in 1833. As with nearly all convicts, he was required to stay with his benefactor for a certain number of years. Convicts sentenced to seven-year terms needed four years of service if all were spent with one master, five years under two masters. The analogous numbers for those with fourteen-year sentences were six and eight years, or twelve years under three masters. And for lifers, eight years were required if only one master, ten years if two, and twelve if three.

Before the *Governor Bourke* was launched, restless and malcontent, Jeremiah sought an alternate position the minute his initial four years were up. He was assigned as a servant to Mr. and Mrs. Francis Beattie in Newcastle in February 1833. Francis was a convict who had been found guilty of forging notes in Lancaster in 1809 and sentenced to fourteen years transportation. He served a year on the hulks before being transported in 1810 on the *Indian*. He married Mary Howarth in 1812, and initially ran a farm. He and his wife had no children.

Fortunes could change rapidly in early colonial days and ironically, Francis, with accomplices, was convicted of receiving stolen goods in 1817 and sentenced to seven years in prison. On release he worked hard, became an innkeeper, and in 1827 established himself as an auctioneer, a respectable business profession of the day. Perhaps he was not the best influence on Jeremiah, who went absent only six months after being re-assigned. On apprehension he endured fourteen days of bread and water in His Majesty's care. Almost immediately Francis and Mary 'loaned' Jeremiah to a good friend, James Barton.

Jeremiah stayed in the district reluctantly waiting for a pardon. In 1835, at the age of fifty-seven, Francis Beattie died, his estate being sold by auction at John Smith's stores in Newcastle. His assets included ten cows, heifers, and steers, a mare, pony, gig and harness, a cart, two saddles and bridles, household furniture, clothes, sofas, bedstead, plates, cooking utensils, and numerous other articles. Francis' wife Mary was very ill and died the following year. No doubt Jeremiah was an unheralded beneficiary of select items prior to auction.

Now, he was without a master. He had six years of servitude behind him and had just turned twenty-three. His shortness at only five feet and one inch tall and the accompanying blarney that dripped off his tongue, however, made him a fascinating and engaging man to many. He could wheedle gift money from gentlemen with relative ease and could disarmingly charm the skirts off women almost as readily. Many females in the latter category ended up quite disappointed, for Jeremiah's limited size extended to his member, which was embarrassingly short and ineffective in sexual efforts. And he was clumsy and semi-abusive in other lovemaking efforts. Askance looks and outright rejection often led him to excessive drink which sometimes resulted in behavior that attracted police involvement and overnight gaol stints.

He entered a phase where his servitude was to the Crown rather than private citizens, for he retreated to old ways and became a criminal again, convicted first in October 1835, again in 1836, and yet again in April 1837. Stealing was his game, the last-mentioned trial written up on page 2 of *The Sydney Gazette and New South Wales Advertiser* of Thursday May 4. "On the 6th April last, the storekeeper of Messrs. S. A. Bryant, observed a carpenter, named Jeremiah Slane, who was employed in the store, removing two Jackets, between which he had secreted, evidently with a view of stealing, two pieces of black handkerchiefs, which were kept upon a shelf within arms' length of Slane. Upon being taxed with stealing, he absconded and was not heard of until Saturday last, when he was casually apprehended in George Street, being intoxicated, having been dealt with for that offence, he has been commuted to take his trial for the robbery."

Things became so serious for Jeremiah that on May 9th he was sent to the Parramatta Stockade, where he served two more years of incarceration. Amazingly he was issued with a Certificate of Freedom in August 1840 shortly after his release. This only served to increase his swagger and self-aggrandizement. The man survived on his wits, epitomizing a much later caricature of certain Irishmen—full of codswallop and flattery, irreverent, with criminal tendencies, wanderlust, and a strange attractiveness due to a 'don't care, doesn't matter, something will turn up, I'll survive' attitude. Survive he did, although constantly in the courts over the following years, exemplified by a charge for assault & robbery on 16 August 1842, and for breach of the peace on 18 March 1844.

He was able to talk his way out of many charges but not the charge for the particularly heinous action of a violent assault on a woman in October 1845. The newspaper *Bell's Life in Sydney and Sporting Reviewer* offered details on page 2 of its 15 November edition. "A Hint to Sureties – Jeremiah Slane, against whom a warrant had been issued for a violent assault on a married female in an advanced stage of pregnancy, and who obtained the indulgence of watch-house bail, thinking it prudent to become "non est," a fresh warrant was directed to be issued on the recognizances of his sureties, John Wald, and Arthur Sheppard, to be forfeited."

For a substantial part of his life up to this point, one government or another had supplied lodging and food for Jeremiah Slane. Not always of the most salubrious and enjoyable formats, but in essence, acceptable. His creative mind told him 'there was more where that came from', and with utter brazenness, once out on the streets again, he applied to be, and was accepted as, a mounted trooper. The city and town police forces were generally not well regarded, being made up primarily of ex-militia and, surprisingly, convicts. Jeremiah's natural Irish lilt, his easy-going camaraderie, and underlying mean streak made him a natural candidate for the force and he maintained his position with gusto. In 1848 and 1849 he was paid one shilling per day to uphold his interpretation of the local laws. He laughed every night with the irony of now being paid to keep order, when he'd grown up practicing multiple forms of thwarting the law. He was in his element.

Jeremiah Slane was short, cocky, and full of himself. A horse gave him stature, physically and metaphorically. He became lord of his mounted kingdom. The mounted troopers had various responsibilities, but they were best recognized for their work in apprehending bushrangers. They roamed the outskirts of Sydney town where escaped convicts sought refuge in bush hideouts and stole from outlying farms and travelers, primarily food, cash, and clothes. Suddenly Jeremiah was no longer a convict per se but a hunter of same.

His primary area of patrol was to the north of Sydney and he'd often be gone for days at a time as part of a small band of troopers tracking down specific escapees or hardened bushrangers. Finally, he had found an occupation he relished. It satisfied his antagonistic demeanour, it offered compromise for his size, and it suited his yearning for adventure and freedom from oppressive oversight. With a natural instinct for finding rogues, he became quite successful in capturing the miscreants. Having been an outlaw himself, he knew their logic and was able to follow what their thinking patterns and planning would be. In mid-1849 he was selected to be part of a special team to help local resources in the region just west of the Blue Mountains where bushrangers were turning to cattle rustling.

The town of Bathurst had been established in 1815 when Governor Macquarie had journeyed along the road that Wentworth, Lawson, Blaxland, Cox, and Evans had surveyed and constructed over the mountains and through the ranges to the large river found 100 miles from Sydney. The town was named after Lord Bathurst, the British secretary of state for the colonies. Later that year a government domain, consisting solely of troopers, government personnel, and convict labourers, was established. Surrounded by a large government stock reserve, it was used as the launching pad for explorations of the interior by Evans in 1815, John Oxley in 1816, Allan Cunningham in 1823, and Charles Sturt in 1828.

Private settlement was forbidden on the west bank of the Macquarie River but Governor Macquarie decided to issue ten 50-acre allotments on the east bank to small landholders in the hope that they would be able to supplement the colony's food supplies. To this end ten 'sober and industrious' grantees were given a cow, a convict servant, and four bushels of wheat seed. However, the problematic nature of transport over the rough Sydney to Bathurst road negated all efforts. And though it was initially known as Bathurst, the settlement on the east bank had, by the early 1820s, become known as Kelso. The Dun Cow Inn opened there around 1817 and the Anglican Church established a parish in 1825.

Bathurst was a frontier town in all ways imaginable. It was blessed, of course, by the governor's visit, which suggested it was not likely to be a town where failure to grow would be acceptable. It was seen as opening the agricultural doors to the vast west and northwest of New South Wales, and many interpreted, correctly, that here was a town offering unparalleled opportunity. 'Frontiership' as a matter of course was fraught with unanticipated circumstances, unforeseen events and activities, and insufficient laws to deal with same. Convicts and free settlers flocked to the town as its public nature became more widely known. But in 1824 the aborigines of the Wiradjuri people staged an uprising which caused Governor Brisbane to declare a state of martial law. Troops were despatched from Sydney and Parramatta and in the consequent reprisals over one hundred twenty aborigines were slaughtered without regard for age or sex. It was one of the more shameful acts of the white man's government and condemned by many. The aborigines eventually gave up their quest and peace reigned.

Five years later authorities quelled a rebellion by eighty convicts after one of their group was flogged for swimming in the purview of Governor Darling and his retinue. Harsh rules applied at the edge of civilization! In 1832 Thomas Mitchell discovered the Victoria Pass and a much improved route across the mountains was quickly established. Consequently, Governor Bourke decided to open up the government reserve at Bathurst to the public. It was surveyed and land sales proceeded, starting in 1833. This new settlement soon became the centre of a major pastoral area and a regular coach service from Sydney was established by 1835. The depression of the 1840s forestalled expansion but by the end of the following decade, things were starting to look up again.

It was to this historic town that Thomas and Eileen now arrived. Working with the innkeeper, Thomas secured two rooms for the night, and with their thirst now quenched the pair decided on a walking tour of the town. There was so much more than Hartley here. In the forty-plus years since its founding in 1815, the town had grown at a remarkable pace. Many buildings had been bought and sold, and changed names and functions. The Female Factory built in 1833 had closed eleven years later, although the building still stood. The hospital dated back to 1824 and had gone through many phases, the latest incarnation adding a women's wing, separate from both the convicts' wing and soldiers' wing. Several hotels had changed ownership over the years and at least four churches were in evidence—two Catholic cathedrals, one Church of England, the other Methodist. Other buildings had seen renovation and modernization, such as the post office, originally established in 1828, and the gaol and courthouse constructed even earlier. An old lumber yard had fallen into disuse although signs still proclaimed its wares.

Frederick Morgan had established himself as a tailor and draper in 1847, and a group of progressive citizens had created a bank back in 1835, as banking in Sydney before then was very inconvenient. Complementing George Flower's General Store was a soap and candle works, W. Purefoy's Law Office, and a storefront for Sloman and Tress, Auctioneers. Several competitive flour mills operated, grinding grain into flour, which was sold locally as well as in Sydney. From being water driven or windmill driven, most had recently progressed to being steam driven. A vacant building had signs indicating a blacksmith was coming, who also happened to be an undertaker with a new hearse! But best of all, from Eileen's point of view, was the existence of a newspaper—*The Bathurst Advocate*, issued on Saturdays and full of advertisements describing all the services and goods available in town. The copy Eileen picked up fascinated her and she spent more than an hour later that evening devouring the contents.

After dinner, with nothing better to do, Thomas headed for the bar, intending to learn more about town lore and current wool prices. He was in the middle of his second pint and a conversation with a grazier when his arm was grabbed from behind, and a throaty voice said, "Hello, handsome, you new in town?" Thomas had seen a couple of flamboyantly dressed women when he entered the saloon but had taken no further notice of them. On turning he now found one of them thrusting an extensive cleavage in his direction and smiling brightly. She bent forward, deliberately exposing more flesh, and asked, "Where are you from, my man?" her fixed smile never changing but watching his eyes dip to her breasts. "Nice, ain't they? More of me is nice too. Want to buy me a drink?"

Thomas blushed and turned away, only to find that his grazier friend was chatting with a man on his other side. "I'm Lila," she continued. "You look young and strong. What's your name?" Sensing his hesitation she added, "Now don't be shy on me. We're all for having a good time here. Where did you say you were from again? We love welcoming newcomers to town." She squeezed her considerable bulk alongside him, turned to the barkeeper, and shouted, "Pete, this gentleman wants to buy me a drink. My favourite, please." The barkeeper raised his eyebrows questioningly in Thomas' direction, who shook his head no vigorously. "Aw, now that's not real sociable, mister. Look what you are missing," and she grabbed his hand and patted her ample breast with it. "Are you sure you don't want to be more friendly?" With that Thomas placed some coins on the counter, pushed the woman aside, and hurriedly walked out into the night.

The fresh air felt good and he inhaled and exhaled several mouthfuls to help him regain his composure. This was his first experience with a prostitute and he was embarrassed. Obviously they were a way of life in the pub, but certainly the types of women he wanted no dealings with. Apparently his newness stuck out. Even so, he wished he'd had something firm to say in response to her first words that would have made it clear he had no interest in her. He wondered what the other men who'd witnessed his hasty departure thought. And whether the red-cheeked woman was laughing at his response, or whether she was already working on other potential customers. He hoped it was the latter. Ah well, he thought, another lesson learned. It made him wonder what else the town might offer. It didn't take long the next morning to find out.

There were two very obvious aspects of life here that were different from Hartley. One was the presence of numerous aborigines, the other the large contingent of military personnel. For the most part the aborigines simply seemed to do nothing more than hang about. Perhaps waiting for handouts, or if they had money to spend from doing odd jobs, waiting to buy alcohol. Some were employed as trackers or interpreters by the local authorities but in general they were not reliable workers, taking off to 'go bush' back in their natural habitat whenever the urge occurred.

Gradually, their natural state of nudity had succumbed to the insistence of white man's interests and most of the men wore loincloths and the women small low aprons, although staying bare breasted. When cold some wore cloaks of skins, but these seemed reserved for older tribesmen only. They had no written communication capabilities so everything was verbal. According to missionaries who worked with them diligently to offer the Christian religion and behaviour to their lives, the natives' stories of the 'dreamtime', that time before their ancestors' ancestors existed, were remarkably consistent as told by separate individuals, thereby showing the power and retention of verbal interchange. Missionaries studied some of the aboriginal dialects and helped willing white soldiers learn enough to work with selected natives for tracking purposes. The relationships so formed were always fraught with concerns and a lack of deep trust on both sides. Some worked, some didn't.

Eileen came out of the baking and confectionary store holding a two-pound loaf of fresh bread she'd bought for fourpence. She nearly walked into a small man on his way inside. As they almost bumped he said politely, "Top of the morning to you, missy. Pardon me," and held the door wider for her to exit. She smiled at the 'missy' bit and headed across the main street to the Edward Austin's general store. There really wasn't anything she wanted, other than to explore the store and see what items were in demand in Bathurst and maybe to learn something about the area from the proprietor. The variety of items available surprised her. Goods ranged from convict slops, drapery, haberdashery, and hosiery, to groceries, ironmongery, stationery, wines, spirits, and tobacco.

The owner was telling her about the aboriginal uprising that had taken place twenty-five years earlier when the doorbell rang and the little man from the bakery encounter entered.

"Mornin' again, miss, and top o' the mornin' to you, sir. I have need of some items for the troopers if you could kindly oblige." And he handed over a handwritten list to the owner, who hastened off to start gathering things.

Eileen took a step back and looked at the man. Definitely on the short side, with a rugged face and dirty uniform, but an air of self-confidence. She wanted to ask a question but was hesitant to appear forward. She was helped out by the visitor's challenge: "Cat got your tongue, miss? I won't bite."

Eileen was mildly annoyed by his brazenness, but also encouraged in an odd way. "I gather you are with the mounted troopers then, sir?"

"That's right, me darlin'. Got in last night."

"How long will you be here then?"

"Well, I really shouldn't be tellin' you this, missy, but..." He looked around furtively to make sure the proprietor wasn't listening, then dropped his voice and conspiratorially whispered, "We're about to head off lookin' for cattle rustlers. My men and me are a special team working for the gov'nor to apprehend these bad'uns. Come all the way from Parramatta we have. Best capture record in the colony. Here to show the local forces how we work."

"How many have you caught in the past?"

"Well, now, missy that would be highly confidential so I can't tell you, but let me just say I've caught fifteen bushrangers on my ownsome in the last year or so. More with my team."

"My gosh. It must be dangerous. How many are loose out there? And aren't most of the bushrangers and rustlers armed?"

"You are right, missy, this isn't a job for the faint of heart. I've been shot at several times. Got a scar between my fingers, here, see? That's where I went to grab a pistol one chap was pointin' at me. Lucky to be alive I am. Yep, the men call me 'Lucky Captain Jerry'."

"I'm glad you weren't killed. Are you staying at the Barracks?"

"Yes, miss. What did you say your name was?"

"Eileen."

"That's a pretty name, but I'll call you Lily. Might see you later." And with that he smiled, doffed his cap, turned, and followed the proprietor, who'd gone into a back room for supplies.

Eileen was a little surprised at the abruptness, but headed to the door, lifted her hemline across the threshold, stepped out onto the boardwalk, and strode back to the hotel with the bread tucked under her arm. Thomas was sitting outside and catching his eye she excitedly said, "I just met the most fascinating man. He's a captain with the mounted troopers, in town to pursue rustlers. Says he's caught many himself single-handed. Short chap but with a huge smile and as Irish in brogue as you'll ever want. I tried to keep him talking just to hear the mother tongue in its richest form."

"I heard that some of the troopers are ex-cons themselves and that gives them an edge in tracking down fugitives. They think the same way, know their fears and hopes, what they need and how devious they can be in getting what they want. Did you get any sense of this captain's background? What's his name?"

"Don't know his last name, but he says the men call him Lucky Jerry, which I guess is short for Jeremy or Jeremiah. It would be fun to meet him again."

"Maybe this evening. Meanwhile, are you going to come out exploring and hunting with me? I want to check out the hills around the river to the northwest. I've heard there's lots of wildlife out there."

"Okay, brother. Let's go get organized."

On the lower slopes of the hills twelve miles out they spotted their first kangaroos. Big reds streaking across the fields in a group of 30 or more. Eileen couldn't help but admire their speed and seemingly boundless energy. Thomas started to withdraw his rifle from its pouch but they were gone too quickly. "Ooh, too bad, I'd love to have brought down one of those big fellows as they moved. Weren't they magnificent? They looked like they owned the world, sprinting around their boundary unchallenged, checking things out, sending a signal to all creatures to stay out of their way. Maybe we'll see some more further on. Let's hope."

It was a vain hope, unfortunately. They saw some wallabies by the bank of the river a couple of miles hence, but even Eileen declined shooting at them. The big reds had raised the desire for a trophy kill, and the wallabies weren't of sufficient stature. So they stopped and had lunch, relaxing under the trees after shooing the wallabies away. Afterwards, Thomas pushed on, and about twenty miles out turned west over a small hill with just a few trees. At the bottom of the western slope a splendid vista opened up to both north and south. It was prime grazing land, fairly dry as the pair viewed it, but surely any person who staked a claim there would be well rewarded.

After stopping to admire the setting Thomas steered back towards Bathurst, but had only gone two hundred and fifty yards when he stopped abruptly and signalled Eileen to hold still. An ill-defined movement at the foot of the far hill had caught his attention. "I think that's a dingo moving between the taller clumps of grass. There's no spinifex here so there must be small mounds of dirt in the fields. Do you see him sis? Watch carefully at that sandy-coloured patch at the base of the hill directly across from us. There he goes. Wonder if he's actually hunting something. Must be, because usually they come out at dawn or dusk."

Dingoes looked uncannily like wild dogs. They could even bark lightly, although some folk mistook them as members of the wolf family because they usually howled. They were very unpopular with farmers as they killed sheep easily by tearing at their throats. Sometimes they simply nipped at the animals' hind legs, wounding them severely enough to cause death later. Thomas thought that the lone animal across the way would indeed be a worthy trophy, making up for missing a large 'roo earlier.

It was impossible to see at a distance what exactly the dingo hunted. But dingoes would eat an amazing variety of food ranging from rabbits, rodents, lizards, red kangaroos, and brushtail possums, to birds such as magpies, crows, and even geese. This one must be stalking something stationary, maybe a rabbit intent on eating, for he stealthily moved from mound to mound at sporadic intervals.

Dingoes were seen as predators that killed wantonly, rather than out of hunger. Additionally, they were seen as having a venomous bite or saliva, and thus, no reservations were required to kill one. They tended to have dens in burrows 'borrowed' from the original owners—rabbits, wombats, or monitor lizards. Often hollow logs would do, or a natural small shelter formed by boulders. It was thought that they had probably arrived in the country four thousand years earlier on Asian seafarer boats. Over the years, dingo trappers gained a kind of prestige for their work, primarily when they managed to kill dingoes that were especially hard to catch. Yes sir, thought Thomas, this one is worthy of the hunt. He's mine.

Eileen had remained quiet, watching Thomas closely. She could tell he was somewhat excited and asked, "How are you going to shoot him? He is so far away."

"I'm going to ask for your indulgence and help. This will be a bit selfish, I'm afraid, but I'd like to have you stay here with all the horses. They don't seem to be bothering the dingo so far—he's too intent on stalking his prey. In fact, you could even head back up the hill and tie them to a tree if you want. Might be easiest. I'm going to crouch-walk to that small swale about 200 yards ahead and use it to cross the flat area until it peters out halfway across. I'm hoping the dingo will soon catch what he's after and stop for a meal. I'll crawl from the end of the depression as far as I can and shoot at the last possible moment. It's going to be a challenge, but I desperately want to try."

"Good luck then. I'll watch from the slope." With a gentle nudge she turned her horse, gathered the extra reins from Thomas, and slowly backtracked. By the time she had tied the horses up to a scrubby acacia Thomas had reached the swale and was moving along it. Every now and then she could see his hat as he popped up to check if the dingo was still present. She marveled at his perseverance and dedication to the task. When the swale eased away he dropped flat on the ground, took off his hat to minimize his profile, and painstakingly inched his way forward. From her position Eileen could no longer see the dingo and had not seen movement since she sat down on the ground. He must be behind one of the mounds with his kill. Apparently Thomas could see him, however, or he would have changed his approach.

The dingo was tearing apart a small animal that was a rodent of some form. He raised his head and seemed to look directly at Thomas, and after sniffing the air, resumed eating. He presented a difficult target head-on and Thomas wished he would sit or lie down, but with one front paw holding the carcass his head was bent down, with the long snout busily chomping away. It was time. Any further movement might be sensed and he could lose his target. It was still a seventy-five yard shot and would have to be highly accurate. He backed up a little until he encountered a small mound on his right. Perfect for resting the rifle. He questioned himself as to what would be best. Shoot the dingo in the head while he was eating or wait till he lifted and rested for a moment and go for the exposed throat. Either would yield a sure kill if accurate. If he aimed for the head and the bullet dropped more than anticipated in flight it might hit the ground in front of the animal's nose and simply scare him away. And when he was tearing at the meat the head would swing vigorously back and forth, so timing would be critical. On the other hand, if he aimed for the exposed neck and the bullet dropped, there was still a chance of hitting the chest. He decided the neck was the better option and patiently waited while the dingo kept eating.

Seconds ticked by, a full minute, two minutes. How long would he stay down? Thomas was working hard to keep his heart from pounding by breathing slowly in and out, forcing himself to stay calm and be patient. Surely it was time. He bent down and sighted along the barrel again. And watched as the narrow head slowly raised, a piece of meat dangling from sharp teeth. Come on, a bit more, a bit more. Where's that light patch on the throat I saw earlier? Ah, here it comes. Yes.

Eileen heard the resounding crack of the rifle and saw Thomas stand up and wave his hat round and round whooping with delight. He turned and waved in her direction, and she could sense his grin, although too far away to actually see it. She untied the horses, mounted hers, and set off in a direct line across the fields. Thomas waited for her to arrive so she could view the beast before he skinned it. He proudly held up the animal's head and showed her the bullet hole in the middle of his throat patch. Right where he'd aimed, hardly spoiling the sandy-coloured fine fur. Up close the dingo was bigger than she had expected and the face had a mean look to it, even in death. Its beady piercing eyes and partly open mouth with protruding canine teeth looked like it was snarling at her. She turned and looked away quickly, then moved off to the side, not particularly wanting to watch the skinning process although she'd seen it before. Finally, Thomas rolled up the furry skin and tied it, letting the horses smell it to quell any fears they might have, and hung it from one of the saddle bags on the pack horse.

Thomas relived his hunt by describing to Eileen in minute detail his thoughts and concerns as he moved into sight of his quarry. She listened patiently, happy that he was so thrilled with his prize, and responding with the appropriate 'oohs' and 'aahs' at just the right spots. Such a good sister, helping massage her brother's ego, yet so easily. Sometimes men were so easy to manipulate. Pump up their egos and one could gain much, including favours, in response. Female wiles to the fore. It was wonderful, however, to see a grown man acting like a little boy. He prattled on nearly all the way back to Bathurst and she was highly thankful when they finally left the horses with the stable boy behind the hotel.

They washed up and went downstairs to the dining room, bypassing the saloon, which was noisy and busy with the local drinking crowd. Their choice for dinner was fish freshly caught that afternoon and served with peas and cabbage from a nearby farm. They were both hungry from the exhilarating day and were finishing off a glass of ale each when a bunch of troopers entered and sat at a large table across the room. It didn't take Jeremiah long to spot Eileen, and after he'd received his drink he rose and crossed the room heading for her table.

"Good evening, Miss Lily. I trust you had a pleasant day?"

"Thank you, I did. That is, we did. May I introduce my brother Thomas?"

Thomas stood and Jeremiah reached out to shake his hand. "Good to meet you, I'll call you Tom."

"Actually everyone calls me Thomas. Never liked Tom much."

"But Tom is so much stronger and easier on the tongue, don't you think. Now what are you two doing in Bathurst?" He sat down on a vacant chair, and Thomas resumed his seat.

"Thomas and I live near Hartley and have simply been out exploring the area and hunting."

"And today was great because I managed to shoot a dingo. Don't see many of them in this area. I was at least one hundred yards away and— "

Jeremiah interrupted: "And did you hunt anything, pretty lady? Or were you a spectator along the way?"

"I shot a monitor lizard and a kangaroo at distance so I contributed for sure."

"Well, good for you. Now Tom, are you a farmer?"

"Yes, my brother and I run sheep and cattle down in Blaxland Swamp. We own a couple hundred acres of prime— "

Jeremiah, again interrupting, "And what do you do, Lily? Are you a teacher? You sound like you could be one."

"No, I live with our parents in Lowther."

"Lowther, is that a real small place? I haven't heard of it before—or the Swamp place."

Thomas weighed in. "Both are small farming communities southwest of Hartley. You must know the stockade in the town."

"Oh yes, we stopped there two nights ago. Bit small but serves its purpose."

"Your accent is very strong. What part of Ireland do you come from? Eileen and I come from Drumcairn, in County Donegal. The family roots there go back generations."

"Well, County Cork was home. I came out in 1828. Y'see, my parents died of consumption and so it was just me left to look after me brother and sister. They was two and four years younger. I got a job in a shipyard, but we got thrown out of our rooms and then lived in the back of a church for a while. I got caught stealing a gent's handkerchief which I was going to pawn to buy food for brother and sister, but they took me away and sent me here."

Eileen felt the lump in her throat. "So what happened to your brother and sister?"

"I have no idea. I suppose the church took care of them. I miss them so badly I can't sleep when I think of them some nights."

"Oh, you poor thing. Sent so far away with no knowledge of what happened to all that remained of your family. You must have been heartbroken."

"I tried to have them come with me, but no one would listen and little kids aren't worth anything in the convict system. You are right—it was a terrible sea voyage out here. I've naught heard of them since."

Tom spoke up: "So you've been in the Colony about twenty years now. When did you get your Certificate of Freedom?"

"It was 1840. Wait, what do you want to know that for?"

"Oh, I was just wondering how long you've been rid of the shackles of punitive Irish law. We came as assisted immigrants but we know how important those certificates are to men like you."

"Well, of course. I started out as a carpenter building ships near Windsor. We did the *Australian* and then the *Governor Bourke*. I became head carpenter for Captain Grono. You must've heard of him, famous shipbuilder who also started the trade in New Zealand seal skins...?"

"No, sorry. Did you ever go hunting seals?"

"No, you had to be a good sailor first and that wasn't me callin' at all. I built 'em. Others sailed 'em."

"What did you do after you finished shipbuilding?"

"My, you ask a lot of questions, Tom."

"But I see you like answering them. Sounds like you've done a lot of different things. Much more exciting than farming."

"Well, let's see. I guess that's when I left to help run an inn. I was the best bar server in the town."

"And then at some point you became a trooper. Eileen tells me you were shot in the hand when apprehending a bushranger. Sounds very scary."

"Well, the bullet went between my fingers when I grabbed the end of his pistol so I was lucky."

"Ugh, that must have hurt horribly. Did you get the rogue anyway, or did he escape after firing at you?"

"I got him. I tripped him when he went off balance after I pulled the gun away, and then he was mine, even though I only had one good hand at the time. I trussed him up good and proper. When me team finally caught up they helped bandage my hand and look after the mongrel."

"I can see the scars on your fingers when you spread your hand around the tankard."

"Not the prettiest, I must admit."

"So how long have you been a trooper?"

"Must be going on five years now. Lots of experience, mainly north and south of Sydney though. This is the first time the team has been west of Penrith. Tell me about living in the Blue Mountains."

"Actually we live just this side of the Blue Mountains. It's beautiful hilly country interspersed with wonderful grazing lands. Lots of creeks running into the Cox's River so well watered. If you continue going south you'd end up at the Fish River Caves. If ever I saw an area where bushrangers could hide out that would be it. But there are a lot of natives in that area so maybe they stay away."

"Don't like the abos. Dirty, lazy, do no good. Just get in the way."

"Then I guess you won't be using any of them locally to help track the rustlers Eileen says you are looking for?"

"We might. Depends how good they are. But just as likely halfway along the track they'll wander off and go 'walkabout' on us. Can't count on 'em. Anyway, better get back to me meal with the men. Good talking to you. Say, miss, if you want to wait a little I could walk you over to the Barracks and show you around the gov'ment buildings if you like. They don't just let anyone in there."

"Oh, that would be fun. I'll wait, thank you."

Thomas spoke up: "I'll come too then."

"No, I meant just the lady. She can tell you all about it later." And with that he stood up and strode across the room.

Eileen leaned across the table and whispered, "Isn't he just the most appealing character, Thomas? I find him oddly attractive. And I love listening to his accent. I think yours and mine have faded over time but his is as strong as ever. Oh, he's just so interesting!"

"Maybe, sister. Maybe. He certainly has an engaging grin, but to me he is a little too shrewd and I'm not sure I believe all his stories."

"Ooh, I do think I detect a touch of jealousy there. Another man showing interest in me? Come on. Be a little supportive. I know he interrupted you a couple of times, but he clearly wasn't educated to the same extent you and I were. But he must be smart to have been a head carpenter and now a captain of the troopers."

"Yes, he certainly doesn't have the best social graces and grammar, but I think he was raised in a harsh environment where there weren't many examples for him to learn from and very little regular schooling. But it's not that. Most convicts are somewhat reluctant to tell why they were transported. He was a bit too ready to tell his story to strangers. And then there's the bullet scars. To me those looked like knife scars. Grabbing a gun barrel would have produced burn scars which would be much wider and far more extensive. There's also a scar on one eyelid that he didn't explain. Not that he was obliged to, but I'm willing to bet that was from a fight with knives. And he sure doesn't want me along with you later. I'd be a little guarded if I were you. Don't say too much. Let him do all the talking."

"Definitely jealous. I haven't seen this in you before. Sort of nice that you care so much. Thank you. I'll be as careful as I can, don't worry."

Thomas watched as they walked down the boardwalk together, Eileen's laughter echoing off the buildings. She towered over Jeremiah and their silhouettes looked incongruous. The little man with slightly bowed legs and a swagger, and the taller woman with a long dress and graceful, flowing strides. He was surprised Eileen seemed so taken with Jeremiah, but knew they'd be headed back homeward tomorrow and that would be the end of it. He wondered what more she'd learn about him in the visit to the government buildings. He got a chuckle out of the fact that he wasn't invited along. Jeremiah must surely want to impress his sister without anyone else hearing his exaggerated tales.

Next morning he knocked three times on the door of Eileen's room before he got a muffled response that sounded like "Go ahead, I'm sleepy." Very unlike her. As he sauntered down to breakfast on his own he wondered how late she had stayed up last night. It was almost mid-morning before she emerged through the front door with her small bags. Thomas had paid the bill, groomed and checked the horses, tipped the stable boy, bought fresh buns at the bakery, plus sugar lumps and apples at the general store for horse treats, and was running out of ways to spend his waiting time productively. Eileen's arrival was timely, as he had just started to pace along the boardwalk when she pranced out through the hotel door and almost bumped into him. A big smile radiated across her face as she swung her bags at him to place on the pack horse. She could sense his questions starting to form and quickly put her fingers to her lips. "Ssshhh. Later."

It was a mile out of town before she volunteered, "I had quite a night last night. Turns out that a number of the men at the post had invited women along for an evening of dancing and singing. Some were wives, some were acquaintances from town, and two were farm widows. And me. All with Irish backgrounds. I think eleven women in total. Maybe fifteen men. They had formed a little band, which was surprisingly good, and we danced and laughed the evening away. That Jeremiah may be small but he has unlimited energy and dances a truly enthusiastic jig. He had everyone laughing at his efforts. Not a shy man. Eventually, though, some of the chaps had too much grog and started to spoil things, so the band shut down and that was it. I think most of us women had had enough anyway by then. Some were going hoarse, and we were all happy from laughing so much, remembering the old songs. Jeremiah and I walked to the edge of the river, and sat and talked for ages about our lives as children growing up. We watched the moon travel across the tree tops and reflect in the water. We had a nice time together."

"I'm glad you had fun. A fitting way to end your visit here. Although I'm wondering from your slightly wistful tone whether you wish you were staying longer to see more of Jeremiah."

"Yes, and no. I want to get home. I'm not as comfortable travelling around in the open as much as you are. And while this has been a wonderful adventure, and I feel you and I have drawn even closer as a result, it's enough for me now. But I will be seeing Jeremiah again as I invited him to come by our place on his way back to Parramatta in about a week. I told him to ask for directions when he got to the general store in Hartley. He said he'd try to get a day away from his team and come and visit. I know you have reservations about him, but he really is a carefree fellow with a great sense of adventure and fun. And while a bit abrupt with men, he can be utterly charming with us ladies. When we sat by the river and it got colder he insisted I wear his jacket to help keep warm. And at the end of the evening he gave me this little lapel pin that he wears when on duty. Says he can get another. Isn't that sweet? I hope you won't voice your concerns too harshly when I talk to Mother and Father about him visiting."

"Well, this is a bit of a surprise to see my sister so taken with a man she just met. Any friend of a family member is always welcome in our homes. You know that. And I think I'll rely on Mother and Father's own intuition to sound him out, so I'll say little ahead of time."

"Thank you. He's just so different from all the other men around. You and others locally are all so hard-working and dedicated to farming, you don't make time for games and community activities as much as I would like. Even back in County Donegal there were fetes and village football matches and craft fairs. Not in Hartley. Bathurst as a town is already growing by leaps and bounds, and will soon offer those broader social doings. Talking with Jeremiah reminded me of those 'extra' parts of community life that we don't have. It made me think that maybe I should look for a position in Parramatta or even Sydney. I mean, look at me, I'm nearly twenty-six years old and never been kissed, let alone anything else. He made me wonder about a lot of things. Can you understand that?"

"I guess so. It's interesting to hear other people's points of view, even if they might be difficult to understand or agree with. In the end I suppose it's what appeals to one's individual make-up. What ideals seem most rewarding, what environments one chooses. Me, I love the country, the open air, the calls of the birds, the smell of the animals, the sound of the breeze in the leaves, and the sunshine above. I don't need much more, definitely not the feel of a cricket bat and ball. But I understand how others do. That's okay. Do tell me one thing, however. I can't resist asking. Did anyone call Jeremiah 'Captain' during your evening?"

"Well, not that I specifically remember. And maybe he is prone to a little exaggeration. But nothing to worry about, Thomas. It was clear he was the boss of his team from the way the others deferred to him. And there were other teams there as well besides his. I don't think it matters what title they really used. Why do you keep raising such issues?"

"I guess I'm concerned for your sake. So I'll say this only once and not raise it again. Maybe I'm being a bit harsh, but I met an Irish salesman in the stockyards at Mulgoa one day and Jeremiah reminds me of him. This chap was full of the blarney. He was thoroughly engaging to talk to, but his stories were too colourful and didn't ring true. I found out later he'd been in and out of gaol many times. Mainly for drunkenness, but also for stealing. He was a con man and good at it. Jeremiah reminds me of him. Similar mannerisms, similar style. I know that's unfair to Jeremiah, but it's my sixth sense talking to me. Some of his exaggeration I suspect is cover for things that may not be all positive. Obviously I don't know for sure. I'm just telling you what my insides are telling me. I'd feel bad if I weren't open and honest in passing my thoughts on. But there, that's it. I've said my piece."

"I appreciate that you are willing to share your concerns and instincts, Thomas, I really am. And who knows what will happen. We'll just see how things evolve. Maybe he won't even stop by, which will be an obvious signal in its own right. All I know at the moment is that he's like a breath of fresh air in my life. And that feels good."

It was an amiable, stress-free journey home. They stayed on the main road, meeting a variety of travellers going in both directions. And with more information about Bathurst under their belts they were able to inform those heading west about the town. Stages rolled by both ways, bullock teams with furniture and a range of supplies for the stores were westward bound, while other bullocks hauled drays piled high with wool bales eastward. They spent two nights in spots by river banks that they'd used on their outbound journey. Eileen shot a small wallaby and Thomas proudly got an eagle on the wing. At night before sleep Eileen would sing Irish folk songs, reliving her night at the soldiers' hall. Once or twice Thomas would hum along, finding himself relaxing as he did so.

In the middle of their last night it started to rain heavily. They moved the tent further under the trees, but got soaked in the process, and they spent six restless, miserably wet hours waiting for first light. At least they had gathered plenty of extra wood the previous evening and had stored it in the burnt-out hollow base of an old gum tree. It had kept dry and the crackling fire and hot tea warmed them as the rain moved on. Thomas looked at the sky. "Can't really complain if this is the only rain we experience in all our time away. Could have been much, much worse. Although I think we'll still have to pass through some light showers before we get home. Those clouds are staying low. We should wear our leather coats and hats. If you'll put the fire out, sis, and pick up, I'll go see a man, and then get the horses ready. Last day. I bet the sun will be shining by the time we reach the front gate. Let's just hope no bullock teams have gotten bogged in the muddy ruts and are blocking the road."

Swollen waters rushed down the creeks carrying small tree limbs and the occasional wild animal carcass, but all the bridges they crossed were still intact and showed no signs of breaching. The road was slippery so the horses moved a little more slowly and surely than usual, and the riders stayed on horseback longer than usual, not wanting to walk in the mud themselves. But there was no long-term escape, and when the hills became steep they got off and calmly paced through the mud along with the horses. Thomas' predictions were right on and they passed through two mini squalls, getting soaked again. The first one found them in the middle of a plain, but for the second they were able to find limited shelter under trees alongside the road. Gradually the clouds lifted, the sun came out, and steam rose off their wet coats and the horses' flanks. They took a shortcut and bypassed Hartley itself, anxious to get home and cleaned up. A mile out Thomas fired three shots in the air, repeating the action half a mile closer in, and again at the main gate. On hearing the shots Patrick had ridden from where he was working in the fields, catching them as they rode up the main track to the house. The young lads came rushing out and Katie and Matthew waved from the veranda as soon as they were in sight. Nothing like a heartfelt reception to make one feel welcome. It felt so good to be home.

19. An outsider steals
a family member

They say that God rested on the seventh day. But not Eileen. For a week she had kept herself busy, cleaning the house to a new degree of shine, baking breads, pies, and scones, making jam, and sorting and re-organizing the vegetables stored in the root cellar. Her usual steady and even-handed demeanour became more fragile as the days passed, and it was Katie who finally took her aside and gently pointed out how snappy and curt she had become. "He'll come when he can, dear, and you can't do a thing about the timing, so please calm down a little, your restlessness is affecting all of us."

Eileen heeded her mother's words for a full day, but on day nine Katie had had enough and sent her off to town in the afternoon to buy some supplies—some necessary, some designed to distract. And in a loving gesture, fully recognizing her daughter's excitement, she also offered to pay for cloth for a new dress should she find material she liked. Eileen rode off, half hoping she'd meet Jeremiah coming the other way. No such luck.

It must have been the new home-sewn dress that did It, for on day ten, she and Mother had just sat down to late morning tea on the front porch when a small dust cloud coming down the track announced the arrival of a lone rider. And suddenly he was right there, dismounting and tying his horse to the post, grinning broadly as Eileen ran to greet him. Their mutual joy was obvious and Eileen proudly introduced Jeremiah to her mother, who offered him tea or lemonade. He opted for the lemonade to quench the thirst he had built up riding hard since morning light.

"It's a delight to meet you, Mrs. Monahan. Eileen has praised you highly and it's very obvious from where she inherited her beautiful looks. This is a very peaceful setting here. I had no trouble finding your homestead."

"We've looked forward to meeting you, Mr. Slane, and you are most welcome to stay with us until you have to head off to Parramatta."

"Well, thank you, ma'am, but please call me Jeremiah or Jerry. I received word in Bathurst that my unit will be repairing to Sydney from Parramatta shortly after I get back, so I do have to return and organize the transfer. I don't think my men can do it on their own, since I'm their leader and all."

"Is that why you were a little delayed getting here?" Eileen asked. "I started to wonder if you were coming."

"No, it took longer to catch the last pair of rustlers, that's all. They were crafty fellas, and kept eluding us. Like they was always one step ahead, you know? But I outsmarted them in the end. I sat down and put my sharp brain to work and thought, where would I go if I was them and knew I was bein' chased. So we rode through the night and got way ahead of them and set up an ambush. They never saw us till the last minute, and while one got off a shot he missed us and we took him down. Miserable bast... oh excuse me, Mrs. Monahan... I do get carried away with me job. Anyways, it took more time for us to capture them. They was sentenced next morning by the judge to be hung but I didn't stay for that."

"Oh dear, that sounds very unpleasant. I feel quite ill at the thought of men being killed that way. You'll have to excuse me. I'll let Eileen look after you." And Katie got up and went inside. Eileen followed quickly but Katie waved her back to the veranda, mouthing, "I'm fine. You have time alone."

They untied Jeremiah's horse and led him around to the stables where there was food and water. "I'd like to brush him down later, he deserves it after the fast ride today." Holding hands, they took a short tour around the house and outbuildings.

"Father will be along later, he's helping the twins with some early lambing today. I do hope you like my parents, Jerry."

"Well, your mother seems very sweet. She reminds me of what I remember of me own mother. Caring and gentle. Now where are your two younger brothers? I thought they would be scampering around here getting in the way and asking me all sorts of questions about being a policeman."

"They'll be here at dinner time, and I'm sure you will feel like the inquisition is under way. They are two very curious lads, so be prepared. Right now they are with my sister Mary Jane at her place up the road a ways."

It was a full complement for dinner, with the twins successfully anticipating that Jeremiah may well have turned up during the day. As predicted, the young boys wanted to see the gun and badge of the hero policeman and hear stories of bushranger captures. Jerry obliged smilingly, in his element talking about his exploits.

Finally, Matthew asked Jeremiah why he had left the shipbuilding business when that was where he was able to practice his carpentry profession. Jeremiah's response was a bit disconcerting. "Well, it was like this. After three years I had worked on every part of the ship and had been made head of the whole team of wood-workers. But I was tired of the long days and the constant complaints of the owner about the quality of the work. He really had no idea of what it took to build some parts, so sometimes we made adjustments for practical reasons, and if he didn't like what we'd done he made us rework it."

"Well, Mr. Grono had an incredible reputation for excellent work on his boat the *Australian*. I remember reading about it. Wouldn't you want that same prestige in what you were building?"

"Well, I sure wasn't going to sail in it, and I don't think the small changes we made would have affected its seaworthiness. My job was carpentry, not sailing, so we tried to do what we could from the tradesman angle."

"I can understand that and I know nothing about sailing, beyond what any of us picked up on our voyage out here, but based on what I saw I can also appreciate that as a ship's captain, equipment had to be reliable and useful from the sailor's perspective, especially when they had to respond to changes needed quickly. So what did you do when you left the boat-building business?"

"I thought it would be fun to own a hotel, and I was able to get a position close by helping an innkeeper with his business. At first I fixed things and made repairs, looked after the buildings, then gradually I learned to help look after the guests. I was starting to learn to write, courtesy of the owner, when he upped and died on me. His wife sold the place and I wasn't in any position to buy it. I didn't like the new owner so I did odd jobs in Sydney for two years until I joined the police force."

"Police work definitely seems a long way from carpentry," said Matthew. "I'm sure you have to deal with all sorts of strange circumstances. I don't think I could ever be a policeman. I much prefer the gentle, somewhat dull life we have here. I think all of us do." The twins voiced their agreement but Eileen remained silent.

"For me, part of the attraction is the unknown and being able to respond to different situations approp... properly. Plus bringing law and order and making the colony a safer place for all its citizens is the major reward. And frankly I also like some of the danger involved. It's exciting to me. There's a challenge in resolving a dangerous situation, and I'm pretty good at it. Which is why I'm the captain of a team of mounted troopers."

"I guess someone has to catch the robbers and murderers and other abusers of society. Eileen, is that a world you want to be closer to?"

Eileen had been admiring and luxuriating in Jeremiah's responses to her father's questions and was caught off-guard and somewhat surprised by what sounded like a veiled challenge, yet also a recognition that she and Jeremiah might be permanently together at some point. Thinking quickly and reinforcing her interests, she said, "I have faith that Jeremiah would be a great protector of me from all things nasty."

The twins' eyebrows shot up and Katie looked more intently at her husband as they all recognized the implications of his question and Eileen's response. Eileen got up and fetched the pie for dessert, allowing the youngsters to fill the silence with their sizing requests and a repeated desire to see Jeremiah's pistol after dinner.

To help out, Thomas suggested that the couple ride over to his and Patrick's property in the morning and help count new lambs born overnight. Even though that wasn't of major interest to Jeremiah he seized the chance to be alone with Eileen again on the ride. She would then accompany him into the village of Hartley before seeing him off on his way across the Blue Mountains.

Katie made breakfast for the couple after the youngsters and their father had eaten. "It's always a pleasure to sleep in a proper bed, Mrs. Monahan. I didn't want to get up this morning. Even our beds at the barracks are not much more than bunks, and most nights on the job I sleep under the stars, or in a tent if raining. Thank you for letting me sleep late this morning and for making breakfast for us. I feel pampered. Is there anything I can do for you before we leave?"

"That's nice of you to offer, Jeremiah, but I think everything is under control. Tell me one thing. though, what were your mother's and father's names?"

"Mother was Mary and Father was Gwilym, bless their souls. I didn't know my father as he left home when I was very young."

"Oh, I thought your parents both died of consumption. Did I get that wrong?"

"Ahhh…. No, that's right. My father left before I was four but later died of consumption as me mother tells it."

"And what were your dear sister and brother called? The ones you had to leave behind?"

"Me brother was Sean two years behind me and the baby was Megan."

"Oh, what a coincidence," Eileen exclaimed. "Those are the names of the Bathurst garrison commander and his wife that we met at the dance night."

"Ooh, I never thought of that before. I hadn't met the commander's wife until that night. I must tell him next time I see him. Anyway, Mrs. Monahan, we'll be going to the twins' place. I imagine there will be more pretty country to see along the way. Thank you for letting me stay overnight. You don't happen to have any pie left over to take along, do you? It was delicious."

As soon as they were out of earshot through the front gate Eileen asked, "So what did you think of Mother and Father, Jerry? Aren't they nice people?"

"Well, I think your mother is a saint. To have eight children and to stay as spry and gracious as she is, is amazing. There's a lot of her in you, I can tell. It was harder to tell with your dad as we didn't have as much time with him. Obviously he doesn't have any problem with us courting based on the questions he asked so he must be pretty nice too."

"Oh, I'm so glad you liked them. It's very important to me as I think the world of them. It would be so hard if you thought otherwise. Now how about a canter to give these animals some exercise. Are you ready? Let's go..."

The morning passed quickly enough at the twins' farm, although by noon Jeremiah had had enough of counting and collecting lambs and marking them. His restlessness started to show, and Eileen was quick to recognize his need to be moving on.

"Well, boys and Father, I want some time alone with Jerry, so we'll head into the village and get him on his way. Is there anything you need me to bring back?"

Matthew, Patrick, and Thomas all shook hands with the little man and wished him a good trip down the mountains. The goodbye conversation was short, which suited everyone. Jerry wanted to be on his way, and the Monahan men had a job to finish.

They rode in silence for thirty minutes, but at a small creek crossing Eileen suggested they dismount and let the horses drink and rest briefly. As Jeremiah finished tying the reins of his stallion over a low tree branch Eileen reached up and drew his arm around her. "There, I've wanted to do that from the minute you arrived." She took off his cap and kissed his forehead. "And that too. Now squish me some so I can remember you when you are gone." And he did.

Jeremiah was the first to break the hugs, his desire to keep moving dominating other considerations. Disappointment flashed across Eileen's face but she held it in check and didn't complain. Her hero and champion's wishes were her command. She rode with him all the way to Victoria Pass, where they said goodbye. She promised to come to Sydney in a month's time, and he promised to wait faithfully for her to turn up. As he turned to ascend the Pass she couldn't hold back the tears, but waved vigorously as he reached the top and doffed his cap. And then he was gone and her life felt empty again. It was a sad, lonely, and long ride home.

Anticipating her daughter's mood, Katie waited patiently on the veranda for her return. As soon as she saw the dust ball on the track she went inside and put the kettle on. By the time Eileen returned from the stables a steaming cup of hot weak tea was ready for her on the small table beside the other rocker.

"You are the best, Mother. Thank you. I needed this. It's been an emotional day. Goodness knows when I'll see him again, although I did promise I'd try to make it to Sydney in about a month."

"Well, we'll just have to find something to keep you busy until then, dear. Am I correct in thinking that if you wrote he wouldn't be able to write back?"

"Yes, he started to learn but never finished. And his job doesn't really require it. He can check boxes on the forms and someone else can write in the prisoner's name. I can write to him at the main police station in Sydney, but he'd have to get someone else to write a message back, and I doubt he'd want to do that."

"Yes, I got the impression he doesn't like to depend on others. Probably because he had to assume responsibility for looking after himself at such an early age. And his sister and brother as well. That was such a coincidence that they have the same names as the Bathurst commander and his wife. And his father's name sounded more Welsh than Irish. Did he ever mention his father's nationality?"

"He and I talked about our childhoods one evening, but he mainly told stories about the other two children, not wanting to talk much about himself. I'd forgotten their names, as he mainly referred to them as brother and baby sister. I think there was also an aunt who helped out somewhat. Not a real aunt but a friend of his mother whom he called 'auntie'."

"I was trying to remember what he did after the innkeeper died. Did he stay in Windsor or move to Parramatta or Sydney?"

"He went to Sydney, where more opportunities were available. He did a lot of odd jobs, everything from serving in a hotel bar to construction work for a group that was commissioned to build government buildings. He's somewhat restless, always looking for something bigger and better to do."

"And is that something you'd be comfortable with if you marry him? Changing jobs often could be a little uncertain and nerve-wracking I would think."

"Well, I think he's settled down a bit now, as he's been a mounted trooper for several years, and I would think that being a policeman would serve well in getting any other job. I have faith that with all the experience he has that he'd always be able to find good employment, just as he has in the past."

"I hope you are right, dear. I'd hate to learn that you had to find a job to support the family."

"What makes you think that would even be necessary, Mother? I'm surprised you raise the thought. I want to stay home and have his children, not be out working. Although I wonder if I went to Sydney shortly whether I could find something to do and save some money for our marriage. Maybe I could find a position as a teacher. What do you think?"

"I have no doubt you would be in demand as a teacher, dear. I just wish there was a position like that in the Hartley area, so you wouldn't have to think about going so far away."

"But Jerry is in Sydney anyway, Mother, so that wouldn't help."

"Oh, I suppose I also wish you could fall in love with some local chap, like Mary Jane did. Perhaps it's too late now..." Silence reigned and both relaxed, rocking gently while the floorboards creaked until eventually Katie sat up and said, "Ah, I see your father coming through the gate. I'd better go and start some dinner for us all. Want to come and help me peel the potatoes?"

Matthew started in as soon as he'd finished the dinner prayer. "Well, your beau didn't seem too comfortable around the lambs today. Looked like he was anxious to leave from the minute he arrived."

"Well, farming is clearly not his interest. He wants to do more exciting things, he says. Like chasing bushrangers."

"A dangerous profession at best. Some of them are totally ruthless and desperate. He could be killed at any time. Are you sure you want to be waiting and wondering whether he'll come home intact from his pursuits?"

"You heard his story about the rustlers. He's smarter than they are."

"So when will you get to see him again? Is he planning to come back this way?"

"I doubt it. With the transfer back to Sydney he says he'll be back to looking for bushrangers hiding beyond the borders of the surrounding towns. Apparently more and more convicts are going bush now that transportation to Sydney is being stopped, and many working for masters feel they should be freed."

"I can't say that he's the sort of man I hoped to see you marry, my dear. When I think of your three sisters' husbands I worry that he will never offer you the same sort of stability they provide their families. There are times he seems a bit sly to me, especially when he praises himself. Maybe he's a modern man but I was uncomfortable at times. Has he asked what you want in life?"

"Father, he came here to meet you all and let you get to know him a little, so of course he talked about himself. How, otherwise, would you get to know him? I'm sorry you didn't feel better about him. And as for me, I want more adventure than my sisters do. I want to see new places, and to learn about other parts of the colony, but yes I want children too. Mother has the patience of Job, but I don't. Jerry provides a sense of excitement and change that is attractive to me."

"Looks like your mind is made up and there's nothing we can do to change it. I just hope it all works out as you want. I suppose that means you'll be off to Sydney soon then?"

"I'm thinking I will go down in a month or so and try to find a position, perhaps as a teacher. At least I'll know Jerry there to help me, especially with his police connections."

Katie interrupted, "And of course there's the Kitchings family as well. You met some of them when you attended Grace and

Robert's wedding and went out on the boat to Manly. Maybe you should write to Robert and have him arrange another introduction. Perhaps you could even end up staying with his uncle Ian if they have room. Whatever you do I hope you will take time and not rush things. You don't want to give the wrong impression."

Eileen smiled at her mother's euphemisms for avoiding becoming too familiar and intimate and being labelled as a 'fallen woman'. She would do what was necessary but wasn't rushing off for coupling purposes.

Six weeks went by faster than Eileen anticipated. Matthew rode into town with her to await the stage. "I do wish you the best, my dear. I am truly sad to see you go and I hope you find what you are looking for in the big city. I have a gift for you to help you along." He reached in his saddle bag and handed her a purse that Katie had retrieved from an old chest in the barn. It was full of English £5 notes.

"Oh, Father, thank you so much. I'm sure this will make life a lot easier. I do love you so." Tears welled up in her eyes and she leant against his shoulder. "Maybe one day I'll be able to repay you."

"That's not necessary, daughter. Just make sure when you have the opportunity that you pass the goodness on. That's all I ask. Now I hear the stage approaching. So one last hug. Say hello to my girls in Penrith and give them my best wishes, and make sure you write to your mother."

Mid-afternoon the coach pulled up in a cloud of dust in front of the Penrith post office. The driver helped Eileen step down, then pulled her two large carpet bags from the roof and placed them on the road beside her. "Good luck to you, ma'am." And with a flick of the reins he was on his way.

George, who had been waiting, ambled across the road waving to Eileen and shouting her name. He kissed her on both cheeks, picked up the bags under one arm, and led her back to the shop. Ann was in the doorway, with the baby in her arms and William and Mary Ann half-hiding behind her long skirt peering shyly at the stranger. "Welcome, Eileen. We're so happy you are here. I'll give you a big hug later. Meanwhile, meet your new niece, she's just over four months old now and a real handful. Come on inside. George, do you want to ride over to the Kitchings' and invite them for dinner?"

Dinner was a lively affair with the three sisters swapping tales and reminiscences, and Eileen having to describe Jeremiah over and over. "I'm hoping I can convince him to come to Hartley for the Christmas community celebration. I know it would be hard for you with three children to cart along, Ann, but it would be so much fun if you and Grace and George and Robert could come. Please think about it, all of you."

Robert was up early next morning and headed off to work, but Grace came by again with four-year-old Eileen, who played contentedly with Ann's children. "Robert says Uncle Ian is looking forward to your coming and living with them all," Grace told Eileen. "His two eldest boys, Cameron and Keith, just left home to open a butcher's shop in Newcastle so their room is available and you will be able to rent it at a price far less than what you would have to pay commercially. I understand that the boys' mother, named Elizabeth, is also looking forward to your coming. With daughters Jane and Susannah that will make four females and four males in the home. She's usually been far outnumbered, now it will be even. Apparently you made a positive impression when you met them all at our wedding. Not that that surprises me. I mean after all you are my twin." Her grin was contagious and they all had a good laugh. It was so good to be with family.

The Sydney Kitchings couldn't have been more accommodating, and made her feel at home immediately. She'd brought small gifts from Grace and Robert as tokens of affection. The pleasure of their aunt and uncle receiving something totally unexpected was a joy to behold.

Over time Eileen simply became another family member, fitting in as if she'd been born there. She actively sought private school teaching positions since she had no formal training as a teacher, but as the school year finished in early December with the summer heat coming on, her timing was off and there were no vacancies. She caught up with Jeremiah and they often strolled in Hyde Park and listened to the bands playing on Sundays when he was free of duties. His work took him away more than she had anticipated so she eagerly looked forward to their limited time together. There were times she felt he used work as an excuse not to be with her and was upset when he made it clear he had no interest in going to Hartley for the village Christmas event. With heavy heart she wrote to Ann and Grace, claiming as a white lie that Jerry would be working and couldn't get away. She wondered to herself if things might be different next year, but told herself not to count on it.

Cameron and Keith came down from Newcastle for Christmas Day and she was intrigued with their entrepreneurship and initiative in setting up business there. Cameron at age twenty-seven was a charismatic fellow and took a clear fancy to her. Keith went back early to the shop but Cameron lingered on, showing her all the new parts of the city. His company was thoroughly enjoyable and contrasted markedly with Jerry's more insular interests and lesser social capabilities. The thought crossed Eileen's mind more than once that Cameron would probably make a good husband. But she really didn't want to be a butcher's wife like Ann. There was far more to the world than that in her view.

In January she got the break she'd been hoping for when the husband of one of the teachers at a nearby Presbyterian church school was transferred to Melbourne and his wife's position became vacant. Eileen readily accepted the appointment and looked forward to having something worthwhile to do every day. Instead of worrying about Jerry, she could worry about the charges in her class.

It wasn't long after she started teaching that she noticed a change in Jerry. He started complaining about his job, which was highly unusual. Small things seemed to be blown out of proportion in importance. She attributed the change to the fact that a new commander had been appointed in Sydney, who spent far more time with Crown lawyers than his predecessor and who had a far tighter and stricter interpretation of the current laws. Some of Jerry's captives seemed to be avoiding convictions on minor technical grounds, and new laws were providing greater recognition of citizens' rights as society progressed from the original basis of a penal colony to that of an English-type city. Sixty years had passed since the First Fleet had pulled into Port Jackson and enormous changes in the colony's make-up had occurred. Immigrants as free citizens were pouring into the country as the messages of continued opportunity in the land of sunshine, space, and water were reinforced with every shipload of wool and wheat heading back to England.

Jerry started talking about running a hotel again, and asked Eileen if she had money he could invest. Next was a scheme to run pleasure boats and ferries on the harbour in competition with existing companies already engaged in such activity. When she asked in what way Jerry's offerings would be different to attract customers away from the current companies, he had no solid answer, except to say there was room for more. Talk in the newspapers about establishing the Sydney Railway Company to build a train line between Sydney and Parramatta made him think about carpenter jobs again, but nothing definite was yet established with the company and in fact wouldn't be for two or more years. The line was proposed to be extended to Goulburn to easily and cheaply transport wool to the coast, and the graziers were big supporters of the notion. It was 1854 before it even made it to Parramatta.

His restlessness and discontent increased over time, and one new scheme after another entered and left his imagination. Eileen was the realist, Jerry the dreamer. Some of his notions were exciting for sure, and some had highly adventuresome overtones, like exploring the interior of the country, but they seemed conjured up more out of desperation than good rationale. During the springtime school holidays Eileen travelled home and shared her frustration with her parents and older brothers. They asked about Robert's cousin Cameron and her interest in him, but she stayed adamant that a butcher's wife she did not want to be.

It was her father who in the end finally summarised the situation and provided sage advice. "It seems to me, daughter, that while you have a good job and are not as restless as Jeremiah, you still have a deep-down desire for adventure. If you really love this man, then I think you have no alternative but to go along with one of his schemes at some point, otherwise he's going to pursue one of them alone and leave you behind. You've told us he always lands on his feet no matter what. Perhaps you have to trust that instinct and be your beau's supporter, and abandon all that conservative thinking your mother and I have instilled in you over the years. The question you probably have to answer is whether you would be happier by his side trying something new, exciting, and probably risky, or whether you would rather stay a maiden teacher, maybe forever single, always looking over your shoulder and wondering about your choice, while he pursues one of his dreams alone. Or... marry a more settled man who doesn't want adventure, challenge, and excitement all the time. Your sisters have made that sort of choice and seem relatively content. But I think you've ruled that option out."

On reflection, Eileen was amazed at her father's advice. He and Mother clearly weren't fond of Jeremiah. She had no hesitation in realising that Father spoke for both parents. Rather than lecture her on what they would like to see happen they had given her free choice, and offered balanced counsel. It didn't make her ultimate decision any easier, but at least she knew they would support her no matter what. She was thankful for their wisdom and love.

Back in Sydney she found Jerry excited about the latest news from California. Gold had been discovered two years earlier in 1848 and through 1849 thousands of fortune seekers had struggled to the gold fields. There was no easy way to get to California. The 'forty-niners' as they were called faced hardship and often death on the way. At first, most travelled by sea. From the east coast of the United States, a sailing voyage around the tip of South America would take five to eight months. One alternative was to sail to the Atlantic side of the Isthmus of Panama, then take canoes and mules through the jungle and wait on the Pacific side for a ship sailing for San Francisco. There was also a route across Mexico starting at Veracruz. But most American gold-seekers took the overland trek across the continental states. Each route had its own deadly hazards, from shipwreck to typhoid fever and cholera. Natives from the Sandwich Islands, later named Hawaii, were some of the first foreigners to reach the Pacific coast en masse. Depending exactly where the prospectors ended up, some would have it easy, picking up nuggets lying on the open ground. Others would find nothing.

To meet the demands of the arrivals, ships bearing goods from around the world headed for San Francisco. But ships' captains found that their crews often deserted to go to the gold fields. By late 1850 the wharves and docks of the city became a forest of masts, as hundreds of ships were abandoned. Enterprising San Franciscans turned the abandoned ships into warehouses, stores, taverns, hotels, and one into a jail.

Then gold was discovered in northern California, and this was what now attracted Jeremiah. New sources of gold had become available. Maybe it wasn't too late to find his fortune! He read the newspapers avidly and through his police connections with the military customs officials was able to talk personally to a few miners who had returned wealthier than when they had left. Their stories were all encouraging. Of course those who had emigrated and failed were still in California, unable to pay their way home. Their stories were of no interest to the newspapers.

Jeremiah started dropping hints about possibly going to California, and Eileen held her tongue, remembering her father's advice, waiting to see how serious her beau might be. It became very serious one Saturday night in late November as they stood by the gap in the Semi-Circular Quay where the Tank Stream entered the harbour. "Eileen, I'm not a man with a fine command of the language like you. So please listen closely. I've had it with the troopers, always following the commander's prissy orders. I can't stand it any longer. It's time to do my own thing, be my own boss, and so I've decided to go to California and find enough gold to live in comfort the rest of me life. I know I've talked about it more and more lately but here's the extra part. I'd like you to come with me on a great adventure there and I'd like us to travel as man and wife. What do you say?"

"Jerry, Jerry, do I hear you correctly, my love? You are asking me to marry you? Oh, you wonderful man, thank you, thank you." And with heady emotion and care cast aside she gasped: "And go to California? Oh yes, oh yes. When do we leave?" Perhaps not the proposal she'd been hoping for, but certainly typical of Jerry's ways. And, my gosh, she'd actually said yes to pulling up roots and heading to San Francisco. It would mean leaving every vestige of family behind. The sudden thought brought tears to her eyes. "It will be hard to leave family, Jerry. Very hard. I'll need you very close by my side in the times ahead." His smile reassured her. They hugged tightly and shared a long kiss, entertaining other passers-by with their passion.

Katie read her daughter's letter for the third time. "Dear Mother, Jerry has at last asked me to marry him. It was on a moonlit night down by the water at Circular Quay and was a complete surprise. There were times I thought he'd never ask. But he's made me very happy. At least in that respect"… Katie cast her mind back, remembering the first time she'd read that phrase and having some trepidation as to what she was about to learn by reading on. "… He's also proposed something truly exciting and different. Remember how you and Father made me think about what would truly make me happy in life—supporting Jerry in a new job or adventure, or being a spinster schoolteacher forever? You made me think long and hard, and finally I decided that life with Jerry would be far more rewarding and satisfying, even with ups and downs and unknown risks, than sitting still all my life wondering what I was missing. Anyway, you'll never guess. A month after we get married in January, we're going to sail to San Francisco and go prospecting for gold in the newly opened northern counties of California. I'm excited to visit another country and Jerry is enthusiastic about his chances to get rich as so many others have done. We plan to come back as soon as we can. Our ship would also stop in the Sandwich Islands, although we wouldn't have much time to look around there. The one thing I'm sad about is leaving everyone behind. I've written to Ann, and she can share my letter with Grace. Perhaps you can share this with Mary Jane. I know just after Christmas is a busy time on the farms but I do hope someone will be able to come to the wedding, which will be at St. Andrews Presbyterian Church on Saturday the 11th of January. Oh Mother, the one thing that scares me is not being in touch with everyone. I hope this finds you and Father and the twins and the youngsters all well. Please pass on my love to them all. Your loving daughter, Eileen."

Silent sobs tore at Katie's soul. Why, why, why? Why so far away? Why? Surely Eileen knew that many never came back, ending up poorer than when they left, owing money to equipment suppliers and the banks, destitute and cast adrift. Maybe Matthew's and her advice to Eileen had been all wrong. Despite her best intentions to think otherwise, she didn't trust Jeremiah. She chastised herself briefly for thinking that a big part of his proposing was purely in order to use Eileen's money to finance the trip. He had never struck her as a highly responsible man and she feared that the union with her daughter would not be a positive one for long. Love could be so blind.

Matthew's reaction to the letter was similar and he sat for a long time with his head in his hands saying nothing. He eventually got up and hugged Katie silently, no words being necessary to share the mutual sense of foreboding. Their instincts to be concerned were prophetic, as they would ultimately discover.

It was a miserable dinner that evening, with the young boys wondering what had upset their parents so much. Being told that Eileen was going further away didn't mean much, as she'd already been gone for well over a year. As an elder sister she lived in a totally different world that they knew nothing about. With the boys asleep Mathew quietly said, "There's nothing we can do, Katie, except be supportive and hope things turn out well. But even so saying I don't think I want to go to the wedding to see the grin on Jeremiah's face and feel the pain of losing our daughter. I feel bad thinking that, but I just can't do it. There is no way she would have elected to remain single. We both knew that in our hearts. No woman wants grow up to be an old spinster maid. I wish she'd picked a George, or Robert, or Andrew type, but too late now. This is a horrible disappointment. I truly wonder if we'll ever hear from her again once she reaches California."

"Perhaps there's one thing you could do, Matthew. Send to Robert's uncle Ian enough money for Eileen to buy a passage home, should she ever need it. He could give it secretly to Eileen with a note from you saying it is for emergencies. That would give us some hope. What do you think?"

"I think you are a very wise mother, my dear. Let's just hope Jeremiah doesn't find out about it. Another option might be to deposit it in a bank here and have them issue a Letter of Credit she could carry. I'll think about it. Oh dear. I dread telling the twins and Mary Jane. I feel so sad."

Jeremiah was only too happy to give up his Catholic background and get married in a Presbyterian church. The value of religion had disappeared years ago in gang fights in the back streets and alleys of Cork. Church had never saved anyone from misery that he had seen, save the priests themselves maybe. Confessions were a joke and he'd given them up after only a few meaningless attempts. Whatever Eileen wanted in a church service he was happy to tolerate. It was his own spirit that drove him, not some divine representation he had never understood.

Two of Jerry's friends were at the wedding service, but no Monahans, Kitchings, Fairweathers, or Dents came. Eileen swallowed her pride temporarily and marched out smiling as Mrs. Slane, determined to be happy no matter what. Deep down inside, however, she was terribly hurt. Her own family had abandoned her, letting her know in advance they wouldn't be present. Yet, when they'd last chatted, her father had seemed to be supportive of her making her own decision. In the end Mother and Father had betrayed her. There was a bitter feeling in the pit of her stomach and her soul felt torn. How could they do this to her? Had all those years of love and affection been thrown out the window so easily? Her brothers too? Maybe going to California would allow her to start a new life and overcome the betrayal and abandonment. At the moment it was still painful to even think about.

She and Jerry stayed at a local Sydney hotel overnight, where she experienced the second indignity of the day. From their time together she anticipated potential reluctance on Jerry's part to engage in any form of intimacy beyond kissing. She knew she was attractive from the glances she received on the streets, the reception she got when introduced to new people, and honest compliments from her family. But her best efforts at seduction failed to elicit a meaningful response from Jerry, who kept making various excuses for his disinterest. She felt devastated to be perceived as undesirable by her new husband. So here was yet another crushing disappointment, one unknowingly she was destined to suffer lifelong.

The British barque *John Calvin*, of five hundred and ten tons, had been built in Greenock, Scotland, and was launched in 1839. She'd first sailed as a merchant ship between London and Calcutta and Bombay, but was then requisitioned by the government for transportation. In September 1846 she transferred 199 male prisoners from London to Norfolk Island and in May 1848 one hundred and seventy female passengers from Dublin to Hobart Town. Thereafter she plied the Pacific between Sydney and San Francisco via the Sandwich Islands.

On Sunday Feb 23rd, 1851, with one hundred and eighty passengers on board, including Jeremiah Slane and his wife, Captain Lacy maneuvered the ship away from the wharf and set sail down the harbour, bound eastward. Compared to the trips which both Jeremiah and Eileen had endured years before between Ireland and Australia, this one was much shorter. Honolulu was reached in 65 days, and on May 25th, the *Daily Alta* California newspaper noted that the boat had arrived safely in San Francisco four days earlier. Unfortunately, like many other ships, the *John Calvin* was never again registered in any port, and probably became one of the collection of abandoned ships in the city harbour.

Sadly, Eileen was never heard from again. Longingly, and desperately, everyone waited for a letter, or a message from returning miners, but none came. They cursed the impetuousness and insincerity of Jeremiah Slane, especially when gold was discovered near Bathurst just six months after the couple left. Jeremiah could have gotten rich locally and Eileen could have stayed in the vicinity of family. The irony was devastating.

There was no way to change the past, to undo the poor decisions that had been made, to rescind well-intended advice and suggestions given. Instead, there was only grief.

Overwhelming, heart-breaking, soul-destroying grief.

Katie and Matthew had lost a daughter for whom they had forsaken their innermost beliefs in order to make her happy. They blamed themselves for not supporting her marriage better, for not attending the ceremony. Was this Eileen's revenge? Deliberately not communicating as payback for what she probably perceived as her family ostracizing her? They'd probably never know.

But it took years before they could forgive themselves.

20. Family expansion
& doings 1851/61

Dawn floated in softly as giant cumulus clouds blotted out the sun's early rays and made the sky unusually overcast for mid-summer. Matthew slept a little longer than normal as his biological clock held back, in apparent deference to the greyness outside. Katie had arisen before him and it was the insistent whistle of the tea kettle that stirred him into consciousness. He stretched and rose, heading a bit clumsily to the kitchen, where he smelled the first indications of fresh bread baking. His nose wrinkled appreciatively as he tipped hot water into the teapot and swirled it around before throwing it out the open window. Reflexively his arm reached back to the sideboard and he grabbed the big glass jar of Assam tea leaves. He spooned a substantial quantity into the pot and added more water. From the cupboard he took the two bone china teacups, then retrieved and checked the milk for sourness, and poured a small amount into each cup. One teaspoon of sugar for Katie, two for himself. Steam rose lazily from the teapot spout as he poured the first weak offering for his wife, then set the pot down on the holder, letting the brew steep and strengthen for his own tastes.

He treasured the small rituals and their sameness each day. Sameness meant nothing was wrong, everything was in order, life was normal. A cup of tea on waking up. Bread or scones baking for the mid-morning break. The ceiling beams creaking as the heat from the stove pipe warmed the room. Just like yesterday, and the day before, and the one before that. Consistency.

Katie checked the bread then sat down and reached for her cup. Her eyes sought her husband's and a gentle smile crossed her face. She asked her standard question: "What are your plans for today, kind sir?" It had started long ago, one of those little idiosyncrasies that was just theirs. Asking as if her lot was to serve and fulfill whatever it was that her husband desired or needed. A small mark of their grateful love for each other. As was his standard reply: "To make you happy, my darling."

He'd made her happy over and over. Eight children were part of his gifts. Working hard and self-sacrificing to do whatever was necessary to raise the children in God's light, having the courage and fortitude to bring them all to Australia, to stand tall when times were tough, and above all to have set an example for family and friends of fairness, honesty, integrity, and unconditional love. Katie thought back to the two times he'd been really hurt when children had disappointed. Mary Jane getting pregnant out of wedlock, and Eileen running off with a philandering con man, never to be heard from again. That had broken his heart. Never had she seen him so torn apart with grief, doubt, and self-recrimination. She knew in a way that it still rankled, more than ten years later, but they no longer talked about it, and she let him think she never dwelled on it, contrary to the truth.

His hair had turned silver gradually, and now, in full flight, it actually made him look quite distinguished. Pity he wasn't running for councilman. His looks would readily support his application. And his wisdom would be well recognized.

But he was content to manage the farm in a more leisurely fashion now, with Patrick doing the hard chores, leaving him time to regularly visit the grandchildren. At least the local ones, of which there were eleven, five boys and six girls. Down in Penrith Ann and George had another five although they had tragically lost their sixth, a bubbling, happy, golden-haired daughter, just sixteen months ago. Her death had affected all of them deeply, especially happening so soon after she'd visited Grandpa and Grandma for the first time. There was no real way to compensate for the little girl's passing, but other events offset the numbing feeling of helplessness.

He was especially proud that Thomas had finally married a lovely local girl, Rebecca Wilson, in Bowenfels six years ago. By coincidence she also came from County Donegal, back home. She'd already borne Thomas four children, first a girl, then three boys.

Rebecca treated Matthew as though he was her father since her own father, Nathaniel, had been held up, shot, and left to die by bushrangers when she was thirteen. He had survived but was crippled for life. Rebecca and her mother, Mary Ann, had scraped along, in part due to the generosity of neighbours. Matthew made sure her parents never wanted again.

Patrick hadn't married and showed no interest in doing so. He had taken time off a few years back and travelled to Melbourne and Van Diemen's Land, exploring the country on foot and horseback, bringing back tales of beautiful forests in the southern isle contrasting with the harsh penal colony at Port Arthur. Melbourne was a busy port with increasing commercialization, which didn't hold much interest. It was the land and nature in all its forms that appealed. He loved the ruggedness of the island shores interspersed with untamed beautiful bays, and animals such as the Tasmanian devil, quolls, and pygmy possums, as well as the endemic birds like the honey eaters and green rosella. Despite the exposure to new flora and fauna and the island's extensive unspoiled wilderness, in the end he was quite happy to return to his farm and its own attractiveness.

And Mary Jane, bless her, the daughter who had wrenched his soul so badly years ago, had mended things by having five children with Andrew, so that now there were two girls and four boys keeping her busy from dawn to dusk and beyond. Daytime silence was an unknown state. He could remember every child's and every grandchild's birthday. He would draw funny pictures on paper for them as gifts, and when they were old enough, at least four, he would carve small figurines or animals out of dead soft wood he found on the property. He was getting better with practice and the animal carvings had become more elaborate and detailed as the years had passed.

He wished he could see all the grandchildren again as had been the case three years ago in 1859. For his fifty-eighth birthday, George and Ann and Robert and Grace, along with all their children, had made the trek from Penrith and Emu Plains to Good Forest. Even with the improvements the government had made to the main western road it was still a several-day trip. And what a trip it had been. They'd all sheltered overnight at Collits' Inn on arrival in town, with the kids having a grand time sleeping all together in one big room. Not long after lights out it started to pour, waking children and adults alike with the incredible pounding noise on the tin roof. Thunder and lightning and torrential rain allowed only fitful sleep and it was nearly noon the next day before the rain finally abated. Streams coursed through the mud on the road outside and the dray they'd parked by the stables was awash with a small pool of water trapped by the metal edges rising above the base boards, soaking the few hay bales the younger children had used to lie on or sit against.

Patrick arrived at the hotel, having anticipated meeting them somewhere along the way. His news was far from reassuring. "We have five creeks to cross. They are all rising fast with floodwaters. We shouldn't have any trouble with the first four, but the last one may be a challenge. The sooner we can get going the better, as they will keep rising with the runoff from the hills."

The two families had six horses in total as the elder children were all given ponies at twelve years old and taught to ride and look after them. Together the men lifted the front of the dray and let the water slosh out over the back end. The two strongest horses were attached and the party set off. Patrick rode in front with one of the youngsters sitting on holding tight behind him. The two sets of parents gamely walked through the mud while the four horse-riding children followed Patrick at a distance and the two smallest children crouched on the wet dray, swaying to and fro sideways as the vehicle moved between uneven ruts in the soggy track.

The creeks were the first the children had encountered with swiftly moving water, swollen above normal levels. Patrick handed the child behind him to Robert and gathered the four mounted children as close as possible. "First rule. Don't rush your horse. He or she needs to feel the solid stones at the base of the creek, for she can't see them with all the silt and dirt that is muddying the water. Second rule, give her time to get used to the current and the temperature of the water. When she's ready, she'll let you know by wanting to move forward. Third rule. Guide her by turning slightly into the current. If you try to go straight across the current will push you too far from the ramp on the opposite side. Last. If floating debris hits your horse, don't panic. Stop, and I'll come and clear it away. Now do you understand what I've told you? I'm going to cross first and show you, so watch carefully. I will wait on the other side, but before each of you crosses I'm going to ask you to repeat back to me the four rules. Do I need to go over them again? No? You'll see that the water doesn't reach your feet in the stirrups. Okay, here I go."

From the other side—not more than ten feet away—Patrick called, "Right, Eileen, tell me the rules and let's see how you do." He had Elizabeth Dent, aged nine, go next, and she did fine. Her sister Mary Ann showed some nervousness mid-stream as a branch full of leaves passed right in front of her mare, which suddenly stopped of its own accord. But she too made it. Finally George's eldest son William crossed. "Well done, all of you," Patrick encouraged. "Now you know. Some of the creeks will be wider and with higher water, some less. Wait down the track a little while I help the other three cross."

Back on the starting side he and his brother-in-law George put George and Ann's three youngest, George Matthew, seven, Thomas aged five, and Rebecca, just two, on his stallion, and they walked across holding the children in place. Ann and Grace volunteered to wade and got their boots and skirt bottoms wet, while Robert walked beside the horses pulling the dray.

The journey was slow going and most unpleasant as the track was muddy, with water constantly dripping from the trees above. They crossed the next three creeks with little problem, the children gaining in confidence each time, getting their horses' sides wet only once, and enjoying seeing their mothers and fathers getting their clothes wetter at each ford.

Their merriment ceased as they viewed the final creek to cross. This was the deepest and widest of all, and at the moment it was almost running its banks, which were five feet tall on either side.

The group stopped and pulled off the track to a large grassy area that sloped down to the creek. The riding children were more than nervous, scared, in fact, of the swirling waters. George asked

Patrick, "Is there any other place where it might be easier to cross?"

"Not really. There's a spot a quarter mile upstream where there are large rocks that can be used as stepping stones when the water is down, but we'd never see them today and there'd be no way to get the wagon across. I know at first glance this doesn't look good but it's not really as bad as it seems. You'll have to take my word for it, but the best part is that the bottom of the rivulet is very even with no holes and in fact the bed is all small stones, so there really is good footing. With the water spread out like it is the current isn't as swift as it would be were the watercourse narrower.

"Here's what I suggest. Since Ann and Grace ride side-saddle they should each take a child's horse, and I will lead them across one at a time. Their clothes will get a bit more wet as the water will be well up over the horses' bellies, but there's no alternative. I will ride on the upstream side to help break the current and ward off any floating branches. Taking them first will make the children feel better to see their mothers safe on the other side. Then the three of us men will take turns going across with a child sitting in front, not behind. I want them to see where they are going and to focus on their mothers waiting for them. If they look too hard at the dirty water and depth it could upset them. When all seven are across, I'll take the extra one, then we can think about getting the dray over to the other side. Does that sound like a good approach or does anyone have better ideas?"

The water was cold and Ann shrieked as her knees got wet. But with Patrick's horse's surefooted guidance she made it. Grace, alerted by Ann's reaction, silently followed Patrick's directions and let her horse be led, also making it safely. Two down, seven to go. William fidgeted in front of George and hung on tight. "I'm coming, Mother. I'm coming," he shouted. Ann lifted him down and held him tight. This was an experience none of the kids would forget. Robert and Eileen had a faltering moment as they started to climb the opposite bank when the horse slipped at one point. The mare recovered quickly, however, and almost before Eileen could complain she was in Grace's arms.

Noting this, the men adopted a slight change in tactics. As they approached the base of the far bank they urged their horse to move faster in order to have more momentum climbing up the bank. Even so, they had more slippages and by the time the last child was safely across, the bank was churned up severely from the horses' hooves.

Robert wondered out loud, "Maybe we should leave the dray here and come back for it when the waters subside. It will be submerged if we try to get it across. And we have the hay bales to move as well. We can take the two horses from the dray, giving us eight in total. That should work okay. What do you think, Patrick?"

"That is a reasonable idea, but frankly I think the waters are only going to go higher, especially as it looks like more heavy rain is on the way. So it may be two days or more before the water level drops enough to come back and pick the dray up. I'd like to try and see what we can do. You've seen the river bed is firm; our only issue is getting up the other side. With two horses pulling—and we could add more—I think we can make it. George?"

"Let's have a go. We can tie the bales to the back end and let them float across pulled behind us. Patrick, maybe you can lead and Robert and I can hop off our horses once we reach the bank and help push from behind."

"Thanks a lot, George. All I need is to get more wet."

"You can run ahead once we get going again, Robert, and dry off that way. How much further is it to the homestead, Patrick?"

"About another three miles. Sure, Robert, you'd be almost dry if you ran."

The humour helped and they secured the bales and maneuvered the dray down the slope. It sank beneath the waters but the two horses moved steadily under Patrick's guidance. With the heavy load they couldn't increase momentum as they approached the opposite bank. And their valiant effort to climb stalled halfway up as first one slipped, then the other. The dray ended up at a forty-five-degree angle with the front end poking up parallel to the bank and the rest under water. Patrick released the two horses and they easily climbed the remainder of the bank. The men hauled in the hay bales and managed to lift them out a little ways downstream directly on to the bank, which no longer sloped at that point.

Two long coils of rope were removed from where they hung in front of the dray. Each was tied to the end of the geldings' harness, now dragging on the ground. The other ends were tied to the stanchions holding the front wheels on the dray. With the two strong horses on flat ground as opposed to the sloping bank, the men felt that the animals would be able to pull the dray up without much difficulty.

Well, that was the theory, anyway. The horses did their job, but just as the front wheels of the dray were about to crest, one of the ropes came untied, the back end of the dray careened sideways, and one of the rear wheels sunk in the soft mud at the side of the track, up to its axle. Luck just wasn't with them.

Even when the rogue rope was refastened, the geldings were no match for the soft clay's sucking power. George slipped off his shirt, dungarees, socks, and boots, and clad only in his drawers waded through the mud alongside the embedded wheel. Patrick stripped down also, and Ann and Grace admired the physique of the two men. Their brother, lean and wiry, was dwarfed by the size of George's chest, his biceps, and shoulder width. Ann loved looking at her man's body.

Patrick and Robert took positions behind and on the up side of the dray. With the horses urged on by Patrick's shouts, George grunted and strained and lifted the wheel out of its mud rut, as the others heaved and pushed, and to everyone's relief the dray rose over the top of the embankment and came to rest.

The kids cheered wildly and clapped their hands, and the men all grinned and muttered a few choice words low enough for the children to miss hearing. They shook hands all round, granting special thanks to George, realising full well that his superior strength was what had saved the day. All three then washed off in the stream and climbed the bank at a dry spot twenty yards further downstream.

What an adventure it had been for everyone. Reflecting back, Matthew remembered how the children couldn't stop talking about the raging waters, how the water was almost over the horses' heads, but how bravely they'd crossed the first four streams, how the dray was totally under water at the last creek, and how their father had gotten undressed and lifted the big dray wheel out when two horses couldn't move it. He loved their exuberance and exaggeration, knowing in a way that for some of them fear had enlarged many aspects of the whole experience. He remembered how the large influx of visitors had had to be accommodated in three homes—Patrick's, Mary Jane's, and his own.

When the sun came out two days later the children even re-enacted parts at a small creek on the property and Matthew couldn't help but laugh with them. It had been a wonderful joyous occasion with the small cousins all getting to know one another better and some getting to know grandparents for the first time.

The years since the visit hadn't yet diminished the memories, although inevitably it was the innocent smile on the face of Rebecca, then two and a half years old, that lingered longest.

From joy to sadness. Matthew, as Grandpa, couldn't stop the old sad feelings from entering and haunting his soul again. Rebecca had just turned four twelve days before the accident. Most of her brothers and sisters were at a friend's house playing, Ann was minding the shop with Rebecca generally hanging around her skirts. George and his eldest son William were out back taking measurements for an extension to the stables. They had measured across the entrance, intending to duplicate it in size, and had walked inside the structure to check the distance from front to back. Unknown to either, the back screen door of the house had unlatched and young Rebecca had wandered into the yard. She heard her father and brother talking inside the stable, and headed in their direction.

She yelled "Daddy" just as young William reached across in front of one of the horses to measure the height of the feed bucket off the ground. Unsure of the boy's intentions, the horse raised his head quickly, backed up two steps, and unknowingly kicked Rebecca in the head. Her "Daddy" changed to a scream, and father and son raced out to find her lying unconscious just two feet from the open end of the stall.

George cradled his daughter in his arms and immediately urged William to ride and bring the doctor, despairing that there was little he would be able to do. At Regentville he'd seen just how serious horse kicks could be. Quickly he bundled Rebecca inside the house, shouting for Ann, who was in the shop out front with a customer. He laid his little girl on the kitchen counter and tried to pull her matted hair out of the bloody indentation behind her temple. As gently as he could, he washed her face and neck and then held her hands. Her eyes had closed, her breathing was almost imperceptible, and her face was getting paler by the minute. George kept muttering over and over, "I'm sorry, I'm sorry, Rebecca. I love you. I love you. Hold on, please hold on."

Ann cried as George explained what happened, and ran back to the bedroom to get a warm blanket. They wrapped her up, her body unmoving, bathed more blood from her face, and took her to the living room. There Ann sat in the rocker, tears streaming down her face, and held her close while George paced up and down, wringing his hands, waiting for the doctor to come. At Ann's request he stopped pacing, kneeled by Ann's feet, and together they prayed for the life of their little girl.

She died in Ann's arms not fifteen minutes later, well before the doctor arrived. One minute she was with them, the next gone. Her utter stillness filled her parents with incredible grief, their feelings of helplessness palpable, as they each alternately hugged and kissed her and cried their silent goodbyes. Life had never been so unfair.

The doctor and William found the two of them utterly heartbroken and distraught, sitting on the living room sofa with the little girl's body between them. William stared at his sister and broke out in huge sobs, his heart grieving, and his mind conjuring up guilt. It was his action that had made his horse back up, causing the terrible injury that was far more than Rebecca's young body could possibly handle.

Ann, recognizing his fear that he would be blamed, rose and held him tight to her skirt, trying to reassure him with words. "It's not your fault, William, not your fault. It's an accident." But he was inconsolable and broke away, running out the front door and down the street. The doctor asked where the other children were, and decided it would be easiest on George and Ann if he told the children the news, at the same time letting the neighbours know about the tragedy. From his experience with the sudden death of children, he knew that at some stage neighbours and friends would become an important ingredient in the eventual healing process. The sooner they got involved, the shorter the healing time would be, for both the parents and the siblings.

Given directions, he rode off to talk to the children, knowing they would be disbelieving and have their own feelings of inexplicable grief. He conjectured that since they had not been present when the accident occurred, they would also assume guilt in part, feeling that had they been playing at home, Rebecca would never have wandered off undetected. Yes, indeed, he mused, life could sometimes be very cruel.

It was the 11th of September, 1860. Spring was showing all her glory. The cootamundra wattle was in gorgeous thick yellow bloom, newborn white lambs frolicked in the paddocks, and the cloudless sky was a vivid blue.

But for a once vibrant four-year-old used to laughing and playing, and being lovingly teased by her elder siblings, the colour of the day was no more. For her, this spring had disappeared in an instant, and all future springs would be absent as well.

They buried Rebecca in the cemetery behind St. Stephen's church the next day.

Katie and Matthew had never lost a child, although other tenant farmers back in Drumcairn had, and they'd been close enough to share some of the grief. They knew, however, it was not the same as losing a member of one's own family. Even with Rebecca's death they couldn't feel the same way Ann and George did. George had become depressed afterwards and Ann indicated in her letter that she had had to work hard to get him back to his old ways. Part of his despondency had been due to the fact that he couldn't help his daughter in any way. According to Ann's letter, he had had an elder sister who'd been born developmentally challenged and had died in her teens where once again he had been helpless to stop her demise.

Christmas became a turning point as George put his energy into making sure personalized gifts were available to the other children so they realised they were still as important and loved as before.

As he aged, Matthew had come to realise that much of what occurred in life was uncontrollable. One made decisions and choices that at the time were well reasoned and perceived to offer the best course forward. But having made them, one was still at the mercy of nature and God's will. Unexpected events occurred no matter how good one's planning. Life was not a smooth line in the sand or a straight path through the woods. Waves rose further than expected, storms changed the routes of creeks, and detours and alternative paths were required.

Compared to some, all the convicts for example, the Monahans had been incredibly fortunate as a family. Even so, he reflected that 'into every life a little rain must fall'. Rebecca's death was probably the first of multiple showers that would inevitably come their way. He turned his head to the heavens. "Please let them be few and far between, Lord!"

A major consequence of the huge birthday gathering three years back was a life-changing decision made by Robert and Grace. For many years Robert had managed the holding pastures and abattoirs for George's butcher shop in Penrith. He'd dreamed of being his own master of a property, but over time another prospect had become attractive—that of going back to his experience of being a shopkeeper. Coincidentally, not three weeks after the family get-together, the current owner of the general store in Hartley announced his retirement and a subsequent move to Sydney, where he and his wife had extended family. His shop was for sale. Matthew wrote to Robert as soon as he heard the news since his daughter and son-in-law had been very open about their commercial interests when visiting.

A week later Robert arrived and stayed five days while negotiating with the current owner. It took time to check inventory and to value all the merchandise, before coming to an agreement on sale price. With the help of a local banker Robert was able to consummate the sale. He didn't stay to rejoice but hurried home to tell Grace and Eileen and to start arrangements to sell the house and help George find a replacement field manager.

It was convenient that they could all stay in one of the family homesteads while Robert took over the store. The big board out front was replaced with the Kitchings name and he rearranged the existing counters and displays to his preferences and checked through the books in more detail on which products were most in demand and how extensive patron credit offerings were. He found a few surprises, unrevealed by the previous incumbent, but nothing that couldn't be corrected with a little effort, empathic relationships, and some creative selling and marketing. He loved what he was doing and Grace noticed an enhanced disposition as the community embraced his presence and actions and his patronage grew.

At times she would help out, as would Eileen, who was now fourteen and very quick with her sums and ability to make correct change for customers. Grace got to meet the local residents and many farmers and their wives, especially on Saturdays, which was when the outlying farm folk tended to come to town. The other invaluable benefit for Grace was being so much closer to family. To see her nieces and nephews up close more often, as well as sister and brothers and parents, warmed her heart. Sharing had always been a part of life growing up in County Donegal. While she and Ann had grown closer together in Penrith and Emu Plains, there were so many more blood relatives in the Hartley area that she felt in a way as if she'd come home again.

Daughter Eileen loved the Cooerwull Academy boarding school, riding home to help out in the shop at weekends. She had an effervescent, outgoing personality that reflected a mature, adventuresome, and lively spirit. There was a restlessness in her, however, and when school holidays came in December of 1860 she pleaded to go to Sydney with her father on his semi-annual trip to evaluate and buy merchandise for the general store. They stayed with Robert's uncle Henry in the heart of Sydney and Eileen became enthralled with the vibrant city.

Henry's son Richard, eight years Eileen's senior, and her cousin once removed, became her constant companion and guide, showing her the sights and sounds of the growing metropolis whenever he could force time away from his father's butcher shop. Eileen marveled at the enormous cargo ships in Darling Harbour, and especially the vast quantities of wool being loaded for export. She wondered if any came from her cousins' and grandparents farms, as shearing had taken place late spring.

The Quay and the main harbour kept drawing her back. Where she had been born and raised there were no inland lakes, just a river or two and numerous rivulets, and she had never been on a motor or sail boat. For a thrill Richard took her up to Parramatta on a rickety ferry. She was like a little girl running from side to side to see all the different islands and views. Where there weren't farms along the river banks there were often parks or bushland, and in some places small factories taking in, or discharging, water. The couple walked around Parramatta admiring the estate houses and other historic buildings, and to finish the day on a high note, caught the steam train back to Sydney. The stories she would be able to tell when she got home kept mounting up.

Five days flew by, at the end of which Eileen and Richard, at the wise young ages of fifteen and twenty-three, realised that through constant propinquity they had fallen in love with one another. Saying good bye became extra hard and they vowed to keep up their relationship by writing frequently. Eileen badgered her father the whole trip home asking when was the earliest he would permit her to get married. She eventually wore him down to get a grudging "close to seventeen" as his final answer. He added one condition—that the local Presbyterian reverend or appropriate state official agree that cousins once removed were permitted to marry in the church's eyes. Eileen hadn't thought much about that issue for her love was blind, and she asked many questions of her father about church and state policies, most of which he couldn't answer. He wondered how much trouble Grace would create for him when she learned he had given in to such a young age, and had mixed emotions about the possible ramifications of the church or state ruling. Permission granted would make his daughter happy.

Permission denied would lead to unpleasant arguments and interminable anguish, of that he had little doubt.

Grace had married at age twenty-one, but her younger sister Ann had married at seventeen. Eileen wielded this knowledge like a club in discussion with her parents, and when the local minister indicated that English royalty and the Church of England for centuries had tolerated even direct cousins marrying, she felt she was on fertile ground. They could find no government official who could determine what office should address the issue, and a letter to the Sydney courthouse elicited no reply.

As a consequence, two related Kitchings, Richard and Eileen, were duly married by the Reverend John Lang at Scots Church, Sydney, in October 1861. Eileen's parents, Robert and Grace, happily gave their permission for the union, and the witnesses present were Richard's elder sister Susan, and her husband of nine years, Samuel Penhall. Initially the couple lived with Richard's parents, but were saving for their own flat, with the intention of possibly opening a butcher's shop adjoining an inn in Hartley in time to come.

Matthew relished the thought of more family living in the area. The timing was good for many reasons. One was the advent of gold. Ever since payable gold had been discovered not far away in 1851, prosperity in the region had increased. Once Edward Hargraves made his historic announcement of his findings in May of that year there began a massive influx of gold seekers from all over the eastern part of the country. They headed for the emerging towns of Ophir and Sofala, out of Bathurst, panning for specks of colour in the numerous creeks in the vicinity. Within two months over four hundred claims were being worked on Lewis Ponds and Summer Hills Creek. As a result, it didn't take long for Bathurst to be converted into a boom town. Matthew was happy that none of his sons or sons-in-law had succumbed to the allure of making it rich from gold fever. Most miners recovered their costs, a few got lucky and did well, but others went home penniless. Prospecting was a risky business.

Miners in general needed accommodation, transport, food, and supplies. They also needed supporting services. New hotels were built, large outfitters established their presence, government offices expanded, more stables and blacksmiths were needed, more farm produce was sold locally instead of being shipped to Sydney, the flour mills worked extra shifts, another grocery store opened, the bakery was enlarged, physicians set up offices, new lawyers arrived, new banks formed, an extra wing was added to the hospital, and a jeweler set up business. The town changed almost overnight.

Trade up and down the road to Penrith and Sydney increased dramatically, which was why Matthew thought Richard's notion of a butcher and hotel in Hartley as an intermediate stopping point made good sense, for Bathurst was still growing as an inland center of commerce and the goldfields were not exhausted yet. New discoveries kept coming to light.

While Bathurst was still fifty miles beyond their village, Robert and Eileen had definitely benefitted from the increased traffic past the front door of their shop. As a shrewd marketing man Robert quickly bought numerous quantities of varied mining supplies and advertised their availability with crude signs at roadside. The tools were often sold as a result of the suggestion that supplies may not be as readily available in Bathurst due to the enormous number of gold seekers buying there. And, further, as an opportunist, any time a heavily loaded wagon of goods stopped in town, Robert would be ready with cash to see if he could pay the driver for certain highly demanded supplies in his load. It didn't always work, depending on how readable, and changeable, was the bill of lading or sale from the Sydney supplier. It was amazing how certain goods could fall off a load and never be missed by the driver. As times changed and new modern conveniences became available, Robert also became an agent selling coal from Scott Brown's mines to those wanting new sources of heat in their homes.

The second most important reason Matthew thought it was a propitious time to build in Hartley was because recent information indicated that Cobb and Co. was moving its headquarters and coach-building factory from Melbourne to Bathurst. Gold had to be safely moved from the new goldfields to Sydney and reliable transport was essential. Existing casual cartage in the mail and other fly-by-night coaches had become an obvious target for bushrangers, which had created a major problem for the authorities.

Cobb and Co. had earned a reputation for guaranteed, on-time, reliable delivery of people and goods. Their coachmen were trained horsemen and gunmen. Their hallmark of quality was the use of relatively comfortable American-designed coaches, fresh horses approximately every twenty miles, quick changeovers, comfortable coaches, and a realistic timetable one could almost set one's watch by. Some changeover stations offered food, some overnight accommodation. Hartley was designated as one of the towns to provide a changeover station, bringing new business and travelers to town.

Matthew saw this as a positive aspect for the town's future. His vision was prophetic, for in the years ahead Cobb and Co. grew to be so successful that it eventually became an Australian transport icon. Many towns benefitted. Hartley was one of them.

21. Progress, family flux, a revelation

1862 had started out well enough. The annual Christmas celebration at the end of 1861 on the Hartley commons had once again been a great success with more people attending than ever before. Indeed, there was talk of having to find a larger venue in the future. It had been a hot day and the heat continued into the new year. But the price of wool and wheat was up and that brought smiles to all the growers in the region. The Europeans must have suffered dismal grain crops and been in short supply of wool from elsewhere. Actually, Australian wool had come into increasing demand, not because of supply issues, but rather because the merino breed of sheep in Australia was producing much finer and softer wool than wool from any other country. Competition to produce the finest fleeces had risen to a national level throughout the colony and local growers were lauded when they won regional competitions.

Shearing, through its art and value, had now become a prideful occupation. Itinerant groups of shearers arranged contracts a year in advance to work sheds on properties in a defined region. On large properties the sheds were huge, capable of having tens of shearers working at the same time. Sometimes neighbouring graziers would share a shed since they were often used only once a year. Most properties with a few thousand sheep would have room for up to ten shearers. The Monahans and Fairweathers shared such a shed on Andrew's land.

There was a well-recognized process to shearing. The sheep were rounded up and their wool washed—usually in a nearby creek—to get rid of burrs, soil, and vegetable matter. Using dogs, they were then moved to large pens attached to, and under, the shed. A sheep would be caught by the shearer from the catching pen and taken to his "stand" on the shearing board, where it was shorn using metal shears. The shearer began by removing the belly wool, which was separated from the main fleece by a roustabout while the sheep was still being shorn. A professional or "gun" shearer would typically remove a fleece, without significantly marking or cutting the sheep, in two to three minutes, depending on the size and condition of the animal. The shorn sheep would be released and removed from the board via a ramped chute in the floor or in a wall, to an exterior counting-out pen.

Men were paid by the number of sheep shorn in an eight-hour period, but were penalized if they cut the sheep too severely or left too much wool on. It was back-breaking work requiring a lot of stamina to hold a heavy sheep in position and efficiently cut off the fleece. Roustabouts would watch for bad cuts and seal them with tar, pick up the fleeces, and throw them clean side down on a large 4' by 6' slatted table. There, a helper would 'skirt the fleece', removing any remaining dirt or poor sections, and then a 'classer' would examine the wool, decide how fine and clean it was, roll the fleece up, and throw it in the appropriate sorting bin. When a bin was full the fleeces would be pressed into 400-pound bales which were banded with metal strips, ready for transport to a coastal city and delivery to a freighter for export.

Shearers were usually wiry, lithe men, with incredibly strong hands to work the heavy 'blade shears'. These shears consisted of two blades arranged similarly to scissors except that the hinge was at the end farthest from the point (not in the middle). The cutting edges passed each other as the shearer squeezed them together, allowing the wool to be cut close to the animal's skin. Fast shearers could make good money. Shearers were so important that they demanded tent or hut accommodation and always travelled with a cook. The bunks had to be comfortable and the cook had to provide not only amazing quantities of food for very hungry men after their exertion, but food of good quality as well. A poor cook was readily replaced. Shearers could actually work almost year round moving from district to district, their worst enemy being rain, which made the fleeces harder to cut smoothly. For the grazier rain made round-up harder and put shorn lambs at greater risk since they now had less natural covering.

Demand for shearers increased as recognition grew around the world of the quality of Australia's merino wool. For station owners like Matthew there was enormous pride in seeing all the bales with the property name and fineness indicator stamped on them. The wagons were loaded high with hessian bales and slowly headed eastward across the Blue Mountains in caravans to Parramatta, where the cargo was loaded onto trains for the final leg of the journey to Sydney. Back home the growers waited nervously to learn the market price they'd achieved. Telegraph links had started in operation in 1858, and were gradually being extended between major Australian towns and cities, but the lines still had not made it far into country centres. Businessmen and government officials alike eagerly awaited its advent in order to change the speed with which information could flow and changes in business decisions could be made. Rural progress was just around the corner.

While January had been a good month for all, things changed dramatically in February.

Not the heat. Although it was ferocious. It was even hot in the shade. In Hartley, all across the Blue Mountains where the bushfire danger was at its peak, and down on the flats by the Nepean River, the heat was oppressive, sapping the strength and motivation of man and animal alike. Wombats, echidnas, possums, wallabies, and other numerous native fauna stayed closer to the river and the water than usual. Swans and ducks gathered on the surface under the drooping branches of the graceful willow trees, their calls strangely muted. A hush settled across the region as wildlife and man minimized activity. Without breeze there was no rustling of the leaves. The cattle lay down rather than stand and the sheep bunched together wherever they could find shade. The water level in the brooks fell and the swishing noise of water over rocks disappeared. Frogs still croaked but without the strength and exuberance of their usual calls. Everyone hoped and prayed for a break in the weather pattern but nothing changed for day after day after scorching day.

One evening in Penrith, when the mountain shadows had already encompassed the town, while Ann and the children were preparing a late supper, they were alerted to the persistent neighing of a horse outside. William went to check and rushed back in a moment later yelling, "It's Maisie, but Dad is not with her." Ann's heart leapt to her mouth as she commanded William and George Jr. to saddle up and help her search for George. She hopped up on Maisie, and with William on his horse and George Jr. on his, they galloped down High Street and set course for the river, anticipating George would have been out on his favourite late afternoon and evening route. William crossed Emu Ford first and headed south, so when Ann and George Jr. followed, they turned north. It wasn't a hundred yards along the bank that William found his father lying on his back on the ground. He jumped down and found his father breathing in a laboured manner, with his eyes closed. There was no response when he asked, "Dad, can you hear me?" So he quickly took off his hat and shirt, bundled them under his father's head, turned to face back the way he had come, and yelled, "Coo-eee, coo-eee, coo-eee" as loudly as he could, to alert his mother and brother.

On arrival, Ann knelt beside her man and followed William's actions, whispering, "George, can you hear me? Please say something, George," but also got no response. She quickly checked for broken bones and bloody injuries but found none, although as she turned him on his side she noticed he'd fallen on top of a large rock. Spittle and foam at George's lips and on his chin were the only outward signs of a problem. She reached for the flask on Maisie's flank but found it empty. To her boys she said, "We'll have to get him to the Benevolent Asylum hospital as quickly as we can. William, you are fastest, rush home and bring back the spring cart. We can't lay him across Maisie in case he has internal injuries. Tell the girls and Thomas to fill two bottles with water and meet us on the way back. The bank is too steep here to fill his flask but I'll get some at the ford. It won't be enough and we'll need more. George Jr., I want you to ride ahead to the hospital and tell them we're coming so they make sure a doctor stays there and waits for us, and doesn't go home since it's near the end of the day. Be quick, lads, your dad is still breathing and we'll see what the doctor says. Go now."

William knew his father was seriously ill, and that his mother was being brave. He rode like the wind through the stifling heat, told his sisters and his brother Thomas what they'd found as he hitched up the cart, and was back on the road going west in short order. The top of the cart was inches above the lowered water level at the ford, so he knew they'd be able to keep his father dry coming back. He shed no tears, just concentrated on maneuvering the cart safely to the opposite bank, raised another "Coo-eee" to tell his mother he was close, and cantered along the bank to her side.

They turned the cart around, and together clumsily managed to lift George on to it and then headed back to the ford. Once there, Ann got off Maisie and walked beside the cart helping maintain stability, creating as comfortable a ride as possible for her man. She'd taken off her bonnet and put it over his face to keep the flies away since his hat seemed to be missing. He still hadn't opened his eyes but more spittle and drool was escaping from his lips, and Ann secretly knew that there was something wrong way beyond her ken.

She filled the flask and held it to his lips, but he wouldn't sip. She took William's folded shirt and soaked it in the water and placed it across George's forehead under the bonnet, hoping to help cool him down. She poured the water from the flask over his hands and ankles, and took off his boots.

The horse pulling the cart kept up a steady pace from the river, and the two girls and Thomas were waiting with more water and some towels at the crossroads to the town. They had managed to remain stoic and hopeful, until they actually saw their father looking so pathetic and weak. Appalled at his visage they all burst into tears, and Ann, unable to comfort them, focused instead on the task of getting George to the hospital.

The doctor had remained behind once he knew they were coming, and the two boys, the doctor, and Ann managed to lift

George to a table, where the doctor and a nurse examined him closely while Ann and the boys sat in the chapel and waited.

As expected, the diagnosis and prognosis was far from good. The doctor gently explained that, in his opinion, George had suffered a severe stroke and that unfortunately he was now dying and that there was essentially nothing that could be done to save him. He was sorry to say, but based on his experience he did not see George lasting the night.

Once again, William was elected to rush home and bring the other three children to the hospital, to say goodbye to their father. None of them relished the idea, but they did it anyway, feeling awkward and embarrassed and confused. Ann sent them all home and stayed behind alone, holding George's hand and whispering her love until her heart broke as her man slipped away.

And so it came to be that Ann's husband, George Clarke, departed the earthly world early in the morning of 12th February 1862. The doctor's assessment was that he died from the combined effect of a paralytic stroke and apoplexy, and this cause was entered into the register of the Penrith District Dispensary.

Word travelled fast through the close-in farm region and over thirty people, including friends, customers, and town officials were present at the burial service conducted by the Church of England minister, Elijah Smith, two days later at St. Stephen's graveyard. A popular citizen was laid to rest, and for his family, an historic era of convict times had come to a close.

Matthew vividly remembered the arrival of the unknown messenger who had been paid to carry the shocking news to remote relatives. It was the day of the planned funeral when he came galloping down the track and through the gates around midday. It was far too late for anyone from Hartley to attend the service, and the messenger only had the barest of information on exactly what had transpired. George had had a stroke, his horse had come home rider-less, and when they eventually found him they'd taken him to the hospital, where he died overnight.

Katie's immediate feelings were for her daughter. Once she had shed her initial disbelief that this could have happened, she fretted about how Ann would cope with five youngsters and a shop to manage. Would she have to give up the shop? Was William old enough to fill much of his father's function with the business? Somehow she doubted it. Perhaps he could help take care of the younger children and do odd jobs around the house. Could or would neighbours help out in the short term? Had Robert and Grace still been living there they would certainly have provided support, but that was no longer the situation. The more she pondered, the more obvious the solution. She and Matthew would make a visit and help where they could. It was the least they could do.

Two days later they boarded the mail coach for the run over the Blue Mountains. It was the first time they'd both been back this way in years and they marveled at the progress that had been made in improving the road, and at all the new establishments either already in place or being built. Little communities were springing up every few miles. They bypassed a number of bullock-led drays laden high with wool bales, and met several coming the opposite way with goods for the shops in Bathurst. The road was no longer just a track for the hardy adventurer as it was when they first walked it, but a major thoroughfare for trade.

The shop seemed closed as they approached so they walked around the house to the back where they found Ann sitting on a tree stump watching the two youngest children poking sticks at a small garter snake. Matthew dropped the bags with their clothes and as the children turned and yelled "Grandma, Grandpa!" Ann rose and hugged her parents. Tears flowed freely as emotions could not be contained. Katie finally managed to whisper between sobs, "We're so sorry, Ann, so terribly sorry."

Matthew's grief was too strong for words, and to mask his feelings he picked up the children who had come running to his side. Thomas, at nine, burst out, "Grandpa. Daddy's gone away and we won't see him again." At which Matthew choked up again but managed to say, "Yes, son, he won't be coming back. You'll have to be a big boy now and help mummy whenever you can." George, at eleven, with only the innocence children can project, asked, "Why did he go away, Grandpa? We saw him at the hospital. He was very sick. Why didn't he get better? We all prayed for him. But God didn't answer our prayers. Why didn't he stop Daddy from dying?" Matthew's only answer was a hug. The boys stared at him wide-eyed.

Katie's arms were around Ann's shoulders as they headed inside to make a pot of tea. "Mother, it just seems so unfair. There are so many ne'er-do-well men around who have little hope to have a fulfilling life. Why couldn't God have taken one of them instead of George, who was so good to me and the children and his friends and customers? What did he do to deserve to die and leave us? I know there's no good answer but I'm haunted by the thought. I know it's selfish but why are the good taken and the bad allowed to stay? I think God must be testing us in some way. For some reason he can't test others. But why us now? George turned fifty only a few years ago. He wasn't an old man so why, why, why?"

Katie let her ramble. She understood the questions, the lack of answers, and the fact that only time could really help her daughter fully absorb her husband's untimely passing. "God doesn't always reveal his answers immediately, Ann. But they will come in time. Probably when you are least expecting them."

The three adults sat at the kitchen table letting the smell of the fine Ceylonese tea waft over them, but ignoring the plate of biscuits Ann had procured. It was hard to say much which wasn't obvious, but eventually Matthew asked, "Have you had a chance to think about what you might like to do with the shop, Ann? "

Her swift response surprised them. "Oh yes, and many others have asked. I'm going to keep it and continue George's work. Over the last two years he'd been teaching me a lot more about the meat cuts and I've even been out to the abattoir a few times. I can add and write the numbers and sales slips now so I feel comfortable that I can serve the customers nearly as well as he did. Plus there's no other butcher shop in town and people depend on us. George had taken to going out riding quite often in late afternoons so I managed the shop then. I think it will be a little hard on the children because I won't have as much time for them as I used to, but we'll adjust. William has just turned sixteen and he's a strapping lad built like his father, and a wonderful help at home. And Mary Ann, who is fourteen-and-a-half, has been helping me make dinner for nearly a year now. Not even George could tell the difference between what she prepared and what I made after a while. I know we'll survive, Father. It won't be easy but we'll make it."

"Spoken like a true Monahan daughter. Perhaps a true Clarke as well, for clearly George had a tremendous will to live through all the trials thrown his way over the years."

"I know I will miss him terribly. I'm only thirty-four and I will be very much alone raising the children in the years ahead. I love them, but we will all miss him in our own ways."

Hesitatingly Katie spoke up. "Well, it's early days, dear, but maybe down the road there could be someone to take his place even."

"I can't even think about that, Mother. Certainly not now, probably not even in the future. He was everything to me and the children. I can't think of anyone else replacing him." Wisely Katie said no more on the topic.

Matthew took over, although his own nervousness and discomfort led him to prattle on more than was necessary. "Well, sweetheart, we've come to help where we can. Maybe William can show me the way to the holding paddocks tomorrow and he and I can bring back some meat for you. Can we help clean up the shop in the meantime? I'm sure you haven't wanted to be working in there but if you are going to continue then we can help you get it organized again. And maybe it would help if you were busy for a bit. Katie and I can work with the children, although I'm sure even the elder ones are very confused. Do they have playmates their own age? How are they all doing? Anything special we need to know?"

"Dad, the others will be home for dinner. They're out playing with friends, for which I'm very thankful. Most of the neighbours have been wonderful. Taking the children to their homes, bringing food for everyone for supper. Sometimes just sitting with me. By the way, there's a big tureen of hearty tomato soup on the counter there that we can heat up if you are hungry. I should have thought, you must both be tired from your journey. That cup of tea will not have been enough. Let me heat the soup and cut some bread. It is good to have you here. I'm sorry if I haven't been as thankful as I should have been."

"Darling, please don't worry about us. We're here for you," Katie responded. "I'll heat the soup. Just show me where the bread is. And we thought we'd stay a week if that's okay. Enough to help you get on your feet again, but not long enough to become a nuisance."

"That will be fine, Mother. This is all so strange and frightening at times. I know eventually I'll be able to cope, but right now losing him is very painful." With that she turned and clung to her mother again and tears fell. Her face was drawn from lack of sleep and her eyes were red from crying. Katie held her close and muttered soothing words of sympathy as best she could. She understood that the healing would not happen overnight.

The warm soup helped everyone feel a little better. Even Elizabeth's and Thomas' cheeks showed some new colour. Thomas sat on his grandfather's knee, and George had his own chair. They didn't say much beyond asking for more bread. And with stomachs partially filled they headed outside to play again.

At the risk of starting tears to flow all over again, Matthew raised a topic that had been on his mind since arrival. "Ann, we'd like to go to the cemetery so we can say our goodbyes to our son-in-law and then to the church to pray for him, bless his soul. We won't be gone long."

"I understand, Father. And thank you. I won't come as I've already been once today, but maybe tomorrow we can go together. That would help."

Silently, Matthew and Katie crossed the road and walked to the graveyard at the back of St. Stephen's church. They passed the enclosure for Sir John Jamison and not far beyond they found the simple headstone marking George's grave. A jar of water with several wilting flowers sat on the earth leaning against the headstone. With heads bowed each offered up their silent prayers, then stood erect and held hands looking into the distance, wondering why, why, why, just as their daughter had done and would continue to do until time enveloped her in its healing powers.

The occasion and location brought new thoughts to each of them. Their own immortality arose unbidden in their hearts and minds, as they both wondered how they would cope when their partner eventually left them. The sobering thoughts helped them understand the decisions and trials that Ann would have to face in the years ahead, and their empathy rose to new levels as small shafts of doubt and fear invaded their souls.

The church was empty, but late afternoon light shone through the stained glass windows creating a warm glow across the walls and pews. They knelt before the altar and once again prayed for George's soul and for Ann and the children's acceptance and recovery.

Exiting through the massive oak doors they both felt a small sense of relief. Instead of heading directly back to the shop, they walked down Main Street and entered several stores, introducing themselves to the merchants, accepting their condolences, and responding to their questions about how Ann was faring. It was clear that George was a well-respected member of the community, and several owners indicated their willingness to keep checking on Ann and the children. Matthew and Katie's hearts lightened as they listened to the widespread recognition and offers of support. While Penrith was bigger than Hartley it was clear that a significant and poignant community spirit still pervaded the town.

On returning to the house they found that the other children had come home and were waiting for them. They were excited to see Grandma and Grandpa but politely waited their turns to get hugs and ask questions. Dinner time was probably the cheeriest Ann had experienced in days, with the children wanting to show off their toys and school work and asking Grandpa if he'd take them swimming in the river tomorrow. Ann said he could borrow George's swim clothes and after that pronouncement there was no way he could escape.

In the morning he borrowed George's horse Maisie, and with William leading the way they rode out to the holding paddocks in Emu Plains. William was a very mature lad and Matthew was impressed with what he had already learned about the meat trade—from animal fattening and health, to slaughter and division, to presentation, tenderness, and taste. He was clearly destined to follow in his father's footsteps as a highly competent butcher. He exuded a certain charisma that his brothers and sisters didn't portray to the same degree and showed he had a developing sense of humour as well. It had been a long time since Matthew had been around a young boy so earnest and well prepared for life ahead. When the subject of his father ultimately came up, William readily recounted what had transpired on the fateful day, and while sad, had clearly reconciled himself to the new situation, and seemed more concerned for his mother than himself and his siblings. "We will be alright, Grandpa, as long as Mother is alright. I'm sure your and Grandma's visit here will help. I'm glad you came."

"And who among your sisters and brothers is having the hardest time, William?"

"That would be Elizabeth. She doted on Rebecca, who died just under eighteen months ago, and now Father is gone too. He never played favorites but I think after Rebecca had gone he spent more time with her than Mary Ann so she feels his loss more. I think it would be nice if Grandma took her for a walk on her own sometime."

"I'll make sure that happens then."

There was little Matthew could help with at the holding yards and abattoir. Everything was well under control. No animals had been killed in the last few days following George's death but there were some fat lambs that were ready and William suggested to the foreman that he and Grandpa would come back tomorrow to collect some offerings for the shop.

The other children were impatiently waiting for their return and were ready to go swimming. After quickly eating a sandwich Matthew changed into George's swim outfit with much approval from his charges, and they set off at an easy pace walking to the river. At an early age the children had all been introduced to the water from a safety perspective and showed no fear of it. As they neared their favorite spot all five of them ran ahead, threw their towels on the bank, and plunged in. While weeping willows provided shade and a swing rope from one of the branches, the heat was still intense and the water was wonderfully refreshing.

Not many females swam in these times but the girls had no hesitation in their home-made chin-to-ankle outfits playing with abandon. Just as George had taught them to ride like boys rather than side-saddle, so he educated and provided them with many practical aspects about living and enjoying the environment about them. There was no reason in his mind why they too shouldn't enjoy the river and learn water safety just as his sons did. To some townsfolk his actions were a little too 'modern'. To others he was a breath of fresh air with his thinking.

Matthew slid down the bank and found himself in chest-high water. The girls started splashing him immediately, at the same time encouraging him to swim across to the other side with them. The two elder boys could swim across under water, but the lungs on the other three weren't quite up to that yet. Matthew had no strokes to speak of but waded across with the girls and trod water when he struck a deep hole. He was exhausted by the time he finally got across, so he begged to be allowed to sit on the bank and just watch everyone else. They let him get away with that for a while, but there was no mercy when they decided it was time to play with the rope to swing out from the bank and drop into the cool water. Summoning up courage, Matthew took a short run and launched himself through the air, landing with a giant splash to enthusiastic cheers from his watchers.

And that was the most talked-about story back home later in the afternoon. How Grandpa had made the biggest splash of all using the jump rope. He endeared himself to all of them with his actions. And as a consequence of his exertions he also fell asleep in the big overstuffed chair after dinner well before the children were sent to bed.

The population in the region had risen to over one thousand two hundred sixty counting St. Mary's and Emu Plains, and the villages of Castlereagh and Mulgoa were also growing rapidly. In response, construction had recently started on a railway station at Penrith. Excitement in the area had been growing ever since surveyors had started planning the extension of the railway from Parramatta. The path for the line had been cleared, and progress extending the rails from Parramatta was in full swing.

More and more farms were being established west of the Blue Mountains but the hills were still a major obstacle to efficient transportation. Penrith was becoming a major staging point for the movement of goods in both directions, and the railway was seen as having a positive impact on the value and vitality of the town. More shops had arrived, a private Church of England school was being built, and it was clear that the town was gaining in stature and recognition.

At the same time, it was realised that only when the trains actually crossed the mountains would truly significant progress occur. Surveyors were already trying to determine appropriate routes, but to date had been unsuccessful. Initial plans for a bridge across the Nepean had been put together, and once the railway station was complete, building the bridge would start.

Parallel to High Street, Henry Street had been completed, and another road was now being built to be called Railway Street, designed to provide access to the new station. Next morning Katie asked Elizabeth if she would take her and show her where the steam trains would soon be coming in to town. Mary Ann, with mature insight, said she'd stay home and help her mother make some bread.

"I'll tell you something that you might find strange, Elizabeth. And that is that I've never seen a steam train. And you will get to see one before I will. In a year or so there will be a grand opening of the station and a magnificent engine will arrive here from Parramatta with all sorts of officials in the carriages it pulls behind. There'll be speeches and ribbons cut, and special tables of drinks and food to celebrate the occasion. I wish I was going to be here to see it. But Grandpa and I will be going home in a few days and probably won't be back before the first train arrives. I wonder... would you be willing to write to us and let us know what happens on that day? We'd love to know. I just feel bad that your father won't be here to be part of the festivities. Do you know why the train is so important?"

"Oh yes, Grandma. It means the wool and wheat that comes from the other side of the mountains and even in the Nepean valley will get to Sydney faster and with less accidents and wastage.

Although doesn't that mean the men who drive the bullocks won't have any more work?"

Katie was pleasantly surprised at Elizabeth's perceptiveness. "Yes, some of them will have to find other jobs, dear, but think of it this way. When the railway arrives here there will be all sorts of new jobs to fill, such as looking after the station, arranging the supply of wood and coal for the engines, managing the water tower, cleaning the engine and carriages, and of course helping load the wagons holding all the wool and bags of wheat and other supplies. Then again someone will have to sell tickets and build special loading pens for the animals that will go to the Sydney markets. Did your dad ever talk about sending any of his fat lambs to the Sydney markets?"

"Oh yes, he was excited about the train coming to Penrith. He said it would be good for the town. Grandma, do you think he will be looking down from Heaven watching on the day the train arrives?"

"I'm absolutely sure he will, darling. He wouldn't miss it for anything. In fact, he's probably listening to us talking about it right now and smiling."

"I know his body is in the ground behind the church, Grandma, but how do we know his soul is in Heaven? I don't know that I really understand."

"It's a bit hard to explain but let me try. When you think about something, you can't actually see the thought, can you? When you like something, you can't actually see the 'like,' can you? And when you feel something—like sadness—you can't actually see your 'sadness,' can you? Yet these are all very real things that affect us. I think of our soul as the owner of all those things inside us that we cannot see. It sort of allows us to experience and understand thoughts, love, and feelings. It helps us understand the difference between right and wrong. It tells us when to help someone. It decides what we will believe in and how we will grow and how much goodness there will be in us. Your daddy was a wonderful man whose soul was so good God wanted it to be in Heaven with Him. Not everyone has a soul that's good. People like bushrangers who steal and hurt others don't have good souls like your daddy and Rebecca had."

"But Rebecca wasn't even four when she died. Did she have a soul?"

"Oh yes. Do you remember how bubbly and smiley and happy she was and how she loved her mummy and daddy and all the things around her? There was only goodness in your little sister, and as much as she was mischievous at times she didn't do anything deliberate to hurt anyone. No doubt her little soul is in Heaven too. In fact, she's probably playing with your daddy right now."

"I like your stories, Grandma. I'll think about them some more."

"You can do that when Grandpa and I have gone home, but now I need you to explain to me what those men are doing on that metal scaffolding over there."

"That's where the signal is going to be that tells the train driver that the line is clear for him to proceed. One of the workmen explained it to Daddy who then told us how it would work. The actual steel rails have already reached St. Mary's so they don't have much further to go to be seen here. But there will be lots of extra sidings and turn-arounds beyond the passenger platform, of course. You can see how they've chopped down so many trees to make room. I don't think we knew how much space it would all take."

Katie reflected how the tentativeness about mentioning 'Daddy' had suddenly disappeared from Elizabeth's discourse. Fingers crossed that she would move on slowly but surely, and become more accepting of life's vagaries with the maturity and perspective that was obviously within her. Katie's children were all good children. But life had already tried them in hard ways, from being raised in a tiny home, then moving to Australia where they knew no one. They had so much to cope with at such young ages. Life wasn't at all simple for them, she mused.

By the time Ann and her children all walked to the courthouse days later to wait for the mail coach to take Matthew and Katie back to Hartley, a sense of emerging stability was being felt within the family. Ann had the shop open every afternoon and the children were back in school, with William and even George Matthew bringing the meat from the holding yards late each day. Mary Ann and Elizabeth had gotten back to making meals with their mother. No doubt all of them still experienced moments of reflection and concern, as they would for some time yet. But at least at breakfast that morning the goodbyes had not been sad, but bright and thankful. "When will you come again, Grandma?" "Do you want to take some sausages and chops home?" "I'll write and tell you about the trains." The children had clamoured for attention, and as the coach finally came into view Ann hugged her parents and said, "I'll be fine, I really will. Thanks for coming. We've all benefited from your stay. You've done wonders for all of us. Say hello to everyone and tell them we'll be fine."

Matthew reflected back on the journey home. It had been years ago and was only the second time they had used the mail coach, but it had been worth every penny of the cost of the ride. He remembered that it was four months later that Cobb & Co. had started their service and helped secure the route for gold, other freight, and travelers alike. Bushranging had changed its character starting in the late fifties and early sixties. No longer were the rogues escaped convicts, but native-born Australians who had turned to evil ways. They'd hung John Peisley in March of that year for stealing cattle and all the robberies he'd made on travelers between Bathurst and Lambing Flat goldfields. But notorious fiends like Frank Gardiner and Ben Hall still roamed the countryside. Gardiner was a horse thief who grew more daring and notorious over time with brazen highway robberies. Along with Ben Hall and John Gilbert in June of 1862 he participated in his most profitable hold up at Coonbong Rock with the gang taking fourteen thousand pounds from a gold escort. In October 1863, a gang of five (including Hall) raided Bathurst, robbed a jeweler's shop, bailed up the Sportsmans Arms Hotel, and tried to steal a racehorse. They returned three days later and held up more businesses. Ben Hall was shot dead in May 1865, but after a gaol term Gardiner eventually went to Hong Kong and America.

But those were the bad memories of the times, Matthew thought. There were many positive events that occurred during the same period which counter-balanced the negative ones. One of the most treasured was in December of 1862 when their only Australian-born child, David, married a local maid at Langford's farm named Mary Jane Peachman. Langford's was where their own Mary Jane had met Andrew so many years before. A Presbyterian minister had travelled to the property to officiate and the wedding was a happy occasion with guests attending from farms scattered widely throughout the region.

A month later in January of 1863 the first train had arrived at Penrith, and Elizabeth had fulfilled her promise of describing the day in a long letter. She painted such a dazzling picture that it made Katie and Matthew wish they'd been there. Apparently entranced with the massive steam-belching machine pulling in to the platform, George Jr. had declared that when he grew up he wanted to be an engine driver. No doubt he would not be the last young boy to so declare.

The rail bridge had been built across the Nepean where they'd all been swimming, and at Lapstone just beyond, with true creativity, the engineers had devised a small zigzag switch designed to help the locomotives conquer the one in thirty grade there.

Mary Jane and Andrew had brought a son, Matthew, their seventh child together, into the world in the October of that year, and Thomas and Rebecca had produced their fifth child, Henry, in May 1864. As well, all the family farms had done very well for three years in a row. There were many positives to appreciate.

And while the newborns extended the Monahan family and prolonged its heritage, and the farm returns assured financial stability, a giant dark cloud had recently settled on Matthew's soul that he could not shake.

Just three months ago in April 1865, Dr. Flatau had drawn him aside after tending to Katie and indicated that in his opinion she had cancer and that regretfully, at best she only had a few months of life left.

The whole family reacted with shock and disbelief. This woman had never been ill in her life. Where had the cancer come from? Was it a curse of the new land, or had she carried it from birth? Did they all carry some seed or germ that would affect them later? Why did some people get cancer and not others? The doctors had no answers, as they simply did not know. All they knew was that it occurred in various forms and usually affected older, not younger, people. What was more upsetting was that there was no known treatment. For a very few people it suddenly went away but for most it only grew worse.

Even though anaesthetics had been discovered in the 1840s, surgery using them was not commonplace, and was still experimental even in Europe. At best there were painkillers, primarily laudanum, or tincture of opium, which contained morphine and codeine, all derived from parent opium. For two months Katie steadfastly refused to resort to their use, but in the last month the pain had become intense at times and the drugs definitely offered relief. She was amazingly stoic over her situation, although it did little to console Matthew's feelings. He was about to lose the person he loved most in his life, and who had been with him for over forty years. She'd brought eight wonderful children into the world and had stood behind him though incredible life trials. What would he do without her? He thought of his daughter Ann losing her husband and how he and Katie had gone to support her. The boot was on the other foot now and he suddenly realised the terror Ann must have first felt at the loss of George. His own anxiety was carefully internalized for he dared not let it show to the surrounding family. They still needed his support. Night-times were the worst. Katie could sleep with the influence of drugs but he would lie awake wishing his wife's pain would disappear and wondering how he would cope in the future without her.

Family members came by to visit, to offer empathy and love, but had a hard time with their emotions, especially when they saw how brave Katie was trying to be. Late autumn drifted into early winter. The major heat of summer had long gone and often she would sit in a rocking chair on the front veranda, alternately dozing, reading, and sipping lemonade or weak tea. She welcomed the distraction of visitors, coping better than they did in recognizing her destiny.

On the second Monday in July, a premonition told her that her time was very near. Matthew had gone into town to buy supplies, uncomfortable in leaving her alone, but reassured by her better than usual disposition. Peace was forming in Katie's soul. Final readiness suddenly suffused her being. She decided she wanted to take one final look at the property and the close-in world she and Matthew had created around them. Her pain eased inexplicably and she gathered her boots, threw a light jacket over her shoulders, and, calling on an inner strength, resolutely set out in the direction of Andrew and Mary Jane's place without really knowing why. Something nagged at her, as she knew she had no intention of making it to their house, but she felt compelled to head that way.

It was one of those unusually balmy winter days with a high blue sky, a gentle breeze, and a temperature several degrees above normal, projecting what spring would surely bring forth a couple of months ahead. The lambs had recovered from shearing and although their coats were no longer white they were a lighter colour than the ewes and with their smaller size stood out easily. They too loved the unusual sunshine and frolicked in the paddocks with renewed energy. The calves, on the other hand, lay down anywhere they liked. She'd never been as comfortable around cattle as she was with sheep. They were slower, heftier, and showed no interest in moving out of her way when she walked among them. They had made plenty of money for the family, so she offered no complaints.

A small wallaby with joey crossed her path, showing no fear, and she mentally marveled at how the tiny thumbnail-sized baby neonates born to these quaint marsupials moved into the pouch after birth and were carried there for nearly eight months until they grew so big their legs poked out. Strange indeed. A screeching pair of sulphur-crested cockatoos flew by and she could hear a large red-tailed black cockatoo up high in one of the eucalypts cracking open nuts and seed clusters from various native trees and dropping the debris to the ground. She carefully crossed over two of the creeks, aware that it was too early in the day to hear the frogs croaking, but as she sat by the bank of one to rest, a swarm of brightly coloured mountain lorikeets alighted in the banksia bushes nearby, and entertained her with their incessant chatter.

The fauna of Australia was incredible and she realised that it was one of the major joys of her life. So different from her country of birth, now so many miles and years behind her. She harboured no regrets in leaving Ireland, certain that had she not done so, the future would have been very bleak indeed for her whole family. Probably the best thing she and Matthew had done in their life together was board that ship twenty-five years ago back in Londonderry. She struggled to remember the ship's name but couldn't. My, did that tell her something, she thought. She and Matthew and the children had braved so much together. She loved them all deeply. There was so much to be thankful for as a result.

And suddenly it came to her as to where she was headed. Not to Mary Jane's place, but to the next creek over the rise ahead. She struggled a bit now, short of breath and feeling tired. But she reached the bank and sat down in the shade, watching and waiting. For here lived the platypus family that Matthew had discovered so long ago. What could better represent the uniqueness of this land she was about to say goodbye to than this incredible creature?

Her mind drifted into reverie but eventually a small splash caught her attention, and there to her surprise a baby platypus was poking its bill through the surface as if to acknowledge her presence. Two larger adult forms came swimming underneath through the crystal clear water and she watched as they taught their youngster what roots to pull and eat. What an amazing experience! Maybe God had arranged it especially for her in what she now knew were her near-final hours.

Totally content and at peace within, she slowly trudged home as some of her pain started up again. Her mind and heart wrestled with the abundance and richness of nature and life itself around her compared to the absence of same back in County Donegal. There, life had been simpler, and nature's offerings more sparse. Variety was severely limited. In that semi-desolate environment they'd birthed and raised seven of their eight children. David was their transition child, born of Irish love under Australian skies. And now in the wider progression of life his wife had recently given birth to their first child, a daughter, Ann. Perhaps it is this child, Katie thought, who is destined to replace me. So be it.

Beyond the now fading memories there was precious left to remind any of them of the old life in Drumcairn. Except that over the years Katie had secretly preserved the two bonnets and the apron that her sisters had made for her at the time of their departure. Also stowed away separately was the diary that held the story of their terrible voyage across the oceans.

On arriving back at the homestead she retrieved all four treasured articles from their hiding places, and placed them on the small table beside her bed, into which she climbed and quickly fell asleep.

The next morning she awoke in a pain-filled haze and called for Matthew, who hastened to her side. She struggled to speak, so he smiled and said, "I see you found some Irish memorabilia, my love. I remember the gifts from your sisters and the diary from my brother. I didn't know you'd been hiding them all these years."

Eventually finding her voice, Katie whispered, "Yes, they are small reminders of our heritage, and represent what once was, and what we left behind. There have been many times when I wished we knew more about what had happened to everyone back home, but something deep inside tells me that the famine would not have been kind given where we lived. And dwelling on unknowns from the past is not a satisfying thing to do.

"But there is something from the past that I need to share with you before I leave, my love. Just over three years ago in the middle of the night I was woken by an apparition. There before me, bathed in a soft diffused light, was the angelic but sad face of a young woman with golden locks of hair falling about her. There was a second face, much smaller and half hidden by the hair, as if not wanting or able to be fully recognized. The image was there for the most fleeting of moments but as it started to fade into nothingness I thought I heard, very faintly, the word 'goodbye'. I have wondered all this time about the spirit that I saw, but now, as I prepare to meet my maker, He has helped me understand that it must have been our daughter Eileen in California telling us that unfortunately, neither she nor her daughter would survive childbirth..."

"Katie, my dear, this is incredibly sad. Such an amazing experience, but why did you not tell me when it occurred?"

"Because I didn't understand what I saw, Matthew. Perhaps deep in my soul I may have thought at the time that it was Eileen and didn't want you to give up hope for her, but I truly do not know why I said nothing. I did not mean to be selfish. Only last night did it finally become clearer."

Her voice weakened. "We still don't know for sure; perhaps one day you will hear from the authorities. But in any case, dear husband, you must forgive her in your heart. When you do perhaps the same dream will visit you too. She only did what she thought would bring her happiness. We cannot criticize her for that."

"I will try, my love. I will really try, especially given your vision."

Katie's voice became hoarse and laboured. "We must forgive all that has darkened our souls or we will never be content. I want you to promise to keep the journal as a reminder of all we've endured but bury the other three small items with me when I go. My love for Ireland will never disappear but the future is here in this wonderful land.

"You know, dear husband of mine, we have twenty grandchildren and two great-grandchildren living today, and our family will continue to grow. I feel blessed and so thankful with all that has come from our union. We have done incredibly well as providers and deserve to be proud."

Matthew's eyes brimmed with tears as he nodded and bent over to kiss her. His voice faltered: "Bless you, my darling. I love you with all my heart. My soul cries to be with you."

Katie kissed him fervently. "I must leave you now," she whispered. "You are the most loving man in the world. I have been blessed spending this time on earth with you. Thank you."

Lying back down, she squeezed Matthew's hand and closed her eyes.

High in the eucalyptus tree by the property entrance a blue-winged kookaburra lifted his head and started his morning welcome call. His joyous warbling laughter was the last sound Katie heard.

About the Author

Warren Dent was born in Sydney, Australia. After gaining Economics degrees in Canberra and Adelaide and a Ph.D. at the University of Minnesota, he taught Econometrics and Business Statistics for many years, before entering the private sector, where he worked for three number one companies – Eli Lilly, American Airlines, and Microsoft - creating new businesses and applying information systems to strategic market applications. Married, with four grown daughters, he now lives with his wife Gail in Seattle. Personal interests include boating and tennis. With numerous academic publications to his credit, and hundreds of business presentations behind him, he has recently turned his writing talents to more personal endeavours. Short story mysteries and longer historical fiction novels are his primary interests. His website is www.warrend.com and email address is warren@warrend.com.